Russia's Rome

Publication of this volume has been made possible in part through the generous support and enduring vision of WARREN G. MOON.

Russia's Rome

Imperial Visions, Messianic Dreams, 1890–1940

Judith E. Kalb

THE UNIVERSITY OF WISCONSIN PRESS

The University of Wisconsin Press
1930 Monroe Street, 3rd Floor
Madison, Wisconsin 53711-2059

www.wisc.edu/wisconsinpress/

3 Henrietta Street
London WC2E 8LU, England

5 4 3 2 1

Printed in the United States of America

Library of Congress Cataloging-in-Publication Data
Kalb, Judith E.
Russia's Rome : imperial visions, messianic dreams, 1890–1940 /
Judith E. Kalb.
p. cm.
Includes bibliographical references and index.
ISBN 978-0-299-22920-7 (cloth : alk. paper)
1. Russian literature—19th century—Classical influences. 2. Russian literature—20th century—Classical influences. 3. Imperialism in literature. 4. Rome—In literature. 5. National characteristics, Russian, in literature. I. Title.
PG2980.5.K28 2008
891.709'35837—dc22
2008011966

for

ALEX

and for

MY PARENTS

Contents

List of Illustrations ix
Acknowledgments xi
Note on Transliteration and Translations xiii

Introduction: Rome Envy 3

1 The Blueprint: Dmitrii Merezhkovskii's *Christ and Antichrist* 34

2 Relinquishing Empire? Valerii Briusov's Roman Novels 76

3 A "Roman Bolshevik": Aleksandr Blok's "Catiline" and the Russian Revolution 106

4 The Third Rome in Exile: Refitting the Pieces in Viacheslav Ivanov's "Roman Sonnets" 129

5 Emperors in Red: The Poet and the Court in Mikhail Kuzmin's *Death of Nero* 162

Conclusion: Bulgakov and Beyond 185

Notes 203
Index 281

Illustrations

1 Statue of Aleksandr Pushkin in the Borghese Gardens, Rome 5
2 Statue of Ovid in Constanta, Romania 8
3 Karl Briullov, *The Last Day of Pompeii,* 1830–1833 13
4 Gymnasium performers of Plautus's *Menaechmi* 14
5 The Appian Way, uncovered and restored in the nineteenth century 19
6 The Catacombs of St. Callistus 20
7 The Roman Forum in 1821 21
8 A page from Fedor Buslaev's *Historical Sketches of Russian Folk Literature and Art* 58
9 Leonardo da Vinci, *John the Baptist,* ca. 1513–1516 60
10 Icon of St. John the Baptist, ca. 1450 61
11 Cesare Maccari, *Cicero Denouncing Catiline before the Senate,* ca. 1888 114
12 Trinità dei Monti Church and Spanish Steps ascending from the Barcaccia Fountain, Rome 143
13 Il Tritone Fountain, Rome 155
14 La Tartarughe Fountain, Rome 157
15 The Third Rome Casino, Yalta, 2003 199

Acknowledgments

As I consider the genesis and evolution of *Russia's Rome,* I am reminded of the 24 April 2006 *New Yorker* cartoon that features one distraught, toga-clad Roman telling another, "My contractor told me Rome would only take a day." The foundations for my version of the city were laid in a Stanford University dissertation (1996), which benefited from the support of the Stanford University Department of Slavic Languages and Literatures, a grant from the Phi Beta Kappa Society of Northern California, and an Educational Foundation Dissertation Fellowship from the American Association of University Women. As I reworked the project into its current form, I was fortunate to receive funding from the Wellesley College Davis Fund for Russian Area Studies, the Kennan Institute at the Woodrow Wilson International Center for Scholars, and the College of Arts and Sciences at the University of South Carolina. I am grateful to the staff of the European Reading Room at the Library of Congress, the Russian State Library in Moscow, the National Library of Russia in St. Petersburg, and the Interlibrary Loan Division of the Thomas Cooper Library at the University of South Carolina for valuable assistance.

I would like to thank Steve Salemson for welcoming this project to the University of Wisconsin Press and Gwen Walker and Sheila Moermond for seeing it through publication. Thanks go as well to Jane Barry for meticulous copyediting.

I am deeply grateful to Avril Pyman and Michael Wachtel, manuscript readers for the University of Wisconsin Press, whose detailed, insightful, and informative comments on my text inspired me and strengthened the final product considerably. I would also like to thank the many additional individuals who have read, commented upon, or more generally discussed aspects of my work. Among them are Stephen Baehr, Peter Barta, Nikolay Bogomolov, Caryl Emerson, Lazar Fleishman, John Malmstad, Irene Masing-Delic, Paul Allen Miller, Stanley Rabinowitz, Paul Robinson, David Sloane, and Andrew Wachtel. My undergraduate advisor at Princeton University, Ellen Chances, introduced me to the study of Russian literature and has responded to my writing ever since with her customary blend of intelligence, excitement, and encouragement. Gregory Freidin, my Stanford dissertation advisor, continues to stimulate and amaze me with his intense commitment to broad-ranging, ambitious ideas and scholarship. The late, extraordinary Mikhail Leonovich Gasparov honored me throughout the creation of this book with his careful attention to my successive drafts and his ongoing support and scholarly generosity.

Yana Yakhnina, in Moscow, and Marianna Landa, Sergei Landa, and Juna Janovna Zek, in St. Petersburg, offered warm hospitality and lively and thought-provoking discussions. My former students Jana H. Copeland, Alexandra Deyneka, André Rembert, and Sara Saylor provided impeccable assistance.

My parents, Madeleine G. Kalb and Marvin Kalb, and my sister, Deborah S. Kalb, instilled in me a love of books and a firm respect for the carefully crafted written word. They have contributed to this project in innumerable ways, and I am very grateful. Finally, heartfelt thanks go to my wonderful husband and fellow Slavist Alexander Ogden, who has provided constant support and intellectual companionship.

Portions of chapter 1 appeared previously in "Merezhkovskii's Third Rome: Imperial Visions and Christian Dreams," *Ab Imperio* 2, no. 1 (March 2001): 125–40. Chapter 3 appeared in an earlier version as "A 'Roman Bolshevik': Aleksandr Blok's 'Catiline' and the Russian Revolution," *Slavic and East European Journal* 44, no. 3 (Fall 2000): 413–28. Chapter 4 was published with minor changes as "Lodestars on the Via Appia: Viacheslav Ivanov's 'Roman Sonnets' in Context," *Die Welt der Slaven* 48 (2003): 23–52. An early draft of chapter 5 was published as "The Politics of an Esoteric Plot: Mikhail Kuzmin's 'Smert' Nerona,'" *Soviet and Post-Soviet Review* 20, no. 1 (1993): 35–49. I thank each of these journals for permission to reprint material. Illustration credit goes to Réunion des Musées Nationaux/Art Resource, N.Y. (Leonardo da Vinci, *Saint John the Baptist*), Scala/Art Resource, N.Y. (Cesare Maccari, *Cicero Denouncing Catiline before the Senate;* Karl Briullov, *The Last Day of Pompeii*), and the Trustees of the British Museum (icon of Saint John the Baptist, ca. 1450).

Note on Transliteration and Translations

I use the Library of Congress transliteration system, simplified to omit ligatures and diacritics. I do, however, use accepted anglicizations of certain well-known Russian and Latin names: Peter I, Nicholas II, Leon Trotsky, Catiline, Sallust, etc. Material quoted from English-language sources preserves the spelling and transliteration of the original.

Translations from Russian and other languages are my own unless otherwise noted. Of the works on which each chapter is focused, all except the two novels by Valerii Briusov discussed in chapter 2 exist in English translation. For readers who wish to consult the works in English, I include a partial list here (in several cases, more than one translation exists):

Dmitri Mérejkowski. *The Death of the Gods.* Translated by Herbert Trench. New York and London: G. P. Putnam's Sons, 1901.

Dmitri Merejkowski. *The Romance of Leonardo da Vinci.* Translated by Bernard Guilbert Guerney. New York: Random House, 1928.

Dmitri Merejkowski. *Peter and Alexis.* New York and London: G. P. Putnam's Sons, 1906.

Aleksandr Blok. "Catiline." Translated by Marian Schwartz. In *A Revolution of the Spirit: Crisis of Value in Russia, 1890–1924,* edited by Bernice Glatzer Rosenthal and Martha Bohachevsky-Chomiak, 293–319. New York: Fordham University Press, 1990.

Vyacheslav Ivanov. "Roman Sonnets." Translated by Lowry Nelson, Jr. In *Vyacheslav Ivanov: Poet, Critic, and Philosopher,* edited by Robert Louis Jackson and Lowry Nelson, Jr., 134–43. New Haven, Conn.: Yale Center for International and Area Studies, 1986.

Mikhail Kuzmin. *The Death of Nero.* In *Mikhail Kuzmin: Selected Writings,* translated and edited by Michael A. Green and Stanislav A. Shvabrin, 131–91. Lewisburg, Pa.: Bucknell University Press, 2005.

Mikhail Bulgakov. *The Master and Margarita.* Translated by Diana Burgin and Katherine Tiernan O'Connor. New York: Vintage International, 1996.

Russia's Rome

Introduction

Rome Envy

Roads to Rome

> And when I finally saw Rome for the second time, oh, how much better it seemed than the first! It felt as if I were seeing my homeland, where I hadn't been for several years, but where my thoughts had been living. But no, it's not that, not my own homeland, but the homeland of my soul that I saw, where my soul was living even before me, before I appeared on this earth.
> Nikolai Gogol', letter to M. P. Balabina, 1838

Not far from the Coliseum, in the heart of Rome, stands the Basilica of San Clemente, named after the Roman Pope Clement, who died in approximately 100 CE. The basilica, which dates back to the twelfth century, is located on the remains of a fourth-century Christian church, which in turn rests upon a first-century Mithraeum, sacred to the pagan god Mithras. The Mithraeum is found above yet another level, consisting of pre-Christian walls dating to Rome's Republican period, before the Roman Empire began. It is startling to observe on the fourth-century level of this architectural palimpsest of Roman history a shrine to Saints Cyril and Methodius, credited with creating the first Slavic alphabet and spreading the words of the Christian Gospels to the Slavs. Grateful plaques and murals from various Slavic peoples—Russians, Slovaks, Bulgarians, Croats, and more—abound. The Russian contribution portrays Methodius on the left, with the initial words of the Gospel of John ("In the beginning was the word . . ."), and Cyril on the right, holding the Cyrillic alphabet. An icon lamp hangs before this celebration of

Russian religion and literacy. The explanation for this geographically unexpected veneration: the bones of St. Cyril, buried by his brother Methodius in the fourth-century church "at the right-hand side of the altar of St. Clement."[1]

How did the apostles to the Slavs end up in Rome, and how is this story relevant to the Rome-related writings of a group of Russian modernist authors in the final years of the nineteenth century and the early decades of the twentieth? The answer to the first question is relatively straightforward. As legend has it, during the reign of the Roman emperor Trajan (98–117 CE), Clement was exiled to the Crimea and ordered to work in the local mines. When he continued despite these hardships to preach the Christian Gospel, anti-Christian representatives of Rome attached him to an anchor and hurled him into the Black Sea; frescoes on the walls of San Clemente depict this tale. Centuries later, the brothers Cyril and Methodius were proselytizing in the Crimea. In 861 Cyril supposedly found Clement's body, albeit in pieces, along with the famous anchor, on an island near Chersonesus. Clement's reconstructed body was brought to San Clemente in 868 with great pomp, and when Cyril died the following year, the pope permitted Cyril's bones to be buried near those of the saint he had returned to Rome.[2]

The answer to the second question is more complex and forms the subject of this book. The Russian contribution to the Basilica of San Clemente stakes a claim to the heritage represented by Rome: in short, the heritage commonly known as Western civilization. A Russian presence in a building that encompasses within itself the best-known features of Roman history and culture, from Republican freedom to the imperial age, from paganism to Christianity, asserts a Russian connection to all those stages and, more importantly perhaps, also makes clear the Russian desire to be recognized as having such a connection. (The statue of Aleksandr Pushkin erected in 2000 in Rome's famed Borghese Gardens as a gift from the Russian government might be said to follow in the same tradition [fig. 1].)

In fact, Russians have claimed Roman origins for centuries, from stories of the first Roman emperor Augustus Caesar's mythical brother Prus, who supposedly was a forebear of Riurik,[3] to the well-known doctrine of "Moscow the Third Rome." Although in some ways these efforts to assert Roman-ness (*Romanitas*) echo those of other nations, the Russian case is to some degree unique. Unlike some other would-be Romes, Russia was never a part of the Roman Empire, nor did it form part of the ensuing Catholic, Latin-dominated realm that the

Fig. 1. Statue of the Russian poet Aleksandr Pushkin erected in Rome's Borghese Gardens in 2000 as a gift from the city of Moscow to the city of Rome

nineteenth-century Russian thinker Petr Chaadaev would later laud, to Russia's disadvantage, as an exemplar of unified culture. Russia was, however, influenced culturally and religiously by the half of the Roman Empire that the West tends to forget: Byzantium, with its capital city, Constantinople, dedicated as a "New Rome" in 330 CE by Rome's first Christian emperor, Constantine. Byzantium provided Russia with its Orthodox Christianity and, through the missionaries Cyril and Methodius, with the spiritually charged Slavic word.

The "first," Western Rome came predominantly to represent secular authority and imperial power to various Russian rulers and their subjects, even as the "second," Eastern Rome, while the inheritor of Rome's secular authority, could function additionally as a symbol of religious piety.[4] Constantinople thus provided Russians with an alternative Roman model, one that emphasized the miracle of faith: the East, after all, was where Clement's mutilated body had been resurrected by an inspired missionary. Generations of Russians would posit and claim Rome's imperial, Western heritage or Byzantium's Eastern, religious stature, at times, as in the Third Rome doctrine, asserting a unique ability to synthesize and surpass the two. In so doing, they would construct a complex myth of a Russian—or, as the poet Marina Tsvetaeva would later term it, a "Scythian"—Rome.[5] The Russian plaque at San Clemente embodies this intricate construction: it announces a Russian stake in Rome, permitting Russia to partake of Rome's cultural and imperial authority even while paradoxically emphasizing Russian spirituality. And it is this process—the process of identifying with, rejecting, emulating, and longing for Rome—that the Russian modernists who wrote about Rome both described and embodied.

In this first book-length study of Russian modernist writings on ancient Rome, I analyze Rome-related texts by six writers: Dmitrii Merezhkovskii, Valerii Briusov, Aleksandr Blok, Viacheslav Ivanov, Mikhail Kuzmin, and Mikhail Bulgakov. I have chosen purposely to discuss a variety of genres—the novel, the essay, the lyric cycle, the play—and to cover a wide-ranging period, from the beginnings of the Symbolist movement in the early 1890s, through the revolutions of the early twentieth century to the Stalinist purges of the 1930s. I seek thereby to demonstrate the staying power of Rome as a powerful symbol for Russian modernist writers, despite differences of genre or radical changes in historical circumstances. This is not a study of Russian modernists *in* Rome, their experiences and reminiscences, though most of the writers I discuss traveled there, and I will make note of this when it is relevant to my arguments.[6] Rather, my analysis focuses on the way these authors used Rome as a mythmaking tool in discussions of their own contemporary Russia to create a Rome-based discourse of Russian national identity neither specifically prerevolutionary nor Soviet but continuous over both periods. Appropriating the multifaceted symbolism and rhetoric associated with Rome, Russian modernist writers attempted to integrate Russia's own history into an archetypal Western narrative and, simultaneously, to assert the crucial role of the often neglected Eastern partner in the Roman model. Following the blueprints of Friedrich Nietzsche, Vladimir Solov'ev, and other figures essential to Russia's modernist period, in their works set in Rome these writers scripted Russia's future by merging it with the Roman past, collapsing historical time into eternal myth in a new and symbolic Russian literary space.[7] The Russian artist cast himself as the central figure in this mythmaking process, able to overcome temporal distances (past-present) and spatial divisions (East-West) to create a lasting, textually unified Third Rome of his own. Before proceeding to further analysis, it is essential to turn to the background of these writings, first to the Western and Russian assumptions about Rome that informed them, as well as previous Russian uses of Rome, including the Third Rome myth, and then to the fin-de-siècle setting, both in Europe and in Russia, that inspired them.

Claims and Inheritances

> There is something amusing, and even a bit alarming, isn't there, in the idea that the East is actually the metaphysical center of mankind?
>
> Joseph Brodsky, "Flight from Byzantium," 1985
> (trans. Joseph Brodsky and Alan Myers)

In the early part of the third century CE, a scholar accustomed to the cultural cosmopolitanism of Rome's imperial age opined, "In . . . all the countries North of Pontus [the Black Sea], . . . no one sees sculptors or painters or perfumers or money changers or poets."[8] This view of the regions beyond the Black Sea as uncultivated and essentially barbaric was a longstanding one: in the world of Greek mythology, one thinks, for example, of the "barbarian" sorceress Medea of Colchis (Western Georgia). It was also a view that many inhabitants of the far-flung Roman Empire shared: for the Roman poet Ovid, exile in 8 CE to Tomis (Romania), on the nearer coast of the Black Sea, was cause enough for the laments of his *Tristia* (fig. 2).[9] Centuries later, after 550 CE, with the Western Roman Empire long since devastated by invading Germanic tribes, other "barbarian" tribes, this time Slavic ones, made their way into the Balkans, eventually arriving in Greece. The areas these Slavs occupied became known as "stateless zones, whose inhabitants no longer paid taxes or provided soldiers for the emperor," zones that "signaled the end of an imperial order."[10] In the ninth century, well over a thousand years after Plato had recorded the dialogues of Socrates and nearly a millennium since Cicero's speeches in the Roman Forum, the Moravian Prince Rastislav summoned help—which came in the form of Cyril and Methodius—to create a Slavic alphabet and a liturgy in Church Slavonic. Kievan Rus' would enter the Christian fold a century later, but a full nine hundred years after this, Russia's great nineteenth-century novelists still ran the risk of being viewed as barbarians by Western Europeans, who often dismissed the idea of Russia as a cultured nation.[11] Not only had Russia missed the Renaissance; it had missed the classical period, which provided Western Europe with much of its assumed cultural heritage, as well.

What I have just presented is essentially a Western narrative, one that diminishes or even negates the importance of the Eastern half of

Fig. 2. Statue of the Roman poet Ovid in Constanta, Romania, formerly Tomis, his place of exile early in the first century CE

the Roman Empire and, correspondingly, its influence on the Slavic world. It is a tale told from an assumed Western "center" about an Eastern "periphery."[12] As such, it ignores complicating factors including the ancient Greek trading colonies around the Black Sea that the Romans perpetuated, or, more significantly, the established relations between Kievan Rus' and the Byzantine Empire during the tenth and eleventh centuries.[13] For in Western eyes, Rome is a quintessentially Western concept. Rome is represented by the Forum, the Senate, and the Coliseum, copies of which proliferate throughout Europe and the United States (another of Rome's would-be heirs).[14] Rome stands for solid masonry and legal codes, for the freedom of the Republic and the power of the Empire. It may stand for Catholicism. It does not stand for Eastern Orthodox Christianity, icons, or Eastern monarchs; these tend to surface only in brief mentions and footnotes.

For Russians, however, the situation is different. Rome holds many of the same associations for Russians as it does for Westerners, and it is these associations that many Westernizing Russians have sought for their own nation. Unlike Westerners, however, Russians do not forget the Eastern half of the Empire, the half that provided them with their alphabet and religion, qualities that set Russia apart from the West.[15]

And yet Constantinople was in fact intended to be a second Rome, defined implicitly at its founding through its Western predecessor.[16] Constantinople's early self-definition through Rome thus provides a model of sorts for Russia's own continual measurements in the modern period of its cultural "progress" against a Western, or Roman, standard.[17] Liah Greenfeld has posited a process according to which reactions to Europe from proud denizens of Peter I's transformed empire were unselfconsciously enthusiastic, while later, less secure evaluations saw Europe as distressingly "superior."[18] Russians sought affirmation through sometimes exaggerated claims of equality—claims, as it turns out, often based on the classical world, with particular reference to Rome. Mikhail Chulkov initiated in a 1766 story a stream of tales of ancient Slavic kingdoms that had come close to or surpassed the strength of Greece and, especially, Rome, while Mikhail Lomonosov wrote of the "equation" between Russia and Rome, given the "general similarity between the order of Russian and Roman events."[19] Europeans failed to recognize Russia as an equal during this period, however, and thus denied Russians a share of the political and cultural authority Rome represents. Greenfeld suggests that the result of this denial was the development on some Russians' part of *ressentiment*, to use Nietzsche's term, along with a corresponding narrative of a Russia stronger, better, than the supposedly paradigmatic West, specifically through Russia's elevated soul, defined against the West's pragmatic and orderly reason.[20] Faith mattered more than an arch or an aqueduct; a holy fool had power over an emperor.[21] The nineteenth-century poet Fedor Tiutchev's "Eti bednye selen'ia" (These Poor Settlements, 1855), which tells the tale of a Russia chosen by Christ specifically because of its poverty, may be read as an example of a such a tendency.[22] And the flip side of Chaadaev's letter condemning Russia's lack of connection to a European heritage is his subsequent "Apologie d'un fou" (Apology of a Madman), written in 1837, in which the former critic of his homeland now argued that it was precisely a "blank slate" quality on the part of pre-Petrine Russia that had made Peter's reforms possible and thus presaged Russia's ability "to perfect most of the ideas which have come up in the old societies, and to decide most of the weighty questions concerning the human race."[23] The very lack Chaadaev had once deplored became in this new exposition the salvation of Russia and the world.

This crowded mixture of competing narratives echoes in a sense Rome's own self-mythologization, which in fact in an early phase provides a useful model of "periphery" turned "central." When Virgil was commissioned by Rome's first emperor, Augustus Caesar, to write an epic of Rome, he consciously drew upon the Greek poet Homer's *Iliad* and *Odyssey* for his models: Virgil needed the cultural authority of Greece to create his own word-based empire.[24] In his *Aeneid,* Virgil told the tale of "pious" Aeneas, survivor of the victorious Greeks' destruction of Troy at the end of the Trojan War. Aeneas gathers his household gods, and, carrying his aged father on his back, he leaves his burning and defeated city in order against all odds to travel to Italy and found there the future Roman Empire.[25] Virgil laid claim to another nation's cultural heritage and used it to bolster the Roman past with a heroic story and to predict an extraordinary Roman future. In so doing, he supplied writers for centuries to come with an inspiring narrative of an insecure but value-laden Eastern state transformed into "empire without end."[26] While Russian rulers, unlike those of various other nations, never explicitly claimed Trojan roots,[27] the story of Aeneas, along with Virgil's model of literary nation-building, held deep resonance for Russian Symbolist writers at the turn of the twentieth century, as they put Virgil's myth and example to work in their own nationally based writings.

Thus the Russian process of self-identification with Rome is one element in a complex and longstanding mythmaking tradition, one begun by the Romans themselves and composed of varying narratives, definitions, and conclusions. While Peter I was the first Russian tsar to incorporate large-scale Romanization into his plans for Russia's imperial development, earlier Russian leaders had initiated the process. Richard S. Wortman writes that as early as the late fifteenth century, Russian monarchs were asserting Roman traits in an effort to claim the status of the Western rulers who were doing the same thing: "Russia found Rome through Europe, then appropriated classical symbols as signs of its own Western character."[28] The eighteenth century then provided fertile ground for these early seeds. As Virgil had acknowledged the authority of Greece, Peter I recognized that in order to join Europe, he needed Rome. Peter ordered various Latin classics translated into Russian, and his reign also saw the production of Latin-Russian-German and Latin-Russian-Dutch dictionaries, along with a Latin grammar.[29] More significantly, Peter and his followers used Rome to promote Peter's imperial ambitions, as he took on the Roman titles of Imperator and Father of the Fatherland, celebrated his military victories with traditional Roman triumphs, and encouraged positive Russian-Roman comparisons. With the establishment of the St. Petersburg Academy of Sciences in 1724–1725 in Peter's new capital city, itself modeled on Rome, Russian scholars gained a venue and imperial support for studying the ancient world, beginning an impressive tradition of respected research in the field.[30]

Catherine II continued Peter's Romanizing tradition, a process symbolized by the "Bronze Horseman" statue of Peter I, based on an ancient Roman rendering of Emperor Marcus Aurelius, that she dedicated to Peter in both Russian and Latin.[31] She also encouraged writers such as Mikhail Kheraskov and Vasilii Maikov to assert Rome, the powerful empire, as the model for her own expanding imperial Russia.[32] In their literary texts, as Stephen L. Baehr writes, "the glory-that-was-Rome iconographically signified the glory-that-was-to-be-Russia."[33] Catherine's imperial conquests, which included Russia's acquisition of the Crimea in 1783, were made with the Roman Empire in mind; mastering territory that had once been a part of the Eastern Roman Empire could be seen as a first step en route to the restoration of Orthodox domination of Constantinople.[34] (Her choice of the name Constantine for one of her grandsons may be read in this light.[35]) Under Alexander I, Russia annexed parts of Georgia as well. These additions to Russia's dominion added a prized geographic element to Russian claims, earlier based predominantly on Russia's reception of Eastern Orthodoxy, to a connection with the ancient world.[36]

Roman-Russian links would also come to function in a manner less pleasing to the empress and her successors when Aleksandr Radishchev compared Catherine's Russia unfavorably with the "freer" Roman Republic.[37] In the early nineteenth century, fascination with the Roman Republic became common among those who sought reform in Russia's autocracy.[38] The Decembrists, who rose up against the Russian regime in 1825, were influenced by ancient writers including Plutarch, Livy, and Cicero, and continued, while in Siberian exile, to assert their importance. Most significant to the Decembrists was Tacitus, author of histories of first-century imperial Rome.[39] Tacitus was also influential for Aleksandr Pushkin, who was reading the Roman historian while composing *Boris Godunov* in 1825. As G. S. Knabe notes, Pushkin derived the mythological names he used in his literary texts from Greek antiquity, but when he was writing about the culture and history of the ancient world or noting its relevance to Russia, he tended to rely upon Roman examples.[40]

At the same time, Russians were becoming acquainted with the object of their comparisons. Peter I's counselor Petr Andreevich Tolstoi stood out among his contemporaries for the journey he made through Italy in the final years of the seventeenth century,[41] but by the early to mid-nineteenth century, many of Russia's leading writers and painters were making trips to the Eternal City, often taking up residence there for extended periods of time, as did Nikolai Gogol' during the writing of part one of the very Russian *Mertvye dushi* (Dead Souls, 1842).[42] The Italian paintings of the Russian artists Karl and Aleksandr Briullov, Aleksandr Ivanov, and Sil'vestr Shchedrin, among others, further bear out the Romantic phenomenon of *toska po Italii*, "longing for Italy," common among educated Russians during the first half of the nineteenth century. Karl Briullov's *Poslednii den' Pompei* (The Last Day of Pompeii, 1830–1833; fig. 3) and Ivanov's *Iavlenie Khrista narodu* (Appearance of Christ before the People, 1837–1857), central works of nineteenth-century Russian art, were created in Rome.[43]

Those Russians who opted to stay at home could take advantage of the numerous Russian translations of Latin texts that proceeded apace during the second half of the nineteenth century in particular, when Afanasii Fet became the most important Russian translator of the Latin poets, with renderings of Virgil, Ovid, and Juvenal.[44] Meanwhile, the

Fig. 3. Karl Briullov, *The Last Day of Pompeii*, 1830–1833 (Scala/Art Resource, N.Y.)

Russian commitment to assimilating the classical heritage was reflected in educational policy: the nineteenth century became the era of the classical gymnasium in Russia, though expectations for students varied widely depending on prevailing policies at the time.[45] Under Sergei Uvarov, who served as minister of education from 1833 to 1849, the Russian gymnasium was reformulated to emphasize both Latin and ancient Greek.[46] Although a school reform of 1849 diminished requirements in ancient languages (Latin was still required for those aspiring to university studies, but Greek was not), the period beginning in 1871 under Minister of Education Dmitrii Tolstoi brought newly rigorous graduation expectations, including an exit exam in ancient languages.[47] Since Tolstoyan classicism stemmed from conservative political ideas focused on buttressing imperial power, Latin, with its imperial associations, was valued more highly under Tolstoi than Greek—despite the focus on Eastern Orthodoxy that tended to coincide with conservative ideals.[48] And yet Tolstoyan classicism proved disappointing and frustrating to many students, since the teaching focus was on grammar rather than content. Merezhkovskii, who attended the Third Classical Gymnasium in St. Petersburg, later wrote unenthusiastically, "That

Участники „Менехмовъ“ Плавта.

Fig. 4. Performers of the Roman poet Plautus's comedy *Menaechmi* at the Kerchensk Gymnasium on 6 January 1914 (pictured in the Russian journal *Hermes*, March 1914)

was the end of the seventies and the beginning of the eighties, the most unenlightened period of classical study: no education, just murderous cramming and corrections."[49] The writer Aleksandr Amfiteatrov recalled as well the distressing preponderance of grammar at the expense of ideas.[50]

As A. A. Nosov notes, however, this picture was by no means a uniform one: excellent teaching at private institutions, including those of Franz Kreiman and Lev Polivanov, led to excitement about the classical world on the part of some receptive students. Andrei Belyi, who attended the latter institution, recalled Polivanov's lively teaching style, which included the energetic pedagogue's parading before his students like a togaed Roman senator.[51] Nonetheless, complaints and doubts endured, and following Tolstoi's reign at the Ministry of Education, guidelines were changed once again in 1890, reducing the stress on ancient languages.

Its shortcomings notwithstanding, the classical gymnasium, and particularly its emphasis on Latin, provided an academic grounding for the texts Russian modernists produced about ancient Rome.[52] By the end of the nineteenth century, Russian readers, especially those who had attended the classical gymnasium, had been exposed to the best-known works of the Latin literary tradition (fig. 4). This secular, Western-dominated path of Rome-fascination developed simultaneously with a tradition that brought Russia's Eastern, religious roots to the fore: the tradition of Moscow, representative of Russia, as the Third Rome.

Filofei and His Interpreters

> When Constantinople fell, and along with it the Greek tsar, by birth the defender of Orthodoxy, and when Ivan Vasil'evich married the Greek princess, then along with the royal crown and regalia he inherited the lawful title, rights, and responsibilities of the great and sole champion of the true faith. . . . And it was not only the Russian people who thought thus.
> Apollon Maikov, "Moscow the Third Rome," 1869

The formula, at this point, has become a cliché: "All the empires of the Orthodox Christian Faith have come together in thy single Empire. Thou art the sole Emperor of all the Christians in the whole universe. . . . For two Romes have fallen, but the Third [i.e., Moscow] stands, and a Fourth shall not be."[53] Perhaps the best-known instance of Russia's self-identification with Rome, the Third Rome doctrine had its origins in the early sixteenth century, when a Pskovian monk named Filofei purportedly wrote a series of letters to various officials, including Tsar Vasilii III.[54] The doctrine has been taken in subsequent years to support an interpretation of an expansionist-minded Muscovite state,[55] but initially it was based on the predominantly religious premise that Russia had assumed the Orthodox Christian mantle that the Byzantines had lost when conquered in 1453 by the Moslem Turks. As keeper of the Orthodox faith, Russia was to value that faith and its ecclesiastical representatives in the face of growing worldly power.[56] This religiously focused concept of a Russian Third Rome drew upon earlier tales such as the "Povest' o belom klobuke" (Tale of the White Cowl), a late fifteenth-century legend in which a holy garment is sent from Rome to Constantinople to Russia, the lone remaining defender of the "true" Christian religion. Such insistence on the orthodoxy of Russia's holy traditions provided fuel for Russia's "Old Believers," who continued to promulgate the Third Rome formula as a vision for an ideal Russia—one apocalyptically betrayed, in their opinion, by the actual Russian state's Church reforms—even when the doctrine had fallen out of general use in the seventeenth and eighteenth centuries.[57]

During the middle of the nineteenth century, interest in the Third Rome revived, particularly when various sources of the doctrine were published, including the "Tale of the White Cowl" and one of Filofei's letters, both of which appeared in 1861.[58] Marshall Poe suggests that a further turning point came with Vladimir Ikonnikov's 1869 study of the cultural significance of Byzantium for Russia. Ikonnikov's view of the Third Rome doctrine as a statement of Russian messianism—Russia could redeem the world from apocalypse through its religious faith—would become a standard reading of Filofei's words into the twentieth century.[59] By the late nineteenth century, the doctrine was common knowledge, found in publications from prestigious scholarly journals to daily newspapers. After Tsar Nicholas II visited Moscow for Easter in 1903, for instance, the newspaper *Moskovskie vedomosti* (Moscow News) asserted the city's holy status through a reference to the Third Rome: "Here, among the national shrines of the Kremlin, one's lips involuntarily whisper, 'This is the Third Rome. There will be no fourth.'"[60]

While the idea of Moscow as the Third Rome was based initially on Filofei's formulation, an imperial element within the myth is inescapable. Rome is, after all, the West's archetypal empire, and the Third Rome doctrine as such may be seen as an example of *translatio imperii,* or translation of empire, a medieval term meant to describe the passage of political power from one empire to another. (The fact that the Third Rome doctrine does not permit a "Fourth" Rome to exist imparts a messianic coloring to what may be viewed as an imperialist claim.) Filofei himself may have been concerned exclusively with Russian religiousness, but the formula he chose, combined with its known political background, came to suggest to subsequent generations of Russians—and Western critics—an imperial subtext. The doctrine emerged in the face of growing Muscovite stature: in 1472 Ivan III married Zoe Paleologue, niece of the last Byzantine emperor, adopted the title of "tsar," derived from the Latin *caesar,* and added Byzantium's two-headed eagle to the symbols representing the Russian monarchy. Aware of Muscovy's emerging power, in the late fifteenth and the sixteenth centuries Papal emissaries interested in a reunion of the Eastern and

Western churches and a recovery of Constantinople approached the Russians. The Russians, while not terribly receptive to Rome's plans, visited the Vatican for further discussions at various points during Russia's medieval period.[61] Vasilii Kliuchevskii interpreted this history in an 1872 article, writing that Filofei had been "thoroughly imbued with the functioning of world events that had changed Russia's ecclesiastical position"; in other words, Filofei was not focused simply on the world beyond, but had been aware, as Kliuchevskii wrote, of the specifically secular "growth that had led to Russia's ecclesiastical autonomy."[62] In Nicholas II's coronation album, the idea of the Third Rome was brought out in simultaneously religious and imperial terms: as Wortman notes, citing the album, when Byzantium proved untrue to Orthodoxy, "the office of Emperor, 'created by the political life of the rulers of the world, the Romans, now became the property of the Russian Orthodox Autocracy alone.'"[63] In a 1914 book on the Third Rome theme, the writer I. Kirillov characterized Filofei as "one of the first Russian political thinkers" and as a representative of a burgeoning Russian nationalism.[64] Thus in the idea of the Third Rome, earlier worries about Russia's status vis-à-vis Europe could be dismissed. The Russian theocracy, anointed by God, could surpass all previous kingdoms and cultures, the first and second Romes, with their particular identities, included.

The idea of Russia as a messianic combination of Eastern and Western tendencies is prevalent in the Third Rome writings of the Russian philosopher Vladimir Solov'ev, a vastly influential figure for Russian Symbolists in the early years of the twentieth century. Influenced by Fedor Dostoevskii's view of Russia, stated in his 1880 Pushkin Speech, as able to encompass the characteristics of all nations within itself, Solov'ev maintained that the power of Russia as the Third Rome lay in Russia's selfless ability to synthesize East and West. For Solov'ev, who was interested in a union of the Eastern and Western churches, Russia represented a "third principle," one that could overcome the differences between the East's "Godman," focused on religious faith, and the West's "Mangod," intent on human, worldly potential. Solov'ev lauded Peter I, whose Westernizing activities had made possible Russia's involvement in the West and, therefore, its mediating role. In his 1896 article "Vizantizm i Rossiia" (Byzantinism and Russia), Solov'ev wrote that "pagan" Rome had fallen because of its worship of Caesar, and Byzantium had fallen because it failed to practice the Christian principles it professed to represent. It had been left to Russia to prove the practicability of a Christian state.[65]

But over the years Solov'ev had developed intermittent doubts about his nation's ability to live up to the mission he had assigned to it. A major disappointment came as early as 1881, when Tsar Alexander III refused to pardon the murderers of his father, Alexander II. In his 1894 poem "Panmongolizm" (Panmongolism), later cited by Aleksandr Blok as the epigraph to his own 1918 poem "Skify" (The Scythians), Solov'ev warned his readers of a new Mongol invasion from the East and rejected his earlier faith in Russia as the Third Rome. Russia had not learned from Byzantium's fate and had forgotten the "rule of love," Solov'ev proclaimed, and as such was prey to the destructive forces of the East. The poem's concluding lines read, "The Third Rome lies in the dust, / And there will be no fourth."[66] In Solov'ev's 1899 "Kratkaia povest' ob Antikhriste" (A Short Story of the Antichrist), a deceptively attractive Antichrist is able to unify the world under his power; because he does not believe in God, however, this unity is false and presages the apocalypse. Orthodox Christians, aided by other Christian denominations and Jews, recognize the Antichrist and, after much bloodshed, find true unity under Jesus Christ and reign with him for one thousand years. The religiously inspired conjunction of East and West occurs not in historical Russia, but in a postapocalyptic framework, as the New Jerusalem replaces Rome.

Solov'ev's vision of a synthesizing Third Rome provided an apocalyptically tinged geographic vocabulary that the Symbolists seized upon while constructing their own Rome-related texts. As Solov'ev had demonstrated, "East" was a fluid term, with wide-ranging and at times contradictory associations, from Christian holiness to barbarian Mongolism.[67] Associating the East with the irrational, faith, and the origins of Christianity, the Symbolists populated the region with Scythians, "Eastern despots," and "barbarians," all of whom stood in contrast to the "rationality" these authors associated with a European "West."[68] These writers drew on Solov'ev's ideas and synthesized them with earlier coursework in the classics, established Russian myths, and new discoveries in Russia and Europe about the classical world and the relevance of this world to the modern age. Their works and those they inspired represent a combination of these influences; they also bear witness to the belief these writers shared in the role art could play in conceptualizing a unified and balanced world.

The Fin-de-siècle Environment

It was all around one—that smoothly built world of old classical taste, an accomplished fact.
Walter Pater, *Marius the Epicurean*, 1885

By the end of the nineteenth century, archaeological excavations of the Roman Forum, the Appian Way (fig. 5), and early Christian catacombs had brought the physical remnants of ancient Rome to the direct gaze of modern Europeans.[69] Under Napoleon in 1810 the French government had created a Commission for Antique Monuments and Civic Buildings in Rome, and ensuing areas of excavation had included the Forum of Emperor Trajan, the Temple of Jupiter, and the first-century emperor Nero's Golden House; the latter would figure in the belletristic writings of Valerii Briusov and Mikhail Kuzmin. By the middle of the century, Italian researchers were uncovering and restoring paths traced

Via Appia. (Chap. IX, No. 206.)

Fig. 5. The Appian Way, ancient Rome's "Queen of the Roads," which had been substantially uncovered and restored in the nineteenth century (from P. J. Chandlery, *Pilgrim-Walks in Rome*, 1908)

Catacombs of S. Callisto: Tomb of St. Cornelius, P.M.
(Chap. IX, No. 202.)

Fig. 6. The Catacombs of St. Callistus, newly accessible to travelers and researchers in the nineteenth century (from P. J. Chandlery, *Pilgrim-Walks in Rome*, 1908)

by the Appian Way, Rome's "Queen of the Roads," which would make an appearance in Viacheslav Ivanov's poetry; the first-century House of Livia, wife of Emperor Augustus; and the Catacombs of St. Callistus (fig. 6), which had been inaccessible for the preceding millennium. Catacombs provided rich scholarly information on the customs of early Christians, and pilgrims flocked to explore graves, paintings, and inscriptions; Merezhkovskii would describe such inscriptions in his early work.[70] The erudite German historian Theodor Mommsen (who in subsequent years would prove inspirational to Ivanov, who wrote a dissertation in Latin on the Roman taxation system) assisted archaeologists mid-century in identifying specific locations in the Roman Forum (fig. 7), which had been largely redeemed by that point from its recent status as a cow pasture.[71]

Excitement over the ancient world gained added fire with the discovery in 1871 by the German amateur excavator Heinrich Schliemann of what he claimed to be Homer's Troy. While in fact Schliemann's

Fig. 7. The Roman Forum in 1821, with ancient and modern layers visible (engraving from Rodolfo Lanciani, *The Destruction of Ancient Rome*, 1903)

treasure trove of discoveries dated back a millennium earlier than the supposed timeframe of the *Iliad,* classical enthusiasts thrilled to the idea that Homer's tales, which provided the cultural background to Virgil's own legend of Rome's founding, seemed to be historically based. Archaeologists in Russia took active part in the general European search for remnants of the classical past. Under the aegis of Russia's Imperial Archaeological Commission, created in 1859, excavations in southern Russia and the Crimea built upon earlier expeditions to reveal the remains of the ancient Scythians and of the Greek trading colonies along the Black Sea coast, notably Chersonesus.[72] Reports on these excavations, which featured among their participants and planners such prominent Russian scholars as Ivan Zabelin, Ivan Tsvetaev, and Vasilii Kliuchevskii, were found in leading journals and newspapers.[73] Anna Akhmatova, who spent time in the Crimea as a child, later recalled the excavations ongoing there at the time and referred to herself as "the last inhabitant of Chersonesus."[74]

Scholars of the day assigned a crucial role to the bridging of the academic and the popular. University lectures on ancient history came to attract avid audiences: as I. S. Sventsitskaia writes, Merezhkovskii was one of the many enraptured students of the historian Fedor Sokolov, and Kliuchevskii wrote in his memoirs that he had tended to be absent from Russian historian Sergei Solov'ev's lectures when they coincided with those of Fedor Buslaev and G. I. Ivanov on the ancient world.[75] Tsvetaev's success in 1912 in founding the Museum of Fine Arts (today known as the Pushkin State Museum of Fine Arts) in cooperation with Moscow University attests not only to his commitment to bringing the ancient world to Russian viewers, but also to journalistic interest in this venture, as reported, for instance, in the journal *Germes* (Hermes), billed as an "illustrated scholarly-popular bulletin of the ancient world."[76] In a further example of the committed popularization of ancient studies in Russia, the works of European historians with particular appeal, including the French scholar Gaston Boissier, were translated into Russian (indeed, in 1894 Boissier was elected to the Petersburg Academy of Sciences).[77] Gibbon's *Decline and Fall of the Roman Empire,* first published in 1776, was translated into Russian in 1883–1886.[78]

Particularly influential both for leading Symbolist writers and their successors and for the Russian general public in their reception of antiquity was the classicist Faddei Zelinskii (Tadeusz Zielinski), a native Pole who was brought up in Russia, studied and traveled abroad, and in 1887 became a professor at St. Petersburg University, where one of the students he inspired was Aleksandr Blok.[79] Zelinskii was a friend to Viacheslav Ivanov and Innokentii Annenskii, a regular at gatherings of St. Petersburg's literary elite in the early years of the twentieth century, and a renowned translator and scholar.[80] Yet in his capacity as a public intellectual he also served as an intermediary and spokesperson to the Russian populace, bringing the ancient world to life through a series of well-received lectures, articles, and books intended for general consumption. In his faith in the connections between ancient Rome and modern Russia, and in his conviction that a Slavic return to antiquity could provide unity to an increasingly fractured world, Zelinskii epitomized many of the characteristic features of the Russian reception of Rome at the turn of the twentieth century. In *Drevnii mir i my,* translated in 1909 as *Our Debt to Antiquity,* he told readers that "our intellectual and moral culture has never been so closely bound up with Antiquity, has never stood in more pressing need of it, and never been so qualified to comprehend and assimilate it as at the present day."[81]

Zelinskii valued antiquity specifically because he believed that through studying and appreciating the classics, a nation could enter into "civilization," the basis of which, he argued, was the classical heritage.[82] Entering into civilization entailed major responsibilities: as Nikolai Bakhtin, who along with his brother Mikhail Bakhtin studied with Zelinskii, would later recall, "Studying classical philology was not simply training, but, above all else, a means to re-create life."[83] Specifically, the resurrection of the classics was intended to inspire what Zelinskii termed a "Slavic Renaissance," a third renaissance following those of fourteenth-century Italy and eighteenth-century Germany.[84] Based on Zelinskii's conviction that "the link which connects and unites all European nations independently of their national and racial differences is their common descent from Antiquity,"[85] his Slavic Renaissance was intended to provide a potential bulwark against the impending new period of barbarism that he feared was menacing Europe. Iu. Asoian and A. Malafeev suggest that Zelinskii believed that the revival and strengthening of what unified Western civilization—its classical base—could forestall this eventuality.[86] Aware of Russia's actual distance from Rome (Zelinskii even argued that the Latin and Russian languages were at two extremities in terms of their focus on the intellect and the senses respectively),[87] Zelinskii nonetheless claimed a major role for the Slavic nations in rescuing the heritage Rome embodied. Slavs were to embrace the West's classical heritage and then, having embodied it, proceed to unite with the West and thereby save it.

Zelinskii's emphasis on the role of the past in interpreting the present was typical of a transition in historical thought in the late nineteenth century. In the 1860s and 1870s, historical studies had been marked by the dominance of positivist tendencies, which applied the techniques of the natural sciences to the study of the past.[88] In a backlash against historicism, as the century progressed, a new generation of thinkers posited alternative methods of historiography. Rejecting positivism, some turned to historical idealism, according to which the goal of the historian was to resurrect the spirit of a vanished era, not only through painstaking research, but through active imagination. Others adopted cyclical views of history and created new narratives of the rise and fall of nations and the relevance of prior experience to the modern age.[89]

In a related approach to history, myth was proposed as a way of assigning meaning to the present by seeking its roots in a distant past.[90] Mythical narratives, based as they were on accounts of sacred origins, added a spiritual dimension to the study of bygone eras.[91] As a presentation of "the actual in terms of the ideal," the present, or the "temporal and immediate," could be seen in the light of a corresponding "eternal and transcendental."[92] As Mircea Eliade argues, historians sought through their writings to "awaken" ancient worlds through a process of anamnesis, or recovery of the past, that would result, for modern researchers, in a sense of "solidarity" with an earlier age.[93] "Tell me what legends you have, and I will tell you what kind of a people you are," Merezhkovskii wrote.[94]

For many Russian modernists, the seminal figure in this wide-ranging transformation of historical thought was Friedrich Nietzsche, who in *On the Advantage and Disadvantage of History for Life* (1874) warned his contemporaries against "an excess of history," but acknowledged nonetheless that history reconceived could serve an important purpose: "only through the power to use the past for life and to refashion what has happened into history, does man become man."[95] Trained as a classicist, in his *Birth of Tragedy* (1872) Nietzsche railed against the staleness of modern European thought and proposed an enormously influential, radical reinterpretation of the classical world. He rejected Johann Winckelmann's concept of classical Greece as the setting for "a noble simplicity and a quiet grandeur"[96] and described a civilization marked instead by an opposition between the rational, individualistic Apollonian tendency and the orgiastic, collective Dionysian. Further, in his *Thus Spake Zarathustra* (1883–1885), Nietzsche suggested his notion of "eternal return," the idea that one moment could repeat itself indefinitely. Thus past, present, and future merged: as Stephen Kern comments, "In the *fin de siècle,* time's arrow did not always fly straight and true."[97]

New modes of thought called for new modes of expression. Just as positivist approaches to history had been deemed insufficient, the language of the past was seen as inappropriate in a world in which longstanding concepts such as causality, rationality, and time itself were being called into question.[98] As Briusov wrote in an 1893 diary entry, one could scarcely use the language of Pushkin to describe the sensations of the end of the century.[99] Writers throughout Europe seized upon the language of symbols and myths: "logical" speech was contrasted with "mythological" speech, as Ivanov would later write, and the symbol was the concept, or "subject," which myth, its "predicate," would then develop.[100] "Myth is born of the symbol," Ivanov explained.[101]

Rome proved a fruitful and attractive symbol to poets and artists; the "golden bough" of James Frazer's eponymous 1890 study of myth was, after all, the limb that Aeneas had plucked on his way to the underworld. Furthermore, as a city that simultaneously epitomized both empire and, through its "ruined" status, imperial dissolution by new forces such as Christianity or "barbarians," Rome evoked associations with the incipient waning of modern Europe's own imperial age. "Decadents" portrayed Rome's well-known decline and fall and called for new "barbarians" to sweep away a world overrun, as they saw it, by meaningless "bourgeois" mechanization and corruptive progress.[102]

Russians, with their long history of ambivalence toward Europe and Western Christianity, joined in this mythmaking process. For Russia's new poetic movement of Symbolism, arising in the 1890s in response to the similar earlier movement in France and continuing until approximately 1910, Rome provided a rich and multivalent symbol through which the Symbolists and then subsequent generations of Russian writers could convey historiosophical views tinged to varying degrees with Solov'evian Christian idealism and apocalypticism and a Nietzschean fascination with Dionysus.[103] Russian writers took advantage of Rome's "essential semiotic polyglottism," to use Iurii Lotman's phrase,[104] and invoked longstanding prior associations: Rome as eternal or archetypal city, as imperial, republican, decadent, pagan, or Christian. Yet Russia's high level of revolutionary unrest at the turn of the twentieth century, combined with the messianic import some Russians assigned to the revolutionary movement, once again added a peculiarly Russian twist to the widespread European phenomenon of Rome-identification at the fin de siècle.

With Russian imperial forces attempting to withstand the "new Christianity," as some Russians termed it, of socialism, the period of Roman history characterized by the pagan-Christian clash,[105] when a firmly entrenched empire of this world was challenged by a revolutionary "City of God," was seen as particularly relevant to Russia's own revolutionary age. Russian modernists recast Rome's well-known ancient story to create narratives that resonated with their own fraught present. Early Christians had risen up against an empire, and therefore modern Russian revolutionaries were associated—despite their widespread atheistic Marxism—with Christianity. Rome, meanwhile, the archetypal empire under siege, could be linked with a Russian autocracy similarly beset, as these writers saw it, by revolutionary opposition. Further, according to Russia's Rome-based narrative of national identity, Christianity tended to be identified with the East, while empire, exemplified in the carefully plotted streets of Peter I's capital, was associated with the "rational" West. Various Symbolist authors availed themselves of these associations to narrate revolution in geographic terms, as the Eastern "faithful" battled the Western "imperialists."

The dominant Russia-Rome paradigm created at the turn of the twentieth century would endure to a large degree through revolution and the consolidation of Soviet rule, though roles would shift along with power and allegiances. Once entrenched, revolutionaries would take on imperial stature, their formerly rebellious footprints now filled by the intellectuals who, to their newfound chagrin, had helped bring the Soviets to power. While early modernist Rome texts link the intelligentsia with revolutionaries in opposition to the state, later texts, such as those of Kuzmin and Bulgakov, link the Bolsheviks with the Roman Empire in opposition to a narrative of artistic revelation and faith.[106]

The divisions and uncertainties in Russian society during this turbulent period led to confusion and alarm. "We are experiencing a crisis," Andrei Belyi proclaimed in the early years of the twentieth century.[107] "We experienced everything happening around us as an omen," Vladislav Khodasevich would later recall of this period. "But of what?"[108] Looking back, Zinaida Hippius would claim that "one could feel tragedy in the air of Russia."[109] Aware of the disunity that surrounded them, these writers sought a way out of what Belyi termed the "apocalyptic rhythm of the time."[110] For while modernist literature marked in ways a break with the civic literature of the past, focused as it had been on the betterment of Russia's social conditions, the Rome-based texts of the Russian Symbolists and those they inspired were also affected by and geared toward contemporary Russian reality, albeit understood through sometimes murky Symbolist spectacles. Convinced that culture as they knew it faced a stark choice between unifying transformation and negation, writers strove in different ways through their work to counteract the disunity in the world around them.

These authors were engaging in the complex, mythmaking phenomenon of *zhiznetvorchestvo,* according to which, as Irina Paperno writes, "Art was proclaimed to be a force capable of, and destined for, the 'creation of life' (*tvorchestvo zhizni*), while 'life' was viewed as an object of artistic creation or a creative act."[111] In the context of Russia's self-identification with Rome, the consequences of this phenomenon were twofold. First, the artistic text became a place where the transformation of "reality" through art could be envisaged and, according to the terms of *zhiznetvorchestvo,* effected. Describing disunity, writers could alert readers to it, explain its consequences, and call for its resolution. Rome thus provided a framework for a given author to present his particular understanding of contemporary Russian national identity and the issues facing Russians at a crucial stage in their history. Second, in keeping with the more cyclical and personal ideas of history prevalent during this period, writers came to view their surroundings and lives as extensions or repetitions of a Roman past. Elizaveta Kuz'mina-Karavaeva, for example, would describe the Russia of 1910 as "Rome in the age of decline."[112] Correspondingly, the Roman characters who populated these writers' texts could function as their alter egos, as literature based in ancient Rome came to serve as a medium for discussions of emotional, artistic, or political issues important in modern-day Russia. Rome thus functioned as a trope on both a national and a personal level.

The Texts

Once out of nature I shall never take
My bodily form from any natural thing,
But such a form as Grecian goldsmiths make
Of hammered gold and gold enamelling
To keep a drowsy Emperor awake;
Or set upon a golden bough to sing
To lords and ladies of Byzantium
Of what is past, or passing, or to come.
William Butler Yeats, "Sailing to Byzantium," 1926

When faced with so rich and wide-ranging a topic as Rome, it is extremely difficult to choose from the many relevant texts available for discussion. I am concerned primarily with the Russian Symbolists, though the final two texts I discuss extend beyond that movement to demonstrate the longevity of the associations the Symbolists had developed. From a gallery of possibilities, I have chosen for the most part those texts that have been under-studied despite the prominence of their authors.[113] A lack of sustained scholarly focus on these works has meant a corresponding neglect of the broader phenomenon they reflect: that of Russian writers' participation in and reworking of the European mythologization of Rome during the modernist period. In chapter 1 I argue that this process began with Merezhkovskii's popular and influential Rome-based trilogy *Khristos i Antikhrist* (Christ and Antichrist), which consisted of the novels *Smert' bogov: Iulian otstupnik* (The Death of the Gods: Julian the Apostate, 1895), *Voskresshie bogi: Leonardo da Vinchi* (The Resurrected Gods: Leonardo da Vinci, 1900), and *Antikhrist: Petr i Aleksei* (The Antichrist: Peter and Alexis, 1904–1905). The trilogy, which only recently has begun to attract the scholarly notice its turn-of-the-century influence merits, was written over a period of more than ten tumultuous years in Russian history, and attracted ample attention at the time in literary circles and in the press. The literary critic D. S. Mirsky would later assert that Merezhkovskii's *Julian the Apostate* was "an excellent 'home university' book that has probably interested more Russian readers in antiquity than any other single book ever did."[114]

In this first in-depth examination of the Rome theme as it unfolds throughout Merezhkovskii's trilogy and relates to other Merezhkovskiian writings of the period, I suggest that Merezhkovskii strove in his first two novels to inspire Russia to fulfill its potential to become a unifying Third Rome, combining Western secularism and Eastern spirituality in a transcendent mix. In his third novel, disillusioned in Solov'evian fashion by the increasing disunity that characterized his nation, he abandoned his former faith in Russia's imperial state, linked repeatedly in this final novel to ancient Rome. In so doing, he rejected the notion of a theocratic Third Rome and proclaimed instead an impending apocalypse.

Christ and Antichrist came to serve as a rich thesaurus of the Roman world for Russian readers and for later Russian writers, as Merezhkovskii availed himself of Rome's myriad associations to suggest allegorically the resonances and parallels of these associations in a Russian context. Merezhkovskii's Julian the Apostate, for instance, craving a return to the pagan gods but paradoxically in need of Christ, shed light on Merezhkovskii himself and his fellow modernists in the early to mid-1890s. In *Leonardo da Vinci,* a Russian icon-painter's vision of Russia as the Third Rome presaged the Slavic artistic Renaissance Merezhkovskii hoped to see at the turn of the twentieth century. And Merezhkovskii's Roman-style Peter the Great, by slaughtering the Tsarevich Alexis, set in motion the tensions that would lead to Russia's 1905 Revolution. Throughout the trilogy, Merezhkovskii maintained his faith in the Russian artist, first as one able to synthesize through his art East and West, Christianity and paganism, and then as one to whom the "final revelation" would be made manifest. Merezhkovskii had claimed Rome, in its various guises, for Russia, and had demonstrated to his contemporaries Rome's power as a tool in discussions of Russia's own identity and path.

Tracing the development of the Rome-Russia associations that Merezhkovskii, through his trilogy, had rendered part of Russia's cultural discourse, I next examine the Rome-related texts of his fellow Symbolists Briusov, Blok, and Ivanov, as well as those of the post-Symbolist writers Kuzmin and Bulgakov. Each writer deals with specific, historical events in ancient Roman history. And each employs, in some cases explicitly, elements of the "Roman" paradigm of Russia's mission and culture that Merezhkovskii had initiated, but in a manner consistent both with the individual writer's historical and cultural beliefs and with the time in which he was writing. Finally, each revisits Merezhkovskii's early belief that the Russian artist, creator of myths, had a particular role in forging a relationship between Eastern spirituality and Western, secular imperialism—a concern not surprising in the Symbolists, known for their faith in the connection between art and life, and those they similarly inspired.

I turn first to Briusov's 1911–1912 novel *Altar' pobedy* (The Altar of Victory), along with its unfinished sequel *Iupiter poverzhennyi* (Jupiter Overthrown, written mainly between 1912 and 1913 and first published in 1934), as the subjects of chapter 2. Unlike Briusov's earlier and better-known novel *Ognennyi angel* (The Fiery Angel, 1907–1908), his Rome-related novels have received only rare scholarly notice and remain unfamiliar to most readers, despite the author's famed attraction to ancient Rome. Situating Briusov's novels in the context of Merezhkovskii's trilogy and contemporary debates on art and politics between the 1905 and 1917 Revolutions, I treat Briusov's texts as an overt, negative response to Merezhkovskii's messianic and apocalyptic visions of Russia and of the Russian artist. Predominantly a Westernizer and imperialist, in his novels, devoted like *Julian the Apostate* to the pagan-Christian clash of fourth-century Rome, Briusov mourns the fall of the Western Roman Empire at the hands of Christians, whom he represents as unappealing, dangerous members of an orgiastic Eastern sect. His leading character, Junius Norbanus, is a pragmatist, however, who in the end embraces the victorious Christian faith he has previously rejected. Upon the Bolshevik seizure of power, Briusov the supporter of autocracy would follow his character's lead and welcome the socialism he had initially found barbaric, comparable to the forces that had attacked the Roman Empire. I read Briusov's acceptance of Bolshevik power, therefore, not simply as political expediency, as has been assumed, but as a difficult and yet logical outgrowth of his commitment to adopting new "faiths," however uncongenial they might initially appear.

In the artistic realm, I maintain, Briusov's novels serve as a postscript to the Symbolist "crisis" of 1910, when Briusov, who had largely created the Symbolist movement, showed himself to have moved far from the views of many of his Symbolist colleagues. At the time he was writing his Roman novels, Briusov had made a painful decision to relinquish Symbolism for what he termed the new artistic "faith" of "scientific poetry." And yet despite his much vaunted faith in "the new" in politics and art, his novels of the period in fact portray a synthesis of past and present forces, both historical and literary. The formerly pagan Junius and his contemporaries create a Christian church that ends up resembling the empire it has replaced, as faith and imperialism merge. Similarly, notwithstanding their "scientific" aspects, stylistically and thematically Briusov's novels demonstrate his inability to move definitively away from his earlier literary practices. Like his earlier texts, the Roman novels are in fact a celebration of human achievement, the highest of which, for Briusov, continued to be art itself. His novels presage his own eventual conviction, despite his best efforts to become a part of the new Soviet state, that socialist Russia should not entirely cut itself off from its imperial past. Rome-based art, with its unifying vision, pointed the way to Briusov's complex reception of Soviet life.

Blok's 1918 essay "Katilina" (Catiline), written shortly after the Bolshevik takeover, forms the subject of chapter 3. Like Briusov's Roman novels, Blok's essay has met with limited scholarly attention. Blok describes the Roman rebel Catiline, who in the first century BCE raised a rebellion against the Roman state and then was defeated by Cicero and the Roman army. In Blok's retelling, Catiline's inspired uprising heralds the revolutionary changes that Jesus Christ will later bring to the Roman Empire. Catiline is also a "Roman Bolshevik"; thus Blok assigns a sacred task to Russia's Red Guards, linking them to Jesus and lauding their revolutionary mission. Desiring all of Russia to follow in this path but acknowledging the unlikelihood of this scenario, Blok calls upon the writer to keep the spirit of revolution alive through his art even when surrounded by deadening, imperial-style bureaucracy. Blok associates Catiline with the mythical Phrygian figure Attis, asserting an Eastern subtext to Catiline's—and the Bolsheviks'—rebellion against the Western state. Incorporating Blok's better-known "Dvenadtsat'" (The Twelve, 1918) and "Skify" (The Scythians, 1918) into my argument, I conclude that for this writer, spiritually imbued revolution recurs eternally, with the Russian artist, once again, as keeper of the myths.

Chapter 4 is devoted to Ivanov's "Rimskie sonety" (Roman Sonnets), written after the poet had fled Bolshevik Russia for the haven of Rome in 1924 and seldom analyzed as a cycle in the context of the poet's pre-emigration work. The subtext in these poems is the theme of fallen empires—Roman, Russian, and Trojan. Ivanov connects himself both to Aeneas, legendary founder of the Roman state who left his vanquished Trojan homeland in order to establish a new empire, and to Virgil, who captured in verse this shift from East to West and in so doing defined his own nation's identity through holy, inspired mythmaking. Like Aeneas and Virgil, Ivanov the artist-émigré becomes the creator of a new kingdom, in his case one defined specifically by art, memory, and religion. Claiming his place in the world of the "first" Rome, with its vestiges of empire preserved in monuments and myth, and connecting it through his verse to Russia, Ivanov the émigré paradoxically achieves on a personal, artistic level the all-encompassing character he had linked, in a 1909 essay, to Russia the Third Rome, ideal unifier of East and West.

Kuzmin's 1928–1929 play *Smert' Nerona* (The Death of Nero), the subject of chapter 5, returns to Russia and to the theme of the artist-revolutionary encountered in Blok's work, but in this case with a somewhat different focus. Conceived during Stalin's rise to power and devoted to the reign of the first-century emperor Nero, Kuzmin's text suggests a parallel between the Roman dictator and Bolshevik leaders including Lenin and Stalin. At the same time, through the figure of a twentieth-century artist who is linked specifically to Nero throughout the text, Kuzmin implies that the prerevolutionary intelligentsia was complicit in the creation of the Bolsheviks' oppressive rule. Rejecting this rule and the utopian-style dreams that inspired it, Kuzmin calls for mutual forgiveness and respect between artist and tyrant—but only on an individual level, in keeping with the Gnostic and neo-Platonic views he valued. Unpublished until 1977, Kuzmin's play provides a fascinating example of the author's intense interest, so typical of his era, in the early Christian period and its links to his own day.

Kuzmin's vision of Russia is echoed to a degree in that of Mikhail Bulgakov, whose *Master i Margarita* (The Master and Margarita), begun in 1928 and left virtually complete at the time of the writer's death in 1940, I discuss briefly in the conclusion. I have chosen to end with Bulgakov's novel in order to situate this widely familiar text in a little-studied framework, thereby providing a new context and identifying possible further predecessors for Bulgakov's novel. Focusing on the Roman themes, I suggest that in *The Master and Margarita* Bulgakov was adapting an established paradigm in Russian cultural discourse. Like Kuzmin's play, Bulgakov's novel connects the Soviet world and the Roman Empire through the writings of a twentieth-century Russian author. Furthermore, at the end of his novel, Bulgakov offers a potential reconciliation between the spiritual or artistic (linked in the novel) and the secular, as the Galilean Yeshua Ha-Notsri (Jesus) and the Roman Pontius Pilate find common ground through the Russian Master's art. Bulgakov's conclusion comes only after a pseudo-apocalypse: like Solov'ev and Merezhkovskii, Bulgakov did not vouchsafe his vision of a synthesized Russia—seen, as ever, through a Roman prism—to the tense times in which he lived.

Thus several decades after Solov'ev's apocalyptic imaginings and Merezhkovskii's messianic visions, with a new, Soviet government firmly in place, Bulgakov returned to the narrative of a secular empire where the Russian artist could—indeed, had a responsibility to—find common ground between spirituality and secular imperialism, unifying and transforming Russia and the world. Revolution had not changed the basic outline of Russia's Rome-based self-mythologization, though the godly revolutionaries of earlier texts had turned, once in power, into their antithesis. Throughout a period of turbulent change, the worldly empire and the Kingdom of God, both archetypal "Rome texts," took center stage in leading Russian writers' discussions of Russian national identity. Now, in the wake of another Russian empire's dissolution and at the beginning of a new century, Rome once again has become a dominant trope in Russia's literary discourse. As I demonstrate in the final portion of my conclusion, a tradition begun in Russia's medieval period has continued into a new millennium.

The Rome texts of the Russian modernists present a unique and crucial window onto Russian modernism and fin-de-siècle Russian thought. The texts reveal a striking concern with history, conceived for the most part cyclically and mythically, and with Russia's place in history and culture. These writers had been schooled in the classical tradition, and they inhabited a world in which the classical past was a living, powerful presence in cultural discourse. Seizing upon Rome as a crucial symbol and rewriting it, sometimes anachronistically, to suit their own modern-day purposes, they created new, individual, and at times subversive narratives of Russian national identity. The Russian Romes they created drew upon aspects of the "First Rome," that complex republican and then imperial capital, as well as the Byzantine "Second Rome" that coexisted with and then succeeded it, in the process inspiring Russians to adopt the Eastern Orthodox Christian faith. They also drew upon the tradition of the Third Rome, as several of the authors I discuss explicitly term it, with its echoes of messianism and its striving for synthesis. "Russia's Rome" is, then, a modernist and at times iconoclastic literary rendering of a Third Rome, a varying combination of the many influences—political, cultural, and religious—that to modernist eyes had helped to create the complicated contemporary "Russias" they wrote into their diverse Rome-based texts. These influences, in their opinion, had provided a variety of terms for scripting a future Russia as well. Taken as a whole, the series of works under discussion in this book form a tradition of their own in Russian literature and self-understanding, and also take part in a larger chain: an age-old and widespread tradition that seeks to locate meaning and self-understanding in Rome.

1

The Blueprint

Dmitrii Merezhkovskii's *Christ and Antichrist*

Oh, will we not find the kind of faith that could once again
Unite on earth all tribes and peoples?
Where are you, unknown God, where are you, O future Rome?
Dmitrii Merezhkovskii, "The Future Rome," 1891

Dmitrii Merezhkovskii's trilogy *Khristos i Antikhrist* (Christ and Antichrist), comprising the novels *Smert' bogov: Iulian otstupnik* (The Death of the Gods: Julian the Apostate, 1895); *Voskresshie bogi: Leonardo da Vinchi* (The Resurrected Gods: Leonardo da Vinci, 1900); and *Antikhrist: Petr i Aleksei* (The Antichrist: Peter and Alexis, 1904–5), represents a milestone in Russian letters.[1] As the philosopher Nikolai Berdiaev would later write, Merezhkovskii had "introduced, and was himself expressive of, a whole unknown or forgotten world of cultural values, of Greek and Roman antiquity, of the Italian Renaissance."[2] The critic D. S. Mirsky would use almost identical terms when describing the significance of Merezhkovskii's prose: it had "introduced to the Russian reader a whole unknown world of cultural values; it made familiar and significant to him figures and epochs that had only been names in textbooks."[3] Contemporary readers compared *Julian the Apostate* to works by Henryk Sienkiewicz, Emile Zola, Gustave Flaubert, and Anatole France.[4] Upon the appearance of *Leonardo da Vinci,* an enthusiastic subscriber to the newspaper *Novoe vremia* (New Times) wrote to its literary critic Viktor Burenin that he had just returned from Italy, where as a result of this second novel Merezhkovskii was being mentioned along with Lev Tolstoi and Maksim Gor'kii as a leading Russian writer.[5] Sigmund Freud would later draw upon *Leonardo da Vinci* in his own research on the Renaissance painter.[6]

Meanwhile, Merezhkovskii's depiction in *Peter and Alexis* of the relationship between the Westernized Russian intelligentsia and the religious *narod* (folk) would find echoes in the writings of Aleksandr Blok, Andrei Belyi, Osip Mandel'shtam, and Aleksei N. Tolstoi. The trilogy as a whole marked the beginning of a tradition of Symbolist novels in Russia.[7]

Merezhkovskii brought the cultural heritage commonly associated with Europe to life in Russia, making it relevant to Russian readers, and, with *Peter and Alexis,* inserted Russian history and letters into that European narrative. *Christ and Antichrist* would contribute to Merezhkovskii's being nominated for a Nobel Prize in 1933.[8] In their chronological and cultural sweep and in their focus on Russia's place in world history and culture, the novels of *Christ and Antichrist* form a complex, allegorical epic of Russia's national identity and destiny at the turn of the twentieth century, with Merezhkovskii as author-prophet defining both.

Goals and Influences

I say that one must be a *visionary*—that one must make oneself a VISIONARY.
Arthur Rimbaud, letter of 1887 (Cited in Edmund Wilson, *Axel's Castle*)

To undertake this lofty task, Merezhkovskii turned to Rome, with its longstanding East-West markers and messianic associations, and created a Symbolist Rome reflective of the concerns of Silver Age Russia. He set the first novel in the fourth-century Roman Empire and the third novel in Petrine Russia, and then rendered explicit the implication of Russia's Third Rome status with references throughout the third novel both to Rome and to the Third Rome. In addition, in the second novel of the trilogy, set in the Italian Renaissance, he featured an artist, a Russian icon-painter, who foretold in exalted terms the glory of "Russia, the Third Rome." Because of the novels' popularity, Merezhkovskii's trilogy functioned for Russian readers as an acknowledged thesaurus of Rome's myriad associated themes (imperial power and its decline, differing varieties of Christianity, the relationship between East and West, the role of the artist in society, the ancient, Renaissance, and modern periods), as the author laid out the resonances and parallels of these concepts in a Russian context. Through Merezhkovskii's texts, Rome became a powerful mythmaking tool in the Symbolist construction of Russia's history and future. Merezhkovskii's impassioned literary musings on a Third Rome mission for Russia—and, as Russia's political and social tensions worsened and Merezhkovskii's views changed, on the vanishing feasibility and desirability of such a mission—created an influential set of terms and ideas that would inspire or have an effect upon a series of similarly Rome-focused texts by his contemporaries.

Despite the novels' significant impact and international renown, at the time of their creation they met with a mixed reaction from Russia's critics, particularly those of the older, Populist generation.[9] Bewildered by Merezhkovskii's "Decadent" deviations from the stylistic and ideological norms of the nineteenth-century Russian novel, many critics rejected his texts, finding them unconvincing as "historical" novels and even dangerous to the unschooled Russian reader. A reviewer for *Russkoe bogatstvo* (Russian Riches) argued that Merezhkovskii's central idea in *Julian the Apostate* was a Nietzschean-style "rejection of an altruistic morality," and expressed his concern at the effect that such an argument might have on the "undeveloped" Russian public, "ill equipped for philosophical thought."[10] Similarly, writing for *Knizhki nedeli* (Booklets of the Week), L. Obolenskii argued that the novel undermined the idea of progress by lauding the paganism that had preceded Christianity.[11] V. Mirskii, reviewing Merezhkovskii's first two novels for *Zhurnal dlia vsekh* (Journal for All), asserted that the novels were too "Western": the Russian author had failed to take into account the "religiously moral" basis crucial to Russian literature.[12] And an outraged Aleksandr Skabichevskii condemned the novels from an artistic and ideological point of view, predicting hopefully, "Twenty or thirty years from now, there won't be even the slightest recollection of this entire divine trilogy."[13]

The critics' discomfort was in a sense justified, for *Christ and Antichrist* represents a distinct departure from the nineteenth-century Realist tradition. Merezhkovskii eschewed positivist-style historicism and the development of plot and character in his novels in favor of a system of interlocking leitmotifs and character types repeated throughout the trilogy. Wide-ranging differences in time and setting among the novels thus became irrelevant, as commonalities among epochs were stressed over the particularities of a given age, and cyclicity gained primacy over historical progression as certain themes were repeated from one novel to the next.[14] In keeping with their essentially atemporal status, the characters in the trilogy voiced philosophical opinions significantly more modern than the characters themselves. Merezhkovskii's fourth-century Emperor Julian is, as critics have noted, an obviously Nietzschean figure,[15] while many of the Renaissance characters might well have emerged from a fin-de-siècle salon.[16] In contrast to the complex psychological portraits readers had enjoyed in the writings of Fedor Dostoevskii or Lev Tolstoi, Merezhkovskii's characters were not well developed: Andrei Belyi wrote that they were interesting only as symbols, rather than as independent individuals.[17] Moreover, even as some of his characters bore resemblances to turn-of-the-century Decadents, Merezhkovskii broke with the Realist tradition of using the novel as an obvious platform for the discussion of Russia's contemporary socio-economic conditions, thus gaining a reputation, in fact inaccurate, as a proponent of "art for art's sake."[18] Stylistically and thematically surprising, the novels of *Christ and Antichrist* drew on the recent discoveries both of the French Symbolists and of the archaeologists unearthing ancient Rome, gave voice to the "dangerous" new philosophy of Friedrich Nietzsche, and fed contemporary artistic debates. They thus exemplify that inherently novelistic openendedness that comes, according to Mikhail Bakhtin, from the novel's link to contemporary reality, "itself in the process of unfolding": "only that which is itself developing can comprehend development as a process."[19] For those unwilling to relinquish the socially focused Realist novel, this process was not appealing, and Merezhkovskii, a promulgator of a new Russian aesthetic, was found wanting.

And yet Merezhkovskii had not turned his back entirely on the nineteenth-century tradition. While his novels amounted to a renunciation of civic literature, he nonetheless was as committed as his nineteenth-century predecessors had been to transforming the Russia of his day through the power of the word. At the time he began the trilogy, Merezhkovskii believed that Russia was at a crucial stage in its development, its inhabitants overwhelmed by dehumanizing industrialization, urbanization, and Marxist materialism, its intellectuals yearning despite themselves for a long-dismissed spirituality. Having passed through stages of positivism, mediated by Christian faith, and then Populism, before being pulled in yet another direction by the writings of Nietzsche as well as Charles Baudelaire and Edgar Allan Poe, Merezhkovskii himself embodied the philosophical confusion he attributed to his era as a whole. He proposed to counter this malaise through an inspirational combination of "two truths," to be promoted and exemplified in works of the new Symbolist art. The first of his "truths," associated in his mind with the East and specifically with Russia, consisted of renewed Christian faith and self-sacrifice. The second consisted of the "pagan" appreciation of beauty, joy, knowledge, and power that Merezhkovskii associated both with Western Europe and, following Nietzsche, with Hellenic Greece and pre-Christian Rome. Influenced additionally by Vladimir Solov'ev, Merezhkovskii believed that Russia was the kingdom of the Godman, for Christ had come to earth to become man, and Russia had not yet lost all its faith in Christ. Europe, on the contrary, was the kingdom of the Mangod, of those who aspire through beauty, wisdom, and power to equal God. The union of Christ and Antichrist, or Christianity and paganism, became for Merezhkovskii a way of expressing the union of the "East," symbolized by the Russian Christian Godman, and the "West," symbolized by the European pagan Mangod.[20]

Merezhkovskii felt that the Russian Orthodox Church of his day was characterized by what he termed "Historic Christianity," unremittingly pious, self-effacing, devoid of life and thought, and thus akin to Nietzsche's "slave morality."[21] But because Russia had received Christianity from the Greek Orthodox Church, Merezhkovskii reasoned that Russian Christianity had a connection through its Greek roots to a Dionysian appreciation of classical "pagan" traits. If Russian Orthodox Christians could rediscover these roots, he believed, Russia would be inherently well equipped to bridge the gap currently existing between Russian and European culture. One might view *Christ and Antichrist*, characterized by a contemporary combination of European and Russian cultural and religious associations, as an attempt to produce the new art Merezhkovskii sought. With its emphasis on Russian messianism, the Third Rome concept, presented by Merezhkovskii in an updated, post-Nietzschean incarnation, provided an ideal vehicle to analyze Russia's past and future.

In attempting to assign a messianic mission both to Russia and to his novels, Merezhkovskii was participating in a tradition of what Frederick T. Griffiths and Stanley J. Rabinowitz have termed "novel epics," those novels that claim a place in a chain of epic works including the exemplary texts of Homer, Virgil, Dante, and Milton.[22] Griffiths and Rabinowitz locate in the novels of Dostoevskii and Gogol' an epic tendency defined by a "double plot: partly about heroes, partly about its own durability as a form."[23] Epic plot, they write, "will concern at most the emergence of a single sense of nationhood or creed, another Rome, while the embedded record of literary genealogy traces the movement of culture from nation to nation, language to language, religion to religion: *Iliad* to *Odyssey* to *Aeneid* to *Divine Comedy*."[24] Thus epic, like the novel, can be seen as a constantly evolving genre, since epic adapts both to a nation's desire to claim another's past authority for its own and to an author's similar desire to wrap himself in a previous master's literary mantle. Griffiths and Rabinowitz note the critic Vissarion Belinskii's proclamation that "the epic of our time is the novel," as they point to the Russian desire to expand the novel's purview, "making it monumental, that is, epic."[25]

Merezhkovskii's authorial predecessors in the trilogy are both Russian and European: Dostoevskii's holy monks coexist with Dante's worldly Italians. Combining these referents, Merezhkovskii asserted continuity between Russia's own cultural tradition and that of Europe. Similarly, on a national level, like the Russians' plaque at San Clemente, the movement of the trilogy from Rome to Russia asserts inheritance: Merezhkovskii laid claim to the Roman Empire and the Italian Renaissance and wrote them as Russia's own past, linked both to Petrine Russia and, by connection, to the Russia of his own day. As the author of this blend, he appropriated the role of the epic writer who enters into the narrative as a participant in epic's "double plot"; one thinks, for example, of Dante-the-poet's relationship with Virgil and of Dante-the-wanderer's journeys.[26] Creating his own three-part narrative of pagan and Christian elements, Merezhkovskii attempted to take part in an illustrious lineage, one focused on remaking a national literature. While he did not insert himself explicitly into his texts, in each novel of his trilogy he presented wanderer-thinkers, evocative of Dante's pilgrim, who through various encounters with actual historical figures strive to make sense of the two forces with which Merezhkovskii himself had struggled for years. His trilogy of "novel-epics" thus represents a record of the author's own evolution over a significant decade in Russian cultural and political life.

Julian the Apostate: Ancient Rome and Modern Russia

> Let's return to Olympus. For some time now, I've had all of Olympus at my heels, and I'm suffering from it quite a bit. Gods have been falling on my head like chimney pots.
> Charles Baudelaire, "The Pagan School," 1852

In the first novel of his trilogy, *The Death of the Gods: Julian the Apostate,* Merezhkovskii allegorically asserted the modern-day relevance of the fourth-century Roman Empire, when the relatively new faith of Christianity gained predominance over the dying religion of the pagan gods.[27] He told the story of the Roman emperor Julian, who ruled from 361 to 363 CE. Julian's reign occurred shortly after Constantine the Great, the first Christian emperor of Rome, had established Constantinople as the new imperial capital, replacing Rome itself, and had taken measures to establish Christianity as the Empire's dominant religion. Despite the brevity of his reign, Julian earned a lasting place in history and literature for his failed attempt to reverse the spread of Christianity and restore popular allegiance to the gods of the Greco-Roman pantheon.[28] Merezhkovskii presented Julian as a passionate devotee of the beauty he finds in the culture of Hellenic Greece and of the power he seeks in Rome's imperial throne, while the reigning Christianity is for the most part portrayed critically. And yet Merezhkovskii's Julian actually craves Christ and remains conflicted throughout the text. It is left to the artists of the tale—the sculptor Arsinoe and the writer-historian Ammianus Marcellinus, both friends of the emperor—to recognize the need for a synthesis of Christ and Antichrist, or Christianity and paganism, which they predict for the future.[29]

Merezhkovskii's choice of the fourth-century Roman Empire at the time of its West-to-East power shift as the setting for his novel, and of Julian "the Apostate" as its failed hero, are significant. He thereby linked the capital's geographic shift with the victory of Christianity over the gods, associating paganism with the Western Empire and the new, triumphant faith of Christianity with the Empire's Eastern half. In addition, by portraying the *translatio imperii* from Rome to Constantinople, Merezhkovskii implicitly raised the subject of his own country, the final destination in the Russian-constructed Third Rome scenario. Indeed, Julian was a stand-in for those Westernized Russian fin-de-siècle intellectuals, including Merezhkovskii himself, who were torn between their dedication to Western ideas and a desire, at times unacknowledged, for the Christian spirituality of the Russian *narod*.[30] Merezhkovskii had explained in his 1893 collection "O prichinakh upadka i o novykh techeniiakh sovremennoi russkoi literatury" (On the Reasons for the Decline and on New Tendencies in Contemporary Russian Literature), "Never before have people so felt in their hearts the necessity of believing and understood with their minds the impossibility of believing."[31] Julian's tortured existence portrayed the dangerously dispirited state of mind Merezhkovskii deplored in his compatriots. The emperor's visionary artist friends showed how to escape from this fate:

through the acceptance of the equal importance of Merezhkovskii's "two truths," Christian and pagan. In such a way, Russia, represented by an intelligentsia connected at last to its Christian roots, could move beyond spiritual stagnation to fulfill its potential as a world leader and unifier, or a Merezhkovskiian variant of the Third Rome.

Throughout *Julian the Apostate,* Merezhkovskii portrayed the fourth century CE as a period when the old and the new gods coexisted. The novel's first scene features a spring, originally dedicated to Castor and Pollux and now sacred to Saints Cosmas and Damian; Julian's childhood nurse is both a sorceress and a Christian; and an innkeeper in an early scene swears by pagan and Christian gods simultaneously. Despite this intermingling, however, each faith has clearly marked characteristics. Julian and his fellow pagans laud human potential, freedom, and the beauty they find in art, rhetoric, philosophy, and literature, and they scorn the Christians as "barbarians" for their lack of such appreciation.[32] Julian insists, against Christian doctrine, that "the strong are the victors" (264). He glories in the adulation of the soldiers who proclaim him emperor after serving under him on the Western borders of the Empire, and he rejoices when his soldiers compare him to the war god Mars and the warrior Alexander the Great. Meanwhile, Julian's prayerful, secret obeisance as a small boy to a beautiful statue of Aphrodite is mirrored in his later attraction to Arsinoe, who is compared to the goddess Artemis. Capturing the essence of paganism as Merezhkovskii presents it, Arsinoe suggests to Julian that as a pair they embody beauty and power, respectively.

By contrast, the Christianity that Merezhkovskii portrays is almost entirely "Historic," defined in Nietzschean fashion as "the victory of the weak over the strong, of slaves over masters" (232). The Arian Christian church where Julian is forced to pray in his youth is filled with miserably sick and maimed people, who listen in fear as Julian reads apocalyptic prophecies from the book of Revelation.[33] Christian monks in the novel profess their dedication to the mortification of the flesh. In addition, many of the Christians Julian encounters are hypocrites, who, despite their protestations of brotherly love, engage in vituperative arguments about doctrinal issues.[34] Christians are also associated with intolerance that approaches or results in violence: as a child, Julian is instructed to swear loyalty to Constantius, Constantine's son and the reigning emperor, by kissing a cross that is stained with the blood of Julian's father, one of the relatives Constantius has murdered en route to the throne.

Despite the overriding distaste with which "Historic" Christianity is portrayed in the novel, the author, looking back after an additional fifteen centuries of Christianity, makes the triumph of the new faith over the old abundantly clear. Julian's efforts to reestablish the worship of the pagan gods meet with derision from most of his subjects. He arranges a Bacchic procession and learns that the women playing the role of Bacchantes are in fact the city's prostitutes: all the upper-class women who in earlier times would have played the role are Christians. Most of Julian's subjects who profess paganism do so mockingly, out of political expediency. They turn readily to Christianity again after Julian's final, vain effort to duplicate the military feats of Alexander the Great ends in his death. The figure of Juventinus, the last son of an ancient Roman family who denies his heritage to become a Christian, is representative of the death of the old, proud Rome, and of the power of the new faith of Christianity.[35] Julian's friend and fellow pagan Antoninus explains that the days of the gods are over: "We are sick, too weak" (74). Arsinoe sadly notes the "rotting body of Greece and Rome" (109), and a pagan priest, soon to be murdered by a Christian mob, worries that the gods have abandoned the earth.[36]

Indeed, Julian himself participates in Christianity's vanquishing of the glorious pagan past. In his efforts before he becomes emperor to simulate dedication to the Christian cause, he joins a group of Christian rabble-rousers who are destroying a pagan temple; Julian himself strikes a statue of the goddess Diana, helping to deface it. While this episode speaks to some of Julian's less attractive qualities—his fear of Constantius and his tendency toward dissimulation—it is also indicative of the "apostate" emperor's conflicted views. On the one hand, filled with pagan zeal, he refers to himself as the Antichrist and exalts the virtues of the gods. Merezhkovskii's Julian also displays decidedly cruel behavior worthy of the most pitiless Olympians when he rapes his Christian wife and turns an elderly Christian couple out of their home to make room for a pagan temple. On the other hand, he gives charity to the poor, albeit in the name of the earth goddess Cybele, and orders the bloody Roman circuses closed. Most startlingly, as Julian lies dying he admits that he has loved Christ throughout his life, even as he has fought against him. Here Merezhkovskii diverges from assumed historical veracity, taking part instead in a Christian tradition that attempted to invent a Christian Julian. The tradition apparently began when Bishop Theodoret of Cyprus, writing nearly a century after Julian's death, asserted that the emperor's dying words had been, "Thou hast conquered, Galilean!"[37] For Merezhkovskii, intent on demonstrating that his Europeanized compatriots actually craved Christ, a somewhat Christianized Julian was ideal. His Julian dies confused, unable to understand his attraction to "the Galilean" who haunts him despite himself. The delirium that precedes his death demonstrates this conflict: "What do you want from me, Galilean? Your love is more terrible than death. Your burden is the heaviest burden. . . . Why are You watching like that? How I loved You, Good Shepherd, You alone. . . . No, no! Pierced hands and feet? Blood? Darkness? I want the sun, the sun! . . . Why are You covering the sun?" (291).

Julian does not realize that the Good Shepherd of his deathbed delirium is the non-"Historic," "true" Christ of the faith's beginnings. Julian encounters this "true" Christianity earlier in the novel as well, in a scene devoted to his childhood. In the gloomy Arian church, amid the portrayals of tortured saints and sinners alike, Julian notes a rendering of Christ that dates back to the earliest years of Christianity:

> But meanwhile, there, below, in the semi-darkness, where only one icon lamp glimmered, a marble bas-relief could be seen on a tomb from the earliest times of Christianity. On it were sculpted small, tender Nereids, panthers, happy Tritons; and next to them—Moses, Jonah with the whale, Orpheus, who was taming beasts of prey with the sounds of his lyre; a small olive branch, a dove and a fish—the simple symbols of a childish faith; among them—the Good Shepherd, carrying a sheep on his shoulders, a lost and found sheep—the soul of a sinner. He was happy and simple, this barelegged young man, with a beardless face, peaceful and gentle, like the faces of poor peasants; he had a smile of quiet joy. It seemed to Julian that no one knew or saw the Good Shepherd any longer; and this little depiction from other times was linked for him with some sort of distant, childish dream, one which at times he wanted to recall but could not. (47)

This portrait of a joyous Christianity, one that accepts the beauty of the pagan gods, is found additionally in the drawings of a Christian monk who paints pagan river gods along with John the Baptist. In the scenes Merezhkovskii devoted to the Christian faith of Arsinoe's sister Mirra, he further demonstrated the ideal form Christianity could take. Mirra and her fellow worshippers are not Arians, and as such they are forced to pray underground in ancient catacombs, hiding from the authorities. Their Christianity is one of everlasting life, as opposed to the morbidity of Merezhkovskii's "Historic" Christianity, and their customs, such as the kiss of peace, recall those of the faith's first days. Mirra, representative of his vision of the early, inclusive days of Christianity, dies, but her sister Arsinoe is inspired by her example to attempt to develop a Christian faith of her own. One of Merezhkovskii's perennial searchers, Arsinoe joins a religious community and then eventually leaves it to return to her work as an artist, now incorporating "true" Christianity and pagan self-love and power in her sculptures.

Arsinoe tries to share her newfound knowledge with Julian, but his hatred of "Historic" Christianity overwhelms the image of the "true" Christ that he has seen. She insists, however, that Christ "loved children, freedom, revelry, and white lilies" (284).[38] She tells Julian that those Christians who reject art and the beauty of the flesh are in fact apostates from the "true" Christianity; Julian, she asserts, is no apostate, as he worships the "true" Christ despite himself.[39] Casting doubt on Julian's vaunted paganism, Arsinoe argues that the Olympians would have scorned his charitable innovations. "Blood and human suffering are the nectar and ambrosia of the gods" (219), she claims, adding that despite his occasional cruelty, Julian appears to lack the stomach for a wholly pagan way of life. Julian's pagan mentor Maximus seems to second this opinion when he tells Julian that the Hellas he loves never in fact existed.

Merezhkovskii ends his novel with a discussion of a sculpture Arsinoe creates after Julian's death, a sculpture that embodies the "two truths" of Christ and Antichrist that have so tortured her friend. This figure, she says, will be "inexorable and terrible, like Mithras-Dionysus in all his glory and strength, yet kind-hearted and gentle like Jesus the Galilean" (304). Arsinoe and her companion Ammianus Marcellinus, who appreciates her art, thus are granted a unique vision that Julian himself could sense only vaguely. Julian is presented as a forerunner of a new era that will encompass the warring entities he could not reconcile. *Julian the Apostate* ends with the mingled notes of a boy's reed-pipe song to the god Pan and the hymns of Christian monks, as Arsinoe and her friends foretell the approach of the Renaissance. Merezhkovskii leaves it to another artist of that later age, Leonardo da Vinci, to spread the word of the unity of Christ and Antichrist—if not to his own countrymen, then to Russia.

Significantly, this final scene of *Julian the Apostate* is set in Italy, in the Western half of the Empire. This placement points the way to the next novel of the trilogy, much of which takes place in Renaissance Italy, where Merezhkovskii hoped to find an example of his ideal synthesis. It also plays a role in the overall geography of the novel: despite the *dvoeverie,* or double faith, common to the fourth century, for Merezhkovskii the Western Empire is associated principally with paganism and the Eastern Empire with Christianity. More specifically, the West, dominated by Rome and its history, is the seat of power and of human ambition and potential. Julian, who in the East was a weak, spindly student feigning Christian devotion, goes west to Milan upon Constantius's orders and becomes a power-driven Caesar. He goes further into Rome's Western Empire, to the northern provinces, and becomes a successful warrior, gaining each day in physical strength through military training and discipline. During one decisive battle, following Julian's silent prayer to the Olympian gods, Julian's best—and oldest—soldiers cry out, "For Rome!" as they lead his army to victory in the name of the Eternal City (145); Constantinople has no place in their war cry. Conversely, Julian dies in the Eastern half of the Empire, where his renowned military strength fails to function. His doomed final campaign against the Persian Empire demonstrates that despite his earlier victories, the age of Rome's powerful pagan warriors is waning.

For in following Constantine's call to rule in the Christian East, thus acknowledging the diminished stature of Rome, the former imperial capital, Julian himself condemns the anti-Christian agenda he has set. It is in a sense fitting, then, that Julian brings about his own downfall when he succumbs to the flattery of an enemy Persian spy, who labels the emperor "King of East and West" (276) and compares him to a god. The would-be Mangod Julian, enticed by the illusion that "my will is the will of the gods" (277), is deceived into the disastrous step of burning his own ships. Having been born into the Christian era, Julian must eventually recognize that his plans, military and religious, will not succeed. Christ's appearance is irrevocable.

With his conflicted feelings, Julian recalls Merezhkovskii's vision of himself and his Russian contemporaries, intent on the pursuit of European-style individualism, freedom, philosophy, and art, and at the same time hard pressed to admit their need for God.[40] Merezhkovskii hoped that by learning from the fourth century, his fellow intellectuals might echo the artists of *Julian the Apostate* and create the unity he sought. He began work on the novel in 1892, shortly after writing the poems found in his 1892 book of verse, *Simvoly* (Symbols).[41] A comparison of the ideas found in *Julian the Apostate* with those expressed in Merezhkovskii's poetry, combined with other Merezhkovskiian concepts of this period, helps to establish the connections he suggested between Julian's day and his own.

In *Symbols,* Merezhkovskii set up an opposition between Europe, represented by modern Paris and ancient Rome, and Russia. In a series of poems titled "Konets veka: Ocherki sovremennogo Parizha" (The End of the Century: Sketches of Contemporary Paris), he described a Paris filled with exponents of the "new art," who pursue "truth" and "beauty" freely, as different religious, political, and artistic groups, including the "godless," join in a search for "discoveries."[42] Paris is compared to the sun, object in Merezhkovskii's novel of Julian's pagan worship; it is also linked repeatedly with freedom.[43] Merezhkovskii made clear the correlation he posited between modern Paris and ancient Rome when he referred to Paris in the opening stanzas of the same cycle as a "new Rome."[44] And in his specifically Rome-related poems in the collection, he explicitly associated Rome, too, with freedom, human potential, and godlessness or paganism. For example, in "Panteon" (The Pantheon), devoted to Rome's famed pagan temple turned Christian church, he referred to the pagan gods native to Rome.[45] And in the poem "Rim" (Rome), written in 1891, he asked, "Who created you, O Rome? The genius of popular freedom!" He ended the poem with a characterization of Rome's spirit: "Man is equal to the gods!"[46]

Given the connections Merezhkovskii posited in his poetry between ancient Rome, with its "pagan" characteristics, and contemporary European society, one can conclude that his similar portrayal of Roman paganism in *Julian the Apostate* was equally reflective of his views of fin-de-siècle Europe: possessed of freedom, beauty, and a celebration of humankind. What fourth-century Western Rome and modern Europe were missing, however, was a firm commitment to Christ: as Merezhkovskii wrote in "The End of the Century," the Europeans had "forgotten" about God.[47] In "The Pantheon," he contrasted the Olympians with the "unknown God," crucified, pierced by nails, and clad in a crown of thorns, who had supplanted them. While the pagan gods stand for worldly beauty in the poem, Christ represents heavenly love and suffering. Recalling Julian's anguished confusion at his death, Merezhkovskii's lyric "I" confesses his own bewilderment at this choice:

"There He is, crucified, pierced with nails, in a crown of thorns . . .
This is my God! . . . Before Him I involuntarily bend my knees . . .
I believe in You, O God; let me renounce life,
Let me die with You in the name of love! . . .
I glanced back; the sun, the open sky . . .
Light streams from the cupola in the ancient pagan temple. . . .
The sun's light is sweet to us, life is a precious gift! . . .
Where are you, truth? . . . In death, in heavenly love and sufferings,
Or, O shades of the gods, in your earthly beauty?"[48]

Once again, paganism is associated with the sun and beauty, while Christ represents a radically different alternative, one to which the poet appears drawn despite himself.[49]

In the poems, the Christian alternative is located in Russia, a country that the fourth-century Julian obviously would not have known, to which the poet proclaims his allegiance notwithstanding his attraction to Europe. "No! The heart can never forget the fatherland!" he announces in "Vozvrashchenie" (The Return).[50] And in "Volny" (Waves), Merezhkovskii associates Russia with God, writing, "I love my homeland and God."[51] In the final stanza of "The End of the Century," he lauds Russia, noting in particular the country's natural beauty and the verses of Pushkin. "No matter what happens," he claims, "I believe in you!"[52] Like Gogol' writing about Russia in Rome, Merezhkovskii writes these lines in Paris in 1891, noting the location at the end of the poem. Through the word "veriu" (I believe), however, he links faith with Russia, rather than Europe.

Europe, lacking Christian conviction, hangs over an abyss, Merezhkovskii claims, doomed to destruction. Indeed, the ruins of Rome reflect the death of powerful empires that lose their guiding faith. Merezhkovskii points in his poems to the once-mighty Coliseum as an example of the vestiges of fallen empires, predicting that "our proud capitals" will fall into similar disrepair.[53] Further, in an 1891 essay on the Roman emperor Marcus Aurelius, Merezhkovskii related the ancient Roman environment to that of modern Europe, asserting that both worlds had been condemned to death and were filled with a sense of impending disaster, as external well-being masked internal alarm.[54] In his poetry Merezhkovskii associates Westernized Russians as well with this threatening fate. Using the first-person plural "my" (we) for much of the final section of his cycle "Peterburgskaia poema" (Petersburg Poem), in the last stanza he cites in Latin the traditional phrase of Roman gladiators facing death: "Salutant, Caesar Imperator, / Te morituri!"[55] For in rapidly industrializing Russia, filled with revolutionary murmurings and discussions of Marxism, "capital" threatens to become a god, supplanting Christ and thus harming Russia.[56]

And yet even as European or Europeanized intellectuals abstain from Christian faith, preferring the enticements of the pagan West, in fact they are not pure pagans, as demonstrated by Merezhkovskii's own painful attraction to the Christ of "The Pantheon." Bringing to mind Arsinoe's characterization of Julian, Merezhkovskii admits in "The End of the Century" that the Europeans of his day are not in fact fully "pagan," at one with the ancient Romans who loved the blood and cruelty of the amphitheaters. "Our ways softened long ago," he acknowledges, including himself in this characterization through the first-person plural pronoun.[57] Hence Merezhkovskii's call in his poem "The Future Rome" for a new faith, a new Rome, intended to unify the world. This faith is to encompass within itself both Christ and Aphrodite, to whom the poet, like Julian, prays at various points in *Symbols*.[58]

For just as pure paganism is no longer a possibility, a Christianity entirely devoid of pagan influences is also worthy of dismissal. Turning to Merezhkovskii's portrayal in his novel of Constantius's Arian Christianity, with its state-sponsored rejection of art, human potential, knowledge, and beauty, and its corresponding stress on suffering and self-denial, one can draw a direct connection to Merezhkovskii's Russia. The Russian Orthodox Church of his day had been characterized for centuries by a lack of knowledge of religious doctrine and an abiding suspicion of education, as well as a longstanding subordinate status vis-à-vis the repressive state.[59] By the end of the nineteenth century, the official Russian Orthodox Church had therefore lost adherents both in the *narod* and among the educated classes. Old Believers, sectarians, and other dissenters numbered in the millions, even as educated Russians rejected religion or sought variants of the faith more in keeping with modern, Western European secular values or, alternatively, with the varied spiritual and mystical quests common in Europe and Russia at the fin de siècle.[60] When the Orthodox clergy realized that artistic inclinations were making slight inroads even into the peasantry, as villagers expressed appreciation of local theatrical performances, priests threatened their flocks with excommunication, as one contemporary account describing the 1880s and 1890s makes clear: "During both rehearsals and performances, the priest, taking advantage of the fact that his home was located across from the theater, sat on the bench at his hut or stood on the path and excommunicated all of the actors and spectators; he threatened them with all of the tortures of hell; . . . he called the theater sinful, the devil's amusement."[61]

Of course the Church did not refrain from excommunicating representatives of Russia's cultural elite, as exemplified by the experience of Lev Tolstoi. The cultural intolerance and anti-intellectualism of the Orthodox Church of Merezhkovskii's day are mirrored in the ignorant, antiartistic pronouncements of the "Historic" Christians of *Julian the Apostate*, thereby occasioning the epithet of "barbarian" given the church figures by the pagans. The Christian crusade against art would be echoed in the next two novels of the trilogy as well.

For Merezhkovskii, passionately devoted both to Russia and to the Western European cultural tradition, and seeking a Christianity that could accommodate the latter, the Russian Orthodox Church of his day was sorely disappointing. And yet, he suggested in *Julian the Apostate,* there could be an alternative Russian Christianity, one based not on the doctrines of the official Church but on the simpler faith of the Russian *narod.* As noted, the novel's leading exemplar of a popularly based Christianity is Arsinoe's sister, worshipping as the first Christians did, in a manner opposed by the official, state-sanctioned church of her day. The former Populist Merezhkovskii's choice of the name "Mirra" is significant: it recalls the Russian *mir,* the peasant village commune lauded by Russia's mid-nineteenth-century Slavophiles. A faith based in the Russian *narod,* he seemed to suggest, was a "truer" form of Christianity than that practiced by Russia's official Church. Indeed, in his "On the Reasons for the Decline and on New Tendencies in Contemporary Russian Literature," Merezhkovskii had written that the Christian faith that Dostoevskii and Tolstoi expressed in their works was powerful precisely because it flowed from the faith of the *narod.* It was this more accepting brand of Christianity that was to enter Western Europe, joining with it and learning from it to create a truly new, synthetic religion that would encompass the truths of East and West. "Only a movement emerging from the very heart of the people can make literature truly national and at the same time all-human [*vse-chelovecheskii*]," Merezhkovskii maintained, echoing Dostoevskii's claim in his 1880 Pushkin Speech that Russians possessed a unique ability to embrace the characteristics of foreign nations.[62] Since *mir* also means "world," its collective connotations could be understood as universal, particularly given that the word in reverse is *Rim* (Rome), symbol for Merezhkovskii of world unity.[63]

Thus as Merezhkovskii conceived it, the Christian faith of the Russian folk was an essential element in Russia's quest to become a universalizing Third Rome. And yet this faith on its own could not bring about the desired conclusion. Russian Christianity was to enter Europe specifically through art, he claimed. Arsinoe's statue uniting Christ and Dionysus presaged the art emerging at the end of the nineteenth century, the art of the Symbolists. "You are triumphing once again in the art of our day, o Galilean," Merezhkovskii proclaimed in "The End of the Century," several lines after acknowledging Venus's role in the cultural revival of the day.[64] He thus underlined the importance of the Westernized artists of Russian society in bringing about a new state of being for Russia and Europe. Calling for these Russian artists to produce a world-unifying culture with Christian content absorbed from the *narod,* Merezhkovskii defined his concept of the Third Rome: a cultural and holy space where East, West, and all they signified could come together in a powerful union.

The lively discussions that surrounded the publication of *Julian the Apostate* attest to the connections contemporary readers acknowledged between Julian's day and their own. As Berdiaev and Mirsky noted, Merezhkovskii made the past come alive for Russians, as fourth-century Rome shed light on the issues facing modern Russia. In *Leonardo da Vinci,* Merezhkovskii would explicitly resurrect the theme of the Third Rome, developing an idea that had been suggested in the setting of his first novel. In so doing, he would develop further the Russia-related themes he had laid out in *Julian the Apostate,* this time making it clear that the task of world unification had fallen decisively on Russia's shoulders.

Leonardo da Vinci, Evtikhii Gagara, and the Third Rome

Prophet, or demon, or sorcerer,
Guarding the eternal secret,
O Leonardo, you are the herald
Of a still unknown day.
Dmitrii Merezhkovskii, "Leonardo da Vinci," 1894

In the second novel of his trilogy, *The Resurrected Gods: Leonardo da Vinci* (1900), Merezhkovskii turned to the Italian Renaissance, focusing on an artist he felt was a forerunner of the pagan-Christian synthesis he sought. Again, his choice of theme resonated with discussions in contemporary European and Russian society. At the time he composed his novel, the artist-scientist Leonardo was a figure of immense scholarly and popular interest in Europe: as A. Richard Turner writes, "During the second part of the nineteenth century, Leonardo probably gave rise to more historical and critical literature than any other historical figure."[65] In Russia, thanks to the efforts of Faddei Zelinskii in particular, the idea of a "Slavic Renaissance" was gaining ground among intellectuals, evoking comparisons between previous artistic renaissances and a potential, Slavically inspired religious and cultural rebirth of Europe.

Merezhkovskii was increasingly convinced that the decaying European society he had described through the prism of ancient Rome in *Julian the Apostate* and in his verse of the early 1890s could be saved only by an artistic infusion of Russian, Hellenic-based Christianity. In his critical study *L. Tolstoi i Dostoevskii* (L. Tolstoi and Dostoevskii), written shortly after *Leonardo da Vinci* and somewhat related to it thematically, he noted that Russians could no longer rely on Europe for inspiration as they often had. Rather, the time was near when Europeans would instead turn to Russians for salvation, aware that the fate of Europe depended on the "word" of Russians possessed of "a new religious consciousness." "It is up to us, and no one else," he concluded.[66]

Merezhkovskii had demonstrated in *Julian the Apostate* that the divisions between East and West in his own day had their roots in the Roman Empire, when Christianity arose in the Eastern half of the Empire to defeat the paganism he associated with the West. Since that time, the Schism of 1054 had divided the Christian Church into the Catholic West and the Orthodox East, largely preserving the former imperial boundaries in a new context. Meanwhile, starting in the fifth century, the Western Empire had disintegrated over a period of centuries into a series of smaller principalities and kingdoms, even as the Eastern Empire, Byzantium, continued on for an additional millennium. Crucial for Merezhkovskii in the midst of these continuities and changes was the emergence in the Orthodox East of a Christian Russia at the end of the tenth century. Then, in 1453, a year after the birth of Leonardo da Vinci, the Moslem Turks conquered Constantinople, leaving Russia as the most powerful remaining Orthodox state. Contrary to accepted opinion, Merezhkovskii suggested that Russia did have a connection to the Renaissance. Specifically during the lifetime of Leonardo, Russia itself had been "born" as the potential heir to the Roman Empire. Modern-day Russians could learn from the interactions between Europe and Russia during the Renaissance period in order to envisage the new, Slavic Renaissance that must now occur.

In this second novel, Merezhkovskii, now able to write explicitly of an existing Muscovite state, linked the concept of this modern, Slavic-based Renaissance to his vision of Russia as the Third Rome. Building upon the East-West associations he had suggested in *Julian the Apostate,* he painted the West, represented by Rome, largely as the reborn empire of the Caesars, and the East, particularly Russia, as Christian. In keeping with post-Schism geographic realities, however, he now frequently included Greece in the East, along with Russia. In Merezhkovskii's ongoing attempts to build a case for a uniquely Russian synthesis of paganism and Christianity, associating Greece with the Christian East made it possible for him to claim a foundation for Eastern Orthodox Christianity in classical paganism.

Through the story of a Russian icon-painter named Evtikhii Paiseevich Gagara, Merezhkovskii portrayed the recognition on the part of a Russian artist of the classical pagan roots of the Russian Orthodox faith he loves. The novel ends with Evtikhii's realization that Russia's identity as the Third Rome is embodied in the union of Russia and Europe. Alone among his European contemporaries, Leonardo, inspired by a visit to Evtikhii Gagara's workroom, recognizes the glory awaiting Russia in its unique, salvational role. In *Leonardo da Vinci,* therefore, Merezhkovskii in effect used Leonardo and the Italian Renaissance to sanction the future Russian Renaissance that Merezhkovskii envisaged.

Amid these messianic overtones, Merezhkovskii's novel is, like *Julian the Apostate,* a compendium of carefully researched historical facts to which Merezhkovskii added his own religio-philosophical emphases and creative inventions. *Leonardo da Vinci* covers the span of the artist's long life (1452–1519), addressing his childhood in Tuscany and his subsequent service to Duke Ludovico Sforza, "Il Moro," in Milan; Cesare Borgia, duke of Valentino, in Rome; the government of the Republic of Florence; and, finally, Louis XII and then François I of France. Merezhkovskii and his wife, Zinaida Hippius, retraced the artist's steps to all these places as Merezhkovskii prepared to write his novel; he also immersed himself in historical artifacts, including transcripts of Leonardo's diaries, excerpts of which are included in the novel. Merezhkovskii portrayed the creation of several of Leonardo's artistic works, including *The Last Supper,* the *Colossus, Mona Lisa,* and a painting of John the Baptist evocative of Dionysus, and he posited relationships between Leonardo and other noted Renaissance figures, including Niccolo Machiavelli, author of *The Prince.* In addition, Merezhkovskii devoted attention to Leonardo's relationships with his students.[67] He focused on the conflicted Giovanni Beltraffio—evocative in his search for "truth" of Merezhkovskii himself and his contemporaries—who vacillates between the beauty and knowledge he finds at Leonardo's atelier and the "Historic" Christianity of the monk Savonarola. When pressured by his friend Cassandra to accept the idea of a pagan-Christian synthesis, Giovanni commits suicide. Other students include the Salieri-like Cesare da Sesto, furiously jealous of Leonardo's talent yet drawn to him nonetheless, and the ever-loving Francesco Melzi, who functions as a son to Leonardo in the latter's old age. Merezhkovskii allegorically suggested the relevance of these characters' milieu to his own, as the Renaissance period became a bridge between the ancient Rome of Merezhkovskii's first novel and his own modern-day Russia.

Renaissance Italy in Merezhkovskii's telling resembles a reborn, would-be Roman Empire. He describes leaders who epitomize Nietzsche's superman (or Merezhkovskii's Mangod), as they seize power, glory, and beauty with impunity. Il Moro, who has come to the throne of Milan by deposing the legitimate heir, dreams of having the pope as his confessor and the Holy Roman Emperor as the head of his armies, and he names the son his beautiful mistress bears him "Caesar." This imperial name also belongs to Cesare Borgia, hero of Machiavelli's *Prince.* Using his personal beauty (he is thought to resemble a god) and that of his highly artistic court to charm all he meets, Cesare Borgia murders everyone who stands in his path to power. Cesare's father, the Borgia Pope Alexander VI, further epitomizes in his murderous lust for power the pagan, imperial nature of Rome, here spread to the Vatican, the seat of the Catholic Church. When Alexander honors Cesare as the potential future unifier of Italy, the theme chosen for the celebration is "The Triumph of Julius Caesar."[68] The ceremony is arranged according to ancient Roman books and monuments: the laurel-crowned Cesare in his chariot is surrounded by soldiers whose uniforms recall those of ancient Roman legionnaires. Alexander's papal successor, Leo X, promotes the greatest artistic talents of the Renaissance and announces that he would rather give away the remains of Peter the Apostle than the recently discovered *Laocoön.* Nonetheless, as in *Julian the Apostate,* the time has passed for a thoroughly pagan kingdom. Il Moro and Cesare Borgia are defeated, Pope Alexander dies, and the first stirrings of the Reformation begin to threaten the Vatican's authority.

As in the first novel, Merezhkovskii presents "Historic" Christianity, now exemplified by Savonarola, and linked in Nietzschean fashion to Judaism. Savonarola seeks to dance as the Biblical David did before the Ark of the Covenant, and the crowd around his "bonfire of the vanities," which consumes the works of Botticelli and of Leonardo himself, sings about King David.[69] "Historic" Christianity is operative in the Inquisition, which condemns the pagan Cassandra to death as a witch, and it is also found in those Russians, such as Evtikhii's supervisor Il'ia Potapych Kopyla, who travel to Europe only to reject all they find there, so entrenched are they in their abhorrence of the body and beauty.

Yet once again there is a unifying antidote to this incomplete version of the faith: "true" Christianity, portrayed with Greek pagan roots, is found in Russia, as demonstrated through Evtikhii's story and even his name. While the name contains a Russian root (*tikh*) that suggests quiet or meekness, a quality affiliated with Russian Orthodoxy, in fact its derivation is Greek, meaning "good fortune" (*eu* + *tyche*). Evtikhii thus nominally embodies the central, inclusive features of "true" Christianity. It is fitting, therefore, that he alone will understand Leonardo's painting of John the Baptist as Dionysus, a pagan-Christian mix that has confused and discomfited all other viewers. By portraying Evtikhii's recognition of the classical pagan roots of his Christian faith, as well as his consequent vision of a synthesizing Russian Third Rome, Merezhkovskii created a character who could inspire his twentieth-century Russian artistic counterparts.[70]

Merezhkovskii made it clear that the path to the Third Rome would not be an easy one. Indeed, the first scene of the book featuring Russians provides scant hope for enlightenment from that quarter—or for acceptance by Westerners of this important Russian message. Il Moro holds a banquet that is attended by various Europeans, including Leonardo, and by a delegation of visiting Russians. Chief among the latter is Danilo Mamyrov, the envoy of the Grand Prince of Muscovy. Mamyrov, a "Historic" Christian, dismisses statues of the Olympian gods as "abominations of the Antichrist" and Il Moro's festivities as "pagan nastiness" (1.510). He is convinced that he is the representative of the "true" Christian faith, and as such he demands a place of honor at the table as he ponders the glory of Russia: "The Grand Muscovite Prince had already been declared sole heir of the two-headed eagle of Byzantium, having united under the protection of its wings East and West, as the Lord All-powerful, as it was told in the tale, having cast down for heresies both Romes, the old and the new, had raised up a third secret city, in order to pour out onto it all His glory, strength and favor—a third, northern Rome—Orthodox Moscow—and there would never be a fourth Rome" (1:508). Far from advocating Merezhkovskii's synthesis of Eastern, enlightened faith and Western, pagan imperialism, Mamyrov rejects all European influences and seeks rather to extend the sway of a narrowly defined Russian Orthodoxy.[71]

At the same time, most of the assembled European guests are no more interested in understanding Russia than Mamyrov is in understanding them. They take Mamyrov's refusal to sit where he is told as a lack of courtesy, and refer mockingly to the Russians: "What is this?

Unpleasantness with the Muscovites again? A wild people! . . . It is impossible to invite them anywhere. Barbarians! And that language—do you hear it?—it's completely Turkish. A brutal tribe!" (1:507). Settling down to dine on "a naked Andromeda, made out of tender breasts of capon, chained to a rock made out of cottage cheese, and her liberator, the winged Perseus, made out of veal," the Europeans refer to Russia as an "unfortunate land, cursed by God" (1:509).

With his eagerness to accumulate more knowledge and his desire, unique among the Europeans at the banquet, to learn more about Russia, Leonardo alone bridges the gap between Europe and Russia. Indeed, Merezhkovskii presents Leonardo as a remarkable combination of influences. The son of a simple peasant woman, he is kind, beloved of children and animals, religious, and yet transfixed by the wonders of this world and unwilling to dismiss them. He can work with equal concentration on the face of Jesus in *The Last Supper* or on his life-long dream of a flying machine. He makes no separation, because Jesus and the machine are both elements of God's universe, which includes the wonders of Christian faith and of worldly beauty and knowledge. Merezhkovskii compares Leonardo to St. Francis of Assisi, for the novelist one of the few Christians who, with his celebration of nature, achieved "truly" Christian, all-encompassing love.[72]

Leonardo is also nonjudgmental: he will work without question for the amoral leaders who fill Renaissance Europe, planning with equal interest projects relating to art or to war. Merezhkovskii contrasts this all-encompassing worldview with that of the unsynthesizing student Giovanni. The difference between the two emerges clearly when Leonardo takes Giovanni to see his mural *The Last Supper* and then shows him the clay statue of a rider on horseback, known as the *Colossus*, which represents Francesco Sforza, the usurping duke of Milan and father of Leonardo's patron, Il Moro. Sforza is seen as a Nietzschean superman: "strong as a lion and cunning as a fox, he attained the heights of power through evil deeds, exploits, and wisdom—and died on the throne of the dukes of Milan" (1:358). Impressed by this leader's "pagan" feats, with Nietzschean irony Leonardo has inscribed on the monument the words "Ecce deus"—Behold the God (1:358).[73]

Giovanni is horrified by Leonardo's glorification of this Mangod, and he contrasts Sforza with Christ, the Godman:

> "A god," repeated Giovanni, having glanced at the clay *Colossus* and at the human sacrifice, trampled by the horse of the victor, Sforza the oppressor,

> and having recalled the light blue summits of Zion, the heavenly charm of John's face, and the peace of the Last Supper of that God, about whom it was said: "Ecce homo!"—"Behold the man!" . . .
>
> Giovanni stood silently, having cast down his eyes; his face was pale.
>
> "Excuse me, teacher! . . . I ponder and I do not understand, how you could create this *Colossus* and *The Last Supper* together, at the same time?"
>
> Leonardo looked at him with simple surprise.
>
> "What is it you don't understand?"
>
> "Oh, Master Leonardo, do you really not see it yourself? These two cannot go together."
>
> "On the contrary, Giovanni. I think that one helps the other: the best thoughts about *The Last Supper* come to me right here, when I am working on the *Colossus*, and, on the contrary, there, in the monastery, I like to think about the monument. These two are twins." (1:358)

Giovanni is unable to understand Leonardo's linking of Mangod and Godman, or Antichrist and Christ. He believes that the two are separate entities, and is convinced that Leonardo must in fact have an allegiance to one side or the other. Driven mad by his fears of Leonardo as Antichrist, Giovanni imagines that his beloved teacher has a double, as Christ and Antichrist merge within him. Leonardo, meanwhile, is unable to explain his vision to his contemporaries, for in fact he is not entirely aware of the significance of his worldview. His lack of awareness combines with the ambivalence one saw in Julian—here expressed in Leonardo's inability to finish projects, for example, and his difficulties promoting himself to his various patrons—to render him almost entirely incapable of passing on his beliefs to others.[74]

The exception, of course, is Evtikhii. Significantly for Merezhkovskii, Evtikhii's origins are humble: like Leonardo, whose maternal roots Merezhkovskii stresses, he is the son of a poor peasant woman. Evtikhii travels to Europe in the spring of 1517, twenty years after Il Moro's ill-fated banquet, as a result of discussions between Pope Leo X and the Muscovites regarding the pope's desire to reunite the two churches and form an alliance against the Turks. While the Russians do not commit themselves to any such plan, they send two ambassadors, Dmitrii Gerasimov and the aforementioned Mamyrov, to discuss it further. Gerasimov, a historical figure, provides a connection between the first novel of the trilogy and the second. He is said to have composed the "Tale of the White Cowl," which describes the progression of power and sanctity, symbolized by the cowl, from Constantine the Great to Byzantium and then to Russia.[75] Evtikhii will use this tale at the end of the novel to predict Russia's future messianic role.

While Evtikhii's supervisor, Il'ia Potapych, is horrified by the Western art the group encounters in Europe, Evtikhii's colleague Fedor finds it appealing. On one occasion, Fedor dares to suggest to Il'ia Potapych that Russian icon-painters might learn from the Western painters, particularly in the area of perspective. The suggestion strikes Il'ia Potapych as heretical, but Evtikhii is intrigued. Later that day, he is paging through his psalter, written in the town of Uglich in 1485, an element of the novel apparently inspired by an actual psalter that Merezhkovskii seems to have known, both from visits to the St. Petersburg Imperial Public Library and from a detailed discussion of the manuscript by the well-known nineteenth-century ethnographer Fedor Buslaev (fig. 8). Evtikhii is astounded to note among the illustrations in the book some that recall figures of Western pagan antiquity, now familiar to him from his travels in Europe. He recognizes Apollo the sun god in a young man with a crown who is harnessed to two horses, and he sees a river god in a figure with an overflowing bowl of water (2:277). Evtikhii realizes that the pagan Hellenic figures are linked to the Christian ones, and that somehow they have made their way from Greece to Uglich. Demonstrating his acceptance of his Hellenic origins and rejecting the "Historically" Christian admonitions of his superior, Evtikhii, representative of the simple Russian *narod,* paints pagan figures into one of his own icons.[76]

Shortly thereafter, Evtikhii receives a visitor to his workroom: the ever-curious Leonardo, now an old man, who has heard that the Russians have arrived in Amboise, where he now serves the French king. In the studio, Leonardo looks through Evtikhii's collection of prototypes of Eastern Orthodox icons. Leonardo is intrigued by the Byzantine tendency to portray John the Baptist with wings, having spent much of his own life endeavoring to learn how to fly. That interest has been deplored by his contemporaries, particularly after one of his students was crippled in Leonardo's nonfunctional flying machine, but Leonardo is fascinated by the idea that a Russian "barbarian" appears to associate flight with sanctity (2:291). Having visited the Byzantine-period mosaics in Ravenna, he notes a resemblance between them and the icons, describing the icons in Evtikhii's book as possessed of "a secret twilight, in which the last ray of Hellenic charm has merged with the first ray of a still unknown dawn" (2:291).

Fig. 8. A page from Fedor Buslaev's *Historical Sketches of Russian Folk Literature and Art*, 1861, with drawings from a 1485 Uglich psalter

At the end of the novel, after Leonardo's death, Evtikhii returns to France and becomes fascinated by Leonardo's enigmatic portrait of an androgynous, Dionysian John the Baptist (fig. 9). That night, unable to sleep, Evtikhii pulls out two of his favorite stories: "The Tale of the White Cowl," devoted to Russia's heavenly splendor, and "About the Babylonian Kingdom," which foretells Russia's future earthly glory. Just as the white cowl makes its way to Russia after stopping in Rome and Byzantium, the crown of Nebuchadnezzar in the second tale is taken from Babylon to Constantinople to Russia. Both narratives are variations on the developing doctrine of the Third Rome. Trying to understand how the crown of the pagan ruler Nebuchadnezzar can fulfill the same role as the holy white cowl, Evtikhii intimates that Mangod and Godman will come together, transformed, in Russia the Third Rome. Overwhelmed by his discovery, Evtikhii finally falls asleep and has a dream in which Leonardo appears as the Prophet Elijah. A winged John the Baptist also appears, with a scroll on which is written, "Behold, I am sending My Angel, and he shall prepare the way before Me" (2:315).[77] Evtikhii awakes and resumes work on an icon showing a winged John the Baptist (fig. 10). Inspired by his dream, he paints into the Baptist's scroll the words he has seen in his dream; on this note, the novel ends. The Russian Evtikhii realizes that Leonardo is himself a forerunner of this future synthesis of East and West[78]—and also of those who will recognize Russia's role in the creation and propagation of such a union.

Evtikhii's story demonstrates Merezhkovskii's goals for his own contemporaries: Evtikhii, too, is a forerunner, of later Russian artists. Particularly significant is the icon-painter's affinity for Leonardo's art, an affinity he shares with Merezhkovskii's own Decadent contemporaries in Russia and Europe. Walter Pater's much-quoted 1869 characterization of Leonardo's "Lady Lisa" as a "symbol of the modern idea" is typical of the attempts of fin-de-siècle modernists, most notably Oscar Wilde, to claim Leonardo as one of their own.[79] The icon-painter Evtikhii Gagara of Uglich thus becomes Merezhkovskii's prototypical Decadent, a Russian, Christian artist in tune with Western modernist artistic ideals. For Merezhkovskii remained convinced, as he had been while writing *Julian the Apostate* and the poems of *Symbols,* that Europe was a modern version of the pagan Roman Empire in decline. And yet, he wrote in *L. Tolstoi and Dostoevskii,* citing Dostoevskii's Pushkin Speech, Europe was the Russian's homeland as much as Russia itself was. In order to save Europe, Russians needed to learn from it, as Evtikhii had done. They also needed to embrace the "true" Christianity

Fig. 9. Leonardo da Vinci, *Saint John the Baptist*, ca. 1513–1516 (Réunion des Musées Nationaux / Art Resource, N.Y.)

Fig. 10. Icon of Saint John the Baptist, Crete, ca. 1450 (The Trustees of the British Museum)

still found in the heart of the *narod*, bringing that faith, through art, to the West. Members of the Russian intelligentsia were to bring about the new artistic and religious Renaissance so crucial to contemporary Europe. Europe, meanwhile, represented in Merezhkovskii's novel by Leonardo himself, was to learn to appreciate what the Russians had to offer through their Western-influenced but Christian-infused Russian Symbolist art. As Merezhkovskii had written in the introduction to his 1896 translation *Dafnis i Khloia* (Daphnis and Chloe), "On the verge of an unknown twentieth century, we stand before the same great and unresolved contradiction of Olympus and Golgotha, paganism and Christianity. And again we hope, and again we await a new Rinascimento [*sic*], the first dim murmur of which we call Symbolism."[80]

As he finished his novel, Merezhkovskii had reason to hope that his vision of fruitful Russian and Western cultural ties was an apt one. While he would later claim that the title of his 1892 poetry collection had been the first mention of the word "symbol" in Russia,[81] by the end of the century he had been joined in his search for a "new," Symbolist art by Valerii Briusov, in particular, on the literary front and by the visual-arts-focused World of Art group. The moving force behind this group was Sergei Diagilev. Diagilev, whom Andrei Belyi compared in his plump self-assurance to the Roman emperor Nero, resembled Merezhkovskii and Briusov in his determination to bridge the gap between Russian and European culture. Lauding Peter the Great, who had opened Russia decisively to Western influences, Diagilev, who later founded the Ballets Russes, sought to introduce to Europeans the Russians they feared; as he proclaimed, "We must make our entrance at once, reveal our whole selves with all the good and the bad qualities of our nationality."[82] He and his colleagues sent examples of the "new" Russian art to European exhibitions and brought the work of foreign artists to Russia. These efforts were not always successful. Diagilev was appalled when few Russians chose to send their work to a German exhibit despite an invitation from their European hosts, for instance, and when an official watercolor exhibition in St. Petersburg in 1897 barred foreign works of art, he exploded. "A new generation is coming with demands of its own and it will make itself heard and say what it has to say," he warned the Russian "establishment." "Your panic fear of the West, of everything that is new and talented, is the beginning of your divorce from the public, your dying sigh."[83]

Evtikhii's Third Rome coincided with Diagilev's wish to bring native Russian cultural traditions, reworked by modern-day Russian artists, to Europe. In addition, though Diagilev himself was certainly not messianically motivated, through the World of Art group Merezhkovskii encountered several individuals who were interested, as he and Hippius were, in spiritual questions.[84] When the World of Art group founded the first Russian modernist journal, *Mir iskusstva* (The World of Art), Merezhkovskii published *L. Tolstoi and Dostoevskii,* with its messianic vision of Russia's future, in the new journal. And in 1901 Merezhkovskii, Hippius, and their companion Dmitrii Filosofov went a step further, founding the Religious-Philosophical Meetings of St. Petersburg. The meetings were meant to bring together members of the Russian intelligentsia and the Russian Orthodox clergy for open discussions of such issues as Merezhkovskii's views on "true" Christianity's appreciation of the beauty of the human body and of human sexuality. Merezhkovskii hoped that the Russian intellectuals who, Julian-like, rejected Christ would instead admit their Christian spirituality, as Julian had so painfully done. He also hoped that the disturbingly "Historic" Russian Orthodox clergy would recognize the validity of Merezhkovskii's "pagan" vision of their faith. The journal *Novyi put'* (The New Path) started publication in 1903 to disseminate to a broader audience the contents of the discussions between these two groups of Russian society.[85]

Merezhkovskii was attempting to bring Evtikhii's vision of Russia as the Third Rome to fruition. The Slavic Renaissance discussed among Russian intellectuals at the turn of the twentieth century had a special significance for Merezhkovskii, one linked to the idea of the Third Rome.[86] More than fifteen centuries after Arsinoe had sculpted her Galilean Dionysus, a world characterized by mutual appreciation between East and West and inspired by Russian faith-filled art would at last come into being.

Subverting the Epic: *Peter and Alexis*

Rome worshipped her founder as a god after she had been built and dedicated; but this Heavenly Jerusalem put Christ as the foundation of her faith, so that she might be built and dedicated.
St. Augustine, *City of God,* fifth century CE (trans. Henry Bettenson)

For the final novel of his trilogy, *Peter and Alexis,* Merezhkovskii chose an exclusively Russian theme: the relationship between Tsar Peter the Great, who ruled from 1694 to 1725, and his son Alexis. The previous novels had set the stage for a glorious portrayal of Peter's Russia: it would open itself to the West even as it retained a Christian faith that would make possible Russia's unifying rescue mission to Europe in the novelist's own day. And yet in *Peter and Alexis,* he tore down the epic of Russian national destiny that he had begun in *Julian the Apostate.* Merezhkovskii presented Peter's "Roman" reign as the start of the social, religious, and political divisions he saw in Russian society at the turn of the twentieth century. He portrayed Peter in many ways as a throwback to the Roman Caesars, one so committed to expanding and modernizing Russia that he is willing to subjugate the Russian Orthodox Church and murder his Christian son in the process. Through this damning portrayal, Merezhkovskii redefined as oppression the powerful Roman imperialism Peter had emulated. Correspondingly, he also abandoned his faith in a Third Rome that would combine within itself imperialism and a refreshed Russian Orthodoxy. Still intent on finding a way to unite all peoples, he substituted for the Third Rome his "Third Testament," an anarchic, apocalyptic form of Christianity envisaged in the novel both by Alexis and by the final seeker of the trilogy, the young Russian wanderer Tikhon Zapol'skii. In other, related writings of this period, Merezhkovskii assigned an apocalyptic, Christian significance to the revolutionary movement of his own day. He called upon Russia's revolutionaries and religious dissenters, successors to Alexis and Tikhon, to come together to vanquish autocracy and Orthodoxy, the two elements of his once-desired Third Rome. In its place they were to substitute the "City of the Future" that Alexis and Tikhon had foreseen. In this final novel of the trilogy, Merezhkovskii turned firmly from Rome to an anarchic, postapocalyptic Christ.

Instrumental in Merezhkovskii's change of heart was the failure of the Religious-Philosophical Meetings to achieve the unifying goals he had projected. The religious and secular sides could not seem to bridge the mistrust between them; as Avril Pyman explains, "If the men of the Church, cowled, long-haired, and long-skirted, with their pale faces and measured movements, seemed exotically medieval to the assembled intelligentsia, what were *they* to think of the gaunt revolutionaries . . . , the powdered and painted dandies . . . and Zinaida Hippius herself, clad in a black lace dress over a flesh-coloured slip which made her appear naked when she moved?"[87] Far from welcoming the religious interest of these Decadents, the clergy instead sought to convert them, ignoring the fact that the intellectuals before them already considered themselves Christian. In 1903, when the tsarist government closed down the meetings, Merezhkovskii's disenchantment with Russia's Orthodox Church was compounded by a newfound mistrust of the Russian autocracy.[88] In *L. Tolstoi and Dostoevskii,* he had praised Peter the Great for subordinating the Russian Orthodox Church to the Russian imperial state, thus keeping it from taking the route of the Roman Catholic Church toward domination of worldly affairs.[89] Now, however, Merezhkovskii came to view the Russian state as anti-Christian and condemned the Church as the tool of the tsarist government. In the early years of the twentieth century, Merezhkovskii became increasingly interested in the Russian revolutionary movement; by 1904 he had effectively renounced his former allegiance to the Russian autocracy and declared that the state was the product of the Antichrist. In his third novel, Merezhkovskii posited imperial Rome as the dominant model for the Russian state he now despised, as the Mangod-Antichrists he had earlier lauded as necessary to Russia became anathema to him.[90] As he explained in a 1911 preface to the trilogy, "When I began the trilogy *Christ and Antichrist,* it seemed to me that there existed two truths: Christianity, the truth of the heavens, and paganism, the truth of the earth. . . . But by the time I was finishing the trilogy, I realized that the union of Christ and Antichrist was a blasphemous lie; I knew that both truths, that of the heavens and that of the earth, are already united in Jesus Christ."[91]

Peter's ties to ancient Rome are brought out from the beginning of the novel. One of the novel's first scenes features the arrival in St. Petersburg of a statue of Venus, once a powerful influence on the boy Julian, in accordance with Peter's request to the Roman pope. As Peter embraces the statue, a bystander compares him to the Roman war god Mars; the narrator adds that the Russian tsar is worthy of the goddess. Peter's desire to produce Russian translations of Latin texts such as those by Ovid and Virgil is mentioned in the novel's second chapter, followed shortly by a description of the Latin phrases spelled out in the fireworks Peter himself organizes and explains. Merezhkovskii notes that, in the Roman tradition, Peter created a Senate and then, like Augustus Caesar, accepted from it the titles "Father of the Fatherland" and "Imperator." In addition, Merezhkovskii's Peter recalls Julian in his desire to unite East and West militarily, rather than in the Christian-inspired manner projected in *Leonardo da Vinci.* Like Cesare Borgia, another latter-day Roman, Peter celebrates his military victories with triumphs modeled on those of ancient Rome: members of his court respond to his efforts with cries of "Vivat Imperator Peter!"[92] In fact, in his Roman qualities Peter outdoes Emperor Julian, who had outlawed Rome's traditional gladiatorial bloodbaths. Peter suffers no such "Christian" qualms. He delights in causing pain, killing and torturing his subjects with impunity, and meetings of his court at times resemble orgies. He is compared to the Roman emperor Caligula, who was notorious for his arbitrary cruelty and sexual licentiousness.

Hippius recalls that she took her husband to task for what she saw as an overly critical portrayal of Peter, and perhaps her remonstrances are responsible for the more positive elements of Merezhkovskii's description.[93] For his Peter firmly believes that he is acting in his nation's best interests. His intent is to improve Russia by strengthening it militarily and culturally, thereby gaining the world's respect. He is determined to bring his country into the fold of "civilized" Western nations, even though this goal may take more than a lifetime to accomplish. Peter prays to God the Father for guidance as he ponders what to do about his own son, Alexis, who he feels will not be able or willing to advance Russia's Westernization once Peter is gone. As Merezhkovskii portrays it, Peter's torturous decision to murder his son is, in his own eyes, a sacrifice for Russia. Peter loves Alexis, just as Alexis loves him, despite their disagreements over their country's future. In his creativity—for Peter is the primary artist of the text, shaping Russia into a new empire—the tsar is compared to Leonardo da Vinci.

Nevertheless, in this third, Eastern-based novel, set predominantly in Russia with a brief interlude in Italy, Peter's Romanizing efforts, along with his cruelty, are presented as inappropriate and harmful. First, his reforms are ineffective: despite his pride in his growing empire, Russia does not in fact measure up to Europe. In one of several such observations, the narrator notes that the tsar's garden, modeled on that of Versailles, is inferior to the French original. Representative of Europe's ongoing scorn for Russia is Fraulein Arnheim, attendant to Alexis's German wife. Arnheim writes scathingly in her journal of the Russians, and Peter in particular, as "stinking savages," "barbarians" dangerous to civilized Europe (392, 432). Indeed, she portrays Peter the self-styled Roman tsar not only as a reborn Caesar, but also as a stereotypical "Eastern despot," creator of a culture of slaves (431). Pressing the point of Russia's actual distance from the European model that has inspired Peter, Merezhkovskii attributes feelings of alienation to the newly arrived statue of Venus, which wonders at finding itself in "Hyperborean Scythia," a land as "hopeless . . . as Hades" (339–40). Upon visiting Europe, Alexis, too, concludes that "the third Rome, as the old men called Moscow, was as far away from the first, real Rome, as Petersburg's Europe was from the real one" (547).

Further, rather than uniting with the Russian Church in a productive manner as Merezhkovskii had once imagined, Peter seems to seek—with more conviction than Julian the Apostate—to undermine Christian faith. Peter views the Church as the root of Russia's parochialism, and he tries to "enlighten" his subjects by ridiculing what they hold most holy. He demonstrates to a gathering of his subjects how a "weeping" icon depicting the Virgin Mary functions, as he squeezes a sponge at the icon's back. He takes steps to hinder monasticism and listens approvingly as Feodosii, his administrator of public affairs, plans various antimonastic measures: "Abolish once and for all the sale of mead and oil in the churches. Forbid the lighting of candles in front of icons standing outside of churches. Demolish chapels. Do not display relics. Do not invent miracles. Arrest beggars and beat them relentlessly with sticks" (463). Nikolai Berdiaev would later write, "[Peter] wanted to destroy the old Muscovite Russia, to tear up by the roots those feelings which lay in the very foundation of its life."[94] Most significantly, even as the Roman Borgias ended up ruling the papacy, Peter sets himself at the head of the Russian Church, subordinating it to the state when he announces his desire to become its "one leader" (422).

Peter's aides and the official Church support him as he dismantles Russian Orthodox traditions and autonomy. Feodosii tells Peter that the tsar is "the Christ of the Lord" (638) and "the earthly god" (423), and instructs him "in what sense the Roman emperors, pagan and Christian alike, designated themselves pontifexes and high priests of the polytheistic law" (422). Impressed by Feodosii's arguments, Peter later proclaims that he is "both together—the patriarch and the tsar!" (453). And, crucially, an official Church figure is instrumental in bringing Alexis to his death: after Alexis confesses to his priest about a plot against his father, the priest breaks the holy seal of confession as a Petrine law dictates. When Peter learns of his son's rebellious words, he looks upon them as justification to kill Alexis. Aided by the subservient Church, imperial Rome has vanquished Christianity in Peter's state. Alexis has reacted in his diary to the changes Peter has implemented, including the new capital city based on imperial, pagan Rome, and questioned his father's actions: "Jesus Christ struck and destroyed the Roman Empire and broke its clay feet into dust. But again we create and build what God destroyed. Is this not fighting with God?" (455).

Merezhkovskii's 1907 article "Religion et révolution" (Religion and Revolution), written under the shadow cast by the 1905 Revolution but linked nonetheless to his prerevolutionary writings, underscores the sacrilege Merezhkovskii perceived in Peter's Roman aspirations and in the degradation of the Russian Church that began during his reign. "The decidedly pagan Caesar of the *First Rome* became the dubiously Christian pontiff of the *Third Rome*," Merezhkovskii wrote. Peter's Russia had duplicated the harmfully secular focus of the Vatican, portrayed in *Leonardo da Vinci,* in which "the kingdom of heaven" had become "a terrestrial kingdom." In Russia's case, the state had taken over the church, rather than the church's becoming a state of its own as the Vatican had, but the effect was essentially the same. In both situations, a harmful and erroneous linkage of church and state had occurred, and church and state had been compromised irrevocably.[95] Implying a condemnation of Peter, Merezhkovskii wrote of the demonic nature of "the Man who would be God, of the Human Kingdom that seeks to replace that of God." He also rejected the idea of a theocracy, a Christian state—or, correspondingly, a Third Rome. He described the "impure soul of the Roman-Byzantine 'Holy Empire,' the soul of the adulterous fusion of the State and the Church, of Orthodoxy and autocracy."[96] And he called for a revolution centered on Christ alone, not on the official Church, but on a "City of the Future" that would negate the very concept of the Rome-based state. He associated such an anti-Roman revolution with the Russian religious dissenters and with the Russian intelligentsia of his day, both committed, according to Merezhkovskii at this point, to Christ, and both opposed to autocracy and Orthodoxy.

Of the Old Believers, or *raskol'niki,* of the Petrine period, Merezhkovskii wrote in "Religion and Revolution," "In their conscious element, one finds shadows, slavery, immobility, an infinite static quality—but in their unconscious element, a blinding light, the strength of religious creativity, and an infinite dynamism, emerging not from the outside, from Europe, but from the depths of the Russian soul. . . . They were the first to declare that the Russian autocracy was the realm of the Antichrist." Thus according to Merezhkovskii, these religious dissenters were the first Russian revolutionaries.[97] This view is reflected throughout *Peter and Alexis,* in which devout Christians express decidedly conservative views that are spared much of the authorial censure typical of Merezhkovskii's previous two novels. In the opening scene of *Peter and Alexis,* an elderly Russian Christian comes to Alexis to complain: "We have mixed ourselves up with infidels, acquired their ways, rejected our Christian vows, and lain waste to the holy churches. We have closed our eyes to the East: we have turned our feet to flight, to the West, and we have gone along strange and unknown paths" (321). Many Russian Christians in fact feel that Peter is the Antichrist, and they proclaim that he is profaning the Third Rome with these Western influences. An Old Believer announces, "In Russia, that is to say the Third Rome, there has appeared that Peter, the son of death, the blasphemer and enemy of God, that is, the Antichrist. . . . That very same Antichrist has arrived, and with him this era ends. Amen!" (362–63). While their xenophobia and their misguided focus on the Third Rome recall the speech of Danilo Mamyrov in *Leonardo da Vinci,* these defensive pronouncements are presented as somewhat understandable in the face of Peter's cruelly anti-Christian Romanization of Russia. Moreover, the apocalyptic tenor of the Old Believers' statements will be echoed in the high points of the novel, when Alexis and Tikhon encounter John of the Apocalypse. In the context of the novel, therefore, as in Merezhkovskii's 1907 essay, some kind of apocalypse is the antidote to autocracy and subservient Orthodoxy. Merezhkovskii's apocalyptic Christians, in their lack of enlightenment, sense the most sacred, revolutionary "truth."[98]

Meanwhile, the respective stories of Alexis and Tikhon provide a window into Merezhkovskii's vision of the character and future path of the revolutionary intelligentsia of his own day. Alexis is linked through his Christian faith to the *narod* and through his little-recognized Westernizing tendencies to his father. The potential synthesis he provides, however, is rendered irrelevant by his inability to communicate his opinions convincingly, particularly to Peter. Rejected by his father, Alexis turns to rebellion. His consequent murder spells the end of any hope for reconciliation between tsar and people, father and son, or autocracy and revolutionary intelligentsia, thus sowing the seeds for the disunity of Merezhkovskii's own era.[99] Tikhon, too, combines within himself a connection to the religious *narod* and an attraction to the clarity and rationality he associates with Europe. Again like Alexis, he will reject the status quo to welcome an apocalyptic epiphany. And yet Tikhon will live on to bear witness to the new era he has glimpsed. His story serves as a model for Merezhkovskii's revolutionary contemporaries, to whom Merezhkovskii idiosyncratically attributed a Christian faith akin to that of the apocalyptically minded dissenters.

Merezhkovskii's Alexis is a complex and rather contradictory character. Known for his Christian piety, he is viewed by the religious, xenophobic folk as their champion, for they are convinced that the tsarevich is firmly committed to Russia's pre-Petrine ways. Early in the novel, for instance, Alexis echoes the views of his religious compatriots when he tells a skeptical Fraulein Arnheim that while the West may have wisdom, strength, and fame, Russia in its poverty and misery has Christ. At various points in the novel, Alexis considers becoming a monk. Further, he dreams of gathering an army to reconquer Constantinople, "liberate the Slavs from the yoke of the infidels," and gather the "peoples from the four corners of the earth" into an eternal Christian kingdom (557).

At the same time, Alexis shares traits with his Westernizing father. For Alexis is not the reactionary his father—and his supporters—assume him to be: as Fraulein Arnheim notes, "I was most surprised to learn that he is not that defender of the old, that enemy of the new, that he is considered by all. . . . The tsar's mistake, it would appear, is in going too fast" (433).[100] Alexis does not condemn Peter's goal of Westernization; rather, he objects to his father's means of achieving it. Moreover, once he has visited Europe, Alexis recognizes that there were once Christian martyrs in the West, and he decides that the West, like Russia, is open to Christ. He also realizes that despite Peter's overwhelming paganism, the tsar has neglected to import from Europe its most precious quality: freedom. Rampant imperialism and cruelty are no substitute: under Peter, a Russian Rome has come to resemble the kingdom of Xerxes that Vladimir Solov'ev had feared. Alexis rebels against his father, hoping to substitute for Peter's reign one that encompasses Western freedom along with the Russian traditions, including Christian faith, that he respects in the *narod*.

Peter remains convinced that his course is correct and that Alexis opposes it entirely. And yet Alexis himself bears some responsibility for this fatal misunderstanding: as Leonardo was unable to convince his contemporaries of the validity of his views, Alexis lacks the courage of his convictions and vacillates among his various allegiances. In addition, along with sharing his father's attraction to the West, Alexis has inherited Peter's brutal temper. Echoing Emperor Julian's treatment of his wife, Alexis rapes and beats his mistress Evrosin'ia, a representative of the Russian *narod* whom he professes to love. In a picture of the vengeful folk that would be echoed in Aleksandr Blok's revolutionary visions, Evrosin'ia avenges this injury when she urges Alexis to return to his father from Europe, although she knows she is driving him to his death.[101] A "superfluous man" unable to realize his most attractive qualities, Alexis fulfills his Christian potential only as he lies dying, killed by his father's bestial blows in the interrogation chamber. His transformation is made possible by John of the Apocalypse, a Merezhkovskiian *deus ex machina* who appears to Alexis in his jail cell in order to administer communion to him.[102] Alexis is filled with joy, and with the everlasting life of Christ's resurrection. Viewing his son's corpse, Peter recognizes that the now Christ-like Alexis, sacrificed to his father's will, has forgiven him and will justify him to God. Moved by this realization, Peter makes the sign of the cross as he weeps for the son he has killed. In Peter's reborn Roman Empire, Christ gains dominion over the Antichrist only in an apocalyptic framework.[103]

Alexis's complicated interactions with the *narod* and with his father combine with his eventual apocalyptic salvation to evoke images of the Russian intelligentsia of Merezhkovskii's day. The Westernizing members of the Russian intelligentsia were sons of Peter, too, as Merezhkovskii implied in an article of this period: they were continuing Peter's plan of Westernization and human progress.[104] Like Alexis, the modern-day intellectuals had participated in decades of the simultaneous exploitation and adulation of the *narod,* along with a complex relationship with the tsarist government. The revolutionary movement, which Merezhkovskii construed as apocalyptic, represented a break in the intelligentsia's previous, indecisive attitude to the people and to the state. For the intelligentsia, filled with suicidal, iconoclastic zeal, was at last ready to renounce its ambivalence, merging with the *narod* in overt rejection of the Russian autocracy. And while many might have questioned the identification of the Christian Alexis with the atheist twentieth-century rebels, Merezhkovskii's views differed. For him, the intellectuals at the fin de siècle professed atheism but manifested a Christian spirit they themselves did not recognize. Like the dissenters who were unwitting revolutionaries, the revolutionaries were unwitting Christians, and thus the two groups were linked. "If one notes not what this latter group says, but what they do, one will recognize that these atheists are actually saints," Merezhkovskii wrote in the introduction to "Religion and Revolution." "Since the first Christian martyrs, there have not been people who died thus—as [the early Christian theologian] Tertullian said, 'They fly to death like bees to honey.' The Russian Revolution is not simply political; it is religious."[105] Alexis, like the modern-day revolutionaries, goes willingly to his death, a death sanctioned religiously and in fact required before a cleansing apocalypse can come to pass, one in which all previous oppositions—tsar and people, fathers and sons, intelligentsia and *narod*—will be resolved. Like Alexis, the modern-day revolutionaries will fulfill their potential in an apocalyptic triumph.

Alexis's journey is thus an important one. He moves from East to West, and then East again, where he is finally made privy to the "truth" of the apocalypse. At the same time, his revelation is a private one between father and son; it affects no other characters. An epiphany similar to the one Alexis experiences comes to Tikhon. He, too, moves in his allegiances between East and West and comes to believe in an apocalyptic future. But Tikhon provides a more productive model for Merezhkovskii's contemporaries than Alexis does, for Tikhon survives his revelation and merges in a nonexploitative manner with the *narod*. His name recalls that of Evtikhii, and the epilepsy from which he suffers recalls Dostoevskii himself and Dostoevskii's Christ-like Prince Myshkin. His name also brings to mind the monk Tikhon Zadonskii, who provided inspiration for Dostoevskii's saintly Father Zosima in *Brat'ia Karamazovy* (The Brothers Karamazov, 1880). This set of associations suggests that in this final novel, Dostoevskiian Christian meekness supplants Roman might. Christ triumphs over Antichrist to create a new universe, rather than merging with him to create a theocratic Third Rome.

The son of a nobleman whom Peter has brutally executed, Tikhon travels a path divided between West and East, rationalism and faith. He is brought up in Moscow by his servant, a member of the *narod* who is firmly convinced that Peter is the Antichrist and that the apocalypse is on its way. But Tikhon loves the scientific study of mathematics, and he is selected by the tsar to complete his education in Western Europe. The night before he is to leave St. Petersburg, however, Tikhon has an epileptic fit prompted by his fear of Peter's city and of Peter himself. At this point, Tihkon has his first intuition of the apocalyptic "truth" that Merezhkovskii promotes in the novel, as he recognizes: "It was all the same . . . where he would go, to the East or to the West; both here and there, at the furthermost reaches of East and West, there was but one thought, one feeling: that of the approaching end" (381). Nonetheless, he does not commit himself to the apocalyptic truth at this point, and he continues to alternate between the religious and rational perspectives he encounters in Peter's Russia. He embarks on a series of experiments with various Christian sects, including self-immolators who repel him with their negation of the human body, sexuality, and life itself, and frenzied Dionysian orgiasts intent on infant sacrifice. He alternates his stints among the sectarians with periods among the Westernizers at Peter's court, but there he is frightened by the "secret thought of all the new philosophers: either with Christ against reason or with reason against Christ" (742). As Tikhon ponders Peter's self-deification, he recalls the beast of Revelation, and he realizes that the apocalyptic beast is founded on the idea of the anti-Christian Mangod, whom he now firmly rejects. He flees yet again to the wilderness, this time finding a home with two Christian hermits, whose dissociation from life distresses him once more. Tikhon is fearfully resigning himself to the idea that perhaps no synthesis of faith and reason is possible after all, when his reverie is broken by the words of the newly arrived John of the Apocalypse: "Are you tired, you poor thing? I have many of you, many little ones. You go all over the world, poor and orphaned. . . . But do not be afraid, dear ones. Wait a little, and I will gather you all into a new Church of the Coming God. There was the ancient Church of Peter, the standing Rock; there will be the new Church of John, the flying thunder. . . . The first testament is the Old, the Kingdom of the Father; the second testament is the New, the Kingdom of the Son; the third testament is the Last, the Kingdom of the Spirit. One in Three, and Three in one" (757). The trilogy ends with Tikhon's—and Merezhkovskii's—joyful paean to this long-awaited unification: "Hosanna! Christ shall defeat the Antichrist!" (759). Although Tikhon is struck dumb by wonder, his face radiates a joy readily visible to others.

Tikhon's story echoes in some respects that of a specific contemporary of Merezhkovskii: Aleksandr Dobroliubov, a Decadent poet turned Christian mystic with whom Merezhkovskii met in 1893 and again in the early days of 1905.[106] Merezhkovskii wrote in "Religion and Revolution" that Dobroliubov had moved through Decadence to a realization of the need to reject the Orthodox Church in order to preach the coming Kingdom of God. Dobroliubov, Merezhkovskii explained, had accomplished what even Tolstoi and Dostoevskii had found impossible: "a miserable Decadent, one who had been mocked, a feeble child, accomplished what was at the base of the strength of titans: *my strength is revealed in weakness*."[107] During their last meeting, Dobroliubov told Merezhkovskii at various intervals that he was tired of talking and would prefer to remain silent, though his eyes were expressive, "illuminated by an inner clarity."[108] Tikhon, too, speechless at the end of *Peter and Alexis*, is portrayed as a childlike man, one who has made his East-West pilgrimages and is now filled not with immense physical strength but with a strong apocalyptic faith. He has been exposed to Western thought and with that "Decadent" background has succeeded in penetrating Merezhkovskii's apocalyptic "final mystery."

Like Dobroliubov, Tikhon provided a model for Merezhkovskii and for his contemporaries. Indeed, Merezhkovskii explained that he himself had had meetings with representatives of the *narod,* to whom he had come with his knowledge of Aeschylus, Plato, and Nietzsche, while they approached him with their faith. The two groups completed each other, he insisted in "Religion and Revolution"; the "Decadence" that had seemed linked to death instead was "the beginning of a new life," one connected to the people and to the joint pursuit of a revolutionary apocalypse.[109] Thus as far as Merezhkovskii was concerned as he concluded his trilogy, the intelligentsia still had an important role to play in transforming Russia. He continued to value the representatives of the "new art," but he now insisted that they cease their previous vacillations and embrace and celebrate Christianity fully. Peter's artistic efforts had excluded Christ and had therefore harmed Russia: he had created a faulty Russian Rome rather than the "City of the Future." Nonetheless, he had opened Russia to Europe, and educated Russians, including twentieth-century Decadents, had benefited.[110] Now they were to move beyond Peter's Russia, joining together with the *narod* to fight Rome through their Christian revolution. In his introduction to "Religion and Revolution," Merezhkovskii called upon Europeans to join Russia in this quest. "The Russian Revolution is universal," he proclaimed. "When you Europeans understand that, you will race to help light the fire. Take heed: you will not put our fire out, but we will set you alight."[111]

Tikhon is fundamentally different from Julian: the first and final "seekers" of Merezhkovskii's trilogy profess varying allegiances and goals. The Roman emperor Julian flourished in the West, fought Christ for much of his life, and ruled firmly in an empire of this world. Tikhon spent his life in Russia, retained an abiding Christian faith, and was transfigured by a vision of an anarchic world to come. And yet both figures resemble Merezhkovskii, albeit at different periods of his life, and therefore they share traits as well. Like him, they experienced East and West, acknowledged Christ, and found Western discoveries enticing. They were anguished in their respective searches. And despite Merezhkovskii's change of setting and mission from his first to his third novel, they lived in worlds with common threads. The Petrine Russia Merezhkovskii portrayed in *Peter and Alexis* is one where Russian Christians fight a newly established Roman Empire. In Julian's Rome, Christians battle the Roman Empire Julian professes to love. In his first two novels, Merezhkovskii situated the resolution of this conflict in a

Russian-led Third Rome. By the time he was writing *Peter and Alexis,* he had concluded that this battle would find its resolution only in apocalypse, and he had rejected the Roman state and the idea of Russia as the Third Rome. Still, Rome remained the prism, now accepted, now rejected, through which he examined and discussed Russia and its prospects.

In a 1912 review, Valerii Briusov wrote that Merezhkovskii had demonstrated a certain continuity throughout his oeuvre, which Briusov characterized as "all one path." Briusov at this stage tended to dismiss Merezhkovskii's work from a "purely aesthetic point of view," but he characterized it nonetheless as an important "chronicle of the searchings of the contemporary spirit, a diary of everything the more sensitive elements of our society have experienced over the past quarter of a century."[112] As other critics noted in their reviews of the trilogy, *Christ and Antichrist* served just such a purpose between 1895 and 1905. Merezhkovskii read and narrated Rome as part of Russia's past, asserting Rome's relevance to Russia—and Russia's relevance to Europe. In so doing, he drew on particular historical moments to create narratives he thought were particularly significant for his contemporaries. As Belyi would later write in a review of the trilogy, "From the pages of world history, familiar, known eyes looked out at us. . . . Through images of the past, Merezhkovskii was able to resurrect the face of an unprecedented future, and all of history was transformed into the search for the unified face."[113] In subsequent years, even those writers who had understandably faulted Merezhkovskii for excessive schematization would draw upon the myths of Russia that he had developed in his novels and make use of them in their own work, as Rome served as a crucial tool in discussions of Russia's national identity. Aspects of the paradigm Merezhkovskii had promoted—that of the relationship between a Roman, imperial West and a Russian, Christian East—along with his attention to the idea of Russia as a synthesizing Third Rome, would resurface in various forms over subsequent decades, the radical changes occasioned by the Bolshevik Revolution notwithstanding. In *Christ and Antichrist,* Merezhkovskii created an influential set of terms, perpetuating and refining a discourse about Rome and Russia that other Russian writers would turn to as they, too, sought to define their nation, their world, and the role of art in this world.

2

Relinquishing Empire?

Valerii Briusov's Roman Novels

All dreams are sweet to me, all speeches dear,
And I dedicate my verse to all gods.
Valerii Briusov, "I," 1899

Reading Merezhkovskii's *Julian the Apostate* as it was serialized in the spring of 1895, Valerii Briusov was delighted. "With every issue of the journal, [the novel] gets better and deeper," he wrote to his friend Petr Pertsov.[1] Having produced such a work, Briusov maintained in a notebook entry the same year, Merezhkovskii ought to assume "one of the first places in Russian literature."[2] Eight years Merezhkovskii's junior, the ambitious Briusov had read of the French Symbolists in the former's "On the Reasons for the Decline,"[3] among other sources, and he was keen to see the creation of a Russian Symbolist movement—and, further, to play a central role in this process. Merezhkovskii, with his stress on idealism and individualism and his attempts at a "new" literature, had despite his intermittent philosophical inconsistencies helped to inaugurate the new literary age Briusov sought.[4] Briusov noted with some satisfaction in an 1893 diary entry that "everyone" had been reading Merezhkovskii's *Symbols*, that he himself was now a "Decadent," and that "others praise Symbolism. Bravo!"[5]

Briusov's own first book of verse, characteristically titled *Chefs d'oeuvre*, appeared in 1895, the same year as Merezhkovskii's first novel. Although it met with predominantly negative reviews, it nonetheless was part of a group of texts that demonstrated that a new movement was indeed gathering steam in Russian letters.[6] By 1899 Briusov had taken a leading role in the new modernist publishing house, Skorpion; a year later he would gain critical acclaim for his verse collection *Tertia vigilia,* whose Latin title referring to the predawn stage of the Roman watch intimated also the changes sensed by Russian writers on the verge of a new century.[7] In 1904, Briusov would go on to serve as the editor of *Vesy* (The Scales), a journal that under his leadership introduced the Russian reading public to a broad range of Western European writers and simultaneously provided a forum for a variety of Russian modernists.[8] Russia's Symbolist movement had come of age, with Valerii Briusov at its head.

Within several years, however, Briusov would break ties with the movement he had done so much to build, leaving *The Scales* in 1909, beginning work at the journal *Russkaia mysl'* (Russian Thought) in 1910, and searching painfully for new artistic "truths" to replace those he had relinquished when he quit the Symbolist camp. At the same time, as war and revolution came to Russia, the rather conservative Briusov would embark on a period of questioning that would lead eventually to his acceptance of and cooperation with the Bolshevik regime until his death in 1924. He would also read and discuss—sometimes with Merezhkovskii himself—the second and third novels of the latter's Rome-based trilogy.[9] And in 1911–12, in the pages of *Russian Thought,* Briusov's own first Roman novel would appear.[10]

Altar' pobedy (The Altar of Victory) and its unfinished, very similar sequel, *Iupiter poverzhennyi* (Jupiter Overthrown, first published in 1934, but written mainly between 1912 and 1913),[11] were devoted to the fourth-century pagan-Christian clash that Merezhkovskii had described in the first novel of his trilogy. Briusov's hero, the young pagan aristocrat Junius Norbanus, concedes by the end of *The Altar of Victory* that despite his love for imperial Rome and its gods, he must bow to the inevitable and become a Christian. Like Merezhkovskii's, Briusov's fourth-century Rome is a world of dying, Western, pagan imperialism vanquished by Eastern, Christian religion. His characters and plots echo Merezhkovskii's to a startling degree. And yet Briusov's message is quite different. Whereas Merezhkovskii had privileged the East in his tale, Briusov, on the contrary, stayed determinedly focused on the West, setting his Merezhkovskiian plot exclusively in the Western Empire. Whereas Merezhkovskii had revealed a surprising pro-Christian bias in his supposedly Nietzschean text, a bias to be borne out in the later novels of his trilogy, Briusov made clear, despite his main character's eventual conversion to Christianity, his distaste for the religion and many of its adherents. And while Merezhkovskii had ended by rejecting empire for faith, Briusov mourned empire's loss and welcomed its replacement only when such acceptance seemed not so much required by "right" or "wrong," but willed by fate itself.

Scholars have compared the two authors in general terms, contrasting the Christian focus of Merezhkovskii's writings with Briusov's known anti-Christian, rationalist approach. Critics have also viewed the plots of Briusov's Roman novels as reflective of the changes the author himself underwent in the decade prior to the first novel's appearance.[12] And yet Briusov's complex polemic with Merezhkovskii's first novel and with his trilogy as a whole, and the significance of this polemic within the world of Russian letters between the 1905 and 1917 Revolutions, remain virtually unexplored topics.[13] Written during a transitional period in Russian history by a long-time devotee of ancient Rome, Briusov's Roman novels are an underappreciated and yet highly revealing link in the chain of Russian texts connecting modern Russia with ancient Rome. An examination of the long-overlooked relationship between these works by two first-generation Russian Symbolists provides ample impetus to read Briusov's Roman novels as subtle commentary on Merezhkovskii's influential trilogy and the ideas it advanced regarding Rome, Russia, and art itself.

Fourth-Century Rome Redux

Not as a stranger did I come
To the Roman Forum—to this country of graves,
But as if to a familiar world . . .
Valerii Briusov, "At the Forum," 1908

As Briusov worked on *The Altar of Victory,* his fervent admiration of Merezhkovskii's 1895 text appears to have faded. "Rereading Merezhkovskii's *Julian the Apostate* after careful study of [the Roman historian] Ammianus Marcellinus," he complained, "I find in Merezhkovskii so many anachronisms and errors in regard to the 'epoch' that I'm now literally afraid of every word I write."[14] Describing his own research in 1914, he explained, "For some time now I have been devoting myself exclusively to ancient Rome and Roman literature: in particular, I studied Virgil and his era, as well as the entire period of the fourth century, from Constantine the Great to Theodosius the Great. In all these areas I am a specialist in the true sense of the word: I have read an entire library about each one of them."[15] Indeed, when Briusov republished the novel in his 1913 incomplete collected works, he appended extensive scholarly notes and a lengthy bibliography to the text.[16]

Briusov's first Roman novel intrigued contemporary readers. Aleksandr Blok pronounced it "interesting,"[17] and A. A. Kondrat'ev lauded it over Merezhkovskii's *Julian*.[18] Others, dazed by the Latinisms and references to Roman literature and customs that abound in the text, acknowledged Briusov's scholarship but failed to appreciate its literary qualities. Briusov's language in this "never-ending" work sounded like "Silver Age Latin," one critic protested.[19] Another maintained that the novel required "scholarly preparation" as well as an "interest in serious historical reading."[20] A third acknowledged that Briusov's portrayals of early Christian sects might prove of interest to contemporary Russians, intrigued as they were by sectarianism, but insisted nonetheless that the work was "distant from contemporary life."[21]

Limiting their comments to Briusov's stylization and historicism, however, these latter critics neglected to note a major aspect of his work: its conscious perpetuation of the terms and plots laid out in Merezhkovskii's popular trilogy, particularly its first novel. Picking up historically where Merezhkovskii's *Julian the Apostate* had left off, *The Altar of Victory* and *Jupiter Overthrown* are devoted to the last official gasp of Roman paganism, and of the Western Roman Empire itself, at the end of the fourth century. Briusov's first novel covers 382–383 CE, and the second, 393–394—mere decades after the end of Julian's reign in 363. Less than one hundred years later, the Goth Odoacer would depose the Western Emperor Romulus Augustulus in what is commonly seen as the end of the Western Roman Empire.

The Altar of Victory deals with the historically documented, unsuccessful attempt by a group of Roman pagan senators, led by the famed orator Symmachus, to persuade the Western Emperor Gratian to reinstate the winged statue of Victory (the "Altar of Victory" of Briusov's title) in the Roman Senate building. The statue had been placed in the Senate originally by Augustus Caesar, and had been removed at the instigation of Ambrosius (bishop of Milan and later St. Ambrose), then Gratian's chief adviser and one of the leading enemies of the Empire's remaining pagans. The senators would repeat their efforts to resurrect paganism, again without success, ten years later, forming the subject of *Jupiter Overthrown*. The pagan senators' hopes this time were fixed upon the puppet emperor Eugenius, a Christian tolerant of the pagans who had raised him to the purple after having his predecessor Valentinian II murdered. In this second case, the pagan efforts would be defeated by the Eastern Emperor Theodosius. He would destroy Eugenius's forces, represented, in keeping with Briusov's title, by an emblem of Jupiter, and establish Christianity once and for all as the religion of the Roman Empire. Since Briusov did not finish the tale, the Christian victory remained unrecorded in his fiction, though Junius Norbanus's thoughts of conversion at the end of *The Altar of Victory* told the same story on an individual level.[22]

Briusov's own heroes thus attempted fruitlessly to achieve the pro-pagan goals that had eluded Emperor Julian. But these characters, like Briusov himself, faced rapidly changing historical circumstances, as their opposition to these changes grew steadily more hopeless. Briusov provides a painstakingly detailed, panoramic picture of fourth-century Rome and its citizens (in contrast to Merezhkovskii's romanticized biography of one "great man"), an approach that in a sense underlines the diminished stature of his pro-pagan characters—particularly his main character, Junius—and their cause. Junius, whose name recalls that of Julian, is no impassioned emperor. Rather, he is a relatively ordinary, well-off, provincial youth from Aquitania, where he has been raised in a traditional pagan family. Related on his father's side to freed slaves and on his mother's to the senator Tiburtinus, the latter a drunken pagan cuckolded by his Christian wife and her priest, Junius becomes infatuated with Tiburtinus's stunningly beautiful, self-serving pagan stepdaughter, Hesperia. When Gratian orders the Altar of Victory removed from the Senate, Junius joins the group, headed by Hesperia, that seeks to reverse the decree and promote the cause of the Roman pantheon. Entrusted by Hesperia with a secret, dangerous, and entirely unrealistic mission—the assassination of the emperor—he travels with Symmachus's embassy to Milan, where the emperor is residing. Junius is caught before making his assassination attempt, thrown into an underground prison for months, and then rescued by the ever-tolerant Symmachus, who packs him off to a luxurious Roman villa to recuperate. The Christian Father Nicholas, who appears in both novels and attempts to convert Junius to the "new faith," goes so far as to call Junius a "little Julian" (523).

Further, like Julian, Junius is in fact conflicted about his mission. Here the conflict is shaped not through imperial orders, as it was in Julian's case, but through the young man's inability to choose between the two women he meets in Rome: the pagan Hesperia and Rhea, an eccentric member of a "heretical," orgiastic Christian sect devoted to the coming of the Antichrist. Despite his sworn allegiance to Hesperia and his constant, rational doubts over Rhea's sanity and attractiveness, he nonetheless leaves Hesperia repeatedly to succumb to the orgiastic sessions Rhea provides. While in Milan to do Hesperia's bidding, for example, Junius reencounters Rhea and finds it difficult at times to remember his earlier commitment. Later, he travels to Britannia with Hesperia to join forces with the rebel Maximus in another bid to gain power and bring paganism back to the Empire, but leaves her en route when he hears that Roman legions are about to attack Rhea's group of sectarians, now hiding in the mountains near Milan. Rhea, her body spread out in the shape of a cross, is killed in battle, and Junius returns yet again to Hesperia. Eventually, like Julian, Junius will accept a more canonical version of Rhea's faith: the preface of *Jupiter Overthrown* is supplied by the monk Bartholomew, who turns out to be Junius himself, filled with professed Christian humility—but still capable of trembling at the very thought of the gorgeous Hesperia. The conflict, like that of the dying, anguished Julian, continues.

Hesperia, whose name recalls the ancient, mythical garden of the Hesperides, located in the westernmost corner of the world, is associated frequently throughout the novel with the Western Empire in general and with the city of Rome—and its imperial mentality—in particular. Making this identification explicit, Junius describes Hesperia's very shape as mirroring the spectacular lines of the imperial city (43). "Hesperia" is also a poetic name for Italy, used, for example, by Virgil in his *Aeneid* when he writes of the land that will become the seat of the Roman Empire. In Briusov's text, the lovestruck Junius underlines this association, admitting that he is drawn to the woman Hesperia as the Trojans had been to their new home (373). As head of the pagan faction in the novel, meanwhile, Hesperia links the Western Empire with paganism, thereby perpetuating—despite Briusov's professed dislike of such Merezhkovskiian bifurcations—the geographic resonances set out in *Christ and Antichrist*.[23] Her other associations include beauty, wisdom, empire, art, and the ruthless, murderous pursuit of power, all of which are also affiliated in the novel with the spirit of ancient Rome—and all of which echo Merezhkovskii's novelistic thesaurus of "pagan" Western civilization. And yet Hesperia, despite her professed allegiance to Rome and its past, converts to Christianity at the end of *The Altar of Victory*. Although this conversion is part of a blatant bid for further power (she becomes the mistress of the usurper Maximus), and the next novel finds her once again dedicated to the pagan cause, it nonetheless points to paganism's pending defeat by the new power of Christianity. As Junius muses at the end of *The Altar of Victory,* "Wherever I look it's the same: success goes to those who, like Constantine, raise the sign of Christ with the words, 'With this sign you shall conquer!'" (407).

The triumphal force of Christianity, meanwhile, is associated primarily with the East, which for Briusov, in keeping with Roman stereotypes, includes both Greece and Jerusalem. Tiburtinus's Christian wife is Greek, and Father Nicholas is described on his first appearance as looking more Greek than Roman (232). Rhea, the primary representative of Christianity in the text, is not originally from the Eastern Empire but is linked to it nonetheless through her faith and her associates, many of whom are depicted as Jews who accept Christ, sing of the New Jerusalem, and speak Hebrew. Indeed, Briusov repeatedly underlines the Jewish basis of the Christian faith through various characters' references to "the Jewish Christ," portrayed as destroying, through his adherents, the Roman Empire. Tiburtinus tells Junius when he first arrives in Rome that the faith of the "Jewish Christ" is proving lethal to the Empire (21); Symmachus rails against emperors who force the descendants of Romulus to worship the "Jewish Christ" (401); and one of Hesperia's associates blames the followers of the "Jewish Christ" for the difficulties the Empire's pagans now face (45). Jews, Jerusalem, and Hebrew are thus pitted against the Roman Empire, Rome itself, and the Latin tongue.

In addition to their associations with Greece and Judaism, fourth-century Christians are linked to barbarism: Rhea in her mystical, uncontrolled ravings is described as filled with a barbaric spirit, and Christianity itself is seen as a barbaric religion (126, 342). This Eastern-based barbarism has produced uncultured, non-Roman emperors and imperial advisers clad, significantly, in Scythian outfits rather than togas (137, 138, 264, 304): while the historian Briusov knows that Russians cannot fit into his fourth-century narrative, he makes frequent reference not only to Scythians but also to the "peoples beyond Scythia," who, it is feared, will invade Rome and help Christianity in its victory over the Empire (44, 78, 103, 115).[24] Briusov thus perpetuates Merezhkovskii's geographic framework, associating the land linked to the future Russia with the Christian, barbarian, mystical faction of his own tale.

Certainly historical hindsight provides sufficient cause to present Christianity as a victorious force, but, as noted in the preceding chapter, scholars disagree on the extent to which Christianity had vanquished paganism by the fourth century. "Up till the close of the fourth century,"

Christopher Hibbert notes in his history of Rome, "pagan shrines had been restored and kept in repair and use beside the places of Christian worship"; following Constantine's death, in fact, "new pagan statues had been erected along the Via Sacra."[25] "To count up the glories of Rome is like counting the stars in the sky," wrote the fourth-century Roman poet Rutilius Namatianus, clearly not anticipating the incipient "fall."[26] But Briusov, like Merezhkovskii before him, stresses the doomed status of paganism and of Rome itself, a situation evident in the "Christian" traits that Junius, like Merezhkovskii's Julian, acknowledges despite himself in the so-called pagan faction of the day. Indeed, shocked by Hesperia's Caesar-like ability to order other human beings killed, Junius realizes that his reaction shows that he has acquired Christian values (268). And when his friend Remigius, distraught over his rejection by a beautiful prostitute, commits suicide, the horrified Junius recognizes that had Caesar or Augustus displayed such weakness, there would have been no Roman Empire (293).

This Christian momentum is portrayed even more strongly in *Jupiter Overthrown.* Symmachus gives up on the pro-pagan group, seeing no point in pursuing its goals, while his former senatorial colleague Flavian, once the epitome of Roman imperial strength, becomes insane. Christianity spreads westward to Aquitania, as Junius's own relatives convert to the new faith. Even Hesperia, reinstated as head of the pagan movement, admits to Junius that their cause is lost. The glories of Rome, pagans mourn, are gone forever. Thus the plot of *Jupiter Overthrown* becomes in a sense superfluous, as Junius's words at the end of *The Altar of Victory* speak for both novels: "Nothing can stand in the way of the whirlwind blowing softly from the low hill of Golgotha: this wind has already thrown the Altar of Victory out of the Curia, and it will bring down the golden-roofed temples of the City, will destroy Rome itself, and maybe the entire Empire. Isn't it time that I, too, came to terms with this victorious storm, that I understood that the Altar of Victory will never again stand in the Senate, and the banner of the Roman legion has been lowered forever before the labarum with the name of Christ! . . . The cross has been thrown onto one scale, and all the gold in the world is not enough to outweigh it!" (407–8).

Beyond the major trajectory of Junius's tale, Briusov's novels echo Merezhkovskii's in numerous minor ways. Most obviously, Briusov incorporates into *The Altar of Victory* a character named Julianius, an unappealing hanger-on in Hesperia's thrall who claims to be the son of Julian the Apostate. A foppish drunk with a painted face and a loose tongue, Julianius, known as "Julianius the Asiatic," tells Junius that he was born in the East but sees himself as a true Roman (45). He boasts that he will become emperor, throw the Christians to the lions, build a house on Rome's Palatine Hill more impressive than Emperor Nero's, and conquer all of Persia. He ends as a suicide, choosing to hang himself rather than open his veins in the traditional Roman way, much to the conservative Tiburtinus's disgust. The imprisoned Junius compares himself to Julian's brother Gallus, who is similarly incarcerated in Merezhkovskii's tale (173). The "divine Julian," the erstwhile emperor of Merezhkovskii's tale, is mentioned repeatedly in such a light throughout *The Altar of Victory* (52, 227, 250). Meanwhile, on the Christian-pagan front, characters combine deities of both persuasions in their speech, as in Merezhkovskii's work, and a procession in honor of the pagan gods is as much of a letdown to Briusov's pagans as it had been to Merezhkovskii's (533–34). And it cannot be a coincidence that Briusov, too, writes of a character named Mirra; far from Merezhkovskii's devoted Christian, however, the nondevout Briusov's Mirra is a prostitute.

Such links extend to the rest of Merezhkovskii's trilogy. A feast Junius enjoys in Milan, for instance, echoes in its location and opulence a Milanese gathering in Merezhkovskii's *Leonardo da Vinci*. The religiously fervent Rhea dreams before her death of a man with a scroll, a vision that appears to mimic that of Evtikhii at the end of Merezhkovskii's second novel. And Rhea's sectarians recall in their orgiastic sessions the various Christian groups of *Peter and Alexis*. In fact, despite his eventual rejection of Merezhkovskii's scholarship in his *Julian*, Briusov's notes from the period when he was working on his own Roman novels reveal that he used Merezhkovskii's writings as a source.[27] The two writers also shared sources, such as the writings of Ammianus Marcellinus and Gustave Flaubert's 1874 novel *The Temptation of Saint Anthony*.[28]

The ironic nature of some of these Merezhkovskiian echoes—ranging from a laughable "descendant" of Julian the Apostate to a sexually charged Mirra—points to the polemic inherent in Briusov's novels. Demonstrating that Julian's quest was doomed and that Christianity had in fact made its way into the heart of Rome's most notoriously pagan emperor was for Merezhkovskii a sacred prescription for contemporary Russian intellectuals and for the future of Russia, a prescription echoed in *Leonardo da Vinci* and reinforced, with an added anti-imperial, revolutionary subtext, in *Peter and Alexis*. Moving from his original goal—the unification of pagan West and Christian East into a Third Rome—to the proclamation of his apocalyptic Third Testament, Merezhkovskii had remained true to his vision of a Russian intelligentsia intended (albeit perhaps obliviously) to fulfill the spiritual goals he ascribed to them. For Briusov, however, showing that paganism and imperial Rome were nearing their end and that a new Christian era was to ensue was a lesson in the vagaries of fate, rather than a call to religious or revolutionary arms. The fact that the Empire would fall, while unarguable, meant not that it was unworthy of existence, but that it was nonetheless time for a newer and therefore more powerful truth to prevail.[29] Indeed, Briusov somewhat surprisingly felt that Rome in many ways had been at its height during the fourth century—and by situating his novel solely in the West, rather than in the "next" Rome, he emphasized this belief. He ascribed no apocalyptic significance to Christianity's triumph, nor did he utilize his narrative of ancient Rome to provide political or religious guidelines to his fellow modernist writers or to his nation. Instead, he lauded the glories of a wide-ranging, Western-style empire and the human potential that made such empires possible in any age, even as he recognized the corresponding power of sometimes unappealing "new truths" that could supplant to large degree those he found so inspiring.[30]

In an 1899 letter Briusov had written, "There are many truths and they often contradict one another. One must accept and understand this. . . . My dream has always been a pantheon, a temple of all gods."[31] His image of the Roman Empire was similarly diverse: its strength for Briusov was rooted in its ability to absorb and integrate new ideas and peoples. As he would explain in a later work:

All the truths that came to light,
Under the hum of victories, under the protection of Roman laws,
Melted powerfully into a new alloy.[32]

In keeping with this all-encompassing, ideal concept, the Rome lauded by many of Briusov's pagan characters in his Roman novels is a constantly evolving kingdom of multiple "truths" and new discoveries. Briusov's ongoing attraction to the world of pagan Rome and his rejection of Merezhkovskii's eventual renunciation of its glories and positive significance are evident from the first lines of *The Altar of Victory,* in which the provincial Junius catches his first glimpse of the imperial city. Thrilled at his opportunity to follow in the steps of such Roman heroes as the "divine Julius" Caesar, Junius brushes aside the city's current difficulties and flatly dismisses the "New Rome" (i.e., Constantinople). He is infatuated with tales of Rome's glory and convinced that it is the "center . . . of greatness, valor, wisdom, and taste" (9).

His friend Remigius, familiar with the city and eager to impress his new companion, offers an impassioned recitation of Rome's marvels: its amphitheaters and circuses, its beautiful palaces and forums, its swimming pools, libraries, and prostitutes. He compares Rome to a thousand-year-old tree that constantly puts forth new shoots as he celebrates its world of differences: "Rome is so immense that it is impossible to embrace it in a glance. In the City, wherever you may be, you are always in the center. What in other countries you see only in parts, in Rome you see united together. In Rome you will find the refinement of the East, the enlightenment of Greece, the fancifulness of the lands far beyond the Ocean, and everything that we have in our native Gaul. The inhabitants of all the provinces and the peoples of all other countries come together here into one crowd. Rome is the world in miniature" (10).

Briusov suggests through Junius's and Remigius's enthralled comments that Rome contains the entire world; Constantinople, the Second Rome, is therefore unnecessary. He thus implicitly rebukes not only Merezhkovskii's anti-imperialism, but his earlier visions of Russia's glory as the Third Rome. For if Constantinople is superfluous, there is clearly no need for a Russian Rome. Briusov's focus remains squarely on the first, Western Rome in its glory, as he enumerates in his text the marvelous advances that fourth-century Rome has made in the cultural, scientific, and social spheres. Significantly, early Christianity has no role in the ideal vision of multiplicity Briusov's characters expound; the glories of the earthly world remain his focus.

And yet Briusov's beloved Rome, that prototypical empire or temple of many truths, had paradoxically produced an environment in which a new "truth" antithetical to it could arise and triumph. Buoyed not by any intrinsic superiority but by its newness and the motivating power of fate, Christianity was gaining strength and thus proving victorious. Briusov presents Christianity in an almost unremittingly unappealing light, with no Merezhkovskiian allowances for the differing traits of a vibrant, "Greek" faith versus a stagnant, intolerant "Historic" Christianity. Father Nicodemus, involved in an affair with Tiburtinus's wife, is a hypocrite and gossip. Tiburtinus's wife and elder daughter are narrow-minded and unpleasant. Rhea's followers are lacking in spirituality and appear committed to her cause simply for the sake of the nightly orgies they enjoy.[33] "If there is a 'miracle' in Christianity, then it's only this one: that a religion so poor in content, compiled out of scraps of Egyptian wisdom, Judaism, Neo-Platonism, and other teachings, could have had such success," Briusov would state in 1919.[34] The only Christian whom Junius and his fellow pagans seem to find continuously worthy of respect is Ambrosius, whose pitiless strength of will and awesome organizational skills remind even the conservative Tibertinus of Roman heroes of old. But Ambrosius, firmly committed to the Christian path, is determined to destroy the pagan past entirely, as he makes clear to his cousin Symmachus during the affair of the Altar of Victory: "'Let Rome perish!' the bishop cried in a thunderous voice. 'Let the Empire perish! On its ruins I shall create another one, eternal and unshakeable. I will erect a new Rome: the City will no longer subjugate various tribes of the earth, but instead, the Christian Church will unite all peoples into one flock!'" (127).

Ambrosius's words as Briusov presents them run directly counter to the novelist's ideal visions of religion and empire. Indeed, Briusov's objection to the Christian mindset he portrays so unsympathetically in his novels lies in the intolerance he finds in the new faith, an intolerance that permits only one narrative to exist, rather than a multitude of voices that then form one diverse whole. "We are the way and the truth and the life; there is no path to God other than through us," Rhea proclaims, surrounded by a group of snake-worshippers (327). It is worth noting that the historian Gaston Boissier, one of Briusov's main sources for the debate between Symmachus and Ambrosius, asserted that the historical Ambrosius in fact was more devoted to religious pluralism than Symmachus, who wanted the Roman gods recognized as the basis of Rome's official religion. Briusov the would-be historian here becomes pure novelist, painting in Ambrosius the vivid picture he desires of an intolerant Christian.[35]

At the same time, it is also important to recognize that in *The Altar of Victory*, the self-proclaimed pagan Junius is powerless to stop himself from visiting Rhea and participating in the religious ceremonies he otherwise finds distasteful. The new faith overwhelms him, particularly when it is combined with the loss of self associated with passion and spiritual frenzy—a frenzy the rather chilly Hesperia, despite her numerous sexual affairs, does not inspire. Junius's occasional, uncomfortable attraction to Christianity and doubts about his commitment to paganism, reflected to a degree in his relationships with these two women, are also highlighted in both novels through his periodic discussions with Father Nicholas, who urges him to recognize that the pagan cause is hopeless. "You believe in strength," he says. "Then open your eyes, and you will see that strength lies on our side" (524). Nicholas explains that every era has its own faith: Jupiter was once sacred, but now Christ is triumphant. Junius resists this message, insisting stubbornly that "truth" is on the pagan side, and that truths cannot die. Nicholas's response is startling: "You are mistaken, young man, truths do die" (525). When Junius asks in some astonishment whether this means that the new Christian truth will also die, Nicholas—here, surely, more Briusov than priest—affirms this supposition, thus negating the idea of the "one eternal truth" to which Ambrosius and the novel's other Christians subscribe. At the same time, Nicholas insists, the Christian truth will last for centuries, and one must follow fate's example in choosing the strong; at present, that strong faith is Christianity.

As Junius sets off again on his Julianesque anti-Christian missions, determined but conflicted, Nicholas's words stay with him, as is evident from Junius's Christian preface to *Jupiter Overthrown.* The power that has intrigued him ends up overcoming him. His conversion is not complete, though: as noted, even as an aged monk he cannot control his agitation at the thought of Hesperia. Her pagan image lives on in the Christian monk, just as Ambrosius runs the church as his ancestors had once ruled an empire, and just as the Christian Trinity, according to one pagan character, recalls the pagan worship of a pantheon of gods (48). In the end, then, a complete conversion is both impossible and undesirable. Rome is perpetuated in its Christian successor, and Junius's previous self retains vestiges of its former vitality even when confined in a monk's cell. "Truths," old and new, merge.

Briusov based his novels structurally and thematically on Merezhkovskii's, but unlike Merezhkovskii he did not write them as thinly veiled portrayals of the challenges facing Russian society. Nevertheless, Briusov did believe that the artist's experiences entered into his text: this was the root of his artistic theory. His poems of the period preceding the composition of *The Altar of Victory* explicitly linked contemporary Russia with ancient Rome in an ongoing exposition of the poet's reactions to current events, and Briusov himself identified throughout his life with ancient Rome. It does not seem farfetched, therefore, to attribute some sort of reflection of Briusov's state of mind and experiences to his later Roman texts as well.[36] Turning to the political, artistic, and personal circumstances that preceded his Roman novels enriches our interpretation of these works and helps to make sense of Briusov's subsequent reactions to changes in Russian cultural and political life.

Rome and Russia

May [our new poetry] sail (and not stand in the same place), for that is the whole point, as Virgil once said.
Valerii Briusov, "We are Experiencing an Epoch of Creativity," 1920

At a crucial point in Virgil's *Aeneid,* the hero, having delayed his departure from the luxurious kingdom and caresses of the Carthaginian Queen Dido, finds himself chastised by the gods for his seeming forgetfulness of the future awaiting him as founder of Rome. Voicing his exasperation with the formerly "dutiful" Trojan hero, Jupiter, king of the gods, wonders:

What has he in mind? What hope, to make him stay
Amid a hostile race, and lose from view
Ausonian progeny, Lavinian lands?
The man should sail: that is the whole point.[37]

Aeneas, of course, does so, and Rome in Virgil's epic telling is permitted to come into being, even as the abandoned Dido's sworn enmity toward her erstwhile lover provides a literary pretext for the later historical conflict between Rome and Carthage. Jupiter's urgent message to go forward, no matter how painful the shift, was one that Briusov would echo consciously—though not always successfully—throughout his career. As he claimed in a speech shortly before his death in 1924, echoing previous statements, he had chosen Virgil's injunction to "sail, for that is the whole point" as a slogan for his own life, trying "above all else to sail, to go forward," in art as in life.[38]

The ailing Briusov's selection of a life "motto" from ancient Rome is not surprising. As he had told the writer Maksimilian Voloshin years earlier, "For me . . . Rome is closest of all. Even Greece is close only insofar as it was reflected in Rome. In essence I relate to the Hellenic world with the same mistrust and lack of comprehension that the Romans did."[39] Briusov's contemporaries were quick to seize and elaborate upon the self-created image of Briusov as Roman. According to Voloshin, for example, Briusov as editor of *The Scales* was a dictatorial Roman emperor, laying down laws as he sought to build a worldwide, literary empire. He had created his own "triumvirate," consisting of himself and his fellow poets Konstantin Bal'mont and Viacheslav Ivanov; he waged civil wars in the literary realm and went into battle against other leaders.

Briusov's poetry had a Roman quality to it, Voloshin asserted: "the strophes of his poems are like aqueducts," his verses seemed "eternal, like a Roman arch."[40] In a similar vein, Vladislav Khodasevich wrote that Briusov "despised democracy. The history of culture, which he worshipped, was for him the history of 'creators,' demi-gods standing apart from the common herd."[41] For Marina Tsvetaeva, meanwhile, disgruntled over Briusov's rejection of her poetry and scornful of his laborious approach to art, "Three times a Roman was Valerii Briusov: through his will and his ox, in poetry; as a wolf (*homo homini lupus est*) in life."[42] And on a different, fonder note, Briusov's former student B. I. Purishev remembered with awe his teacher's lectures on ancient Rome: "He spoke about ancient Rome as if he had spent many years there."[43] Purishev noted that listening to Briusov lecture fluently on such subjects as "the topography of the Eternal City" involuntarily called to mind his 1908 poem "Na Forume" (At the Forum). Affirming Briusov's feeling of connection to Rome, this poem resulted from a visit to the city in 1908, during which he noted in his diary that he was so thrilled by the ancient Roman monuments that the art of the Renaissance left him unmoved. "The entire ancient world seems alive," he commented.[44]

Briusov's initial excitement over Merezhkovskii's first novel may be viewed in the light of this enthusiasm. To be sure, a work that shocked traditional literary critics could only have appealed to the author of the notorious one-line poem "O, cover thy pale legs!"[45] even as Merezhkovskii's rejection of Russian literature's stagnant utilitarian ethos resonated with a young man dedicated to novelty and individualism. But just as importantly, Briusov was already deeply intrigued by the Roman world. The 1890s found him engaged in an attempt to translate Virgil's *Aeneid* (he would continue these efforts while writing his Roman novels). He also worked on a monograph devoted to the emperor Nero and worked hard at Latin while at university, noting in his diary his "brilliant" performance on his Latin examination (as compared with his lackluster results in Greek).[46] Determined from an early age to make a name for himself as a leader, Briusov was fascinated during this period by the "great men" of history and compared himself specifically in his diary to the Roman dictator Sulla, whom he described in Nietzschean fashion as a man admirably "sans foi ni loi."[47]

With the onset of the Russo-Japanese War and then Russia's 1905 Revolution, Rome took on additional significance. Intrigued by its historical particulars, an approach that would mark his Roman novels and other works,[48] he also linked Rome's past to Russia's present in several texts of the early revolutionary period, particularly in the poems that formed part of "Sovremennost'" (The Present), a section of his 1906 volume *Stephanos.* At the time the war began, Briusov yearned for Russia to achieve Rome's worldwide imperial status, and he predicted an easy victory.[49] Committed to Russia's military success, he rejected the revolutionary tendencies afoot there, calling for Russia's "plebeians" to postpone their revolutionary processions until such time as Russia, like Rome, would stand proud and victorious once again.[50] As Russia's military fortunes waned, his Rome-inspired rhetoric continued in a different vein, this time with a particularly Russian cast: in a poem of 1905 reacting to Russia's defeat by the Japanese at Tsushima, he lamented the loss of the crown of the Third Rome, for the areligious Briusov clearly an exclusively worldly and political image.[51] In mid-1905, disillusioned in his dreams of Russia's expansion and appalled by the weakness of the tsarist regime, Briusov relinquished his commitment to it. In the poem "Iulii Tsezar'" (Julius Caesar, 1905), he announced his intention to spur his horse across a (presumably political) Rubicon, the river Julius Caesar had crossed to take the unprecedented and fateful step, for a Roman leader, of invading Italy in what amounted to an act of treason against the Roman state.[52]

The period preceding Briusov's writing of his Roman novels gave him ample opportunity to put to the test his Virgilian maxim to "go forward." Just as Junius had to confront the dissolution of the Empire he revered, the imperialist Briusov faced the failed war with Japan and then the Revolution of 1905 and its aftermath. Again like Junius, though, Briusov found himself unable to dedicate himself fully to any side in the political conflict. He was disgusted by the Russian Empire's failure to defeat its own "Eastern" foe, certainly, and the government's subsequent, ineffectual response to revolution did not appease him. "What have you done with Rome? / You, the consuls, and you, the Senate!" he queried in "Julius Caesar."[53] And yet in "Dovol'nym" (To the Satisfied, 1905), written after the government had submitted to a constitution, he sneered at those members of the opposition who were satisfied with this response: "Your satisfaction is the joy of a herd / That has found a clump of grass."[54]

As Joan Delaney Grossman explains, Briusov's distaste for the spent government and easily pacified liberal opposition is clarified by another line from "To the Satisfied," in which he proclaimed the magnificence of both mighty rulers and passionate rebels.[55] Strength, energy, and will were the essential elements; for Briusov the Roman, they possessed a powerful aesthetic appeal. Therefore, although the revolutionaries' program was not to his liking, as revolution gained force, it provided a wave of excitement that he found attractive. Revolution was the new "truth" displacing the cherished old, and as such it demanded respect. Yet again like Junius, however, much as he had left the autocracy behind, Briusov was still unable to commit himself fully to revolution. In "Griadushchie gunny" (The Coming Huns, 1905), Briusov revealed his discomfort with revolution, celebrating its attractive qualities but fearing its pending annihilation of the culture he loved. Significantly, in keeping with the title and theme of the poem, Briusov chose as his epigraph a line from Viacheslav Ivanov on Attila the Hun: once more, Russia's revolutionary woes found their counterpart in ancient Rome.[56] Briusov's concerns over Russia's revolutionary future entered as well into an article he wrote in 1905 in response to Vladimir Lenin's article "Partiinaia organizatsiia i partiinaia literatura" (Party Organization and Party Literature). Briusov's "Freedom of Speech" was not reprinted in Russia until 1990.[57]

In "Party Organization and Party Literature," Lenin urged the creation of a Party-focused literature, insisting that Russian letters could be free only within the context of service to the proletariat. Lenin took issue with those "superman" writers (i.e., Nietzschean Decadents) who scorned the social-democratic work of the collective and failed to find inspiration in it. Announcing that the big tent of his Social-Democratic Party could find room for all, including such unlikely participants as Christians and mystics, Lenin warned those writers who chose not to participate in his plans that the Party reserved the right to exclude those who did not accept its wisdom.[58]

Briusov responded immediately with a column in *The Scales*. The slave of Plato was still a slave, he noted, adding that even if one was drawn to Russia's recent revolutionary developments, one still reserved the right to criticize them—a right the Party seemed determined to ignore. Comparing the 1905 Revolution to an uprising by Roman plebeians, Briusov took issue with Lenin's vision of required unity of thought. "In this decision," he wrote, "lies the fanaticism of people who do not permit the concept that their convictions may be false. From here it is only one step to the declaration of Caliph Omar: 'Books that contain what is in the Koran are unnecessary, and those that contain anything else are harmful.'"[59] Briusov added that what the modernist poets valued most was the freedom to seek, even if this seeking led only to the destruction of their beliefs and ideals—a seeking Lenin's party sought in its exclusivity to deny. He concluded that although any political party aspired to become the only one, the Social Democrats seemed to want this most of all. Beyond refusing artists the necessary exploratory freedom to create, the Social Democratic goal for literature, he suggested presciently, was to exile anyone who disagreed with them to a Sakhalin of solitude.

Briusov's reaction to Lenin's words recalls his portrayal of an intolerant, dedicated Bishop Ambrosius, intent on destroying all that has come before in the name of creating a new monochromatic empire of the faithful. This impression is strengthened by the reference to Caliph Omar, associated in popular legend with the burning of the library at Alexandria in the seventh century. Furthermore, given the antiartistic agenda Briusov attributes to Lenin, it is useful to note Symmachus's fears in *The Altar of Victory* that the new, Christian-influenced generation will not understand Cicero's speeches or the Latin of Livy. In the context of "The Coming Huns," with its portrayal of culture under siege, one can conclude that Briusov was following Merezhkovskii in connecting the Christian revolutionaries of fourth-century Rome to the Russian revolutionaries at the turn of the twentieth century. (Indeed, when Junius sees Rhea at the camp outside Milan, she is clad in scarlet.) But there was a crucial difference: Briusov left modern-day artists out of this revolutionary, political mix. "Revolution is beautiful and, as a historical phenomenon, magnificent, but it is difficult to live in it for poor poets. They are not necessary," he wrote in a 1905 letter.[60] The excitement of revolution could certainly provide grist for the poet's art in the form of vivid new experiences. But for Briusov, revolution was not possessed of the millenarian overtones Merezhkovskii had ascribed to it, and the writer was not a priest of a new apocalyptic-revolutionary faith.

In the context of these longstanding misgivings about Lenin, it should come as no surprise that Briusov's initial reaction to the Bolshevik takeover was not so positive as his reputation as prorevolution would suggest. His poetry of the early revolutionary period, some only recently published, reveals at times a distinct discomfort with the new regime and its effects. In a poem written in early January 1918 and published for the first time in 1993, for instance, he created a "heartsick" lyric hero with "no strength left for battle."[61] His wife later wrote that Briusov had been unwell at the time of the October Revolution and had not reacted significantly to it.[62] It was during these months that Briusov returned to work on *Jupiter Overthrown,* though once again he did not complete the novel or record the Christian victory.

Nonetheless, in 1918, perhaps in the spirit of Junius, as the Bolsheviks began to consolidate their power, Briusov chose to become part of the new, revolutionary regime, appalling Merezhkovskii and Hippius, among others, in the process. He worked at the state publishing house and organized the literary division of the People's Commissariat of Public Education. Bowing as Junius had to a new, powerful, "fateborne" empire, Briusov became a member of the Communist Party in 1920 and busied himself within the regime's cultural bureaucracy until his death in 1924.[63] His Roman-Russian parallels continued: he told Il'ia Erenburg that socialist culture would differ from capitalist culture as strongly as Christian Rome had differed from the Rome of Augustus.[64]

And yet even as Briusov attempted to make good on his commitment to go forward, he proved incapable of dissociating himself from a past culture he had loved. Undercutting or complicating the views he expressed to Erenburg, he wrote in one 1918 article that just as Christian civilization had learned from antiquity, Communist culture should also grow on the basis of what had preceded it.[65] The years 1920 and 1921 found him advertising his availability as a Latin tutor, and he taught numerous courses on ancient civilization.[66] Further, in a 1918 lecture on Roman history, Briusov attempted to convince his auditors that the past was relevant to the present: "Recalling the lessons of history, we can not only foretell to a degree what awaits us in the future, but we can also find guidance for our activity in the present."[67] In his focus on the past even as he devoted himself to the future, Briusov again echoes Junius, the figure he had described a decade earlier, admitting his longing for Hesperia in the midst of writing a Christian homily on human sin and unworthiness in a monk's cell. Revolution had overtaken the Roman-style empire Briusov sought for his nation, and he had succumbed, as far as he could, to the new faith. His Roman novels presaged both his Virgilian commitment to going forward and his somewhat conflicted or inconclusive decisions.[68]

Junius's story also reflects various changes Briusov underwent in the literary sphere during the years surrounding the writing of his Roman novels, changes that grew out of earlier interactions among Briusov, Merezhkovskii, and other writers. In a sense, Briusov and Merezhkovskii had been conducting a discussion on religion and art for over a decade. At the turn of the century, Briusov had resisted not only Merezhkovskii's attempts to convert him to his new faith, but also the latter's conflation of literature and religious prophecy. Briusov's diary charts his interactions with Merezhkovskii and Hippius, who as early as 1901 began agitating for Briusov to join them in their religious quests (a 1902 entry recorded Merezhkovskii's "despair" when Briusov admitted that he did not believe in Christ).[69] In another entry from the same period, Briusov noted that Merezhkovskii hoped to be "chosen" as one through whom others could be saved.[70] Briusov himself, though intrigued and somewhat tempted by the couple's blandishments, opted not to fall into this latter category. Having agreed in 1902 to serve as the editor for *Novyi put'* (The New Path), newly formed by Hippius and Merezhkovskii, Briusov soon renounced his duties when the "nonliterariness" [*neliteraturnost'*] of the religiously focused journal became more than he could stomach.[71] By 1905, his diary notes, he had broken off relations with "the Merezhkovskiis," who became increasingly caught up in apocalypticism and revolutionary activism.[72]

The Roman novels serve to place Briusov's literary disagreements with Merezhkovskii into the larger context of the debates that split the Symbolist movement into warring groups beginning in 1905 and led eventually to its "crisis" in 1910. Briusov's major role in these debates, one already evident in his reaction to *The New Path,* was to warn his fellow artists against assigning a religious or any other sort of external role to art. In his 1905 article "V zashchitu ot odnoi pokhvaly" (In Defense Against A Certain Praise), for instance, he rejected Andrei Belyi's assertion of a "providential" mission for Russian poetry, arguing instead that poets must be judged only on the merits of their verse.[73] In 1906, in a series of articles in *The Scales,* Briusov attacked the short-lived literary group called "Mystical Anarchists," who included in their ranks Ivanov and, for a time, Blok. He mocked the group's stated rejection of the world around them and the fraught language in which they expounded the tenets of their "cause." Banding together on a nonliterary basis was a return to utilitarianism, he scolded.[74] Several years later, as the crisis in the Symbolist movement came to a head, his well-known 1910 article "O 'rechi rabskoi,' v zashchitu poezii" (On 'Servile Speech,' in Defense of Poetry) took issue with the religiously focused artistic views of writers such as Blok, Belyi, and Ivanov. He proclaimed that insisting "that all poets of necessity be theurgists is as absurd as insisting that they all be members of the State Duma."[75] Briusov told an interviewer in 1910 that he had departed from *The Scales* the previous year "precisely because I sensed how worn out and dated their preaching had become."[76]

With their "preaching" and their promotion of a faith-based "cause," Briusov's fellow participants in the Symbolist debates had sought to erase the boundaries between two distinct entities: art and religion. In so doing, as they promoted their own visions of theurgic literature, they had developed the intolerance characteristic of Briusov's rendering of the Christian faith in his Roman novels (Symbolist religious imagery, of course, tended to privilege Christianity of various, often non-Orthodox, kinds). The "Mystical Anarchist" language Briusov mocked in his 1906 articles is highly reminiscent of Rhea's exalted, high-style pronouncements regarding her fourth-century Christian-associated "cause." His fictional portrayal of mad prophets, therefore, may well have had a polemical purpose beyond his response to Merezhkovskii's trilogy and rejection of Merezhkovskii's turn to religious activism. Once again, Briusov was agitating for a broader separation of church and art, rather than the conflation his contemporaries called for. He was also consciously directing Russian Symbolism away from the religious focus intended, according to his colleagues, to redeem it from European "decadent" values, and back toward its European origins.[77]

It is somewhat fitting, then, that when Briusov stepped forth on a new artistic path, it was one inspired by the French poet and theorist René Ghil. Ghil is generally known for his theory of "verbal instrumentation," an effort to map out with scientific precision the effect of specific sounds in poetry. Briusov's particular interest in Ghil, however, was centered more upon his idea of "scientific poetry," which stressed the complementarity of art and science and shifted away from a strictly personal approach to artistic creation. As with Briusov's move toward revolution, though, this "conversion," too, was not entirely conclusive, nor did it come naturally in every aspect. From his earliest poetic manifestos, Briusov had proclaimed the primacy of the artist's soul as inspiration for his art, and in his article "Kliuchi tain" (Keys to the Mysteries, 1904), he had proclaimed art's superiority to science.[78] And although his article "Sviashchennaia zhertva" (A Holy Sacrifice, 1905) had linked Symbolism and Realism, it did so in the context of a "realistic" vision of the events in one's soul.[79] And yet, as he admitted painfully in a 1906 letter to his lover, Nina Petrovskaia, "I can no longer live by outworn beliefs, those ideals through which I have already passed. I can no longer live by 'Decadence' and 'Nietzscheanism,' in which I believe, I believe."[80] Briusov proclaimed his allegiance to whatever new artistic "truths" might appear to show him the way beyond his creative stalemate.[81]

Ghil's ideas were contrary in central ways to the ideals Briusov lauded, and in a 1904 article he had made clear his opinion that Ghil was too devoted to scientific discipline to reconcile himself to the role of the unconscious in the creative process. In addition, Briusov had been unable at this point to countenance Ghil's dismissal of the artist's soul as a worthy object of study. By January 1907, however, as Briusov desperately sought new artistic ideals to replace those that had lost their novelty and related strength, he conceded in a letter to the French writer, "The more I study your work, the more I am carried away by its greatness and worldwide significance. . . . Its principles seem more and more unshakable to me, and, without a doubt, one fine day I shall surprise my friends with my unexpected conversion."[82] In a 1909 article on Ghil's theories, Briusov now asserted that modern poets were egotists whose sole goal was to express their emotions; these poets were alien to the contemporary world and its scientific advances.[83] Against this useless model of the poet, the seekers of "scientific poetry" proposed their own ideal of art: "conscious, thinking, definitively knowing what it wants, and irrevocably linked to contemporary times."[84] By immersing itself in "reality," poetry was to establish its connections to history and sociology. Briusov concluded, "Evidently, the newest criticism effectively destroys all of the teachings presented until this time about the final goal of art."[85] The appeal of Ghil's scientific poetry notwithstanding, it recalled Ambrosius's church in its lack of tolerance for other ideas, and thus represented a difficult choice for Briusov—but one he attempted to make.

Briusov's Roman novels reveal the writer in the initial stages of integrating Ghil's thoughts into his work: certainly the abundant notes, appendices, and bibliographic references suggest a "scientific" reverence for historical research, though one clearly grounded in Briusov's longstanding fascination with the historical past.[86] Once again, however, he had balked at a full "conversion."[87] Along with their "scientific" historicism, Briusov's novels contain a wealth of longstanding Briusovian themes: art, passion, worship, human achievement, and the relationship between these concepts and the artist's own soul. Briusov's novels are examples of mythmaking; they inherently assert a synthesis of the writer's past and present, even as they portray the mixed world of fourth-century Rome.[88] Like Merezhkovskii, whose Julian had been the first in a series of characters throughout *Christ and Antichrist* who called to mind the spiritually seeking Merezhkovskii himself, Briusov, too, inserted himself into his own text. Yet even as he used Merezhkovskii as a stepping stone, Briusov made Rome his own. For Junius's story and Rome's represent at their core what Briusov, intent on the human ability to "go forward," valued most: the ongoing human search for transcendence that characterizes spirituality, science, passion, and, most importantly, art itself.

The Eternal City

Soon all this will be past; and then will there be but one temple,
Amor's temple alone, where the Initiate may go.
Thou art indeed a world, oh Rome; and yet, were Love absent,
Then would the world be no world, then would e'en Rome be
no Rome.

Johann Wolfgang von Goethe, "Roman Elegies," 1795
(trans. E. A. Bowring)

Junius Norbanus and Valerii Briusov have a great deal in common, biographically and professionally. The writer's 1914 autobiography discusses his paternal grandfather, a cork merchant and former serf who had purchased his freedom; Briusov's early adventures in brothels, which among other factors led to his dismissal from his first school and transfer to another; and his early and then more developed poetic efforts.[89] At the beginning of *Jupiter Overthrown*, told like *The Altar of Victory* in the first person, Junius reveals that he is descended on one side of the family from slaves, that his overwhelming attractiveness (Briusovian hyperbole?) brought him early sexual adventures, and that he had switched tutors in the middle of his education (413–16). Briusov's diary of the 1890s contains references to the author's thirst for fame, as well as his conviction that European Decadence was the key to the glory he sought. At the same time he was devoting himself to writing tales of the ancient Romans.[90] Junius, for his part, looking back at his first trip to Rome at age eighteen, recalls his desire at the time for "universal attention," adding, "Of course these were childish dreams, but it's important to remember what Rome signified to a far-away provincial—that very Rome he'd read about in all his books and stories . . . which alone had the power to make a person great and renowned" (419). Briusov, of course, was a poet and literary activist, one who cared deeply about literature and engaged in spirited discussions on literary subjects with his contemporaries. He also translated many Latin writers, including, while he was at work on *The Altar of Victory*, the fourth-century Ausonius; in fact, he was especially fond of fourth-century Roman writers.[91] Junius, too, is a poet who particularly enjoys the writings of Ausonius, his fellow Gaul (101). He discusses the latter's writings with Symmachus and freely cites other Latin poets throughout his narrative (his twentieth-century counterpart Briusov, meanwhile, provides sources for these citations in his lengthy notes to the novel).[92]

Significantly, Junius writes poems to Hesperia, though he worries that she could not possibly appreciate the efforts of a humble "provincial" such as he (63). Since the glorious Hesperia represents the city of Rome itself, and her name specifically evokes the West, Junius's attraction can be understood in this light as emblematic of Briusov the Russian's own determined, longstanding desire to assimilate and master European culture, using the cultural key to fame and glory that Rome signifies. Decadence for Briusov was, after all, a way to take a leading role in making Russian letters an acknowledged part of the European literary arena: in an 1893 diary entry, he had named Decadence as the artistic trend of the future and had asserted his intention of becoming the movement's leader ("And that leader will be I! Yes, I!").[93] Merezhkovskii had presented a Dostoevskiian vision of a Russia that, in its meekness and faith, as well as its distance from the West, could offer Europe something crucial, and in so doing bring unity to the world. The Westernizer Briusov sought rather to integrate Russia into European letters: the unity he envisaged was literary, and devoid of religious or messianic overtones. This was the purpose of *The Scales,* and this was what the Symbolist debate signified to him. Assigning himself an alter ego whose "provinciality" meant in fact that he hailed from a portion of the Roman Empire was a way for Briusov to assert a latter-day citizenship for Russia, as well.

Junius's worship of Hesperia also recalls the relationship Briusov posited in various texts not only between lover and beloved, but between his lyrical "I" and a stern Muse, an all-consuming relationship well documented by Briusov's contemporaries and by later critics. Khodasevich, for example, wrote that Briusov "loved literature, and only literature. . . . Literature was for him a merciless divinity, eternally demanding blood-sacrifice."[94] Thus, in his early poem "Iunomu poetu" (To the Young Poet, 1896), Briusov exhorted the novice to worship art to the exclusion of all else.[95] The poet was to revere his Muse: "My verses are like the smoke at an altar [*kak dym altarnyi*]," Briusov wrote in 1911.[96] And such adoration had a self-sacrificial element to it; in "A Holy Sacrifice," Briusov had called for Russia's artists to "throw [themselves] onto the altar of our divinity. Only a priest's knife, cutting our breast, gives us the right to be called a poet."[97]

Paralleling this scenario, Junius is drawn hopelessly to Hesperia: even when he recognizes her manipulations, he is powerless to disobey her. Indeed, he swears an oath to her early in *The Altar of Victory,* and announces proudly in *Jupiter Overthrown* that he has never been false to it (87–88, 423). His oath binds him to personal pain, even death, so long as he serves her and no one else. Hesperia underscores the danger inherent in this commitment when she gives him a dagger inscribed with the slogan "Learn to die," the second dagger she has bestowed upon him at a moment of danger (92, 308). Making her point still more explicit, she unhesitatingly—and effectively—demands the death of Julianius, also bound to her, when questions arise about his loyalty (286). Even while drawn to Rhea, even when no longer feeling the intensity of the bond to Hesperia that her enticing proximity inspires, Junius never questions the need to keep his vows to her, including his commission to assassinate the emperor. When he lands in a subterranean cell for his pains, his reaction is to write poetry, often about his hatred for the woman who has placed him in this position, but always revealing the power she has over his life. And when at the beginning of *Jupiter Overthrown,* she summons him after ten years of silence, Junius leaves his wife and dying child without hesitation. He finds Hesperia unchanged: her beauty is eternal.

Junius joins a gallery of Briusovian protagonist-lovers: as Diana Burgin has written of the heroes of Briusov's ballads, many of whom hail from the ancient world, he "so often writes of the passionate encounters between a submissive, nearly impotent poetic persona and a dominating, powerful woman whose greatest cruelties are the proverbial 'blessing in disguise' in that they return creative power to the weak male." Burgin explains that the ballad thus serves for Briusov as a "metatale of the poet's search for the eternal truth of art," as his heroes undergo symbolic death through passion in order to create.[98] The poet's painful relationship with his Muse finds artistic fulfillment in tales of dangerous, transformative passion. Irene Masing-Delic notes further that in Briusov's poetry, pain, which can be represented by "descents into infernal regions," "helps him overcome indifference, stirs up suppressed feelings, and stimulates poetic activity."[99] The imprisoned Junius's experiences in Milan, and his relationship with Hesperia overall, perpetuate this paradigm in another genre.

Junius's comparison of the enticing, regal Hesperia to Cleopatra furthers this parallel: in Briusov's 1899 poem "Kleopatra" (Cleopatra), the famously seductive Egyptian queen notes her ability to dominate the poet.[100] References to Cleopatra also call to mind another Briusovian hero: her lover Mark Antony, whom Briusov celebrated in his 1905 poem "Antonii" for his elevation of passion over power: "But you, beautiful, eternally young (*iunyi*), / Erected a single altar—passion!"[101] In 1904, Briusov published two articles that, read together, make clear the links he advanced between passion and creativity. In "The Keys to the Mysteries," Briusov told his fellow writers that their works must serve as "mystical keys that will open for humankind the doors of its 'blue prison' to eternal freedom."[102] In "Strast'" (Passion), meanwhile, he wrote, "When passion rules us, we are close to those eternal boundaries that delineate our 'blue prison.' . . . Passion is that point at which the physical world touches upon other worlds."[103] In other words, for Briusov, both passion and art can break the earthly boundaries that surround humankind to elevate the lover or artist to a new level of understanding. A poem or novel thematically devoted to passion, therefore, may in fact tell the story of its own creation. The story of Junius (in Russian "Iunyi," as in Briusov's "Antony") and his passion for Hesperia may be viewed in this light as a tale of art itself.

But Junius's story is also one of the opposition between two women, representative of the warring religious forces of their day. It is significant that Junius believes that while supporting Hesperia's plans, he is acting for the Roman pantheon—and while consorting with Rhea, he is succumbing to Christian rites and beliefs. Rhea's importance to Briusov's overall narrative is underlined by the fact that although she dies in *The Altar of Victory, Jupiter Overthrown* features a character named Sylvia, remarkably like Rhea physically and emotionally and, like Rhea, a Christian. The connection between these two characters extends to their names: Rhea Sylvia was the mother of Romulus and Remus, mythical founders of Rome, so Junius is struck by Sylvia's name when he first meets her. The conflict between Hesperia and Rhea, who know of each other's existence, is thus perpetuated from the first novel to the second, introducing two important additional themes into Briusov's narrative of passion and artistic creativity: first, given Junius's status as alter ego, Briusov's own conflicted character, and, second, the relationship of religion to passion and art.

Whereas Maksim Gor'kii considered Briusov the most cultured man in Russia, other contemporaries—and, interestingly, Briusov himself—posited a more complicated picture of the self-styled Roman Westernizer. Voloshin, for example, maintained that in Briusov's most spectacular writing there was nonetheless an absence of artistic taste: he compared Briusov to a warlike centurion arriving in the imperial capital from afar.[104] Mochul'skii writes that Briusov "loved order, proportion and form, but was instinctively drawn to chaos; inside the European Briusov there sat an ancient Hun."[105] And the critic Renato Poggioli claims that Briusov "had mastered the cultural experience of modern Europe with the aggressive spirit of a Scythian taking possession of the learning and wisdom of Greece."[106] As for Briusov himself, even as he worried in "The Coming Huns" about the impact of those revolutionary Huns on his beloved culture, in Decadent fashion he summoned forth their destructive acts, insisting in a letter to Pertsov, "I am for the barbarians, the Huns, the Russians!"[107] In an introduction to a volume of verse by the peasant poet Nikolai Kliuev, Briusov suggested the attraction he felt not only to Western European culture, but to Russia's own cultural roots as well. Paying tribute to the splendor of heavy, centuries-old stones crafted by artists into Gothic cathedrals, Briusov also acknowledged the appeal of the "wild forest" where nothing is planned, nothing is foreseen, and "at every step the unexpected awaits."[108] Rhea, who is constantly surprising Junius, bestowing upon him an illegal purple cloak or enticing him into orgiastic rites, is comparable to just such a wild forest. Hesperia is the splendid Gothic cathedral, evocative in its endurance and elegance of Roman monuments. Both appeal to Junius, even as he proclaims his allegiance to the Roman pantheon, just as both appeal to Briusov, compared by some critics to the Westernizing Peter the Great in the area of Russian culture. "I am a person who is 'rational' to such a degree that these few instants that tear me away from life are very dear to me," Briusov confessed in a 1900 diary entry, in the context of his attraction to spiritualist séances.[109]

Briusov's contradictions, too, find their context in Rome: one recalls Remigius's early description of Rome's many-faceted glories to the neophyte Junius. Briusov the Roman thus embodied the often contrary Roman spirit of inclusiveness and multiplicity that he had lauded in his texts. "The 'I' is that central point where all differences fade, where all boundaries are overcome," he had written in an 1899 letter.[110] The artistic self, then, may be compared to Rome, a world in miniature. Acting out of his life experiences, the artist creates a text in which Russian-Hun and Roman-Westernizer coexist, and these oppositions become fruitful. And religious striving, the other theme underlined in the rivalry between Hesperia and Rhea for Junius's affections, is related to this process. For religion, like passion and creativity, presents similar opportunities for human transcendence.[111] Symmachus's cousin Valeria, who is charged with Junius's care once he is rescued from prison, makes this clear when Junius contrasts his beloved, "clear and reasonable" paganism with Christianity, which he labels "incomprehensible and insane" (185). Valeria explains, "Human beings have a certain attraction to divinity, out of which religion has emerged, just as they have a particular attraction to knowledge, which has led to science, and a particular attraction to imitation, which has led to art. This attraction to divinity is nothing other than the desire to comprehend the hidden secrets of the universe. Religion reveals these secrets, but for each people it reveals them in forms accessible to that group. . . . Thus all religions are equal amongst themselves, and no one teaching is more true, and no faith is more authentic" (186).

Junius notes that because of her "masculine mind," the startlingly wise Valeria is at times called "Valerii" by her relatives in Symmachus's home (188). Her views might well be taken, then, as evidence of Valerii Briusov's continuing faith in the fundamental value of a "kingdom of many truths." Her words also suggest the links Briusov himself posited between religion, art, and, more recently, science. For, as she makes clear, all of these phenomena—religion, science, and art—reflect the human need to seek transcendence of some kind. And through their links to human striving, each of these phenomena is thus connected to Rome, that ultimate symbol for Briusov of human effort and will. As his contemporary S. V. Shervinskii proclaimed in a 1924 speech on Briusov and Rome, "Rome, from the Temple of the Great Mother to the military camp and the barbarian face of Caracalla, from the multilingual forum to Eastern home furnishings—all this hypnotizes Briusov, the worshipper of man."[112]

In his poem "V Damask" (To Damascus, 1903), Briusov described the conversion experience of another (this time Biblical) figure of early Christianity, the New Testament figure Saul, into the Apostle Paul. Briusov's portrayal of Saul's transformation from Jew to Christian takes on sexual trappings, as in the poem Saul's religious "altar" is night ("I noch'—altar'"), which serves, surprisingly, as the setting for a couple's sexual act, equated with Saul's conversion experience.[113] Passion, art, and religion are linked in this poem, and the worshipper finds transcendence at an altar through an act that encompasses a certain loss of self. Turning back to Briusov's angry words to Lenin, one recalls the "seeking" Briusov had endorsed, which could lead to the loss of all one held dear but was nonetheless essential for artistic creation. Set in Rome's plethora of "truths" and allegiances, the newly "scientific" Briusov's "world in miniature," Junius's tale of religious searching, sexual experimentation, and artistic effort becomes indeed the tale of a multifaceted, often painful "altar," as in the novel's title. And the Altar of Victory, symbol for Briusov's characters of the glories of empire, the West, beauty, freedom of religion, and multiple narratives, becomes for the author ultimately a symbol of art itself, art which is the highest of the many transformative, self-sacrificial acts his semiautobiographical hero attempts. One might suggest that Briusov's novels are thus intrinsic, literary Romes, in that they portray various types of human striving and themselves embody Briusov-the-artist's own.

Merezhkovskii's Rome-based trilogy had ended with a rejection of the human ambition represented by the Roman Mangod Peter, as the author called instead for an apocalyptic revolution that would lead to the Kingdom of God, one proclaimed by the spiritually minded Russian artist. Briusov's Roman novels, focusing on the same historical period and utilizing the same schema Merezhkovskii had made popular over a decade earlier, suggested a very different conclusion. Lauding human potential and ability, Briusov saw in Rome their ultimate symbol, represented for him by the altar of his title and by his hero-seeker's adventures. The paganism that appeals to Junius is a faith that bridges the gap between human and god: the Roman Hesperia takes issue with the Christians who reject the fact that pagan gods "love, suffer, and even commit crimes, just like people! . . . And we ourselves become like gods, when we permit these feelings to rule our souls freely" (509). And if paganism is the elevation of humankind to godlike status, artistic creativity is its highest expression, Briusov's most treasured mode of the human attempt to broach new spheres of being. Junius's very human adventures, filled with passion, despair, and confusion in the context of fourth-century Rome, are once again comparable to an artistic quest, one equally possible for a poet in modern-day Russia.

And yet Christ's revolution had come to disrupt Rome, just as Lenin's revolution came to threaten the individualism crucial to Briusov's attempts at creative self-transcendence. Far from propagating Christian revelation and revolution as Merezhkovskii had done, Briusov accepted the "new Christians" specifically for their newness—not because he saw any inherent value in their views or those of their fourth-century predecessors. Illuminating his own controversial later decisions, Briusov defined the role of the Russian artist in revolution as a recorder of events—and eventually as one bound to accept them. This acceptance, contrary to the path of "many truths" Briusov valued, did, however, exemplify the other Roman trait he held dear: the ability to go forward into new, often threatening areas, in art and life, worthy simply for their novelty and corresponding power. In his Roman novels, which reflect both imperial inclusiveness and an acceptance of the new faith of Rhea and Ambrosius, Briusov merges contradictory truths into a new artistic whole: a new Russian Rome. For Briusov, Rome in its commingled contradictions became not just a truth that had died, but an eternal truth: a model of historical continuity, or the merging of opposites—geographic, chronological, religious, political, or artistic—in the midst of change. Despite her resentment of Briusov, therefore, Tsvetaeva's words may stand as a fitting summary of his inclusive Roman spirit:

And my unjust—though searching for justice—heart will not be soothed until in Rome—albeit in some far-off suburb—there will stand (in what, if not marble?) a statue:

> To the Scythian Roman
> From Rome.[114]

For Aleksandr Blok, familiar with Merezhkovskii's trilogy and interested in Briusov's *Altar of Victory*, the paradigm his predecessors had developed was intriguing. In his 1918 essay "Katilina" (Catiline), he continued their Rome-based narrative, focusing on the self-sacrifice inherent in the creative process and in revolutionary struggle, associated for him both with the Bolsheviks and with Christ. Meanwhile, Briusov's warnings about the depersonalizing aspects of Russia's revolutionaries—a trait he attributed to early Christians—would be borne out and recorded in the writings of Ivanov and Kuzmin, as Russia's revolutionary events continued to unfold.

3

A "Roman Bolshevik"

Aleksandr Blok's "Catiline" and the Russian Revolution

I want Ovid, Pushkin, and Catullus once again, and I am not satisfied with the historical Ovid, Pushkin, and Catullus.
Osip Mandel'shtam, "The Word and Culture," 1921

In his 1918 article "Katilina" (Catiline), written only months after the Bolsheviks' November 1917 takeover,[1] Aleksandr Blok explicitly and repeatedly asserted the relevance of Rome's past to Russia's present and future. The ostensible subject of his article, the Roman rebel Catiline, was a notorious figure known for his abortive and much maligned uprising in the year 63 BCE against the Roman state. Blok described this Roman outlaw not only as a herald of the changes Jesus Christ would bring to the world, but also as a "Roman Bolshevik."[2] In so doing, he recast Catiline's uprising as a precursor of the Bolsheviks' first step toward all-encompassing "world revolution." He also claimed a link between Jesus Christ and the Russian revolutionaries, reinforcing and rendering less ambiguous the statement he had made through the appearance of Christ at the end of his controversial revolutionary poem "Dvenadtsat'" (The Twelve, 1918), which featured twelve marauding Red Guardsmen. Finally, by connecting Catiline's rebellion with the Roman poet Catullus's roughly contemporaneous "Attis" (poem 63), Blok affirmed the importance of the artist as one uniquely able to comprehend, seize upon, and preserve an era's "vibration" (86), its meaning, for future generations.

Blok made clear in the article his dislike of "dead schemas . . . between the pagan and Christian worlds, between Venus and the Mother of God, between Christ and Antichrist" (76), thereby calling to mind quite effectively Merezhkovskii's earlier trilogy. Blok insisted that such "parallels" were the domain of "scribes and corpses" (76), but "Catiline" carries forward into a new era crucial elements of the Russia-Rome parallels that Merezhkovskii had laid out.[3] In Blok's ancient Rome, a proto-Christian rebel linked to the East and to the Russian revolutionaries takes on a decaying Roman state, connected (in this essay and other writings of the period) with modern, imperial Russia and its adherents and with Western Europe. And the artist, represented in the ancient world by Catullus and in the modern arena by Blok, is the figure best able to understand and interpret the tumultuous events around him.

Blok's essay is not, like Merezhkovskii's novels, a religiously focused call to arms for the Russian intelligentsia, nor is it a Briusovian story of artistic creation as the ultimate goal, with no higher aim posited or, indeed, possible. Rather, Blok tells a story of revolutionary archetypes, reenacted periodically by figures who renounce themselves and are transformed as they momentarily leave profane, historical time to enter into and relive a sacred, past, and inspirational moment.[4] The artist who takes part in this process sacrifices his own identity to take on that of his changing era. In so doing, he functions not only as supreme mythmaker, able to create and reflect a new world, but also as a revolutionary myth unto himself, identifiable with self-sacrificial and yet powerful figures of the past—and inspiring to figures yet to come. As the upheaval his predecessors had foreseen for their nation now came to a head, Blok recast their Roman model in Symbolist trappings updated for a new age, as he argued that individual, personal transformation on the part of rebels and artists, in ancient Rome or modern Russia, can lead, at least temporarily, to the transfiguration of the world.[5]

A Close, Familiar World

I . . . choose that epoch which, in its historical process, corresponds most to my own time.
Aleksandr Blok, "Catiline," 1918

Although Blok called "Catiline" his favorite essay[6] and maintained its importance as a blueprint of sorts for "The Twelve,"[7] it remains one of his less well-known works. And yet in choosing Catiline as his subject,

Blok was "calling to mind a rather well-known page of ancient history" (76). He could assume his readers' knowledge of the conspiracy that pitted the dissolute aristocrat Catiline against the "new man" Cicero during the Roman consular elections of 63 BCE.[8] Catiline was running on a populist platform that included, among other goals, the cancellation of debts. He had long been opposed by the elitist Optimates, who rallied behind the more conservative Cicero, effectively shutting Catiline out of the consulship and perpetuating their own authority over the Roman government. Catiline, thoroughly frustrated at his lack of political success, took up arms against the Roman state. He was mortally wounded at the battle of Pistoria, and Cicero, who had ordered the execution of the conspirators, was declared Father of the Fatherland for having "saved" Rome. Along with the account left by the Roman historian Sallust, also an opponent of Catiline, and that of Plutarch, Cicero's writings about the affair became standard reading for students of Latin, including the young Aleksandr Blok.[9] Among other horrors, Catiline is said to have killed his brother-in-law and son, seduced a vestal virgin, and sworn adherents to his cause over a shared bowl of human blood.[10] If even one-quarter of these charges were true, Blok remarks, that fraction would be enough to invite condemnation (67).

At the time Blok was writing, however, a reevaluation of Catiline was well under way. Most notably, for Blok's purposes, Henrik Ibsen, inspired by the revolutions in Europe in 1848, had written a play, his first, about Catiline.[11] Ibsen freely acknowledged that although he had "lapped up" the ancient sources, he had also strayed from them to a significant degree.[12] At times almost Christ-like, Ibsen's Catiline forgives the wrongs done him but, driven by his desire to restore freedom to the Roman Republic, stoops to revolt and to murder. Because of the inherent nobility of his goals, however, upon his death he is sent to Elysium rather than to hell. Blok's version of Catiline's story, while deeply influenced in its stress on revolutionary freedom by Ibsen's work, is an evocative, opinionated, and contradictory mix of history, fiction, and literary analysis, an attempted "critical history" in the Nietzschean style that strives to debunk past doctrine in order to serve contemporary reality.[13] Glorifying Catiline's rebellion and condemning Cicero and Sallust, Blok professes to reject the generations of historians who have failed to grasp the profound significance of Catiline's deeds. Although these claims are disingenuous—Blok does in fact rely on previous histories in constructing his own,[14] and he seems to enjoy instructing the reader in the historical background to Catiline's plot—he reworks his inherited material to create a narrative of the Roman past that resonates with revolutionary Russia. "*Catiline.* What a close, FAMILIAR, sad world!" he exclaimed in his notebooks.[15]

Writing mythologized history rather than historicized fiction, Blok was able to lay out his views of history more readily than Merezhkovskii and Briusov—particularly the resemblances he posited between the modern and ancient worlds, and specifically between Rome and Russia, his "favorite historiosophical idea" during the revolutionary period.[16] In the text, he brings out these parallels both semantically and thematically. The connections start with his subtitle, "A Page from the History of the World Revolution" (60), which serves to characterize Catiline's rebellion in terms used in newspapers of Blok's own day to acclaim the Bolshevik takeover and its projected consequences.[17] Blok renders the link more overt through references to the Roman "bourgeoisie" and "urban proletariat" (62) and, most significantly of course, to Catiline as a "Roman Bolshevik" (86). Further parallels include the description of Catullus as a "Latin Pushkin" (80)—an association that once again inserts the Russian poet into the potent mix of Roman and Russian rebels that Blok's essay presents.

The linguistic markers underline the major similarity Blok posited between first-century BCE Rome and twentieth-century Russia: the idea that both worlds, ancient and modern, were undergoing transformations of profound significance. Catiline's Rome was a doomed republic, marked by the constant civil wars that would lead eventually to Julius Caesar's crossing the Rubicon in 49 BCE and then, in 31 BCE, to the consolidation of power by his adopted son Octavian, later called Augustus Caesar, who became Rome's first emperor. The empire of the Caesars, in Blok's mind as in that of many of his contemporaries, would be condemned in turn—and almost immediately—by the appearance of Christ. "Do not forget," Blok admonished in a statement of the early revolutionary period, "that the Roman Empire existed for another five hundred years after the birth of Christ. But it only *existed,* it swelled up, decomposed, and decayed—already dead."[18] Thus Catiline's world was a precursor of the dying Western Roman Empire. In his initial description of Rome, Blok refers to a "corrupt civilization" (61), a society already sated but intent on further conquest, a society characterized by the exploitation of the poor at the hands of the rich. It is also the site of political anarchy: "the government was utterly weak and lacking in authority" (68). Describing "triumphantly decomposing Rome," Blok writes, "The enormous dying body of the beast of state weighed on millions of people—almost all the people of that world. Only a few dozen degenerates danced out on its back their shameless, degenerate, patriotic dance. All this taken together was called the sublime spectacle of Roman state power" (80).

Ancient Rome in its decrepitude and doomed status was comparable in Blok's mind to modern-day Europe, which he had linked for some time with the theme of death. In his essay "Nemye svideteli" (Silent Witnesses), written in 1909 upon his return from a trip to Italy, Blok had described that country as a place where "all the air seems to have been used up by the dead."[19] His preface to *Molnii iskusstva* (Lightning Flashes of Art), the collection of essays to which "Silent Witnesses" belongs, generalized these reactions to include all of Europe: "And the nineteenth century is all atremble. . . . Time rushes on: year by year, day by day, and hour by hour it becomes even more apparent that civilization will collapse over the heads of its builders and crush them with its own weight; but it has not yet begun to crush them and the madness lingers on: everything is premeditated and predetermined, destruction is inescapable, but slow in coming."[20]

Russia, meanwhile, despite its revolutionary present, was as yet still emerging from a European-influenced tsarist past, represented for Blok by those who continued to mourn its demise: monarchist sympathizers, to be sure, but also the deracinated urban "bourgeoisie" and those members of the intelligentsia who preferred "old-world" values to those of the new.[21] Following the first 1917 revolution and the abdication of the tsar in March of that year, Blok described Russia's prerevolutionary status in a diary entry of 25 May 1917: "For a long time those invested with power in Russia had lacked all these qualities [faith, courage, honesty, and genius]. The upper strata declined, demoralizing the lower. All this went on for many years. During the last years, as those invested with power themselves admit, they were already absolutely lost. Nevertheless, the balance was not upset."[22]

Although revolution had now come to Russia, upsetting that "balance," Blok feared that antirevolutionary forces might impede the progress achieved thus far. In "The Twelve," an unseen enemy constantly menaces the twelve marching Red Guardsmen, and the journal that published the poem on its second page devoted its first page to anti–White Guard slogans.[23] After all, Blok himself was convinced that an extraordinary transformation had occurred, but he recognized that most of humanity, including Russian humanity, had failed to grasp the sweeping significance he saw in recent events. As he wrote in "Catiline," "Most people simply cannot imagine that *events take place.* . . . We know . . . that events occur in the life of humanity: there are world wars, there are revolutions; Christ is born. . . . But those who think this way are always in the minority" (84–85).

Blok's scorn for contemporary Europe, including the "reactionary," "bourgeois" elements of his own society, comes out clearly in "Catiline." He claimed an unequivocal kinship between the unthinking Roman society of Catiline's day and the threatened (and yet paradoxically still threatening) state of Europe and Europeanized Russia. He maintained that the goals of Roman education resembled those of modern Europe: "after all, this is how any average person is educated in contemporary Europe: to exercise his will, not to lose heart, always to preserve his courage, to prepare to become good cannon fodder and a good citizen" (66). He asserted that there were Ciceros alive in Russia in his own day (72). He lamented the fact that Roman poets were read as little as modern poets (83).[24] And, most significantly, he proclaimed that both societies were ripe for explosion, both "that 'pagan' old world where Catiline acted and lived" and "this 'Christian' old world, where we live and act" (70, 61, 80). For even as Rome "continued to be governed by an old, provincial, vulgar, positivist morality," Blok claims, it did so "on the eve of that time when a new morality would enter the world" (78). And Roman culture "in several decades would be condemned forever and irreversibly in another court, an unhypocritical court, the court of Jesus Christ" (73). Catiline's plot, Blok insisted, foreshadowed the far more sweeping changes Jesus would bring to the Roman world; therein lay Catiline's significance:

> In [Catiline's] time there blew a wind that grew into a storm, having destroyed the pagan old world. He was seized by the wind that blew before the birth of Jesus Christ, the herald of the new world.
>
> Only with such a premise is it worthwhile to investigate the dark, worldly goals of the plot of Catiline. Without it they become deeply uninteresting, insignificant, and unnecessary; their investigation is transformed into the historical gravedigging of the philologists. (71)[25]

In his sensitivity to the wind of Christ's approaching transformation, Catiline merited comparison to Russia's Bolsheviks, who were also set against an established order and represented to Blok a force of sweeping change that would spread throughout the moldering West. In a diary entry of 11 January 1918, Blok wrote, "Europe (its theme) is *Art and Death.* Russia is life."[26] Writing an (eventually unsent) letter in May

1918 to Zinaida Hippius, who was appalled by Blok's acceptance of the Bolshevik regime, he maintained his belief in the demise of Europe and old Russia and in the onset of a new era akin to the early years of Christianity: "Do you really not know that 'there will be no more Russia,' just as there was no more Rome—not in the fifth century after the birth of Christ, but in the first year of the first century? In addition—there will be no England, no Germany, no France. That the world has already been transformed? That the 'old world' has already disappeared?"[27]

As he explained elsewhere, "The Russia that was is no more and never will be. The Europe that was is no more and never will be. . . . The world has entered into a new era. *That* civilization, *that* idea of the state, *that* religion—have died. . . . We . . . are now condemned to be present at their decomposition and decay."[28]

Thus Blok's world found itself at a fragile moment in its history. The Bolshevik Revolution echoed in its magnitude the birth of Christianity. According to Blok, the Russian state and Europe were now doomed by the Revolution and all it signified, just as ancient Rome had been condemned to transformation by Christ's birth. Events would now determine whether the changes Blok dreamed of would be fully realized. He believed that the answer lay in the hands of Russia's and then the world's citizens, who needed to become aware of the phenomenon of metamorphosis itself in order to appreciate and maintain the transformation that had occurred. In his January 1918 article "Intelligentsiia i revoliutsiia" (The Intelligentsia and the Revolution), he had urged his fellow intellectuals, "With all your body, with all your heart, and with all your consciousness—listen to the Revolution."[29] In "Catiline," he described the Roman rebel as "a revolutionary with all his spirit and all his body" (68). An examination of Blok's portrayal of Catiline deepens one's understanding of the changes he hoped to see in his often unthinking contemporaries and illuminates his portrayal of the violent but lauded Red Guardsmen of "The Twelve," the rebels who stand as Catiline's brothers-in-arms against the Roman-Russian state.

Revolutionary Anger

Whatever did you think? That a revolution was an idyll?
Aleksandr Blok, "The Intelligentsia and the Revolution," 1918

In "Catiline," Blok described revolution as a wind independent of human intent. "The wind arises not according to the will of individual people," he wrote, "individual people feel and seem only to organize it" (70).[30] He divided these receptive individuals into two groups: those who "breathe this wind, live and act by this wind, having inhaled it," and those who "throw themselves into this wind, are seized by it, live and act carried by the wind" (70). The former group, he implied, consisted of writers and artists, who "hide and do not reveal themselves in external activity, concentrating all their forces on internal action." The latter group was made up of active revolutionaries, to whom "stormy, physical, external manifestation is essential" (70). Both groups, he maintained, were "equally filled with the storm," and both groups were eager to "sow the wind," to "destroy correctness, to upset the order of life" (70). Catiline, according to Blok, belonged to the latter group.

Catiline's revolutionary credentials did not ensure an uncritical portrayal, however. Blok accepts much of Sallust's unflattering physical description of the Roman revolutionary: "His complexion was pallid, his eyes hideous, his gait now hurried and now slow. Face and expression clearly marked him as a man distraught."[31] Indeed, according to Blok, Catiline combined the vices of his age "within himself and brought them to a legendary monstrosity" (69). And yet crucially, despite his flaws, Catiline is open to the wind of revolution: he was "created by *social inequality*, suckled in its suffocating atmosphere" (68).[32] Because of his awareness of his surroundings, Catiline in the midst of his dissipation is nonetheless a revolutionary waiting to explode. Upon hearing Cicero's first oration against him (fig. 11) Blok claims, the transformation occurs: "[Catiline] was gripped by a rage that knew no limits" (75). He writes further, "The invective was not a weight around his neck. The very rage that had seized him helped him to shake off its weight, and he appeared to have been subjected to a metamorphosis, a transformation" (84). "It became easier for him," Blok explains, citing the revolutionary anthem "The Marseillaise,"[33] "because he had 'renounced the old world' and 'shaken off the dust' of Rome from his feet" (84). "This is the same Catiline," he concludes, "the recent pet of the lionesses of Roman society and the demimonde, the criminal ringleader of a debauched band. He walks with his same 'now lazy, now hurried' gait, but his fury and rage have communicated a musical rhythm to his walk, as if this were no longer the same mercenary and debauched Catiline; in the tread of this man are revolt, uprising, and the furies of the people's anger" (85).

Thus it is precisely Catiline's explosive fury that marks him as a revolutionary and transforms him into a representative of popular anger and an agent of change. No longer merely receptive to the revolutionary

Fig. 11. Cesare Maccari, *Cicero Denouncing Catiline before the Senate,* ca. 1888 (Scala/Art Resource, N.Y.)

wind, Catiline through his anger has become a full-fledged participant in its merciless impending destruction of the status quo. Referring back to Blok's analyses of postrevolutionary life, one recalls his insistence on the disappearance not only of the tsarist autocracy, but of the very concept of nation-states and indeed of the entire "old" world he and his contemporaries had known. A revolutionary wind, Blok had suggested, is one that brings an end to established categories. When Catiline crosses the line into the revolutionary realm, therefore, he becomes part of a new sphere of being, one incomprehensible to those unaware of its significance. "Such a person is a madman," Blok explains, "a maniac, possessed. Life flows on as if submitting to other laws of causality, space, and time; because of this, his entire make-up—physical and spiritual . . . conforms to a different time and a different space" (69).

In presenting Catiline as one who has broken away from all currently existing restrictive categories, Blok draws on Ibsen's concept of freedom as expressed in his play *Catiline* and in letters to his contemporary George Brandes: "What you call liberty, I call liberties; and what I call the struggle for liberty is nothing but the constant, living assimilation of the idea of freedom. He who possesses liberty other than as a thing to be striven for, possesses it dead and soulless. . . . So that a man who stops in the midst of the struggle and says: 'Now I have it'—thereby shows that he has lost it."[34]

As Blok notes, Ibsen's Catiline "was a friend not of lasting and positive *liberties* that have been thrown from the sky; he was a friend of freedom that eternally flies away" (91). Catiline feels stifled by his surroundings and refuses to be condemned "to the horror of a half-life" (91). In his March 1918 article "Iskusstvo i revoliutsiia" (Art and Revolution), intended as a preface to Richard Wagner's book of the same name, Blok had discussed the Wagnerian "new man" who would come into being in the postrevolutionary period. The "new man" would understand that "the meaning of human life lies in unrest and alarm."[35] Catiline, then, for both Ibsen and Blok, is representative of perpetual revolution, of the constant, unending creation of the new through the destruction of the old.[36] Thus even as he wreaks terror on the habit-bound citizens of Rome, his violence becomes cause for celebration. For it is Catiline's destructive rage, in the name of freedom, that is essential in the "new man" of the revolutionary age. Discussing the end of Ibsen's play, Blok proclaims in the last lines of his own text, "Catiline—precisely that rebel and murderer of what was most holy in life—turns out to be worthy of Elysium and of love" (91).

Like Catiline, who is "carried by the wind" of revolution, the Twelve of Blok's eponymous poem react to a strong wind that blows from the first stanza of the poem: "Wind, wind—/ On all God's earth." Surrounded by darkness, Catiline strides ahead of a group of rebellious men who resemble the Twelve, marching through a "black night."[37] (Indeed, Blok remarks in "Catiline" that "revolution, like all great events, always underlines blackness" [85].) Like Catiline, the Twelve commit murder, when the prostitute Kat'ka is killed during her rendezvous with the traitor-"bourgeois" Van'ka, who has renounced his former Red Guard associates in order to join the Whites.[38] But again like Catiline, the Twelve represent freedom, a freedom devoid of ties to institutional Christianity or the previous regime, which is mourned in the poem by its remaining representatives, who are pitiful and at times despicable. Just as Catiline's very steps represent Roman popular wrath, the marching Twelve embody the spiteful anger of the long-oppressed Russian people, ever ready in Blok's mind to take revenge on those formerly in power—and eminently justified, according to him, in doing so.[39] As he had reasoned in "The Intelligentsia and the Revolution":

> Why do they dig holes in an ancient cathedral? Because for a hundred years an obese priest, hiccupping, took bribes and traded in vodka here.

> Why do they defile the masters' estates, so dear to the heart? Because girls were raped and whipped there; if not at this master's, then at a neighbor's.
>
> Why do they topple centuries-old parks? Because for a hundred years, under the spreading linden trees and maple trees, gentlemen showed their power, flaunting their purse in the faces of the poor, their education in the faces of the simpleton.
>
> Everything is thus.[40]

Hence Blok's respect for Catiline; and hence his impassioned outburst during a January 1918 argument, when he claimed that he saw angels' wings behind the shoulders of every Red Guardsman.[41]

Thus for Blok, transformation, while necessary, entailed pain and sacrifice, and Blok did not exempt himself from the need to give up what he loved most. In the days immediately following the revolution, he told the poet Vladimir Maiakovskii that the revolution was "good," and then added, "They've burned my library in the country."[42] The destruction of Shakhmatovo, the beloved country estate where he had spent many idyllic summers, would haunt Blok despite his faith in the revolution's destructive necessity. He wrote in his notebook on 22 September 1918 that he had dreamed of Shakhmatovo,[43] and on 12 December 1918 noted that he had cried over it in his sleep the night before.[44] He also sympathetically chronicled his wife's tearful but determined welcome of the "new world," adding a laconic "yes" after his account.[45] Nonetheless, he insisted, precisely the violence of the Bolshevik Revolution was necessary to overthrow pre-existing, "old-world" categories. Thus, responding to reports of starvation and famine in the Russian countryside, Blok noted in his notebook on 21 July 1918, "So it will be (the dying out, etc.) as long as everything rests on the state, the church, civilization, 'culture,' nationality, and so on, and so forth."[46] He repeatedly castigated his fellow intellectuals for their unwillingness to accept the revolution, with all its excesses, meant to propel Russia into "living" the myth of revolution, transforming Russia and then the world into a new state of being.

Holy Anger, Holy Revolution

The violation of tradition is also a tradition.
Aleksandr Blok, notebook entry, 30 December 1918

In "Catiline" and "The Twelve," as Blok posited revolutionary forebears—ranging from Catiline to Jesus—for the Bolsheviks, he situated the Russian Revolution in a chain of inspired, transformative acts of rebellion. Joined in their commitment to the explosion of the status quo, these figures nonetheless were taking part in an age-old pattern. Alongside Blok's "wind-sowing" revolutionaries, there was another, equally important group of mythmakers: the thinkers or writers who participated in this chain by telling the revolutionaries' stories. For Blok, intent on explicating the myths of revolutionary Russia, there were several particularly important precursors: Nietzsche and Wagner, Viacheslav Ivanov, who had added a Christian framework to Nietzsche's "Dionysian magic,"[47] and Ernest Renan, whose 1861 biography of Jesus as revolutionary had earned its author the censure but also the fascination of many of his contemporaries.

As Blok worked on "Catiline" and on the preface to Wagner's *Art and Revolution,* his thoughts returned to a book he had once called "a revelation": Nietzsche's *Birth of Tragedy,* complete with its preface to Wagner.[48] Blok had delved into Nietzsche's thought in 1906 and had filled several pages of his December 1906 notebook with a summary, including copious notes, of *The Birth of Tragedy.*[49] Most of his notes are devoted to a discussion of the significance of Greek tragedy and the differences, according to Nietzsche, between Apollo and Dionysus; he noted at one point that he could not write down everything that intrigued him about the book, for it was too long.[50] Nonetheless, Nietzsche's dismissal of his own "spent" culture and his call for "an exuberant, triumphant life in which all things, whether good or evil, are deified" made their way into Blok's pre- and postrevolutionary prose.[51] Convinced that his own culture was doomed, Blok prophesied a Dionysian wind that would sweep away the known world.

Unlike Nietzsche, however, with his "anti-Christian evaluation of life,"[52] Blok insisted that this wind was comparable to that unleashed at the birth of Jesus Christ. In this assertion the influence of Ivanov is readily discernible.[53] In his *Religiia Dionisa* (The Religion of Dionysus, 1905), Ivanov claimed that the Dionysian religion, largely as interpreted by Nietzsche, might be seen as a predecessor of Christianity.[54] The worship of both Dionysus and Christ, Ivanov believed, involved the psychological transformation of the worshipper through a state of orgiastic ecstasy.[55] Ivanov found this condition particularly applicable to early Christianity: "For Christianity as it was in its beginning can be understood only on the assumption of a certain orgiastic condition of souls, before whom the whole world suddenly appeared different, unexpected until then, because they themselves had changed internally."[56]

Through Nietzsche, Blok had discovered the glory of Dionysus's transformative destruction. Through Ivanov, Blok had learned to reinterpret Nietzsche, linking this Dionysian frenzy to Christianity, albeit in an unorthodox form. The influence of both thinkers is apparent in Blok's portrayal of Catiline. Catiline is possessed by an explosive Dionysian frenzy, and then he becomes privy to another order of time and space, perceiving the world differently in his transformed condition. In this state, his mission becomes comparable not only to that of the Bolsheviks, but also to that of Jesus Christ. And yet Catiline's metamorphosis is a specific one: he is transformed into a revolutionary. And it is specifically his status as revolutionary, Blok implies, that makes it possible to associate him with Jesus. The influence of another thinker, the French writer Ernest Renan, is significant in this regard.

Blok was reading Renan's *Life of Jesus* at the time he wrote "Catiline" and "The Twelve," and there are references to Renan throughout Blok's notebooks and diaries of the revolutionary period.[57] In his characterization of Catiline and his significance, Blok drew to a substantial degree upon Renan's assessments of Jesus, who in Renan's telling begins his career as a reformer of Judaism and then, transformed, becomes its angry destroyer. After a frustrating sojourn in Jerusalem, Jesus decides that there is "no union possible between him and the ancient Jewish religion."[58] "Jesus was no longer a Jew," Renan claims.[59] "Filled with revolutionary ardor,"[60] he now seeks to found a new kingdom based on liberty,[61] a liberty that has nothing to do with political forms.[62] Motivating Jesus in this task are the "fire and rage" that go "to the very marrow,"[63] Renan writes, as he elaborates on Jesus's metamorphosis: "Sometimes one would have said that his reason was disturbed. . . . His disciples at times thought him mad. His enemies declared him to be possessed. His excessively impassioned temperament carried him incessantly beyond the bounds of human nature. He laughed at all human systems. . . . His natural gentleness seemed to have abandoned him; he was sometimes harsh and capricious. His disciples at times did not understand him, and experienced in his presence a feeling akin to fear. Sometimes his displeasure at the slightest opposition led him to commit inexplicable and apparently absurd acts."[64]

Like Blok, Ivanov, and Nietzsche, Renan opposes "petty and commonplace ideas" to "extraordinary movements so far above our everyday life,"[65] explaining that modern human beings are limited by their misleading ideas about madness. "A state in which a man says things of which he is not conscious, in which thought is produced without the summons and control of the will, exposes him to being confined as a lunatic. Formerly this was called prophecy and inspiration."[66]

Far from being sinless, in his quest for transformation Renan's Jesus "trampl[es] under foot everything that is human, blood, love, and country," saving himself only for his mission.[67] And Jesus does "not conceal from himself the terrible storm he [is] about to cause in the world," Renan claims, moving on to cite the Gospels: "'Think not,' said he, with much boldness and beauty, 'that I am come to send peace on earth: I came not to send peace, but a sword.'"[68] The resemblances to Blok's portrayal of Catiline are evident. Like Renan's Jesus, Blok's Catiline is a man transformed by rage and a mission. Both men are destroyers who confuse and frighten those around them. Most significantly, both men, according to their creators, are justified in their revolutionary violence. Renan explains, "The most beautiful things in the world are done in a state of fever; every great creation involves a breach of equilibrium, a violent state of the being that draws it forth."[69] And, he states, "No revolution is effected without some harshness."[70] Blok, of course, concurred with this assessment: as he had maintained in his poem "Skify" (The Scythians), written immediately after "The Twelve" in January 1918, "You have forgotten that there exists a love / That both burns and destroys."[71]

Renan's ideas further illuminate Blok's comparison of the outlaw revolutionary Catiline to Jesus and, combined with reference to Nietzsche, shed particular light on the conclusion of "The Twelve."[72] In the final lines of the poem, the reader learns that the twelve marchers are led (unbeknownst to them) by the figure of Jesus Christ, who is clad in a crown of white roses.[73] This image shocked many of Blok's contemporaries. Those who opposed the Bolshevik takeover were appalled by the appearance of Jesus at the head of a gang of cutthroats. Those who supported the revolution wondered why an outmoded Christian symbol concluded what was otherwise a revolutionary poem. Blok himself, in fact, professed to be baffled by the image.[74]

Seen in light of "Catiline," the Christ of "The Twelve" can be viewed not necessarily as a "feminized" vision, as the white roses he wears have been thought to suggest.[75] For the Christ of Renan and of "Catiline" belongs at the head of the twelve Red Guardsmen. He represents revolutionary transformation and therefore condones violence in the name of sacred freedom. The white roses he wears may in fact hark back to Blok's earlier, impassioned reading of Nietzsche. Blok's copy of *The Birth of Tragedy* contained the introduction Nietzsche had added to the text in 1886, his "Attempt at Self-Criticism."[76] In this introduction, cited in Blok's 1906 notebook, Nietzsche had quoted from *Thus*

Spake Zarathustra. Nietzsche's call to his contemporaries "in the language of that Dionysian monster who bears the name of Zarathustra" is significant:

> Raise up your hearts, my brothers, high, higher! And don't forget your legs! Raise up your legs, too, good dancers; and still better: stand on your heads!
>
> This crown of laughter, the rose-wreath crown: I crown myself with this crown; I myself pronounced holy my laughter. I did not find anyone else today strong enough for that. . . .
>
> This crown of laughter, the rose-wreath crown: to you, my brothers, I throw this crown. Laughter I have pronounced holy: you higher men, *learn*—to laugh![77]

In the final stanza of "The Twelve," before Christ's appearance, a menacing wind laughs.[78] Blok's Christ might be viewed in this context as a Dionysian revolutionary in the style of Renan. Crowned with a Dionysian wreath, like the outlaw Catiline and the Russian Bolsheviks, he stands for revolution.

The Revolutionary Artist: Mythologizing the New World

He is at once subject and object, at once poet, actor, and spectator.
Friedrich Nietzsche, *The Birth of Tragedy,* 1872

In his 1919 article "Krushenie gumanizma" (The Collapse of Humanism), Blok drew upon Wagner and Nietzsche in his description of the "new man" he felt the revolution was inspiring: "The entire man has begun to move, he has woken up from the age-long dream of civilization; his spirit, his soul, and his body are seized by stormy motion; in the storm of spiritual, political, social revolutions, possessed of cosmic correspondences . . . a new man is formed: man—a human animal, a social animal, a moral animal is transformed into an *artist,* in the language of Wagner."[79] With this formulation of revolutionary man as artist, Blok was again invoking *The Birth of Tragedy,* in which Nietzsche had written "that existence and the world seem justified only as an aesthetic phenomenon."[80] "The Dionysian," Nietzsche had explained, "with its primordial joy experienced even in pain, is the common source of music and tragic myth."[81]

Thus the Apollonian "age-long dream," Russia's prerevolutionary state, was opposed to the Dionysian awakening inherent in Russia's revolution. In *The Birth of Tragedy,* Nietzsche had contrasted "so-called culture" and "true art," asserting that the two had never been so far apart as they were in nineteenth-century Western Europe.[82] In "The Collapse of Humanism," Blok now developed this theme. He substituted the term "civilization," with its longstanding associations of "the true, the good, and the beautiful," for Nietzsche's "so-called culture," and, somewhat confusingly, substituted the word "culture," which he saw as synonymous with "the spirit of music," for Nietzsche's "true art." Blok declared that it was "the people," rather than the intelligentsia or the "bourgeoisie," who possessed that "spirit of music," associated with nature, life, and freedom. Thus at a time when "civilization" was in a state of decay, new life could be found lying dormant in a nation's "people," though they themselves might be unaware of the power they held. At a reading of "The Collapse of Humanism" during the Russian civil war, Blok explained, "Therefore it is not paradoxical to claim that the barbarian masses, possessing only the spirit of music, turn out to be the guardians of culture in those epochs when civilization, having lost its wings and voice, becomes the enemy of culture, despite the fact that it has at its disposal all the elements of progress—science, technology, law, etc. . . . This music is a wild chorus, . . . almost unbearable for many of us, and at this point it will seem far from amusing if I say that for many of us it will in fact prove fatal."[83]

The transformation Blok sought in his compatriots consisted of their becoming conscious "artists": they were to acknowledge the revolutionary spirit of music within their nation and themselves and awaken to its Dionysian expression, however frightening and alien some of them might find it. In so doing, they were to glory in the destruction of "civilization" as Europe knew it, a destruction comparable to the "barbarian" assault on the decaying Roman Empire. For Rome, like Blok's contemporary Europe, was representative of "civilization," even as both Roman and Russian revolutionaries spoke for "culture," or the "spirit of music." The wind that had swept up Catiline was that same "spirit of music" that the Bolsheviks were now hearing as they initiated the annihilation of Blok's own "old world." "Listening to the Revolution" was for Blok an aesthetic as well as a moral act.

And yet, despite Blok's own dreams of unending revolution, of the transformation of all his contemporaries into his conception of "revolutionaries," he knew how unlikely such an outcome was. Christ's transformative revolution had eventually faded, and so, too, might that of the Bolsheviks.[84] Indeed, even as he worked on "Catiline," Blok feared a diminution of the revolutionary energy that had surrounded him as he composed "The Twelve." In a notebook entry of 16 May 1918, he wrote, "'CATILINE'—all day. The swan song of the revolution? The fever is less."[85] Rome took on further precursory significance in Blok's eyes, then, as he explored what happens when revolutions fade: "And right away: *the bitterness of the fall.* How boring it is, how familiar. So, Christ will come."[86] Summing up the end results of Catiline's rebellion, Blok writes resignedly, "There was a conspiracy, there was a revolution; but the revolution was suppressed, the conspiracy uncovered—and all is well again" (80). Should the Russian revolution also come to an end, should the transformations cease, should the Russian people not lead the rest of the world to a new era, then the violence unleashed during the revolution would lose its moral and aesthetic significance. "Blood-letting . . . becomes nothing but a wearisome banality once it has ceased to be sacred madness," he warned.[87]

Amid his disappointment over the end of Catiline's rebellion and his fears for his own day, however, Blok maintained his faith in the potency of the artist as one capable not only of telling but of reviving revolutionary myths. In the Roman setting, Blok pointed to the poet Catullus, able to hear the windy music of his revolutionary moment and to distill it in his art for generations to come. In his notebook on 27 April 1918, Blok wrote, "*Catiline.* All morning—fruitless attempts. . . . Suddenly, toward the evening, it dawned upon me (the 63rd poem of Juvenal—the key to everything!)."[88] The poem Blok had in mind was in fact the sixty-third poem of Catullus, known as "Attis." It tells the story of a youth who leaves Greece and goes east to Phrygia, where he falls under the orgiastic spell of the goddess Cybele and, in his delirium, castrates himself. Catullus at this point begins to use feminine grammatical endings in his description of Attis.[89] Awakening after a frenzied interlude in the company of the goddess's other priestesses, Attis regrets what she has done, lamenting the loss of her manhood and her homeland. Cybele, however, has no mercy, and sends her lions to summon Attis back to the fold. Terrified, Attis does Cybele's bidding for the rest of her life. Catullus ends the poem with an invocation to the goddess to spare him the pain Attis has experienced, a plea his twentieth-century counterpart Blok, intent on a Symbolist model of self-sacrifice, does not share.[90]

Aleksandr Etkind advances the theory that castration serves for Blok as a metaphor for revolution.[91] Castration is a transformative event that removes the subject's masculine identity and releases him into an unencumbered, androgynous world where previous boundaries have disappeared and revolution is therefore possible. Being a revolutionary with "all" of one's body implies the need to renounce part of it, in keeping with the ideals of the revolutionary sects of Russian castrates that had long fascinated Blok.[92] Etkind joins Irene Masing-Delic in noting the correspondingly androgynous and therefore ideal Christ of "The Twelve."[93] This Christ can also perhaps be identified with the poet himself,[94] who, like Attis, has yielded his own subjectivity to the wind of his own revolutionary age.

One should also consider the myth of Attis's castration in the specific context of revolutionary Rome and its poetry. Dismissing a simplified Russian translation of Catullus's verses, Blok claims that the Latin original's rare galliambic meter, one associated with the orgiastic worship of Cybele, is essential to its interpretation.[95] He characterizes Catullus's language after Attis's castration: "From this minute the verse, like Attis himself, changes; the brokenness leaves it; from the difficult and manly it becomes lighter, as if more feminine. . . . Further, the verse undergoes a new series of changes; it becomes unlike Latin verses; it seems to spill out in lyric tears characteristic of the Christian soul in the place where Attis mourns his homeland, himself, his friends, his parents, his gymnasium, his youth, his manhood" (82).

Blok insists, "Poems whose content can seem perfectly abstract and unrelated to an epoch are called into being by the most nonabstract and topical of events" (83). Thus, he proclaims in a characteristic formulation:[96] "I believe that we not only have the right but indeed are obliged to consider a poet as linked to his time. It does not matter to us in what precise year Catullus wrote 'Attis,' whether it was when Catiline's conspiracy had just matured, or when it flared up, or when it had just been suppressed. That it was precisely during those years is indisputable, because Catullus was writing precisely during those years. 'Attis' is the creation of an inhabitant of a Rome that was torn up by civil war. This is for me the explanation both of the meter of Catullus's poem and even of its theme" (84). Blok goes on to analyze Catiline's rebellion in the light of the poem. Referring back to Catiline's procession out of Rome, he writes, "Do you hear that uneven, hurried step of the condemned man, the step of the revolutionary, the step in which the storm of fury sounds, resolving itself in staccato musical sounds?" (85). He follows this query with a quotation from the initial lines of Catullus's text, comparing the meter of the Latin verse with Catiline's musical fury. In the galliambs of Catullus, Blok asserts, Catiline's angry footsteps reverberate.

Developing these parallels, Blok uses the same word, *neistovstvo* (rage), in his descriptions of Catiline's revolutionary fury and Attis's orgiastic frenzy (84, 80). Both Catiline and Attis are obedient to the spirit of music; each of them hears the wind that will sweep away all that is associated with "civilized," Western society. Catiline is part of the wave that will eventually destroy Roman society. Attis, a creation of the same period, falls victim to a fury that means the end of the world he has known. And Catullus, Blok implies, is well aware of this similarity. For Attis's story is also one of Rome itself. Like Attis, Rome's past will be transformed and swept away by a Dionysian force. As the storm fades, Rome, like Attis's bereft expressions of woe, will take on a Christian cast. Both Rome and Attis are fated to experience first-hand the pain of metamorphosis, so vividly rendered in the description of Attis's passage from male to female.

Thus the poet, according to Blok, is capable of conveying a sense of his epoch that historians and orators, for example, simply do not grasp. Referring to Catiline's revolutionary anger, he adds:

> In vain would we begin to look in the works of historians for reflections of this anger, for recollections of the revolutionary rage of Catiline, for descriptions of that pressured, threatening atmosphere in which the Rome of those days lived. We will not find a word about this either in the lofty phrases of Sallust, in the chatter of Cicero, nor in the moralizing of Plutarch. But we will find this very atmosphere in the work of the poet—in those galliambs of Catullus about which we have been speaking. (85)

For the artist, as Blok explains of himself, pursues a synthetic vision of his surroundings:

> I resort to juxtapositions of phenomena taken from areas of life which appear to have nothing in common; in the given case, for example, I juxtapose the Roman revolution and the verses of Catullus. I am convinced that only with the help of such juxtapositions and others similar to them is it possible to find the key to an epoch, is it possible to feel its vibration, to clarify for oneself its meaning. (86)

In addition to Catullus's poetry, Blok asserts, "our contemporary life" is useful in "restor[ing] the rhythm of Roman life at the time of the revolution" (80). Turning this paradigm on its head, one might suggest that the tempo of Roman life, as expressed in Catullus's galliambs, is useful in reconstructing the mood of revolutionary Russia nearly two thousand years later. For Blok, literary creations are inextricably linked to the artist's surroundings. His attention to Catullus and Attis must then signal their relevance to Blok's own milieu and to Blok himself. In the context of "The Scythians," Attis's story, when added to that of

Catiline and, by extension, the Bolsheviks, serves to flesh out Blok's Russian-Roman myth.

In "The Scythians," written at the time of the negotiations that led ultimately to Russia's official exit from World War I, Blok called for contemporary Europe to renounce war and celebrate the world revolution. In an 11 January 1918 diary entry, he had responded to the "lack of result" of the Brest-Litovsk negotiations by issuing a warning to the European nations. Should they refuse Russia's invitation to peace, he wrote, Russia stood ready to relinquish its role as buffer between Europe and Asia and "open wide the gates to the East," leaving Europe vulnerable to destruction from that quarter. The Russians themselves could metamorphose from Aryans into Asians, he declared, thus becoming a part of that threat: "We will show you just what barbarians are."[97] In the poem, he returned to these themes, referring to the potentially maddened Russians, with their fluid identity, as "Scythians."[98] After invoking in his epigraph Vladimir Solov'ev's poem "Panmongolism," Blok proclaimed, "Yes, we are Scythians! Yes, we are Asiatics! / With slanting and greedy eyes!"[99] "The Scythians" ended with the following warning:

For the last time—come to your senses, old world!
To the brotherly feast of labor and peace,
For the last time, to the bright, brotherly feast
The barbarian lyre calls you![100]

Blok's references to the Russians as potentially "Eastern" and "barbarian" deepen a reader's understanding of his identification of "Attis" as the key to his article "Catiline." Attis, one recalls, moves from West to East when he is overtaken and transformed by the frenzy Cybele has visited upon him. At that point, having dissociated himself from the civilization he knew, Attis mourns the change in himself and his fate but is unable to return to his previous life. Cybele's force is more powerful than any regrets he may have, and he lives out the rest of his life in her thrall. Similarly, by embarking upon the path of revolution, Blok felt, Russia had of necessity renounced the "civilized," Western elements within itself. The Russian Revolution, a response to the "spirit of music" of Blok's own day, meant the end of Western Europe and its centuries-old "civilization." Just as "barbarians" had once attacked ancient Rome, revolutionary Russians now threatened to demolish rotting Europe in a Dionysian wave of destruction. Attis's story served as a warning to Russians and Europeans alike: however difficult and painful the transition might be, the revolutionary wave that carried it was impossible to resist. While this revolution, like its predecessors, might fade, its transformative spirit would resurface whenever a dangerous wind began to blow once more, waiting to inspire a new generation of revolutionaries. Longstanding myths of revolution, kept alive through imaginative art and primed for rebirth, would form part of this wind.

Shortly before Blok wrote "Catiline," at the time he was reading Renan, he planned a play about Jesus, a play that was never written. It was to feature a "sinful" Jesus whose meetings with his apostles resembled Russian revolutionary gatherings. It is interesting to note that Blok characterized this Jesus as "an artist," one who "receives everything from the people."[101] And like the potentially androgynous Jesus of "The Twelve" and like Catullus's castrated Attis, this Jesus is also "neither a man nor a woman."[102] In this figure of Jesus, therefore, many others come together: Catiline, the Red Guards of "The Twelve," Catullus, Attis, and Blok himself. All of these individuals respond to the music of their era, a Dionysian wind residing in the depths of "the people's" revolutionary wrath. Catiline and the Red Guards, while flawed, act in freedom's name and thereby justify their violence. Attis, in his self-inflicted mutilation, resembles the doomed revolutionary Catiline and Blok himself. And, perhaps most importantly, Catullus and Blok, sensitive to the destructive but inspiring music around them, capture the revolutionary fugue in a lasting legacy for future generations. Each of these figures, then, forms a piece of Blok's Jesus: a revolutionary artist living out and resurrecting age-old myths of revolution.

It is a commonplace that Blok died disappointed in the "failure" of the revolution to transform the world and its inhabitants. The turbulent glory of the revolution ended, and bureaucracy, a new state, set in. Although the first anniversary of the revolution was a day Blok celebrated,[103] already in June 1918 he had noted, "How tired I am of the senselessness of meetings!"[104] and in October of the same year he wrote that he was a writer, not a bureaucrat.[105] Anarchic, free revolution was turning into the state organism it had been meant to replace, as the once stateless Bolsheviks laid the seeds for their new empire. Blok summed up his disappointed dreams in a diary entry of 24 December 1920:

> Once again: (the human) conscience prompts a man to seek out the best and helps him to reject at times the old, comfortable, pleasant, but *dying and decomposing* in favor of the new, which is initially uncomfortable and unpleasant, but promises a bright life ahead.
>
> On the other hand: under the yoke of coercion the human conscience falls silent; then man locks himself up in the old; the more overt the coercion, the

more firmly the person locks himself up in the old. That is what happened to Europe under the yoke of war; that is what has happened to Russia—today.[106]

Perpetuating his personal myth of the artist, Blok insisted that he could no longer hear the "music" that had always inspired his verse, for the revolutionary wind had disappeared.[107] "I am . . . gasping for breath . . . and I am not alone; you, too, and all of us are gasping; all of us will choke. The world revolution is becoming a universal heart attack," he told his friend Iurii Annenkov.[108]

Attis submits willingly to Cybele, sacrificing much of his identity, transforming himself, in the process. And yet the Dionysian celebration comes to an end. Only at that point does Attis's true pain begin: self-mutilation is indeed "but a wearisome banality once it has ceased to be sacred madness."[109] Changed despite himself, Attis regrets what he has done, but he is trapped. Cybele demands further madness—madness Attis no longer welcomes but is bound to accept, albeit in a minor key. Blok, too, experienced the pain of loss during the revolution, and was disappointed once the madness faded. Unlike Attis, however, Blok's disappointment stemmed not from having succumbed to the frenzy of the revolution, but from that frenzy's end. His rather prescient portrayal of Catiline and Attis suggests that Blok suspected to a degree what would happen in his country. Aware of the possible failure of his sacrifice, however, he did not reconsider its necessity. Referring to the eradication of the "old world," Blok insisted, "The artist must flame with wrath against everything that tries to resurrect the corpse."[110] Like Catullus, he became a revolutionary mythmaker, telling the ongoing tale of generations of holy rebels and applying it to revolutionary Russia.

Like Briusov's Roman "kingdom of many truths," which combines within itself Western empire, Eastern faith, and all the writer associates with them, Blok's literary Rome encompasses in complex fashion both a decaying Western state and an Eastern, spiritually infused rebellion against it. Writing mythologized history, Blok moved beyond Catiline's Republican Rome to include in his vision of the world that Catiline and Christ had come to "explode" not only the Republic, but the Roman Empire as well. For Blok, Catiline's rebellion was thus a precursor of the transformation Jesus would bring to Rome's imperial age. In Blok's Russia of 1918, the Bolsheviks were resurrecting this struggle for a new era. Linking Russia's erstwhile government and prerevolutionary way of life with the Roman past, Blok evoked images of similar catastrophic upheaval in the old world and the new. At the same time, he recognized the ability of aspects of "old worlds" to resurrect themselves, and he called upon artists like himself to perpetuate the actions of earlier revolutionaries through the merging of life and art.

While Blok in a sense followed Merezhkovskii in calling for the Russian intelligentsia's participation in a Christian-linked path of renewal, one that would then spread to Europe, Blok did not seek to bring European or "Roman" values into his vision. Rather, revolution was to vanquish established "civilization," just as Briusov, predominantly a Westernizer, had feared. Blok, translator of German philosophy and son of a university family, assigned the poet a role in the revolutionary corner of his paradigm: the poet was to ally himself painfully with freedom, and thus with destruction, against the state, and against "old" civilization. For Viacheslav Ivanov, who had taught Blok about orgiastic self-sacrifice, Russia's revolutionary deprivations would prove to be too painful, its cultural amnesia unacceptable. Ivanov, unlike Blok and unlike Attis, would move westward, departing the new, Russian Rome for the first, Italian one in 1924. There he would pen his own responses to Russia's revolution, as he paid tribute to the cultural monuments that in his mind outlasted and mastered history's revolutionary crises. Once again, the Russian writer would become the voice of the changes he sought in his nation; once again, this voice would be grounded in a complex disillusionment with Russia's revolutionary reality.

4

The Third Rome in Exile

Refitting the Pieces in Viacheslav Ivanov's "Roman Sonnets"

Once again, a faithful pilgrim of your ancient arches,
In my twilight hour with an evening "Ave Roma"
I greet you as my own home,
Refuge from wanderings, Eternal Rome.
Viacheslav Ivanov, "Regina Viarum," 1924

In a 1964 article, the Russian émigré writer and priest Kirill Fotiev wrote that following the appearance of Viacheslav Ivanov's "Rimskie sonety" (Roman Sonnets), "no one can doubt any longer that we, the 'barbarians,' have been invited to the feast of the Western European spirit that Rome both was and continues to be." Ivanov, Fotiev concluded, had shown the way to Rome's culturally laden tables.[1] Indeed, in Ivanov's nine sonnets, written shortly after his 1924 emigration from newly Soviet Russia to Rome,[2] the erudite Russian poet masterfully navigated an evocative path through the physical environs of his adopted city—its fountains, monuments, colors, and sounds—as well as its rich panoply of cultural associations, ranging from Greek and Roman mythology to Renaissance palaces and the sculptures of Bernini. Situating himself in the sonnets through repeated first-person references, Ivanov asserted the place of the Russian artist in the world of culture represented by the "first" Rome, calling to his company such compatriots as Nikolai Gogol' and the painter Aleksandr Ivanov.

Moreover, through the act of writing himself into his Rome-based work, and through suggestions within the poems of his life's journey, Ivanov claimed kinship with a series of central, epic literary personages—authors and characters—from the Western cultural tradition. These figures include Virgil and his Aeneas; Augustine, as both author and principal character in the *Confessions;* and Dante-the-author and Dante-the-character in the *Divine Comedy.* Moving from East to West in a disillusioned rejection of Russian political reality, Ivanov included in his sonnets a vision of St. Peter's Dome, thus presaging his own conversion to Catholicism in 1926.

At the same time, even as the sonnets reflect Ivanov's turn from Russia to Rome, they also demonstrate his continuing faith in what he believed to be the ideal task of the twentieth-century Russian artist: the merging of East and West to join in the creation of a Kingdom of God characterized by the religious and cultural unity of humankind and the divine, of time and of space, through the active creativity of sacred memory. For Ivanov as for other Russian Symbolists writing about Rome, the envisaged heavenly dominion coexisted to some degree with earthly power, often associated by Ivanov with nationalism. Whereas previous writers, immersed in Russia's turbulent revolutionary surroundings, had focused on the clash between these two forces, paying particular attention to the early Christian period, the émigré Ivanov, now immersed in the ongoing cultural history of the "Eternal City," approached the junction of the sacred and the imperial-nationalistic somewhat differently. For him, the sacred and the imperial form part of a larger, Rome-based master narrative of death and resurrection in which earthly power, somewhat paradoxically, may be sanctioned by divinity and then reborn into holy universalism. This process is rooted in holy epiphany and myth, as the poet, drawing on the revelatory experiences of his creative predecessors, both prophesies and spurs a nation to fulfill its intended, unifying potential. As Virgil was said to have predicted and embodied in his "messianic" fourth eclogue the transfiguration of worldly Rome into the overarching Christian kingdom sought by Augustine and lauded in its ideal form by Dante, Ivanov, too, claimed his role as Russian poet-prophet of a desired age of Christian unity. In the "Roman Sonnets," Rome, pictured in its multitudinous guises and stages, represents this very state of creative unity, as worldly power is subsumed into the heavenly and both exist within the artistic work. Relinquishing immediate hope for Russia's realization of his vision of the all-encompassing Third Rome status he had earlier sought and turning instead to Rome itself, Ivanov nevertheless asserted a place for the Russian artist and his sacred goals in the complex Rome the sonnets reflect.

Monuments and Spiritual Initiations

The way downward is easy from Avernus.
Black Dis's door stands open night and day.
But to retrace your steps to heaven's air,
There is the trouble, there is the toil.
Virgil, *The Aeneid,* first century BCE (trans. Robert Fitzgerald)

Ivanov's decision to leave Russia in 1924 for "his beloved Rome," as his daughter Lidiia Ivanova would later term it,[3] was hardly incidental. The city was of longstanding historical and cultural interest to him. In 1886 the young graduate student Ivanov had embarked upon five years of studying Roman history in Berlin, under scholars including the German historian Theodor Mommsen; later he spent several years in Rome, completing his dissertation in Latin on the Roman taxation system of the imperial period.[4] Although his intellectual interests turned shortly thereafter to ancient Greek culture, and particularly the cult of Dionysus, Rome continued to play an important role in his life. There, in 1893, Ivanov met his second wife, Lidiia Zinov'eva-Annibal, who was to prove his greatest poetic inspiration. The couple then spent a year in England, where Ivanov, ensconced in the Reading Room at the British Museum, researched "the religious-historical roots of the Roman faith in Rome's universal mission."[5]

Following Zinov'eva-Annibal's death in 1907, Ivanov found his love for her renewed, as he saw it, in his feelings for Vera Shvarsalon, Zinov'eva-Annibal's daughter from her first marriage. In 1910, also in Rome, Ivanov and Shvarsalon decided to marry; their son Dmitrii Ivanov was born in 1912.[6] The Ivanov family passed the winter of 1912/13 in Rome, after which they returned to Russia and to war, revolution, cold, famine, and ill health. After the thirty-year-old Vera's death in 1920, Ivanov and his two children spent four years in Baku, where he taught literature, including the classics, to enraptured students at the newly established Baku University, before returning to Moscow.[7] Thus Ivanov's departure from the Soviet state was also a return to a city, culture, and history he knew intimately.[8] In his poem "Laeta" (Joys), written during his first trip to Rome in 1892, Ivanov had characterized the city as "a new homeland," even as he proclaimed his loyalty to Russia.[9]

Ivanov's "Roman Sonnets" are a joyous paean to this recovered "homeland": as he exclaimed in his diary on 1 December 1924, "To be in Rome—it seemed an unrealizable dream so recently!"[10] Lidiia Ivanova recalls that her father set to work on the sonnets "without an established plan," writing "freely" and incorporating into the poems features of the Via delle Quattro Fontane on which they lived, the statues and fountains they passed en route to Dmitrii's school, and the sights they took in on Sunday evenings after dining at a small café nearby.[11] "The 'Roman Sonnets' were born here," Dmitrii Ivanov later wrote, "in the immediate vicinity of the Four Fountains, Bernini's Tritone, and the via Sistina."[12] Indeed, in the immediacy of their impressions and in their informative details, the sonnets convey the impression of an elite Baedeker guidebook and recall in their emphases the Russian writer Pavel Muratov's 1911 *Obrazy Italii* (Images of Italy), a work that introduced many Russians to Italy and its cultural riches.[13] The sonnets begin with the poet's appearance on the Appian Way, an ancient road leading into the city, whence he proceeds to the Quirinal Hill and then to six of Rome's most famous fountains; he finishes his journey on Monte Pincio, looking out over the city toward St. Peter's Dome. En route he encounters Renaissance palaces, the Piazza di Spagna where, the reader recalls, the poet John Keats once lived, the former haunts of Gogol' and Aleksandr Ivanov, and the gardens at the Villa Giulia. The final sonnet takes place at sunset, as the poet appears to have completed his day's travels around Rome.

And yet the sonnets are much more than a record of Ivanov-the-émigré's day-long peregrinations through Rome. On another level, they represent the complex symbolic journey of Ivanov's lyric hero through a lifetime of poetic creation, and therefore his participation—and, as will be suggested, Rome's own—in what Ivanov saw as an age-old and crucially important spiritual process. A brief overview of the poet's vision of spiritual creativity, which remained in ways constant throughout his life, is therefore essential to further exploration of the poems.

Ivanov's concept of "reality" lies at the heart of his vision of Symbolism. It may be traced back to the "realism" of medieval philosophy, characterized by Vasily Rudich as "the view of reality as a hierarchy of meanings in which each lower element signifies a higher and, by extension, the highest, the transcendental."[14] Thus, as Ivanov famously explained in his 1910 essay "Zavety simvolizma" (The Testaments of

Symbolism), "The artist must . . . harmoniously discover a correlation between what art depicts as outer reality (*realia*) and what it intuits in the outer as the inner and higher reality (*realiora*)."[15]

For Ivanov, then, culture and revelation are synonymous. The artist in his creativity surrenders himself to an ecstatic state that Ivanov links to the rites of Dionysus. In his abandon, he becomes aware of a reality that transcends the "prison of the self," as Dmitrii Ivanov writes, characterizing this phenomenon further as "the death of oneself, the initial impulse of every authentic religious experience."[16] In keeping with Dionysian self-extinction and resurrection and with the Christian narrative that in Ivanov's view represents this process's ultimate fulfillment, the artist's death of self results in new life. Reborn into a recollected awareness of the original, forgotten unity of God and humanity, he descends from the heights of this "truth" to embody it in artistic, Apollonian forms that will be both accessible and recognizable to his audience.[17] For the poet "teaches [his audience] to remember," as Ivanov claimed in his 1944 "Rimskii dnevnik" (Roman Diary).[18] And the art he creates, motivated by and in turn inspiring memory, thus carries within itself the ability to call participants to potential spiritual renewal, suggesting the possibility of a positive transformation of the world around them. As Ivanov explained to Mikhail Gershenzon in their celebrated "Perepiska iz dvukh uglov" (Correspondence from Two Corners), written in 1920 in a Moscow sanatorium room shared serendipitously by the two men, "Culture itself, in its proper sense, is not at all a flat horizontal surface, not a plain of ruins or a field littered with bones. It holds, besides, something truly sacred: the memory, not only of the earthly, external visage of our fathers, but of the high initiations they achieved. . . . In this sense, culture is not only monuments but spiritual initiation."[19] Sacrificial religion and art come together in this vision, as the poet, taking on the attributes of the perpetually deceased and resurrected god and of his celebrants, functions simultaneously as worshipper and worshipped in his ecstasy, mythmaker, priest, and prophet in his creativity.[20]

In the context of Russian Symbolism and the "life-creation" it espoused, Ivanov's view of the poet as mythmaker took on personal as well as artistic significance. Like many of his Symbolist colleagues, Ivanov cast his own life in mythological terms, viewing his personal experiences as examples of the process of death and renewal relevant to the creation of his literary texts. Most significant in Ivanov's personal mythology was his relationship with Zinov'eva-Annibal, complete with her death and then the resurrection of their mutual commitment—a new, creative life—through his marriage to her daughter and then the birth of their son. As Pamela Davidson explains, the relationship between Ivanov and Zinov'eva-Annibal "developed from an initial experience of ecstasy, at first Nietzschean and chaotic in character, but subsequently absorbed into a Christian context through a sense of sacrificial suffering, and eventually sanctified in marriage. The excess of life contained in the original experience of ecstasy resolved itself in death; but this in turn led to a renewal of life through Lidiya Dmitrievna's daughter, Vera, who became Ivanov's third wife."[21]

In his attempts to perpetuate his relationship with Zinov'eva-Annibal beyond the grave, Ivanov was assigning to himself the role of the paradigmatic mythological or epic hero, who descends to the underworld in an attempt to find lost love and to create his future. His poem "Ad Rosam" discusses Orpheus, the poet-musician who travels to the underworld to find his beloved Eurydice, only to lose her again when he turns to look at her while exiting the world of the dead. Like Dionysus and Christ, Orpheus then undergoes a violent death; Ivanov's poem in a sense calls for his resurrection, as it summons a successor to the dismantled artist-hero.[22] Michael Wachtel has discussed Ivanov's own attempts in the years following Zinov'eva-Annibal's death to achieve a reunion with his dead wife, as well as his conviction on various occasions that he had indeed made contact with her (in Ivanov's visions, she spoke to him frequently in foreign languages, particularly Latin and Italian).[23] In mythological terms, he had descended into the underworld and found his lost beloved, emerging from the realm of death to record this journey both in his writings and, through his third marriage, in his life. "No upward step on the ladder of spiritual ascent is possible without a step down on the ladder leading to her subterranean treasures," Ivanov wrote in his "Correspondence." The combined imagery of fire and water that he employs throughout his oeuvre relates to this process, as Ivanov's seeker undergoes Goethe's *Flammentod,* or fiery death, which itself becomes a rebirth: "And death, that is, the personality's rebirth, *is* the liberation desired by man. Cleanse yourself with cold spring water—and be consumed. This is always possible—on any morning of the daily reawakening spirit."[24] The epic hero, of course, must pass through the water that separates the world of the living from the world of the dead before he can once again ascend to life, completing one episode of an endlessly repeating narrative.

Home Is the Hero

... that fair company
Then made me one among them—so as we traveled
Onward toward the light I made a sixth
Amid such store of wisdom.
Dante, *The Inferno,* early fourteenth century (trans. Robert Pinsky)

Ivanov's move to Rome perpetuates his mythologies of art and life, permitting him to draw upon previous paradigms in his arsenal and pointing the way to their future development. His declaration on the eve of his 1924 departure from Russia that he was "going to Rome to die"[25] marks the beginning of a newly reenacted process of death and resurrection that in its identification with and links to Rome ties Ivanov to a series of epic heroes who share aspects of his journey as seeker and creator. Most important among these figures is Virgil's Aeneas, a fellow fugitive to Rome. Aeneas was not a new figure of identification for Ivanov. For instance, in the poem "Kumy" (Cumae), which appeared in his first collection, *Kormchie zvezdy* (Lodestars, 1903), Ivanov had situated the poem's speaker, identified with a first-person dative reference ("mne," to me), in the realm of ancient Greco-Roman prophecy featured in the *Aeneid.* Ivanov referred to Aeneas's father, Anchises, and suggested through a mention of Hades Aeneas's trip, aided by the Cumaean Sibyl, to visit Anchises in the underworld.[26] In the "Roman Sonnets," the connection between Ivanov and Aeneas is developed more explicitly, in keeping with the circumstances of Ivanov's emigration from a Russia torn by strife, like Aeneas's native Troy, at the end of the Trojan War. Indeed, upon his arrival in Rome Ivanov cited the first book of the *Aeneid,* comparing the friends left behind in turbulent Russia to a Virgilian "handful of swimmers in the bottomless deep" and noting that he and his family, by contrast, had found refuge from the storm.[27] Once again, Ivanov had followed Aeneas, emerging from the water to be born anew into a world of creative productivity.

Ivanov's links to Aeneas are brought out from the beginning of sonnet I, which sets up the framework of the poet's journey through the city, and then are perpetuated through further references in sonnet II. In keeping with Aeneas's story and his own prior experiences, Ivanov presents himself both as a newly arrived refugee and as a homecomer destined to inhabit Rome. The first poem of the cycle is titled "Regina

Viarum" (Queen of the Ways)—a reference both to Rome itself ("All roads lead to Rome") and to the Appian Way, the ancient road into Rome traditionally known by that title.[28] Underlining his sonnets' Trojan resonance, Ivanov explains in a note to the first sonnet that in the ancient world, Rome was known as a "new Troy."[29] He refers to Rome as a "skitanii pristan'" (refuge from wanderings), and he invests his arrival with religious significance, calling himself a "vernyi piligrim" (faithful pilgrim) to the city. He ends the initial stanza with an affirmation of the city as "vechnyi Rim" (eternal Rome).

In the sonnet's second quatrain, this perpetuity is juxtaposed with the transitory quality of the world Ivanov is fleeing, as both Troy and Russia become actors in the text. "We are throwing the Troy of our fathers into the flames," he claims. "Tsar of the roads, you see how we burn." Replacing the title's "Regina" with the Russian "Tsar'" brings out the Russian subtext to the Trojan reference, as does the first-person plural pronoun Ivanov chooses for his pronouncement.[30] In a departure from the story of the Trojan War, in which the Greeks laid waste to an enemy society, he suggests that the Russians, unlike the Trojans, have committed themselves to the flames. The flame imagery associated with both Russia and Troy brings to mind Ivanov's assertion, voiced in his "Lettre à Charles Du Bos" (Letter to Charles Du Bos, 1930) and evocative once again of Aeneas's tale, that in fleeing Russia he had left "the fire devouring the sanctuaries of my ancestors."[31]

And yet, Ivanov suggests in the two tercets that follow, this death in flames gives hope for renewal. Regardless of the source of Troy's woes, it succumbed to flames and then, miraculously, "rose from the ashes." "Troy grew stronger," he claims in the sonnet's final lines, "When Troy lay in flames." In other words, the human vestiges of Troy, led by Aeneas, went on to found an even mightier kingdom, that of Rome. Death, then, in keeping with Ivanov's master narrative, makes future life possible: after all, inherent in the word "gorim" (we are burning), is its opposite—"Rim" (Rome)—symbolic of continuity, but dependent on its periodic phoenixlike resurrections. And this process is thus applicable both to individuals—epic heroes such as Aeneas and his twentieth-century counterpart Ivanov—and to nations, as Troy's glorious rebirth as Rome attests. The crucial role of memory in this resurrection is brought out in the poem's final stanza through the words "pamiatlivaia" (retentive), which characterizes the blue of the Roman skies, and "pomnit" (remembers), linked to the cypress tree that observes Rome's resurrection.[32] As Ivanov will demonstrate in the cycle's subsequent sonnets, the art that fills Rome bears witness, like the cypress tree, to the city's lengthy creative history, as earlier generations inspire meaningful creativity in generations to come.

Of course the *Aeneid* is dominated by Aeneas's quest to found Rome: this mission underlies his flight from Troy and justifies his decisions throughout the narrative. Despite his alien origins, Aeneas belongs in Rome and is fated to be there.[33] In a further parallel to Aeneas, the Russian Ivanov, too, asserts his ownership of the city to which he comes as a pilgrim. In the third line of poem I, he welcomes the city, addressed with the familiar "tebia" (you), as his own home. His repeated visits to the city are brought out in the cycle's initial word ("vnov'" [again]), a theme that will be echoed in sonnet VIII, in which the poet refers to the custom of throwing coins into the Trevi Fountain as a hopeful pledge of returning to the city.[34] In sonnet VIII, Ivanov affirms that the vows have been carried out: the fountain has returned the fortunate pilgrim to his holy places. New personal sanctuaries have risen from the ashes of the old. The exiled poet's journey is elevated in sonnet VIII, as in sonnet I, by a preponderance of archaic pronunciations and high-style words ("reve" [roar], here rhymed with "Trevi" in the first stanza, the "vodometov" [fountains] of line 4),[35] and yet at the same time personalized, humanized, through an imperative-form address in line 3 in the second-person singular—the only imperative addressed, apparently, to an individual in the cycle. Through such personal references and repetitions in the early and later stages of the cycle, Ivanov reminds the reader that Rome is a place to which he has paid homage throughout his life: a place where he, like his fellow traveler Aeneas, has roots and connections—a resurrected home.

The Trojan theme, with its various resonances, continues in the second sonnet, devoted to the myths surrounding the semidivine Dioscuri, the "horse-tamers" Castor and Pollux, brothers of Helen of Troy. Helen, the beautiful wife of the Greek warrior Menelaus, was abducted by the Trojan Paris in the act that initiated the Trojan War. In this sonnet, titled "Monte Cavallo" in reference to the hill on which two statues of the Dioscuri are found, Ivanov refers to the legendary role played by the brothers in the battle of Lake Regillus in 496 BCE, specifically mentioned in the second note he appended to the poems. In this battle between the Romans and Latins, the long-dead Castor and Pollux are said to have intervened on the side of the Roman *quirites* (citizens). They then announced to the Romans that the battle was won. In gratitude, the Roman citizens established a cult to honor them. The Roman citizens, who have received help, are thus paralleled with the poet's lyric "I," whose prayers to return to Rome are answered in sonnet VIII by the waters of the Trevi Fountain. Like the Romans', Ivanov's presence in Rome, or his participation in Rome's story, has been sanctioned by the sacred forces of ancient popular legend.

The mention in line 6 of sonnet II of Castor and Pollux's stop "u Iuturnskoi vlagi" (by Juturna's pool), where they lead their horses to drink before announcing their victory, signals a further Virgilian reference. In the *Aeneid,* Juturna is sister and helpmeet to Turnus, the champion of the Latins. At the end of the epic, a merciless Aeneas, filled with a rage far removed from his usual *pietas,* defeats Turnus in a struggle for the hand of the Latin princess Lavinia and the kingdom of her father, Latinus. With Turnus's defeat, Roman stock will take root in the destined union of Aeneas and Lavinia, as the exiled invader and the invaded are, in Virgil's telling, unified as intended by the will of the gods. It is important for Virgil, writing under Rome's first emperor, Augustus, in the first century BCE, to assert this idea of specifically predestined unity between Romans and Italians: literature and divine sanction thus justify future imperialism.[36] The well-known Roman mandate is proclaimed by Anchises to his son in the kingdom of the dead:

. . . remember by your strength to rule
Earth's peoples—for your arts are to be these:
To pacify, to impose the rule of law,
To spare the conquered, battle down the proud.[37]

Virgil purports in his epic to return to supernaturally inspired commandments in order to bring them to pass—through his writing—in his nation.

Virgil's significance to Ivanov lies precisely in the Roman poet's assertion of a predestined, nationally based, and divinely sanctioned universalism. In a 1931 article devoted to Virgil's philosophy of history, Ivanov argued that through his use of the older gods of Rome and popular legend to ordain Aeneas's mission and, correspondingly, Rome's empire, Virgil had in fact demonstrated the longstanding religious intent inherent in Rome's sway over much of the then-known world.[38] Moreover, as Ivanov had noted somewhat paradoxically in his 1909 essay "O russkoi idee" (On the Russian Idea), the universality of the Roman mission—"remember by your strength to rule / Earth's peoples"—"shows clearly that there was no national egoism in Virgil's words."[39] Rather, Ivanov insisted, Rome's mission as formulated by

Virgil, born in Aeneas's distress and culminating in his far-reaching triumph, had been a religious one,[40] in that it reflected divine guidance and promoted world unity.[41] Thus national self-determination and universalism could be joined into a "harmonious whole," so long as a nation's individual mission was foreordained and sanctioned. The mission would then take on the role of "ecumenical entelechy" as it propelled the nation to fulfill its highest, spiritually unifying potential.[42] This potential would eventually find its ultimate form in Rome's later conversion to a Christianity that would spread over the globe. Linking the pagan Virgil to this Christian future, Ivanov explained that through such works as Virgil's fourth eclogue—ostensibly a laudatory celebration of the first-century BCE consulship of the Roman Gaius Asinius Pollio but later interpreted as a prediction of the coming Christian era—the Roman poet had demonstrated a prophetically Christian sensibility.[43] Virgil, akin to Catullus in Blok's "Catiline," had stood, inspired, on the threshold of a new world, one he sensed and voiced in his art: again, the artist had insights others were denied. Virgil represented a bridge between the pagan past and the Christian future. Ironically, therefore, Ivanov used the pre-Christian Virgil to justify a vision of the Roman Empire as predecessor to a universal Kingdom of God.

Ivanov's treatment of Virgil points to an inherent inconsistency in his reactions to the state power epitomized by the Roman Empire. As Rudich explains, Ivanov echoed St. Augustine in his general mistrust and condemnation of such power. Particularly in his 1916 article "Legion i sobornost'" (Legion and *Sobornost'*), for instance, Ivanov contrasted the legions evocative of imperial might with the spiritually unifying tendencies he sought as Russia's ideal form of self-expression.[44] Nonetheless, in his writings related to Virgil, Ivanov managed in a sense to justify Rome's empire by recasting it in a religious, epiphanic light.[45]

The Virgilian subtext of the "Roman Sonnets" thus provides Ivanov with powerful models of exile, empire-building, and prophesied, complex transfiguration. Like Aeneas, Ivanov leaves a home in ruins; like Aeneas, he finds a new, predestined home in Rome. Aeneas goes on to found the Roman Empire, as prophesied and approved by Anchises and the gods. Ivanov, too, is fated to take part in the formation of a widespread kingdom, but in his case it is a creative kingdom of God, rooted in the unifying nature of Aeneas's mission and then embodied both in Ivanov's Rome-based sonnets and in his life. For when he chose eventually to make St. Peter's Dome the final vision of his cycle, Ivanov was reflecting in part a milestone not only in Rome's history but in his own personal journey as a Russian, a humanist, and a Christian: his choice in 1926 to join the Catholic faith. In Ivanov's eyes, this shift represented a unification within himself of Russian Orthodoxy and Catholicism, rather than a rejection of the former for the latter; he thus was taking part in creating an ecumenical construct of faith that others, such as Vladimir Solov'ev, had foretold.[46] Ivanov told Du Bos that his religious conversion came once he recognized that "it was high time to hasten my steps in order to arrive at the end of that long road that I had been following at first unconsciously (this was the time in my life when my faith began to reaffirm itself bit by bit on the debris of my pagan humanism)."[47] Ivanov implied that he was moving from the classics to a new understanding of Christ in life; as a Symbolist, he embodied these stages simultaneously in his art. Fedor Stepun later wrote that Ivanov's "Roman Sonnets" reflected the poet's journey from his youthful, "Dionysian" meetings with Zinov'eva-Annibal in the Coliseum in the 1890s to his eventual, more peaceful Christian conversion experience decades later.[48] In his Rome-based poetry, with its Christian elements, Ivanov was presaging later developments and in so doing was following in the prophetic footsteps he assigned to the "proto-Christian" Virgil.

Through the structure of his text—its rich inclusion of both Aeneas and himself—and through its Rome-based vision of Christian ascendance, Ivanov calls to mind other literary models. Both Augustine and Dante moved through Virgil to Christianity via Rome and wrote of this experience. While neither is mentioned explicitly in the "Roman Sonnets," their enduring importance to Ivanov has been documented, as has his tendency to respond to other thinkers in his work. Thus the similarities between the journeys described in their works and Ivanov's own path in the sonnets deserve attention.[49] Both writers become further "forefathers" upon whom Ivanov relies as he constructs his own literary call for holy unity, even as their literary alter egos provide him with more epic heroes with whom to identify.

The Ivanov family left Russia for Italy in August of 1924 on St. Augustine's Day, a day that Ivanov, according to his daughter Lidiia, always considered significant.[50] Ivanov had echoed the author of the *City of God* when he titled a portion of his 1915 work *Chelovek* (Man) "Dva grada" (Two Cities), and in "Legion and *Sobornost'*" he had referred quite clearly to Augustine's opus, characterizing the "City of Man" as the result of the love of self to the exclusion of God, and the "City of God" as the result of the love of God to the exclusion of self.[51] In the years immediately following his emigration, Ivanov turned to

Augustine repeatedly, on separate occasions in 1925 and 1928 naming the fourth-century priest the thinker closest to his spirit[52] and writing of *City of God* as his favorite book.[53] Given the autobiographical thrust of Ivanov's own work, it is understandable that he would have been drawn as well to Augustine's *Confessions*—a book that did in fact form part of his library—in which the future saint movingly described his intellectual and emotional passage through the culture of the pagan classical world to the faith of Christianity.[54] For Augustine's *Confessions* may be read in a sense as an anti-*Aeneid*. Like Aeneas, who stops on his way to Italy in the Carthage ruled by his lover-to-be Dido, Augustine, a native of North Africa, spends time in Carthage before moving on to Rome. Again like Aeneas, early in his tale Augustine is involved in a physical relationship that precedes—and impedes—his greater mission. In fact, Augustine refers explicitly to the *Aeneid,* writing of the relationship between Aeneas and Dido and noting to his discredit the tears he shed over Dido's fate while neglecting his own soul. "These were the stages of my pitiful fall into the depths of hell," Augustine would later recall, adding that God had redeemed him from "the depths of this darkness," his "spiritual death."[55] And like Aeneas, who is the son of the goddess Venus, Augustine is blessed with a mother possessed of divine insights and determined to see her son succeed in accordance with God's plans.[56] Aeneas, of course, goes on to found Rome, while Augustine moves beyond Rome literally and figuratively, meeting St. Ambrose in Milan and explicitly rejecting Virgil's paganism when he converts to Christianity. And yet Augustine then returns to North Africa, in a sense integrating his past with his present and future. There he would become a priest of the Rome-based Church. More importantly, in writing about his past he would use Virgil as a literary model.[57]

Dante, meanwhile, was of enormous importance to various Russian Symbolists, but as Davidson writes, Ivanov's approach to the Italian writer differed from that of his contemporaries: "first, it was based on a much closer knowledge of Dante's works and deeper understanding of his ideas; and second, Ivanov turned to Dante for guidance in the context of his own spiritual outlook on a much more profound level than the other Symbolists did."[58] Ivanov translated portions of Dante's works, including the *Divine Comedy,* into Russian, and at the University of Baku he taught Italian using Dante's *Vita nuova* as his textbook.[59] He also employed Dantean images and themes throughout his own oeuvre, finding inspiration in Dante's thought, and particularly in Dante's love-inspired search for unity with the divine.[60] This inspiration is evident in the "Roman Sonnets."

Like Augustine's text and Ivanov's, Dante's *Divine Comedy* describes the "path of our life," as the first line of his work characterizes it, as the poet inserts himself into his text as an example and then chooses Virgil as his guide.[61] Dante-the-character professes his admiration for and identification with Virgil, describing Virgil as his "Master" and telling him, "You are my guide and author, whose verses teach / The graceful style whose model has done me honor."[62] In fact, from one perspective Virgil has created Dante-the-author by inspiring his verse—verse that then features Dante-the-character, who proclaims his own author's allegiance to Virgil. While both Dante-the-author and his lyric hero rely on Virgil until Paradise nears, Dante-the-author dismisses Virgil at that crucial point, asserting that Virgil as a pre-Christian cannot partake of the Christian God's heavenly salvation. Indeed, by recreating Virgil as a character in his own text, Dante in a sense diminishes him even as he relies upon and lauds him. Dante thus asserts his own power, as both author and Christian, over the Roman poet.

Nonetheless, Virgil, and particularly his vision of Rome, remain essential to Dante, who accepts the glorified Rome that Virgil presents and then, somewhat as Ivanov does, takes it one crucial step further. Rome for Dante becomes the empire that was "later established Holy, / Seat of great Peter's heir."[63] The Roman Empire, in other words, paved the way for the Church that has replaced it. Thus Dante-the-author can place in the depths of hell Brutus and Cassius, murderers of Julius Caesar, who was adoptive father of Rome's first emperor, Augustus. Both men are in Giudecca, the region of hell Dante names for Judas, the betrayer of Christ. Aeneas, meanwhile, is linked to St. Paul, as they both, according to Dante, descended into Hell and then ascended to the world of the living. As in the Christian interpretation of the Pentateuch, the classical world in this model constitutes a text that can be read as "prefiguring" the Christian era. Dante, of course, will echo Aeneas and Paul in his own text, after which he will move on to the mountain of the Lord and then return to write of what he has seen.

Thus both Augustine and Dante undergo experiences that involve figurative descents into hell and ascents to heaven, a combination of pagan humanism and Christianity, an increased knowledge of God, and an awareness of Rome's complex role in this process. And each author writes himself into his text, thereby asserting a similarity or equivalency with those who have gone before, such as Aeneas and Saint

Paul. In the "Roman Sonnets," Ivanov follows in the footsteps of Augustine and Dante, styling himself a successor to Aeneas, finishing his journey on a mountaintop overlooking God's dome, and perpetuating the self-referential quality of the cycle's first stanza through a series of first-person references that continue throughout the text. In sonnets IV, V, VI, VIII, and IX, for instance, he employs a first-person singular verb; sonnet VII, meanwhile, contains the first-person plural "nas" (us). Through such personal references Ivanov underlines his active participation in the story that is Rome: he welcomes, loves, rejoices, catches echoes of the past, and drinks in the Roman sunset. In keeping with the shift of his predecessors' allegiances from the earthly to the heavenly, the image of ascent, physical and spiritual, dominates the cycle. In sonnet III, the water of the Acqua Felice aqueduct splashes into sarcophaguslike depths and then shoots up into the sky like a column. The rising water is echoed in sonnet IV's soaring Spanish Steps, which, as Ivanov describes in the second stanza of this poem, split into two as they mount the hill to the Trinità dei Monti Church (fig. 12). The final image of this stanza is the obelisk, surrounded by two towers set off against

Trinità de' Monti. (Chap. XVII, No. 344.)

Fig. 12. View of Trinità dei Monti Church and the Spanish Steps ascending from the Barcaccia Fountain, Rome (from P. J. Chandlery, *Pilgrim-Walks in Rome*, 1908)

the blue sky, that dominates the Piazza di Spagna. In sonnet V, devoted to the fountain known as "Il Tritone," the ancient sea demon Triton blows into a conch shell, out of which spurts a stream of water, which in turn once again pierces the blue sky. The blueness of the Roman sky, noted throughout the cycle, will turn to gold at day's end in sonnet IX, while St. Peter's Dome will take on its blueness in the evening light. Nature and art, ancient sea demon and church of Christ are connected in a swirl of colors, sounds, and images, as Ivanov shows himself to have been reborn, resurrected, in the "cold spring water" of the fountains of Rome.

And yet the unabashed syncretism of Ivanov's imagery sets him somewhat apart from both Augustine and Dante, who despite their textual and mythological dependency must reject the pagan Virgil in accepting Christ fully. While Ivanov did wonder in his 1927 poem "Palinodiia" (Palinode) whether he had ceased to love Hellas,[64] following this poem with his words to Du Bos regarding the "debris of [his] pagan humanism," his conversion did not in fact signal an end to his devotion to the humanistic, classical tradition. Nor did Ivanov's conversion mark a completely new allegiance to Christianity on his part, though clearly his particular turn to the Catholic Church represents both a significant new departure and an intensification within an ongoing Christian context.[65] With the exception of a brief spell of atheism in his teens, Ivanov had never moved far from Christian faith, instilled in him by his highly devout Russian Orthodox mother, though he had immersed himself for a time in Nietzscheanism and searched, as Merezhkovskii did, for a Christianity revitalized by Hellenism.[66] Ivanov's oeuvre may be seen rather as an ongoing effort to merge the classical-humanistic and Christian traditions. As Davidson writes, "To this day his work provides the most important model in the Russian tradition of an artist who sought to integrate religion and culture, both in theory and in practice, rather than regarding them as distinct or conflicting forces."[67] Christ joins with epic heroes and their authors to inspire Ivanov in his creative quest.

The religious significance with which Ivanov invested culture meant once again that in his view Christianity was a sacred extension of the classical world, rather than a replacement of it, just as Dionysus was a precursor of Christ, and, in the context of the art portrayed in the sonnets, the spiritual was an extension of the material. This is why the *pax romana* could herald a greater, Christian peace. And this is why, in sonnet IV, a fountain in the shape of a half-drowned boat can give way within several lines to a church. The earthly can become spiritual, particularly when baptized in water; art leads to initiation.[68] Thus the pagan half-men, half-gods featured in the sonnets, from the semidivine Aeneas to the Dioscuri, prepare the way for the Godman Christ celebrated in the cycle's final sonnet, even as this repeated combination of human and divine reminds the reader of their ultimate, ideal unity. And Ivanov, immersed poetically and repeatedly in Rome's fountains and blue sky, follows in their footsteps, reborn and ascending "on any morning of the daily reawakening spirit." Augustine-the-character weeps for Dido, but Augustine-the-author condemns his tears. Dante-the-character despairs when Virgil cannot join him in Paradise, while Dante-the-author enforces this prohibition. For Ivanov the Symbolist, however, art and life are in no such conflict. Accepting the past and looking toward the future, he celebrates the creative potentiality of both, incorporating classical humanism and Christianity freely into his sonnets' broad vision of Christian faith. In keeping with Ivanov's Virgilian vision of Rome, worldly power, too, becomes a part of this larger kingdom of faith, as kingdoms of this world are reborn, transformed, through sublimation into the creative text. As further explanation and analysis will suggest, the syncretistic and mythologically focused portrait of Rome that the Russian poet presents in the sonnets both evokes and moves beyond the vision he had held earlier of an ideal Russia as a Third Rome.

The Russian Poet and the Third Rome

For what else is the strength of the Russian national spirit than the aspiration, in its ultimate goal, for universality and all-embracing humanitarianism?

Fedor Dostoevskii, "Pushkin (A Sketch)," in *Diary of a Writer*, 1880 (trans. Boris Brasol)

In a diary entry of 2 December 1924, Ivanov recorded his state of mind as he was writing the sixth sonnet in the cycle: "Wrote 'Fontana delle Tartarughe.' Constant thoughts about our revolution, and about the spread of propaganda, about what tomorrow will hold for Europe."[69] Ivanov's portrayal of one of Rome's most playful fountains, which features a group of boys dancing on dolphins, would appear to have little in common with Russia's revolution, though the poet tempers the joyous mood of the boys' play with a reference to the "melancholies" afflicting

Lorenzo de Medici, the fifteenth-century patron of Michelangelo and Botticelli (whose title "Lorenzo the Magnificent" inspired Ivanov's own sobriquet, "Viacheslav the Magnificent").[70] His entry the following day elaborated upon this theme: "The entire time I've been abroad, I've been maintaining, 'Hannibal *ad portas.*' I mean communism. Everyone said in unison that it wasn't true. Now all of France is crying out fearfully about the communist danger."[71] The Roman-Russian connection thus becomes clear: the communism that had captured Ivanov's own country, and the menace a potential westward spread of communism posed to Europe, were comparable in the poet's mind to the events of the third-century BCE Second Punic War, during which the Carthaginian Hannibal invaded and conquered parts of Italy.[72] Russia had met its own Hannibal, and the battle could now spread to Europe, threatening its centuries-old, spiritually imbued culture.

Such a linkage of Russian and Roman history was not unusual for the cyclically minded Ivanov, who previously had viewed such major events in Russian history as the 1905 Revolution and Russia's involvement in World War I through a Roman prism. In his comments about Hannibal, for instance, Ivanov was harking back to his 1909 essay "On the Russian Idea." Writing in response to events that followed the 1905 Revolution, Ivanov had characterized the Russo-Japanese War as Russia's "First Punic War," a conflict between Russia and a non-Christian "Yellow Asia" that would determine "whether Christ is still alive and vital in Europe."[73] Russia at this time had not lived up to the Christ-bearing role Ivanov assigned to his nation. Divided in spirit, opting "neither to mount the Beast and raise high its scepter, nor to take up wholly the easy yoke of Christ," Russia had battled unsuccessfully "in no one's name."[74]

Despite this failure, however, Ivanov had referred explicitly in this essay to the concept of Russia in its ideal form as a Third Rome. Warning against the nationalism often associated with the concept, he had gone on to assert an image of a Russian Rome in terms characteristic of Merezhkovskii's increasingly Christian vision of Russia in *Christ and Antichrist* and also clearly linked to Dostoevskii, to Virgil, and to Ivanov's own master narrative of descent and resurrection. "The very christening of our universal idea (for 'Rome' is always 'the universe') with the name of the 'Third Rome,' the 'Rome of the Spirit,' reveals to us: 'You, Russian, must remember one thing: universal truth is your truth and if you want to preserve your soul, do not be afraid to lose it.'"[75] Continuing his professions against nationalism and imperialism, Ivanov had described the Russian intelligentsia's "historically unprecedented example of a will to poverty, simplification, self-abnegation, and descent," as well as the general Russian "love of descent"—for him "the distinguishing feature of our national psychology."[76] The Russian soul, he had concluded, expressed the "central content of the Christian idea, the categorical imperative of descent and burial of the Light," and, through its stress on Easter, "the categorical postulate of resurrection."[77] Having characterized Dionysus in an earlier essay as "our barbarian, our Slavic god,"[78] Ivanov linked Russia's Christian character with its Dionysian roots, finding in the dissolution of self he associated with Dionysus a central feature of the Russian character. "Our most attractive and noble aspirations are sealed with a craving for self-destruction, as if we were secretly bound to the inescapable charms of a peculiar Dionysus . . . , as if other peoples were deadly selfish, whereas we, a nation of self-immolators, represented the vital principle in life, which Goethe saw as the butterfly Psyche who yearned for a fiery death."[79] Ivanov's rhetoric of national death followed by universal resurrection presages his portrayal of Troy/Rome's fiery, phoenix-like death and rebirth in the "Roman Sonnets," further linking Russia and Rome.

Thus Russia's talent for loss of self, for descent, would culminate in its resurrection, as Russians in losing their own identities would follow in Rome's footsteps to be reborn into a glorious, holy universality. The loss of boundaries and the overall unity associated with this process embodied what Ivanov termed in a Russian context *sobornost'*, defined by his associate Olga Deschartes as "the principle of unity in the City of God; it unifies the living with the living and the living with the dead, it springs from the *Memoria Aeterna* and creates the *Communio Sanctorum*."[80] *Sobornost'* "must surmount spiritual entropy and alienation," Tomas Venclova explains.[81] *Sobornost'*, then, can be identified with Ivanov's vision of an ideal Russia, a self-sacrificing, descending and ascending Third Rome that unifies time and space and negates the barriers of nationalism and individualism.[82] In the same essay, after quoting Anchises' words to Aeneas about Rome's destiny (in terms he would echo in his 1931 essay on Virgil), Ivanov noted "the providential will and idea of imperial Rome, which was becoming the world."[83] He added that the *pax romana* had been "developed through a complex process of collective mythopoesis: they needed both the legend of the Trojan Aeneas and the Hellenic and oriental Sibylline prophesying in order gradually to strengthen the vital sense of Rome's universal role."[84] The creation of religious unity, therefore, was in essence an artistic act, one in line with

Ivanov's concept of the poet's holy creativity and here associated with national destiny, be it that of Rome or, in Ivanov's case, Russia.

For it was now Russia's turn to assume this "Roman," unifying role in the world, Ivanov had insisted in 1909: "Mystics of East and West alike are agreed that Slavdom, and particularly Russia, is being handed a certain torch precisely at this moment; whether our nation carries it high or lets it fall is a question of world destiny. If our nation . . . carries [the torch] aloft, it will benefit the entire world."[85] Russia could follow Virgil's and Aeneas's paths in the recognition and creation of holy unity.

At the time of Russia's entrance into World War I, Ivanov once again proclaimed his faith in that country's fated mission as witness to Christ. Again, he couched this conception in terms of Rome, this time focusing upon Rome's Eastern, Christian successor, Constantinople. As Ben Hellman notes, Ivanov came to construe the entire war as a struggle for "Tsar'grad" between two adversaries: Germany, associated in Ivanov's mind—perhaps because of its alliance with the Moslem Turks—with the non-Christian East and thus with the Mongols, and Orthodox Russia, by implication heir to Byzantium and its specifically Christian Eastern heritage.[86] In his 1916 poem "Budi, budi" (So Be It, So Be It), for instance, he proclaimed, "Rus', in Constantinople's purple / Robed . . . / Do not serve the prince of this world!"[87] And in poems such as "Chasha Sviatoi Sofii" (The Chalice of Holy Sophia, 1915), and essays including "Pol'skii messianizm kak zhivaia sila" (Polish Messianism as a Living Force, 1916) and "Dukhovnyi lik slavianstva" (The Spiritual Face of Slavdom, 1917), he called for the "liberation" of Constantinople from Turkish, Moslem rule, insisting that the city should return to Christianity and become the capital of a united, Christian Slavic community that would then speak its holy "word" to the rest of the world.[88] Thus, as in 1905, the Russians had an important task before them during World War I: the fervent affirmation of a Christianity under threat from the non-Christian "East," with its paradoxical associations in this case with both Islam and Germany. "I believe this war to be holy in its inner essence and a war of liberation, and I regard it as something very positive," Ivanov wrote in a 1914 letter.[89]

When the February Revolution of 1917 occurred, Ivanov rejoiced, convinced that the time had now come for Russia to fulfill its Christian mission to the rest of the world. Poems such as "Gimn" (Hymn, April 1917) proclaimed, "Peace on earth! Freedom in holy Russia!"[90] As the months passed, however, Ivanov became concerned that Kerenskii's government was insufficiently religious, a failing to which he would attribute the Bolsheviks' success in November.[91] Horrified by the Soviets' overt rejection of Christianity, which he excoriated particularly in a series of poems written between 1917 and 1918, Ivanov exhorted Russians to remember their faith in God, the only force that could resurrect their nation.[92] In his 1918 poem "Lazar'" (Lazarus), for instance, he called for the rebirth of Russia in Christ, akin to Lazarus's own resurrection—a rebirth that would come with the defeat of the Bolshevik regime.[93] Ivanov's stress in his wartime works on Constantinople as the head of a Christian, Slavic entity, bolstered by his continuing emphasis throughout the revolutionary period on Russia's need to be a sanctifying, universalizing force, echoes his earlier vision of Russia as a Third Rome—though beyond his somewhat myopic pronouncements during the First World War, he never provided any details on how this desired vision was to be realized.

In the difficult years following the revolution, Ivanov's opposition to the atheistic Soviet regime deepened, and throughout the 1920s and 1930s, when he wrote and then published his "Roman Sonnets," he became increasingly disillusioned over Russia's contemporary state and its current ability as a nation to achieve the goals he had envisioned for it. As he was writing his "Roman Sonnets," he acknowledged in his diary the dangerous appeal of communism for those unable to withstand its seductive but misleading qualities: "Communism . . . can be a surrogate for faith, and answers the question about the meaning of life in terms that are nearly cosmic."[94] Communism, therefore, was the opposite of Russia in its ideal form—Russia as a universal and unifying Rome. It had created an imperial collective supported by legions, rather than the free, prophesied Kingdom of God Ivanov had envisaged. As he wrote to Du Bos in 1930, the Bolsheviks, with their opposition to Christianity, had posed the question, "Are you with us or with God?"[95] Ivanov explained that he had realized in the period following his emigration that "the Boat of the Fisherman was the only bulwark against the flood that had submerged my native country and threatened to swallow up all of Christendom."[96] His gradual embrace of Catholicism upon his emigration may be viewed in this light.

Ivanov's sonnets reflect his complex and evolving views during this period of Rome and its links to Russia.[97] He had not in fact renounced his ideal vision of Russians as universal: he reaffirmed the concept in a 1935 letter, referring to Dostoevskii's belief that "a truly Russian person is above all a 'universal person' [*vsechelovek*]." "You mourn the 'destruction of Russian culture,'" he wrote, "but it is not destroyed, but rather called to new accomplishments, to a new spiritual consciousness."[98] Indeed, it was in this "universalizing" context that he explicated his own move to Catholicism,[99] telling Du Bos in 1930 that with the conversion he had fulfilled his own "duty" and, as far as he could, "that of [his] nation."[100] In addition, he republished "On the Russian Idea" in German translation in 1930, with revisions but few substantive changes to the essay's major ideas.[101] But a move from Russia to Rome, both physical and metaphorical, had taken place, as Ivanov journeyed along the path marked by his predecessors and sought in the Catholic Church the unity he desired. His sonnets paradoxically reflect both his consistency—his continued, nonnationalistic vision of an all-embracing Russian character, and his individual commitment to revive and fulfill it—and his long journey from East to West, to the "bulwark" provided by Roman Catholicism and the "first" Rome.

In his 1907 essay "O veselom remesle i umnom veselii" (On the Joyful Craft and the Joy of the Spirit), in terms he would reuse in a 1917 essay, Ivanov had, as noted, linked Russia and Dionysus. He had then gone on to characterize both as "barbarian," in contrast with the "formal harmony" of Apollo and the West. "The old tale of Helen's abduction by her uncivilized lovers is repeated eternally: eternally the barbarian Faust falls in love with the Beautiful One, eternally Chaos seeks harmony and an image, and the Scythian Anacharsis travels to Hellas for the wisdom of form and measure."[102] Russia the "barbarian," therefore, was comparable to the Scythians and to Paris, the Trojan who had spirited Helen away from her Greek husband. Paris's compatriot Aeneas, to continue the thread of the argument, was thus a barbarian as well, again comparable to the Russians. The "oriental Sibylline prophesying" to which this barbarian had been privy as he moved from East to "civilized," Apollonian West had led to world unity when sung by the poet Virgil. Twenty-three years after "On the Joyful Craft and the Joy of the Spirit," Ivanov wrote to Du Bos that with his emigration he had left the provenance of "Sibylline prophecies" and ended his difficult journeys.[103] Once in Rome, Ivanov the Russian "barbarian" had proceeded to become Virgil, recording the universalizing prophecies of his native land through formal, Western, Apollonian poetic structure.[104]

In the formal and thematic unity they demonstrate—"for 'Rome' is always 'the universe'"—his "Roman Sonnets" embody the unifying Slavic "word" Ivanov had once proclaimed. The poems reflect *sobornost'*, and the world of the sonnets is one in which a series of Russian "words" melds with other cultures, time periods, and individuals, and with Rome in various guises. While the cycle is clearly focused on the city of Rome, it is also grounded in the specifics of Russian culture and the Russian poetic tradition through specific allusions and word choices. Ivanov thus makes a place for Russian culture within the world of Rome, as creative colleagues such as Gogol' and the painter Ivanov join him in a journey to the "Eternal City."[105] In Ivanov's text, Russia becomes associated yet again with the universality and unifying tendencies that Rome represents throughout the cycle. The phoenix-like resurrection ascribed in Ivanov's first sonnet to Troy becomes in that sense potentially applicable to Russia—though this rebirth occurs not on the national level, but within an individual artistic text. Out of the chaos of loss, new, unified life is created through the holy and memorializing act of art. Ivanov's country was unable at this point to fulfill its Christian, artistic task, but that task had been shouldered by the Russian poet, now newly grounded in the "first" Rome, and yet faithful through his art and life to his role as voice of what he still believed should be the Russian national idea.[106]

Sobornost' in the Sonnets

So said the ready-voiced daughters of great Zeus, and they plucked and gave me a rod, a shoot of sturdy laurel, a marvellous thing, and breathed into me a divine voice to celebrate things that shall be and things there were aforetime.
Hesiod, *The Theogony*, ca. 700 BCE (trans. Hugh G. Evelyn-White)

Ivanov's choice of the Petrarchan sonnet for his tribute to Rome was a fitting one, both because the form originated in Italy, and because of his long-term mastery of the sonnet form, which he had used repeatedly throughout his poetic life and considered to have a particularly "didactic, philosophical" nature.[107] Although he had told Gershenzon in their "Correspondence" that the world around them was "disjointed and scattered,"[108] he countered that disunity in the sonnets by painting through words and images a religiously inspired cultural domain that spans genres, cultures, and centuries.[109] More specifically, the sonnets encapsulate Rome in all its stages and ramifications as viewed by a Russian poet: ancient, Renaissance, Catholic, modern, and, through the links Ivanov establishes between Rome and Russia throughout the text, Russian. Time periods come together into one simultaneously apprehended poetic space. Emblematic of this space and of Ivanov's message of culturally inspired, holy unity is Rome, the City of Man resurrected into an artistic City of God.

In lines 2 and 3 of sonnet I, Ivanov's lyric hero greets Rome with a Latin salutation: "Ave Roma." The introduction of the Latin alphabet into an otherwise Cyrillic text semantically links Russia to the Western world, thus echoing the poet's own journey from Russia to Rome. This union is underlined through the rhyme scheme of both quatrains, throughout which the morphemes *rim* ("Rome" in Russian) and *roma* ("Rome" in Italian) are repeated. Alexis Klimoff notes that such repetitions emphasize "the pilgrim's prayerful attitude" toward the city, adding, "Repeated invocation of the object of worship is, after all, the central feature of all liturgical language."[110] The repeated rhyming of a Russian and an Italian Rome also serves to link the two, underlining the connection between Troy and Russia that is made explicit in these two quatrains. The final line of the second quatrain, with its reference to the "Tsar of the roads," linguistically links the two "Romes" further. Along with space, various times also merge, as words connoting temporality—"drevnikh" (ancient), "pozdnii" (late), "vechernii" (evening)—are juxtaposed with "vechnyi" (eternal) Rome. This melding of time periods, or indeed disregard of expected order, is reflected in Ivanov's rhythms, as in line 10, with its unusual three skipped stresses ("I pamiatlivaia golubizna" [and the retentive blueness]). Concepts synaesthetically take on color, with blue linked to memory and gold linked to the caress of a dream, as the senses, too, merge in this first sonnet.[111]

Sonnet II continues the Trojan focus, recalling the first sonnet's linkage of Ivanov and Aeneas. It combines the Greek mythological tales of the Dioscuri with the ancient Roman statuary that has commemorated them. Ivanov uses the plural form of the rare Germanic loan-word *saga* to characterize the tales of the brothers' miraculous postdeath appearance at Juturna's Pool, as cultures, popular memory, and time periods come together in the context of divine epiphany. Republican Rome takes center stage in Ivanov's text and then merges with the modern world the poet inhabits, as in the poem's final tercet he explicitly asserts the statues' contemporary location on the Quirinal Hill, one of the legendary seven hills of Rome.[112] Through this reference, the poet evokes the legends that in sonnet VIII's description of the Trevi Fountain will sanction his own presence in the city. Echoes of earlier Russian poets enter into this sonnet and correspondingly into the multilayered world of Rome through Ivanov's rhymes (the combination of "mira" [world] and "kumira" [idol] used by Pushkin in part II of his *Mednyi vsadnik*

[Bronze Horseman, 1837]), and particular word choices ("saga," for instance, recalls Lermontov's use of the word in his 1837 "Kogda volnuetsia zhelteiushchaia niva" [When the Yellow Grainfield Ripples], virtually the only such use in nineteenth-century Russian poetry[113]), as Greek and Roman tales and statues merge with Russian culture to perpetuate the connections already established.

Sonnet III continues the linkage of cultural forms and worlds, as it features literature, music, and architecture, with references to the fifth-century BCE Greek poet Pindar, the play of water in fountains, and sculpted aqueducts. Meanwhile, the title of the sonnet, "l'acqua felice," suggests both the aqueduct of this name, built between 1583 and 1587 in the reign of Pope Sixtus V, and the fountain near Dmitrii Ivanov's school, as chronological periods come together once more and the Russian émigré interacts with Rome.[114] As Ivanov wrote in a note to the sonnets, the aqueduct feeds several of Rome's fountains (their quantity is suggested through the plural "rodnikov schastlivykh" [happy springs]); one is adjacent to the statues of the Dioscuri. In a further link between sonnets II and III, the poet Pindar was known for his poem celebrating Olympic victories, while the Dioscuri participated in the Olympic games. Line 11, with its mention of "morskie bogi" (sea gods), ancient gods of Greco-Roman legend, provides another connection to the preceding sonnet, with its own ancient gods; the fact that a "rezets" (chisel) shapes these gods links Rome's past, along with its former religion, to its art. Meanwhile, Ivanov's combination in line 5 of "kladiaz'" (well) and "sarkofaga" (sarcophagus), one word of Old Church Slavic descent and the other found in both Greek and Latin, again semantically suggests the linkage of Russia and the classical tradition.[115] The final tercet of the sonnet serves, as did the tercets of sonnet II, to bring the reader from Rome's past to the present, as the reader takes in the sleepy, evocatively deserted Renaissance-period halls that listen to the voices of the fountains.

Sonnet IV, "La Barcaccia," is named for the fountain in the shape of a half-sunken boat, said to have been created in memory of the flood of 1598 that brought a capsized boat to this segment of the city, at the foot of the Piazza di Spagna.[116] Ivanov evokes through that location both the Spanish Steps behind the fountain and the Caffè Greco nearby, known to have been frequented by artists, including Gogol', who will appear in the next sonnet.[117] As in previous sonnets of the cycle, Ivanov uses the tercets to establish a connection between Rome's past and its present: in line 9, in his first appearance since sonnet I, the poet uses a first-person verb ("liubliu," I love) to paint himself into the portrayal of the piazza filled with crowds, musicians, palms, and old orange walls. The "brodiachei . . . mandoliny" (strolling mandolin) of the poem's final line adds music to the mix of writers featured or implied in the sonnet and recalls the singing of the poet Pindar (line 1) and the running water (line 14) of sonnet III.

Sonnet V, "Il Tritone," takes its title from the fountain of that name (fig. 13), sculpted by Lorenzo Bernini for Pope Urban VIII in 1632–1637.[118] It is found in the Piazza Barberini, at the end of the Via Sistina. Gogol' lived at 126 Via Sistina from 1838 until 1842 (a plaque identifies the building as the location of the composition of his *Dead Souls*),[119] and the Ivanovs' first Roman apartment in 1924 was located nearby, as Dmitrii Ivanov later recalled. Thus the location of sonnet V follows directly from that of the preceding poem, in keeping with the poet's stroll through the city and with Rome's own chronology, spanning Renaissance popes and modern Russian émigrés. The fountain features several dolphins with their tails extending upward. On top of the tails is a large shell, upon which sits the pre-Greek sea "demon" Triton; Ivanov's use of the high-style "demon" echoes the word's ancient usage as a generalized term for a divinity. As Triton blows into his snail-shaped shell, here identified with the unusual term "ulita," rather than "ulitka," the reader notes once again Ivanov's stress on the interrelationships among various modes of art and the senses: there emerges "ne zychnyi ton" (not a strident note), but a "struia luchom" (stream of light), which pierces the blue sky. The connection between art and nature is brought out further in the second quatrain, in which the Italian heat, which causes the stone slabs of the fountain metaphorically to cry out for the shade of the Italian pines, is juxtaposed with the green moss growing on the Triton. Ivanov renders explicit the theme of the interrelationship of nature and culture in lines 7 and 8, as he notes the similarities between the fanciful qualities of the "starinnyi son" (ancient dream) of Bernini's chisel and of nature's own lines. The dream of this sonnet recalls the sleeping palaces of sonnet III (line 12), as Ivanov's poems once again unite in an intricate artistic and chronological system in which the remnants of the powerful live on as inspirational art.

As in earlier sonnets, Ivanov employs the tercets of sonnet V to inject himself into the poem, here employing "veselius'" (I rejoice) to commend Bernini's work and, further, describing his walks from the Four Fountains to the Pincio, previously visited by Gogol', Aleksandr Ivanov, and the eighteenth-century sculptor and engraver Piranesi. Ivanov

Fig. 13. Il Tritone Fountain, Rome (from Mrs. Charles MacVeagh, *Fountains of Papal Rome*, 1915)

places himself explicitly in the company of earlier Rome-based artists, evoking Dante-the-character's communion with the epic poets of the past in the *Inferno*.[120] The Russian writers and painters thus take their place with the Italian sculptor and engraver, while the mention of Rome's pines suggests further a reference to the composer Ottorino Respighi's "Pines of Rome," a composition with which Ivanov was familiar.[121] All the artists come together in a celebration of both nature and memory: in line 14, Ivanov refers to the Titans, one of whom was Mnemosyne, or Memory, mother of the Muses. Ivanov's rhyme of "Titanov" (Titans) with "Fontanov" (Fountains) underlines the crucial links between the two: the water that perpetually ascends and descends in the fountain suggests the sacred path that results in the remembering of self through recollection of human and divine unity, a recollection then embodied in spiritually inspiring artistic forms. Thus Rome and Russia continue to be linked through their artists, past and present, who perpetuate their holy, eternal assignment of resurrecting the substance of this world into a religiously coherent vision of unity.

Sonnet VI, featuring the fountain of the Tartarughe, presents a visual picture of the present, complete with the poet, joined with the fountain's roots once again in an aristocratic Roman past (fig. 14). The sculpted "otroki" (youths) who dance on the dolphins in the sixteenth-century fountain recall the dancing sea gods Ivanov mentions in sonnet III (lines 10–11). Contrary to his usual practice of introducing a new theme in the tercets, the first tercet of this sixth sonnet continues the themes brought out in the two quatrains: the boys continue, in a happy picture, to gambol. In the final tercet, however, the poet appears once again in the present tense, as he catches the echo of Lorenzo's melancholies and notes the "nege leni i privolii" (languor of indolence and expanses) created by the fountain. Ivanov's use of "leni," followed by "privolii," is a clear instance of poetic language evocative of the Pushkin era in Russian poetry. And yet the profusion of plurals in this tercet ("privolii" [expanses], "melankholii" [melancholies]), meanwhile, is a Symbolist-style innovation, as Russian literary language describing Rome reflects once again Ivanov's goal of merging time periods as well as locations.

In sonnet VII, "Valle Giulia," the poet describes the fountain of Asclepius, found near an avenue leading to the Villa Giulia and commemorating the Greek god of healing who, according to legend, brought the dismembered youth Hippolytus back to life in an ancient episode of death and resurrection. In a further Trojan reference, Asclepius was also the

Fig. 14. La Tartarughe Fountain, Rome (from Mrs. Charles MacVeagh, *Fountains of Papal Rome*, 1915)

father of two Trojan heroes.[122] His fountain is located near the Pincio, as the poet's walk through the city continues. The fact that the grounds of the Villa Giulia originally belonged to a prince but were given to the city of Rome in 1902 illuminates the reference in line 2 to the "Bagriantsem nishchim tsarstvennykh otrepii" (the beggarly purple of kingly rags), though Ivanov's combination of "tsarstvennykh" (kingly, with its root "tsar'") with "otrepii" (rags) also suggests the end of tsardom in his native country and continues the theme of empire turned to art. The arch under which Asclepius stands in line 4 recalls the Roman arches first mentioned in Ivanov's greeting to the city in sonnet I, upon his arrival in Rome from Russia, as does the "sinii svod" (dark blue vault) of line 5. Art and nature are associated yet again as he compares the enveloping leaves mentioned in line 7 to a picture frame. Further connections among the sonnets are brought out through the use of "mkhov i skal" (moss and stone) in line 3, which recalls the Triton covered in moss in sonnet V, as well as through the autumnal focus of the poem (the "vodoem osennii" [autumnal reservoir] of line 1; the foliage of line 7), which in conjunction with "beggarly" and "rags" perpetuates the melancholy of the preceding sonnet's conclusion. In a twist from previous sonnets in the cycle, however, Ivanov here broadens the circle of contemporaries in the poems and, instead of a first-person singular verb form, uses here the word "nas" (us), bringing a companion—or, in an ever-widening circle of participants in the world of Rome, the reader—into the picture. The poet and his companion are viewed sadly by the "Blazhennye" (Blessed), an adjectival form used without a noun and without antecedent, whose mood once again peacefully echoes the slight sadness of the preceding lines and sonnet. The "Blazhennye" appear to look at "us" as the sun would look at a withered plane tree, an image of dryness counteracted, though, in the same line, which again introduces the theme of water. The final image of the poem—"Asklepii, klen, i nebo, i fontan" (Asclepius, the maple, and the sky, and the fountain), which appear "oprokinuty" (capsized) in their reflection in the water—recalls La Barcaccia, with its associations of baptismal resurrection, thus joining the Asclepius of the first quatrain with the sonnet's ending and with the cycle's overall vision of death and resurrection.[123]

Sonnet VIII, "Aqua Virgo," derives its name from the aqueduct that feeds the fountain the poem describes: the Trevi, constructed in 1762 under Clement XIII and known as one of Rome's most famous sights.[124] The figure of Neptune, the Roman sea god, is in the middle of the fountain, in a chariot drawn by two sea horses and two tritons (one recalls the triton of sonnet V). The sonnet differs in mood from the two preceding ones, as it is filled with images of ongoing power, brought out from the second word of the poem ("moshchnykh" [mighty]). Ivanov evokes the "rastushchem reve" (the growing roar) of the fountain, advising his unidentified companion through the singular, imperative "idi" (go) to follow its "gul" (rumble), which is significantly more powerful than the palaces near it: art and life-giving water continue to overcome worldly power. The fountain itself is described as the "Tsaritsa vodometov" (the Queen of fountains), an appellation that recalls the "Tsar of the roads" of the initial sonnet as well as the demoted royalty of sonnet VII and thus further links Russia and Rome as sites of vanquished imperialism reborn into art. Ivanov uses the tercets to identify himself as a "beglets nevol'nyi Rima" (an unwilling fugitive from Rome), and then proceeds in the poem's remaining lines to note his earlier dreams of returning to the Eternal City, expressed through coins thrown into the Trevi Fountain, and to give thanks for his return. By resurrecting the self-image of pilgrim first found in sonnet I, and through his reference to his resurrected "holy places," the poet reestablishes the religious framework of the first sonnet and prepares the reader for the concluding sonnet, which ties together the themes of the preceding poems.

The cycle's final sonnet, "Monte Pincio," is named for the hill Ivanov has visited in sonnet V. Standing atop the hill, it is possible to look across the whole of central Rome directly to St. Peter's Dome, evoked as the cycle's last image. Ivanov's lyric hero thus is overlooking the location of the Apostle Peter's martyrdom and, through his sacrifice, Rome's transformation from pagan to Christian.[125] The poet ends his journey at sunset in a thoughtful mood: his spirit is filled with a "pechal'iu bespechal'noi" (griefless grief) as he reflects on the city he now inhabits and its significance. He refers to Day as a "kubok venchal'nyi" (wedding goblet), filled with the honey of resurrected years, and, continuing the wedding imagery, writes that Eternity has given Day a wedding ring. Thus time and events contain an eternality, made possible, as Ivanov has suggested throughout the cycle, by memory. For memory is that unifying force which serves to bring together time periods and people, as well as humankind and the divine, an idea underlined by the nuptial imagery of the sonnet's two quatrains. Forging his own present with the city's rich associations one last time, Ivanov is present from the sonnet's initial word ("P'iu" [I drink]). The trajectory of the sonnet moves from sunset in the quatrains to the sun's "drowning" in a golden "nebesnogo rasplava" (heavenly fusion) atop the pines of Rome in the tercets. The image of the sun's splendor is replaced at that point with St. Peter's Dome, circling in its blueness the gold of the sky. Ivanov's use in his cycle's final image óf two such favorite Symbolist colors as blue and gold, often emblematic of heavenly unity, suggests his faith in St. Peter's as a potential source of such unity. This is in keeping with his views regarding his refuge—not only in Rome, but in Catholicism as a gateway to an all-Christian culture following his departure from Soviet Russia. The cupola of the church echoes the arches found earlier in the cycle, as Rome in all its phases, ancient and modern, republican, imperial, and Catholic, comes together, subsumed into one final image of unity celebrated by the Russian poet.

Ivanov's poems are thus a reminder and embodiment of the individual's reach upward toward unity with God, a unity reflected in the world that art, remembering that unity, can create. This is the spiritual kingdom that Ivanov creates for himself by evoking the mythology of Rome; this is the newly recreated "holy place," infused with an Ivanovian, paradoxically non-nationalistic Russianness, into which he invites the reader. It is a spiritual setting that asserts the unity of humankind and the divine and celebrates the potential for rebirth out of death: in the poems, Ivanov is repeatedly resurrected by the fountains of Rome; Rome itself—and by association, one might suggest, Russia—emerges from ashes; and Asclepius and Christ bring humankind back to life. The world of the sonnets, therefore, is one in keeping with Ivanov's master narrative of life, death, and resurrection, one that echoes the hero's path and asserts his closeness to an all-embracing God. Celebrating the art made possible by Rome's earthly power, Ivanov sublimates this power by placing Rome's artistic glory into a spiritual framework, as the City of God overcomes a City of Man, not through condemnation but through inclusion and holy resurrection in art. The worldly and the spiritual, both facets of Rome, are sanctified in artistic, catholically Roman unity. And Ivanov the Russian poet, having made a home for himself in Western culture, succeeds in giving Apollonian structure to the message of unity he brings along with his own cultural heritage, linked significantly to that of Rome. *Sobornost'* takes form in the sonnets, therefore, as the barriers of space, time, and nationality are overcome through ecphrasis to provide unifying communion with the living and the dead of East and West.

In a discussion of Ivanov's poetry, Mikhail Bakhtin claimed that all the themes of Ivanov's verse may be viewed as participating in one complex system. "His thematic world is as unified, separate moments of his thematics are just as mutually dependent, as in a philosophical tractate. Thanks to such strength of thought, strength of penetration, and strength of erudition, it is impossible to imitate him."[126] Introducing an Italian audience to Ivanov's work in a 1933 article, Faddei Zelinskii shared Bakhtin's awe, noting that when one has evaluated Ivanov as a poet, a philosopher, and a philologist, "all that remains is to marvel."[127] Studying Ivanov's "Roman Sonnets" in the context of other Ivanovian texts provides an example of the "marvelous" erudition and unifying systematization lauded by his contemporaries.

And yet Ivanov's Symbolist construction of the poet as magus to the people and voice of his nation, along with the concept of the union of humankind and divine, would take on new and dangerous life in the Soviet period, as the Soviets appropriated such powerful ideas for decidedly worldly goals. In a reversal of the paradigm celebrated in Ivanov's art, the Kingdom of Man would subsume the spiritual.[128] Rather than being associated with a Russian Third Rome of the spirit, writers would be pressed into service by a new Roman Empire that forced them to mediate, not always successfully, between the spiritual and the imperial, as man and God merged in a manner Ivanov had feared and deplored. Subsequent Russian modernist texts devoted to Rome would explore the complicated dynamic between literature and power, condemning the writer as complicit in the construction of a Roman-style state and yet celebrating him, as ever, as one uniquely equipped to redeem his world through a unifying spirituality.

5

Emperors in Red

The Poet and the Court in Mikhail Kuzmin's *Death of Nero*

So we shall be justified in not admitting [the poet] into a well-ordered commonwealth, because he stimulates and strengthens an element which threatens to undermine the reason.
Plato, *The Republic*, fourth century BCE
(trans. Francis MacDonald Cornford)

Poets are not to blame . . .
Homer, *The Odyssey*, eighth century BCE
(trans. Robert Fitzgerald)

"We, the *humanists*, the freethinking *philosophers* who decry and lament violence, are the most refined oppressors, executioners and tyrants. The state monopoly of thought is the reflection of ourselves: we are the 'gate keepers,' and, oh yes, we are the Bolsheviks," proclaimed Andrei Belyi in 1921.[1] In a subsequent review article, Mikhail Kuzmin rejected Belyi's lamentations,[2] but the professedly apolitical Kuzmin would in the following years create a drama that would effectively echo and explore Belyi's shocking conflation of humanist and tyrant in the new Soviet state. In *Smert' Nerona* (The Death of Nero), conceived following Lenin's death in 1924 but written predominantly from 1928 to 1929,[3] Kuzmin divided his narrative between the tale of Rome's notorious first-century emperor Nero, clearly presented as a precursor to both Lenin and Stalin, and the story of a Russian writer named Pavel Lukin, who is visiting

Rome in 1919 and writing a play about Nero. In keeping with Kuzmin's expressionistic art of the 1920s, the play, characterized by leading Kuzmin scholars John Malmstad and Nikolai Bogomolov as "arguably [Kuzmin's] dramatic masterpiece,"[4] features a series of interlocking themes and motifs that serve to link the two characters' stories, as the action alternates almost scene by scene between emperor and artist at various stages of their lives. Each man moves from early poverty to sudden wealth, which enables him to put into motion utopian dreams of helping a generalized humanity; and then, finally, each arrives at the eventual rejection of utopianism in favor of individual relationships and self-knowledge. Through the parallel tales of Nero and Pavel, whose active idealism leads to tragedy for those around them, Kuzmin underlined the danger of bringing world-altering dreams to life and drew an equal sign between the modern-day "emperors" remaking Russia and the susceptible artists who had fallen prey to socialism's dangerous lure. Demonstrating the staying power of Rome as a mythmaking tool in discussions of Russian national identity, in his Russian Rome Kuzmin showed clearly that the ancient world continued to illuminate Russia's postrevolutionary present.

Kuzmin's Rome is simultaneously the capital of the Roman Empire during Nero's lifetime (37–68 CE) and the twentieth-century setting for Pavel's literary musings on that earlier period. In its former guise, Rome witnesses yet again the interaction of a pagan empire and the new Christian force that will eventually replace it. Diverging from his major source on Nero's life, the writings of the first-century Roman historian Suetonius, Kuzmin paints Nero's mistress Acte as a Christian,[5] and through Nero's condemnation of her beliefs introduces the theme of the clash between paganism and Christianity. And yet by extending the circle of connections in his play to include a parodic link between Nero and Jesus Christ, Kuzmin achieves two further effects. He suggests a correspondence between the newly developing religion, with its utopianism and deification of the individual, and the worldly empire it aspires to displace; and, at the same time, he satirizes the godlike status the powerful can assume. Moreover, through the links he implies between Nero and the Soviet leaders, as well as in other texts he wrote during this period, Kuzmin manages to join Russia's socialism both to Nero's empire and to the dreams and goals of early Christianity. In his text, therefore, socialism, Christianity, and imperialism merge, as the warlike clash of Blok's "Catiline" turns in Kuzmin's postrevolutionary work into a mood of generalized disenchantment with all revolutionary dreams.

In its latter guise, meanwhile, Kuzmin's Rome is a place where the modern-day Russian writer joins into this mix, a place where he can go, either literally or metaphorically, to explore through the creative act the potent combination of utopian visions and power. In his own literary text Kuzmin thus responds to previous Russian treatments of Rome by demonstrating the devastating effects of such a combination. Reflecting his own journey through Russia's revolutionary period, Kuzmin admits the appeal of such visions for rulers, subjects, and artists alike, but calls nonetheless for a crucial alternative: the personal, intimate quest of each individual soul for creative self-realization through love. Depicting the path followed by Pavel and Nero, who serve in a sense as alter egos for the author's artistic self, Kuzmin manages to provide potential redemption for both characters. In so doing, he renounces self-assigned complicity in the state's admittedly dangerous dreams. Instead, he claims a complex but eventually sanctified and redemptive place for the writer in a postrevolutionary Russia turned into a Third Rome, or a Moscow-led combination of politics and faith, gone decidedly wrong.

Background: Politics and Rome

"Nay," cried Glaucus, "no cold and trite director for us: no dictator of the banquet; no *rex convivii.*"
Edward Bulwer-Lytton, *The Last Days of Pompeii*, 1834

Throughout his life, Kuzmin professed to find politics devoid of interest, unappealing, or both, and his friends and acquaintances both bolstered and reported the largely justified ensuing image of Kuzmin as thoroughly apolitical. As early as 1904, for instance, Georgii Chicherin, who began the century as close friend and confidant to the Decadent Kuzmin and then became Commissar of Foreign Affairs under the Soviets, wrote him a letter in which he contrasted "two parallel streams" of the day: "the spiritually aristocratic new art and the democratic social movement." Noting his own involvement in the latter, Chicherin suggested that this realm was entirely "alien" to Kuzmin, occupied as he was with "hymns of praise to the earth, the new mysticism, the new, more intense human being."[6] Rounding out the picture, in a December 1936 diary entry, Kuzmin's friend Erikh Gollerbakh recalled that the recently deceased Kuzmin "used to say that it was absolutely all the same to him who was 'there, at the top'—'let even a horse rule us, I don't care.'"[7]

Certainly Kuzmin was never seriously involved in political parties, nor did he attempt to curry favor with any political regime—choices in keeping with his dismissal of all mass groupings, be they literary schools or political movements. This does not mean, however, that the observant and sensitive Kuzmin had no opinions regarding the revolutionary events his lifetime spanned, nor does it mean that he left no record of these reactions as they evolved over a period of several decades. His initial lack of mention in his diary of the political events of 1905—entries from the autumn of that year feature predominantly his successful readings,[8] visits to the Chicherins', and conversations with barbers, friends, and lovers—would eventually give way to grudging recognition of the revolutionary unrest he could no longer ignore.[9] In an August 1905 letter to Chicherin, meanwhile, he acknowledged that he was "less indifferent to social questions" than he previously had been.[10] His annoyance at disruptive political disturbances such as antigovernment strikes comes through strongly in his diaries, as in an entry from 13 October 1905: "Anyone can express his fair protest through idleness, but to interrupt by force the carrying out of the most urgent functions of cultural life is barbarism and a crime."[11] Frustrated by the consuming interest in politics he found around him, even among his friends, he wondered in an 18 October 1905 diary entry where the aesthetes were "who would not speak of meetings and universal voting rights."[12]

In the passage in which he described revolutionary disruptions of his daily routine as "barbarism," Kuzmin went on to blame both strikers and the ineffectual government for such inconveniences. However, his sympathy with the monarchy and antipathy toward the revolutionaries would emerge in subsequent entries and in his correspondence with Chicherin, as, for example, when he voiced his support for the notorious Black Hundreds, and in his decision in November 1905 to join the Union of the Russian People, a right-wing, anti-Semitic organization that asked potential members whether they were Orthodox Christians and "patriots."[13] As Malmstad and Bogomolov explain, although Kuzmin did not apparently become involved in the group's activities, he "was convinced that liberal and radical opinion, which he, like many others, identified with the Jews, was making this revolution, not the traditionalist mass of common people who were standing silently apart from the events in the capital."[14] Standing with the "common people" and their tsar, in a 2 December 1905 diary entry, Kuzmin wrote that the revolutionaries were "cursed," and claimed that "yids and those insolent types that act like them, traitors and villains are destroying Russia. . . . What do they care about Russia, Russian culture, history, riches?"[15]

In his diary, Kuzmin linked what he saw as "Jewish" socialism to Christianity. "They are comparing socialism with Christianity (also a Jewish utopia)," he wrote, noting that socialism would require enormous changes that would affect the very nature of the movement before it would become appropriate to Russia.[16] As early as 1905, then, Kuzmin rejected the impracticability of what he felt to be utopian visions. Significantly, he expressed this opinion while associating events of his own time with those of the first centuries of the common era, when the "utopian" religion of Christianity had first emerged as a Jewish sect in an eastern province of the Roman Empire.

In fact, Kuzmin's interest in the birth of Christianity dated back to a trip to Italy in 1897, during which, as he would later recall, Rome had "intoxicated" him, particularly in its blend of pagan and Christian cultures.[17] Having become fascinated with Hellenistic philosophy during an 1895 journey to Alexandria,[18] Kuzmin rediscovered in Rome's pagan roots the culture that had attracted him in Alexandria and simultaneously found a new, more appealing vision of Christianity in its earliest stages.[19] Writing to Chicherin on 16 April 1897, he exclaimed in terms very similar to those Merezhkovskii had employed in his *Julian the Apostate,* "And what a new light for me on the earliest Christianity—meek, dear, simple, almost idyllic, still in contact with classical antiquity, somewhat mystical, and not at all gloomy: Jesus is everywhere without a beard, handsome and gentle; the attendant spirits gathering grapes; the good shepherds."[20]

It is unclear whether Kuzmin's 1905 association of Christianity both with the socialism he disdained and with Judaism marks a change in his views of Christianity since 1897, when he had associated the religion in its early years with paganism in a positive way. Clearly his views on the subject of Christianity were not entirely consistent. It is important, however, to distinguish Kuzmin's life-long individual Christian faith,[21] which he married to an abiding interest in neo-Platonism and Gnosticism,[22] from his attitude toward Christianity as a utopian mass movement or an official, monolithic institution. Dissatisfied, like many of his artistic contemporaries at the turn of the century, with the official Russian Orthodox Church, Kuzmin explored the religion of Russia's Old

Believers and Catholicism, though his 1905 diary records his attendance at Orthodox services.[23] At the same time, he would continue to link Christianity as a movement with Judaism and with socialism, and in the Soviet period would increasingly condemn both Christianity and socialism for a utopianism that was not only unrealistic but also harmful and for anti-individualistic extremism. Meanwhile, his ongoing interest in Italy and ancient Rome, with its various associations, would reappear in numerous literary works throughout his career, including *The Death of Nero*.[24]

Given Kuzmin's outraged reactions to the revolutionary excitement of 1905, as well as his general rejection of socialism, his initial reception of the events of 1917 comes as a surprise. For Kuzmin succumbed for a time to the revolutionary utopianism he had long rejected. Carried away by the chiliastic tendencies that swept the Russian intelligentsia during this period, as well as by his strong opposition to Russia's involvement in the first World War, he appears to have been moved by dreams of a new culture, in which, as Charles Rougle writes, "social and philosophical differences would be resolved in a humanist spirit of mutual respect."[25] After the February Revolution, Kuzmin greeted the revolutionaries with joy, awaiting the era of peace and harmony he believed they would inaugurate. He characterized the revolution as an event possessed of religious overtones, portraying it as "an angel in a worker's blouse," and proclaiming his view of all human beings as "brothers."[26] In the spring of 1917, Kuzmin joined the new Union of Art Workers, and was elected with his fellow writers Blok, Vladimir Maiakovskii, and Nikolai Punin to its executive committee. Along with Maiakovskii and Vsevolod Meierkhol'd, Kuzmin also became involved in Freedom to Art, a leftist organization within the Union that rejected conservative involvement in the world of art.[27]

Many members of the intelligentsia found their revolutionary enthusiasm noticeably abating after the Bolshevik takeover in October. Kuzmin, however, remained committed to the revolution. In a diary entry of 26 October 1917, he wrote, "Miracles are happening. Everything is occupied by the Bolsheviks."[28] He told his fellow writer Georgii Chulkov, "It goes without saying that I am a Bolshevik," and added that Lenin, who opposed Russia's continued participation in World War I, was more attractive to him than "all our liberals who cry out about the defense of the fatherland." When asked whether he had changed his previous views on socialism, he replied, "Socialism? I don't have anything against it. It's all the same to me." On 4 December 1917, he wrote in his diary that the takeover was "blessed." Chulkov recorded his astonishment at the "metamorphosis of the decadent Black Hundreds member into a revolutionary Bolshevik."[29]

And yet by March 1918, Kuzmin had grown thoroughly disenchanted with his erstwhile revolutionary dreams. A 10 March diary entry noted that "the comrades," now in power, were behaving like Attila the Hun.[30] Subsequently he would refer to the Bolsheviks as "cursed," as his sympathies seemed to swing back to his earlier anti-"barbarian" and antirevolutionary mentality of 1905. Several months later, when the young poet Leonid Kannegiser assassinated Moisei Uritskii, head of Petrograd's secret police, Kuzmin underwent an ordeal that sealed his opposition to the new regime he had lauded so recently. Kuzmin's longtime lover and companion Iurii Iurkun, mentioned in Kannegiser's address book, was arrested as part of the "Red Terror" of September 1918.[31] Though Iurkun was released after several months,[32] Kuzmin's ensuing emotional stress, combined with the physical difficulties of the period, were longer-lasting. In his poetic cycle "Plen" (Captivity), written during the difficult winter of 1919, Kuzmin juxtaposed the aesthetically pleasing images of past literary, culinary, and erotic delights with outraged protests against the new order. Rather than bringing the freedom it had promised ("They said: / 'Live and be free!'"), he asserted, the Bolshevik regime had imposed general deprivation and a lack of humanity, which had resulted in a corresponding lack of creativity.[33] He was further horrified by the execution of the poet Nikolai Gumilev in August 1921.[34]

As the decade progressed, Kuzmin's fears for art's freedom and survival under the new regime intensified and found further justification. In 1923 the journal *Abraksas,* which he co-edited, was closed because of its "literary incomprehensibility."[35] The next year found Leon Trotsky proclaiming in his *Literatura i revoliutsiia* (Literature and Revolution) that Kuzmin was an "internal émigré of the Revolution," and describing a journal to which Kuzmin had contributed as "completely and entirely superfluous to a modern post-October man."[36] The following year, Viktor Pertsov attacked Kuzmin in an article in *Zhizn' iskusstva* (The Life of Art), where he stated that "no possible current could galvanize a writer like Kuzmin for our contemporary time."[37] (Ironically, Kuzmin had helped found *The Life of Art* in October 1918, and indeed had served on its original editorial board.[38]) Kuzmin found it ever more difficult to earn a living through publishing, which was increasingly barred to him throughout the 1920s. He refused to alter his style or content to make it more palatable to the new regime and produced works of growing abstraction and mysticism that in some cases baffled even critics long familiar with his work.[39]

During this difficult period, Kuzmin turned once again to ancient Rome to make sense of his own nation's present. In his 1922 collection of musings titled "Cheshuia v nevode" (Scales in the Net), for instance, he suggested that Russia's postrevolutionary period, "the crucible of the future," was "similar to the second century."[40] As before, he portrayed Rome as a place where various forces came together in an intriguing mix. In belletristic works such as the unfinished novel *Rimskie chudesa* (Roman Marvels) and the poetic cycle "Sofiia" (Sophia), he explored the syncretistic Gnostic visions that had long captivated him. And in his 1925 article "Struzhki" (Shavings), he returned to his earlier discussion of Christianity, socialism, and contemporary culture. He claimed that "the analogy between the origins of Christianity and the development of socialism is indubitable." Among the factors joining the two philosophies were their "racial provenance" (i.e., as he saw it, their Jewishness) and their "internationalism."[41]

Having connected the two movements, Kuzmin proceeded in the same article to record his current objections to Christianity—and, by extension, to socialism: "Any hint of the diversity and variety of the world, external and spiritual, national, and personal, must be hateful to primitive Christianity: the gloomiest misanthropic asceticism, the lack of acceptance of the 'diabolical' world, the rush toward death, toward abstraction, toward nonexistence, where, of course, the most intractable problems can be solved with ease."[42] He concluded by relating these observations to a discussion of contemporary literature, also dominated, as he saw it, by an anti-individualistic, monolithic mindset that he rejected: "One must be either a fanatic (that is, a one-sided and blinded person) or a charlatan in order to act as a member of a school."[43] In other articles, Kuzmin lauded those writers of the day who avoided regimentation and instead created works characterized by stylistic innovation, a combination of shifting planes and time periods, and a rejection of noncontemporary tranquility and composure.[44] Kuzmin's concerns over the anti-individualism of the revolutionary period resonate with Briusov's earlier warnings.[45]

In its stylistics and setting, *The Death of Nero* reflects Kuzmin's artistic and political ideas and reactions during the first decade of Soviet rule. He used the figure of one of his main characters, Nero, as an allegorical warning of the disturbing political and artistic trends he saw in his own day. Determined at the beginning of his reign to bring joy to all his subjects, Nero soon realizes that "power destroys all illusions."[46] Some of his subjects, however, remain entranced by the impossible ideals the emperor has presented, and Nero as the powerful representative of these ideals becomes an object of worship in a pointed satire both of the erroneous deification of human power and of the impracticable dreams that power can attempt, dangerously, to fulfill. Meanwhile, Kuzmin takes advantage of the legends associated with "Nero the artist" to present a ludicrous parody of the truly creative being: infeasible dreams of any sort when put into action lead to the destruction of the individual—and, therefore, of art and culture.

The Imperial Bolsheviks

I wish all you Romans had only one neck!
Caligula, emperor of Rome, in Suetonius, *The Twelve Caesars*, early second century CE (trans. Robert Graves)

When we first encounter Kuzmin's version of the future emperor Nero in Act One of the play, he is a fatherless, poverty-stricken, six-year-old who has been sent, following the exile of his mother, Agrippina, to live with his aunt Lepida. The young Nero enjoys performing the new dances he has learned from his instructor, Pertinax, and he craves attention and love.[47] Five years later, foreshadowing his eventual burning of sections of Rome, Nero tells Pertinax of his love for drownings, fires, and earthquakes—for "something unusual" (333). In Kuzmin's tale, Nero has his first sexual experience at the age of fourteen with a young man named Servilius. Thrilled by Servilius's affection and wishing to prove himself a worthy partner, in Christ-like fashion Nero takes upon himself the punishment for stealing apples from his aunt's favorite tree, a theft actually committed by two local boys. When Servilius comments that he finds Nero a bit lacking in height, however, Nero turns on his former lover, swearing that he will have his legs broken. The stage is set for Nero's future as performer, dreamer, false Christ—and emperor.

For Nero soon has a change of luck. His mother marries Emperor Claudius, her uncle, and Claudius agrees to adopt Nero, thereby putting him next in line for succession to the throne.[48] Upon this reversal of his fortunes, Nero longs to do good, to be perceived as a benefactor. Directing his magnanimity toward all of humanity, he proclaims, "I swear that everyone will be happy; not a minute will pass without good deeds, not a drop of blood will be shed, I will give away everything, I will judge kindly, no one will leave me with empty hands, I will hide my face from no one, I will dance for everyone. I will bring joy, consolation, and support to one and all. The very name Nero will resound like glad tidings!" (340). Nero's words are met with ecstasy from his new attendants, who in the language of the Orthodox Christian Church declare him "holy" ("sviat Neron," 340).[49]

We find out in Act Two, however, that Nero's far-reaching goals have proved unattainable. From the time of his ascension to the throne, it is rumored that he conspired with his mother Agrippina to kill Claudius, and once on the throne Nero proceeds to kill both Agrippina herself, after several attempts, and his own pregnant wife, Poppaea—murders that will haunt him for the rest of his life.[50] Meanwhile, as a result of Nero's lack of respect for his subjects and Rome's loss of several provinces under his reign, the Roman citizens are in revolt. Nero himself realizes by the middle of the play that his plans have gone awry, and wonders why, "in order to benefit all of humanity, it is impossible to do good to any one individual!" (360).[51] And yet he has already answered this conundrum: "having become emperor, one is soon convinced that there are no decent people" (350). Thus, when his treasurer informs him that the Roman people are starving, Nero, who has been planning the construction of his new palace, replies simply that he has heard that "in India, there are people with such self-control that they can go three years without eating" (353). Despite his early, exalted intentions, the third act of the play features Nero's attempted escape from the betrayed and enraged Roman citizenry and ends with his unwilling death by suicide, as implacable centurions approach to execute him as an "enemy of the people" ("vrag naroda," 369). Given the power to put his ideals into action on a large scale, Nero instead turns out to be a murderer—feared, shunned, lethal to many of those close to him, and eventually forced into death by those he had planned to assist.

In keeping with Kuzmin's fears for art under the new regime, his Nero is the emperor who "fiddled while Rome burned," making a mockery of true artistic creativity. Kuzmin follows Suetonius in portraying Nero's recitals as so painfully long that women in the audience give birth during them and men feign death to escape them.[52] Significantly, Kuzmin associates these vaunted and ludicrous artistic displays with bouts of cruelty: Nero is lying in bed resting his voice, for example, when Poppaea enters the room, reproaches him for his lack of constructive deeds as emperor, and then receives for her pains three fatal kicks in the stomach. Nero's appalled and somewhat bewildered subjects mock his artistic pretensions. "Why is his throat all wrapped up? Is he sick?" one spectator queries at the sight of Nero "the singer" swathed in a muffler (345). Nero's delusions about his own creativity reach their pinnacle in his famous dying words, drawn from Suetonius: "In me the world loses a great artist" (376).[53] Kuzmin demonstrates emphatically that the obliviously tyrannical Nero cannot produce art worthy of respect.

Kuzmin's rendering of Nero, the utopian thinker gone fatally wrong, appears to reflect his horrified reactions to the Soviet leaders, their worldview, and their effect on Russia. Indeed, in a diary entry of 28 January 1924, he responded to the demonstrations of mourning throughout Russia that followed Lenin's death.[54] He characterized the speeches dedicated to Lenin's memory as "complete rubbish and charlatanism," and added, "The whole world through drunken vomit—that's the Communist world order. . . . It occurred to me to write *The Death of Nero*."[55] As Gleb Morev has shown, Kuzmin's association of Bolshevik plans and actions with bodily excretions is one he repeated during the 1920s: in his 1925 work "Piat' razgovorov i odin sluchai" (Five Conversations and One Event), he linked the revolution's aftermath with fecal matter.[56] It is tempting to speculate that through such associations, Kuzmin was once again commenting on the unimpressive results of the Bolsheviks' "creativity" in sculpting a new society and on their artistic policies.

One particular speech commemorating Lenin—that of Stalin—may have influenced the creation of the play as well. Iurkun's common-law wife, the actress Ol'ga Gildebrandt-Arbenina, recalls in her memoirs that Kuzmin tended to rework subjects first dreamed up by Iurkun, a habit that drove Iurkun to tears of frustration early in their relationship—particularly since Kuzmin was the more talented, "Mozartian" member of the duo. One such subject was Nero, whom Iurkun had planned to compare to Lermontov. While Gildebrandt-Arbenina writes that Iurkun's concept was quite different from Kuzmin's eventual depiction of Nero, she also notes Iurkun's recognition of the significance of Stalin's speech on Lenin's death. "He predicted Stalin's fame immediately after his speech on Lenin's death—like the speech of Augustus over the grave of Caesar—and he said that this was an enormous political step for Stalin," she notes, adding that Iurkun had a knack for spotting talent and predicting the future.[57]

Perhaps Kuzmin noted Iurkun's association of Stalin's speech and Roman history, as well as his proposed linkage of Bolshevik leader and writer. In any case, in *The Death of Nero* Stalin's accelerated Five-Year Plan is echoed in Nero's intended schedule for the next four years of his reign: "Within four years, we will have outlived all social ills: hunger, mass epidemics, fires, poverty, we will restrain the very elements. This plan itself is already our victory and our achievement" (353). And Nero's dismissal of the famine his subjects face recalls the plight of Russia's peasants during the collectivization of agriculture, mandated by Stalin as Kuzmin was writing his play.[58]

Suetonius ends his description of Nero's reign by noting various reactions to the tyrant's death. Most Roman citizens, he writes, "ran through the streets wearing caps of liberty."[59] Others, however, mourned the dead tyrant and established a cult to his memory. These subjects insisted either that Nero had not really died or that he would return from the dead. In keeping with Suetonius's characterization of this latter group, Kuzmin ends his play with a scene at Nero's grave, where women simultaneously mourn the emperor and refuse to accept the idea of his death. They are joined by a young woman named Tiukhe (Greek for "fortune"), who recalls her one meeting with Nero several years earlier in Greece. She speaks of him in Christ-like terms, declaring that if Nero were to call her name, even if she were dead she would arise to respond to him. In an ironic echo of Nero's grandiose promises, Tiukhe reports that the tyrant's name "resounds for me like glad tidings" (380).

The theme of ruler-worship emphasized at the end of the play links the figure of Nero figure to that of Lenin: as Robert Tucker points out, the Lenin cult was "an established institution of public life in 1929," when Kuzmin completed his play.[60] As early as 1924, however, immediately after his death, Lenin was declared to be a religious figure, one approaching Christ-like status. He was said to be immortal, as was his cause, and in some cases he was perceived to be both man and god simultaneously.[61] In one instance, a group of peasants from Kaluga Province requested from the Central Committee of the Communist Party "a short history of Lenin's life, that we may insert it in place of the Gospel."[62] Soviet institutions began to feature "Lenin Corners," reminiscent of Russian Orthodox icon corners. Observing one such "Lenin Corner," an English visitor to Moscow could not help remarking that "Lenin had replaced Christ."[63] Tiukhe's adoring descriptions of Nero might well be interpreted as Kuzmin's sardonic comment on the burgeoning beatification of Lenin as well as on the near sanctity that power and those invested with it can assume.[64]

Indeed, Kuzmin repeatedly invokes Christ in the Nero sections of the text—obliquely in the apple tree episode and in Tiukhe's characterization of Nero's abilities, or overtly through the emperor's discussions of Christianity with Acte. These references are absent from Suetonius, who mentions Jesus only once in his biography of Nero to note that during Nero's reign, "punishments were also inflicted on the Christians, a sect professing a new and mischievous religious belief."[65] Kuzmin's Nero purports to scorn Christianity: when Acte attempts to explain her allegiance to the faith, he replies that he remembers quite well the "nonsense" she has told him about her "sect" (361). Rejecting Christ, Nero instead asserts his own power. Acte counters by asking whether Nero would be able to raise a corpse from the dead, and inquires whether he would worship someone capable of such a feat. "I would crucify him," the emperor replies, "so that there wouldn't be any temptation." At this Acte calls him "Antichrist" (361), evoking Nero's long association with that figure by religious Christians. Nero's rumored abilities and Christ-associated actions may be read in this context as parodic, as can the emperor's desire, expressed in Christ-like fashion as he steels himself for death, that "this cup might pass" from him (376). His life, of course, ends with his unfounded assertion of his own creativity.

Yet Acte is one of the women attending Nero's grave at the end of the play, as the emperor in death is declared "godlike" by other attendants (379), blurring the line between her devotion to Christ and her participation in a scene of emperor-worship. Further, in singling out three of the women, Kuzmin invites a parallel to his 1926 poem "Tri Marii" (Three Marys), which opens with a portrayal of three mourning women who surround the body of Jesus.[66] Such a conflation is well in keeping with Kuzmin's longstanding interest in the syncretism of the Roman world. In the context of "Shavings," of Kuzmin's portrayal of the effects of Nero's reign, and of the links established between Christ, Nero, and the Bolsheviks, it suggests once again a condemnation on the author's part of large-scale utopian dreams of all kinds, ancient and modern, imperial, socialist, or religious, and of the antiartistic tyrannies they can create.

Nero, Pavel, Kuzmin

Shall I awaken in another homeland,
Not in this gloomy land?
Aleksandr Blok, "Venice," 1909

Nero is not the only main character of *The Death of Nero:* the action of the play alternates between Nero's story and that of the writer Pavel. At first glance, Pavel appears to have little in common with the Roman emperor, apart from composing a play about Nero that meets with notable lack of success when read to a group of listeners in the second scene of Kuzmin's text. Judging by the audience's reaction, however, Pavel's play about Nero appears to have a good deal in common with Kuzmin's own play, though the two texts are not one and the same. Like Pavel, for example, who is reproached by his audience for his lack of "historical accuracy," Kuzmin does not follow his historical sources with precision. They both assign "to the Romans our feelings and concepts," create female characters who "verge on stereotypes," and do not make it clear "with which side the author sympathizes" (323). Further, like Kuzmin in the 1920s, Pavel is told that the time for "decadence" in art has passed. It is possible therefore to read Pavel as Kuzmin's alter ego and to contrast the tyrant and the artist as Kuzmin's much-loved Plato does in his *Phaedrus,* where he writes that there are nine levels of the soul. The first, the most positive, is a "seeker after wisdom or beauty or a follower of the muses and a lover"; the ninth and last belongs to the tyrant.[67]

Upon further examination, however, Pavel's story bears a striking similarity to Nero's, and the situation thus becomes significantly more complicated. Pavel's narrative begins in Italy, where Pavel and Marie are vacationing in 1919. The scenes devoted to Pavel in Act Two, however, return to an earlier period of his life and serve to supply the circumstances of Pavel and Marie's relationship and their current travels abroad. We learn in Act Two that after growing up in poverty, Pavel finds at age twenty-four that the extremely wealthy father whom he never knew has died and left him a fortune. Like Nero, Pavel swears that he will help others. He instantly proves his lofty intentions by offering a large portion of his new wealth to Marie, the proud daughter of the vice governor. Having spurned Pavel's affections, she is disgraced when her father is arrested for embezzling state funds. Grateful for Pavel's largesse, she agrees to marry him.[68] And yet the naive Pavel's sweeping plans for helping all of humanity ultimately lead him into the clutches of a group of Italian criminals, who are available for hire by various political factions to create provocations. Under the guise of making an idealistic political statement, the gang persuades Pavel to become involved in setting his hotel on fire, and they steal from the hotel guests during the ensuing chaos. Act One ends with Pavel on the roof of the flaming hotel, scattering his money into the air and proclaiming ironic "glad tidings," reminiscent of Nero's, to the guests he has displaced from the hotel and the police who have come to assist them.

The fire in the hotel prefigures Nero's own efforts to burn the city of Rome; it also puts the finishing touches on Pavel's increasingly strained relationship with his wife, who resents the gratitude she feels Pavel requires. Desperately unhappy, Marie kills herself and her new companion, Friedrich von Steinbach, who initially had appeared more taken with her husband. Pavel, meanwhile, finds himself in a home for the mentally ill, where a fellow patient identifies him as a modern-day incarnation of Nero. Rescued by Marianna, a reluctant associate of the gang that has duped him, the confused Pavel wakes in Act Three in a sanatorium in Switzerland, where he is left in his brother Fedia's charge. A wise doctor counsels the now penniless Pavel to forget his utopian ideals and informs him that this is advice he might receive from anyone "uninfected by an abstract dream" (378). "You are a human being—focus on another human being," Pavel's doctor encourages him. "And don't consider yourself a benefactor. At present you are like a child, without strength, . . . but you know where strength is not to be found. . . . You know the false path, and that is already a good deal to know" (377). Meeting Fedia once again after many years, Pavel remarks on his brother's beauty and compares him to an angel.

Pavel's story echoes Nero's thematically and stylistically. Both men grow up in straitened circumstances, which are then alleviated by heretofore missing father figures. Both show human potential in their desire to help others, to improve their lives. Both gain the means to do so and then discover that money may allow them to fulfill their dreams, but that dreams that do not take into account individual emotions and well-being are doomed to failure. Both men have failed marriages and find more fulfillment with other men. Words are repeated from one section of the text to another (the ironic "good tidings"; the phrase "How wet you are!" applied by Marie to Pavel and by Nero to his nearly drowned mother), as are images: Nero and Marie, two thousand years apart, take the same road out of Rome.

Thus, a simple contrast between ruler and artist is not tenable. For Kuzmin's anger at Russia's postrevolutionary state was not confined to its political leaders: he also blamed himself and the rest of the prorevolutionary intelligentsia for their utopian-minded acceptance of the February Revolution and the Bolsheviks' rise to power. In "Captivity," he acknowledged the responsibility he felt for Russia's current woes: "And you are horrified by the failure, / For it was you who savagely led the song / At the beginning of the senseless funeral feast."[69] And in "Five Conversations and One Event," one character asserts, "I think that the worst counterrevolutionaries are those who originally supported the revolution. This happens as a result of idealism, . . . not very clever, I would say, like any idealism."[70] Another character in the play insists that the intelligentsia "behaved shamefully, shamefully," during the revolutionary period.[71] The tale of the dangerously idealistic Russian writer Pavel serves to characterize Kuzmin's own early hopes and subsequent disillusionment in the revolutionary period.

On another level, Pavel's story also provides an alternative, hopeful model for writers and rulers alike. His rehabilitation at the end of the play suggests some positive significance for Nero as well. For despite Nero's evident faults and outrages, Kuzmin's Nero is not the thoroughly depraved emperor (despite his early attempts to govern wisely) that Suetonius portrays. Suetonius's horror at Nero's "wedding" to the castrate Sporus is different from Kuzmin's accepting portrayal of that relationship, and Suetonius's disgusted and rather extensive renderings of Nero's sexual exploits with men and women alike (including Agrippina) are suggested only briefly in the play, mainly through Poppaea's speech chastising her husband for staying out late at night.

Moreover, like Pavel, Nero undergoes an important transformation during the course of the play. For the "Antichrist" Nero, in an echo of Merezhkovskii's Julian "the Apostate," is in fact attracted to the Christianity he seeks to oppose: killing Christ, after all, is a means to repudiate the temptation to worship him. In the midst of his nightmares about his murdered wife and mother, Nero tells his companions of another part of his dream, one missing from Suetonius's narrative. A woman wipes water from the face of Agrippina, who has emerged from the lake where Nero attempted to have her drowned. Then the woman hands Nero an egg decorated in purple and announces that "Christ is risen" (360). Acte interprets the dream to mean that Nero ought to accept the teachings of Christ, but the emperor tells her not to pin her hopes on a "moment of weakness" (361). It is at this point in the text, however, that he comments on the impossibility of helping all of humanity. Through the chinks in Nero's anti-Christian armor, the playwright seems to point to a possible redemption for his tyrant, one in keeping with Kuzmin's own transformative, personally focused Christian faith, rather than with an institution. Shortly before his death, the emperor arrives at a moment of clarity: "Loyalty, betrayal, honor, dishonor, people, the gods, fate, myself—I'm beginning to understand everything all at once, as if I were living for the first time" (372). His supporters urge him to fly to safety, noting that "dawn is not far away" (372).

Pavel, arriving in the sanatorium, is uncertain whether he is alive or dead; the first words of the sickbed scene are Pavel's "Tell me, didn't I die?" (377). His words come directly after Nero's dying words in the preceding scene ("Nero. 'Ah, what fidelity.' He dies. The sun rises." [376]). In addition, the identical words describing Nero's death conclude Pavel's play about Nero, read by Pavel in the second scene of Kuzmin's play. Through the participation of both men in this hopeful discourse of resurrection, and through the joining of Pavel's play to Kuzmin's own work of art, Pavel's redemption becomes applicable to Nero and to Kuzmin himself.

In fact, as early as "Five Conversations and One Event," Kuzmin had arrived at some sort of self-absolution for his brief lapse into utopianism. For in response to the scornful assessment, quoted above, of the intelligentsia's behavior during the revolutionary period, another character responds, "At that time all the markers changed for us, all shame, society, and conventions disappeared, the most primitive needs were what remained, very simple perhaps, not always plausible at another time."[72] *The Death of Nero* might be said to conclude this process of self-forgiveness, then, after a thorough examination of the original transgression of utopian idealism. In addition, through the end of Pavel's story, Kuzmin moved beyond transgression and forgiveness to offer an alternative to the totalitarian-minded Soviet reality and utopianism he had come to reject. This alternative was based on his long-held, neo-Platonic belief in the importance of individualized love as the basis of a creative existence.

The Alternative: Art, Love, and Creativity

We are travelers: motion is our vow,
We are the children of God: creativity is our vow,
Motion and creativity are life,
Which is called Love.
Mikhail Kuzmin, "The Ladder," *Parabolas*, 1923

In his *Ideology and Utopia*, Karl Mannheim describes the fate of intellectuals who have contributed to the founding of a new order and then find themselves excluded from it. Mannheim discusses three possible responses to this situation. Some bereft intellectuals respond with skepticism to the state of affairs they have encountered, others develop a mystical worldview, and still others shut themselves off from the world.[73] Mannheim asserts that this third group participates "in the great historical process of disillusionment, in which every concrete meaning of things as well as myths and beliefs are slowly cast aside"—"modern expressionistic art" tends to depict this state of lost meaning.[74] Kuzmin's intermittently expressionistic art of the 1920s as well as his disillusionment during this period might therefore suggest his potential connection to Mannheim's third group of displaced intellectuals.[75]

And yet Kuzmin believed that true art was always linked to contemporary life, rather than divorced from it. In "Shavings," he wrote of expressionism as the art form associated with socialism: as socialism had developed out of dying capitalism, so too had expressionism arisen out of earlier European culture.[76] Expressionism was for him a response to the new, socialist era. While the style of *The Death of Nero* is expressionistic, the content is tied specifically to Soviet reality. Kuzmin rejected his own foray into Soviet utopianism and offered instead a choice based on his enduring fascination with the Gnosticism and neo-Platonism of the ancient world. His views as expressed in *The Death of Nero* are also consistent, therefore, with Mannheim's second group of displaced intellectuals, those who approach the world mystically. Mannheim writes that this "group takes refuge in the past and attempts to find there an epoch or society in which an extinct form of reality-transcendence dominated the world, and through this romantic reconstruction it seeks to respiritualize the present. The same function, from this point of view, is fulfilled by attempts to revive religious feeling, idealism, symbols, and myths."[77] Still focused on the Roman past, Kuzmin chose the apolitical world of Gnostic-based mysticism and individualized creativity, rather than that of the imperial court or a Christian "movement." An exploration of his longstanding, personally focused "symbols and myths" helps to clarify the fate of both of his heroes, and sheds light on the writer himself as well.

Kuzmin's style changed in the 1920s, but his thematic base remained in many ways consistent; his oeuvre is marked by a recurring set of ideas and images.[78] Kuzmin combined Plato's idea of the soul's aspiration to the Good with the Gnostics' vision of an errant World Soul longing to return to the Pleroma. To this he added Plotinus's image of the soul, led by a watchful spirit, journeying through various stages (or hypostases) of existence, ending ideally at unity with what Plotinus termed "the One."[79] This idea of the journeying soul who attempts, albeit at times futilely, to achieve some sort of self-understanding and unity is reflected in many Kuzminian texts, ranging from the early

Kryl'ia (Wings, 1906) to *The Death of Nero*. As Kuzmin wrote in the introduction to his 1916 novel *Chudesnaia zhizn' Iosifa Bal'zamo, grafa Kaliostro* (The Miraculous Life of Joseph Balsamo, Count Cagliostro): "For the most part, I am interested in the Spirit's varied paths, which lead to one goal. Sometimes, however, these paths do not reach their goal, and they force the traveler to end up in side alleys, where he will undoubtedly lose his way."[80]

In Kuzmin's poetic system, the individual soul arrives at unity through male homosexual love. His works frequently feature a homosexual relationship between the protagonist and his beloved, who at times is seen as an otherworldly figure. The hero and his beloved go through various transformations throughout the course of the narrative; the beloved, in fact, can be equated in some of his guises with the Plotinian guiding spirit (in Kuzmin's terminology, the *vozhatyi* [guide]). As Malmstad and Gennadii Shmakov write, Kuzmin "uses [Plotinus' system of the striving soul] as a poetic model of love, substituting for the Plotinian soul the lover who moves endlessly through stages of seeming death, transformation, and resurrection. Love and the loved one ascending through different phases are seen here in the various guises of the lyrical hero himself who moves, as though on a journey, toward ultimate unity with the lover, the poet himself." The two scholars note further that "an associative chain is preserved" as hypostases of lover and beloved take form throughout the text.[81]

Kuzmin often employs the imagery of the twin to describe the eventual, hoped-for merging process between the two men: the beloved is seen, in Platonic fashion, as his lover's other half, or as the lover's double. Irina Paperno summarizes this process: "Thus there arises in Kuzmin's poetry a constant thematic pattern: the appearance to the hero of a double (a messenger from the other world and a beloved) and the merging with this double after overcoming the barriers separating them." Paperno notes further that Kuzmin's plots feature a triangle consisting of hero, identified with the poet's lyric self; his beloved, also portrayed as a brother, twin, or double to the hero; and a woman who separates the two.[82] These triangles reflect Kuzmin's own life experiences, as the poet was involved with three men who then left him for a woman (in Iurkun's case, he returned to Kuzmin despite an ongoing relationship with Gildebrandt-Arbenina).

Kuzmin's own experiences—though substantially reworked in his texts[83]—are relevant, because in his view the artist too longs to achieve unity, in this case a coherent artistic product. And in this creative process, he, too, is inspired by love. Kuzmin viewed artistic creation as a process of recapturing one's past through memory, and, further, of uniting disparate elements of one's past with various facets of the present and future into an integral structure.[84] Thus the artistic process becomes in a sense for Kuzmin a resurrecting, or life-creating, force, as the past is made to live again through the present in the artistic text. This concept of art as a unifying, vivifying force can be compared to God's creation of the world: out of the original chaos of the artist's multitude of individual experiences, art creates a combined whole.[85] Love is the initial impetus that lies at the root of artistic creation; love counteracts the living death of the mundane and leads to unity through art. And, crucially, it is love for a particular person, or some specific element of God's universe, which inspires creativity, rather than a generalized emotion. In his 1923 article "Emotsional'nost' i faktura" (Emotionalism and Style), Kuzmin wrote: "Love is the inspiration for art. Love toward the world, the material, a person. Not schematic, not abstract, but simple, concrete, individually directed love."[86] The love one feels for a specific individual and the emotional and physical unity achieved by two lovers are reflected in the unifying aspects of the artistic text. Kuzmin's arsenal of inspirational thinkers may be esoteric, but his focus is decidedly of this world. His goal, to return to Mannheim's vocabulary, is to "respiritualize" his present-day surroundings.

Thus Kuzmin's play, while challenging and unusual, can be seen as linked to much of his prior writing.[87] Pavel is the classic Kuzminian hero: a naive, well-meaning man, deluded by his professed love for all of mankind, rather than for a specific male soul mate, and by his overwhelming obsession with a woman. When Pavel encounters his brother at the end of the play, he notes that Fedia looks just like him. The otherworldly double has now arrived, and Pavel, free of the murderous Marie (who earlier thwarted his potential romance with Friedrich), can give himself up to his brother's affection. The paradigm is intact: the soul has completed its journeys and has found its true path, unity through love for another man.

Kuzmin's Nero, meanwhile, may be viewed as another searching soul and, through his rebirth as Pavel, even as a hypostasis of Pavel and of Kuzmin's creative self. For Kuzmin's some-time Christ-seeking emperor has a merit that Suetonius's ruler clearly lacks. And while the final scene of the play appears parodic and cynical, as Tiukhe proceeds to worship her deceased ruler as a god, a different interpretation becomes possible when one looks at *The Death of Nero* in the wider context of Kuzmin's oeuvre, and particularly with regard to his poetic cycle "Forel' razbivaet led" (The Trout Breaks the Ice), written in 1927.

In "The Trout Breaks the Ice," the poet's lyrical hero is separated from his lover. Eventually, however, the two are reunited: the lover returns from various travels and near-death experiences, and, in the reunion that ensues, the poet and his lover are referred to as identical twins. The merging between the two men is reflected in the fact that the trout of the poem's title succeeds, after many attempts throughout the narrative, in breaking through the ice that is trapping it. Ice and other watery substances often serve in Kuzmin's oeuvre as barriers separating lover from beloved.[88] Since otherworldly connotations are often associated with the figure of the beloved, one can also see water and ice as representative of the barriers separating the living from the other world, or the kingdom of the dead. When the trout breaks through the restricting ice, therefore, a crossing-over has occurred between life and death: love and, by association, art are seen as resurrecting forces.

The final scene of *The Death of Nero* recalls that unifying moment from "The Trout Breaks the Ice." The women mourning at Nero's grave remember his good luck charm, a doll significantly named Tiukhe. "When he was fishing, she fell in the water and it was impossible to find her," one woman recalls (379).[89] Immediately after this recollection, the grief-stricken woman named Tiukhe appears to the group and is seen as an "unearthly" embodiment of the lost doll. Tiukhe, from one perspective an ironic symbol of a Russian people ready to worship a dictator, becomes in this context a symbol of artistic creativity. For the perceived resurfacing of this otherworldly symbol from the water, like the trout in "The Trout Breaks the Ice," can also be read as a potentially hopeful statement about Nero's future.[90] Tiukhe's listeners support this idea, as they speak the play's last words: "Tiukhe! Tiukhe! She has been found, she's not lost, they've gotten her out of the water. . . . Thrice blessed are you, stranger, messenger of life!" (380). Kuzmin thus joins Nero and Pavel, separated by two thousand years but joined by their common story, in one resurrection, and he suggests a creative future for the new being that Pavel/Nero, now schooled in the importance of the individual, has become.

In *The Death of Nero,* Kuzmin fulfilled his poetic task of unifying past and present into one work of art. Reacting to a new empire, he contrasted it with faith, love, and artistic inspiration. At the same time, curiously, he linked the figures of the earth-bound tyrant and the ethereal artist, as the two merged to create a new society. Representative of Kuzmin himself, Pavel succumbed to a metaphorical death after repeating a first-century Roman emperor's mistakes. And yet the redemption he found granted him and, through him, his tyrannical Roman counterpart a second chance at living a creative life focused on individualized love. The lack of vindictiveness in Kuzmin's message is striking: repentance through acceptance of one's own path is open to writers and rulers alike. Rewriting accepted history, Kuzmin demonstrated the potential existing in one of the world's most hated dictators. That this potential existed only within the artistic text, and not in Kuzmin's own Soviet environment, was no doubt clear to the author, in retreat from a monolithic, utopian-inspired Russian Rome he could no longer accept.

With its continued linkage of modern Russia and ancient Rome, Kuzmin's play serves as a bridge between the Symbolist texts that form the basis of discussion for much of this study and the post-Symbolist period with which it concludes: in fact, Kuzmin's play of the late 1920s has been called "the only authentically symbolist play this poet ever wrote."[91] Certainly Kuzmin would have been aware of his Russian predecessors' writings on a theme that had interested him throughout his life. Kuzmin's perusal of Merezhkovskii's pathbreaking "Roman" trilogy is well documented: his 1905 diary refers to Merezhkovskii's third novel, with an entry the next day that mentions the figure of Leonardo da Vinci, and in a review of Merezhkovskii's 1920 play *Tsarevich Aleksei* (Tsarevich Alexis), based on *Peter and Alexis,* Kuzmin compared that novel to the preceding two.[92] And while Kuzmin wrote negatively at times of the Merezhkovskiis' historiosophical views and preaching,[93] in his own Rome-related play he echoed to a certain extent some of the earlier conclusions of his predecessor. He rejected a disillusioning earthly Rome, linked to the Russian state, in order to embrace an alternative Rome related by the Russian artist.

Unlike Merezhkovskii's Third Testament, though, Kuzmin's goal, while narrated through the imagery of an esoteric philosophy, was centered in essence on the glories of this world: love, beauty, and art. For Kuzmin himself, perhaps in the spirit of his 1897 letter to Chicherin, Christ could be a part of this world of joyous simplicity. When he construed Christianity as a sweeping anti-imperial movement or official church, however, he saw yet another all-encompassing and erroneous utopia, one he linked with power in his text as he rejected Third-Rome-style visions.[94] In *The Death of Nero,* the apolitical and anti-institutional writer comes decisively to the fore.

The Death of Nero, never performed but read in the theatrical circles of St. Petersburg and Moscow at the time Bulgakov was beginning work on his *Master and Margarita,* also points the way to that novel.[95] Bulgakov's work, too, features interlocking chronological planes, the motif of "glad tidings," and chronological and thematic reversals of expectations that echo Kuzmin's; one notes, for instance, Kuzmin's placement of the Biblically named Pavel, Marie, and Peter (Marie's father) in the modern, Russian sections of his text, as well as the links he suggests between Jesus Christ and a figure representative of Roman power. Unlike Kuzmin, Bulgakov would not flee decisively from his Russian Rome. He would, however, explore—as Kuzmin had, but more ambiguously—the connections between a compromised writer and a potentially artistic dictator, as he, too, interpolated elements of his own experience with Soviet power into his Rome-related text and demonstrated the ongoing relevance of ancient Rome to modern Russia in a newly imperial stage of its history.

Conclusion

Bulgakov and Beyond

I shall see Cyprus, dear to the Goddess,
I shall see Tyre, Ephesus, and Smyrna,
I shall see Athens, the dream of my youth,
Corinth and far-off Byzantium
and the crown of all desires,
the goal of all strivings—
I shall see Rome the great!
Mikhail Kuzmin, *Alexandrian Songs*, 1905–1908

Each of the writers discussed in this book turned his attention to the relationship between pagans and Christians in ancient Rome and applied the lessons he took from it to his own nation's turbulent present. In the process, he showed that for Russia, "opposites" in fact could be co-participants in a complex creation of national identity. And yet although the birth of Christianity often took center stage, starting with Merezhkovskii's popular *Julian the Apostate*, none of these leading writers devoted his major Rome-related literature of the revolutionary period to the life and milieu of Jesus—surely the key figure in the ancient transformations they described, and symbolic prototype, for many of them, of Russia's early twentieth-century revolutionaries. Focusing on Catiline, who staged his rebellion before Jesus's birth, or on Julian, ruling several centuries after Jesus had been crucified, Blok, Merezhkovskii, and Briusov, for instance, clearly referred to the birth of Christianity and envisaged Jesus, and yet they chose in central "Roman" texts not to describe him in detail.[1] In a sense, such a focus was irrelevant to them: as Blok proclaimed, the "old world" was dead from the moment Jesus appeared in it, and thus revolutionary figures of the preceding period were precursors, and those of subsequent periods, successors. But their works left a gap.

In his novel *Master i Margarita* (The Master and Margarita, written from 1928 to 1940), Mikhail Bulgakov, clearly influenced by Silver Age discussions of cities of God and of man,[2] filled this gap, turning his attention to Jesus's surroundings and to Jesus himself. Intrigued, as Blok was, by Renan's vision of a human Jesus,[3] Bulgakov created a figure grounded in the variegated Roman empire of his day. Like his predecessors, Bulgakov then linked Jesus's Roman world to his own modern-day Russia, then under the rule of Joseph Stalin. Like Ivanov, he showed in the process of such application that the Bolsheviks had created a world alien to Christ. Then, like Kuzmin, he undercut this model of separation between holy and imperial by positing links between the two, links closely tied to his complicated vision of the relationship between the Russian writer and Stalin's Soviet state. The following discussion seeks not to provide a new interpretation of Bulgakov's novel, but, rather, to situate it in an underacknowledged context: that of Russia's "Rome text" in the early decades of the twentieth century.[4] I will examine the Roman setting of Bulgakov's "sunset novel":[5] the historical context for his narrative, the Rome he portrays, and the relationship of this Rome to those of other Russian modernists of the Silver Age. I will then conclude this study of Russia's Rome by turning briefly to the resurrection of the Third Rome formula in post-Soviet Russia.

Bulgakov's *Master and Margarita* in a Roman Context

> Woland spoke, "What an interesting city, [Moscow,] don't you think?"
>
> Azazello stirred and replied respectfully, "Messire, I prefer Rome!"
>
> Mikhail Bulgakov, *The Master and Margarita*, 1928–1940
> (trans. Diana Burgin and Katherine Tiernan O'Connor)

In 63 BCE, as Catiline was leading his failed insurrection against the Roman state, the Roman military leader Pompey was laying successful siege to the city of Jerusalem, thereafter part of the Roman orbit. Rome's approved local man to rule Jerusalem and its environs from the 30s BCE to 4 CE was King Herod, early on a supporter of Mark Antony in Rome's ongoing civil wars, but quick to switch to Octavian when the latter defeated Antony in 31 BCE and then went on to become Rome's first emperor, Augustus Caesar.[6] The politically savvy Herod built up the city of Jerusalem to include a palace for himself (later, Roman procurators would be housed there), towers, fortresses, and the beginnings of a spectacular temple. Starting with Augustus's reign, the lands Herod controlled were considered to be part of the larger imperial province of Syria, which itself was governed by a Roman legate who ruled from Antioch.[7]

Upon Herod's death, his territories were divided among three of his sons: Philip, Herod Antipas, and Archelaus. The land Herod Antipas inherited included Galilee, site of Nazareth, while Archelaus was deeded regions to the south: Samaria and Judea, the latter including Jerusalem. When Archelaus proved an unacceptable ruler, Rome banished him to Gaul in 6 CE and from then on installed Roman procurators to rule Judea and Samaria. From 26 to 36 CE, while Tiberius, adopted son of Augustus, was emperor of Rome, the procurator in question was Pontius Pilate, a man so cruel that his subjects, particularly Jews, complained bitterly about him. After supplication by outraged Samaritans, Rome finally removed him from his post.[8] Jewish protests against Roman rule continued, as did the growing conviction that an apocalyptic age—one that would bring an end to Roman power—was nearing. In the 60s CE, Emperor Nero dispatched the army commander Vespasian to vanquish Judean opposition to Roman rule. Two years after Nero's suicide in 68 CE, Vespasian's son Titus led Roman troops in demolishing the recently completed Jewish Temple and slaughtering or taking captive much of the Jewish population (the Arch of Titus in the Roman Forum recalls this event). By this time Vespasian had become emperor of Rome. It has been postulated that the spoils from the savage sacking of Jerusalem later went toward the creation of the Flavian Amphitheater, now known as the Coliseum, built under Vespasian and the sons who succeeded him.[9]

Jesus, a Jew, was born during the rule of King Herod and Emperor Augustus and lived his life under Herod Antipas in Galilee, where he began his ministry, and then under Pontius Pilate in Judea. The dominant language of the region was Aramaic, related to Hebrew. Jesus's crucifixion—a punishment typically meted out to slaves and noncitizens of Rome—occurred under Pilate in approximately 30 CE; the Roman emperor at the time was Tiberius, then living on the island of

Capri, off the Italian coast. Christians would be persecuted by the Roman state for centuries to come, at times in the Coliseum, until the fourth-century emperor Constantine chose to make the faith inspired by the Galilean Jesus the dominant religion of the Roman Empire, with its new, Eastern capital, Constantinople. Despite the efforts of "pagans" such as Julian "the Apostate" and Senator Symmachus, Rome's Christianity would hold. The tensions of the preceding centuries, however, when provincial faith clashed with world *imperium,* would inspire countless creative works, among them those of Russian modernist writers, including Mikhail Bulgakov, during Russia's revolutionary age.

Though different in genre, *The Master and Margarita* is quite similar in its structure to Kuzmin's *The Death of Nero.* Like Kuzmin's play, Bulgakov's text is explicitly set in both the ancient world and the modern world: its settings are Jerusalem at the time of Jesus and Moscow in the late 1920s and 1930s. And as in Kuzmin's work, Bulgakov's two time periods are linked through the figure of a Russian artist, who writes during the modern period about the ancient one. Bulgakov's artist, the Master, tells the story of Jesus's meeting with Pontius Pilate, followed by Jesus's execution and Pilate's almost simultaneous remorse.[10] The Master's work meets with derision from the Soviet literary hierarchy, and he ends up in a clinic for the mentally ill. When the devil comes to modern-day Moscow in the guise of the magician Woland, the Master's faithful lover Margarita agrees to serve Woland for an evening as the hostess at his ball in order to have the Master returned to her. Even as Woland and his gang wreak havoc on Moscow and on its literary world in particular, they restore the Master to Margarita. Chapters featuring this contemporary Russian tale are interspersed with chapters devoted to Jesus's story and its effects on Pontius Pilate, chapters presumed to be identical to the Master's own text (and significantly different, one should note, from the established Gospel narratives). At the end of Bulgakov's novel, the now immortal Master finishes his tale with another meeting, long desired by Pilate, between Pilate and Jesus, as Woland hints at a future agreement between the two.

That Jesus is a subject of the Roman Empire in the early years of the first century CE is made clear from the first section of the novel dedicated to the ancient world. A reader's first image in this section is one of Roman power: "the procurator of Judea, Pontius Pilate" walks "into the roofed colonnade that connected the two wings of the palace of Herod the Great" (30; 13). As we learn in a later section, Pilate hates his current posting to this troublesome eastern province: the "absurd construction of Herod's" that he must inhabit, the climate that makes him ill, the need to "transfer troops around" in response to the apocalyptically motivated uprisings of the day. "Oh, if it weren't for the imperial service," he laments to Afranius, the head of his secret police (307; 259). And yet Pilate, terrified of Tiberius, whom he pictures as a powerful and threatening degenerate in the gardens of Capri, must fulfill his obligations as a Roman ruler loyal to Rome's emperor. He must represent Rome before the Jewish high priest and engage in political jousting with him. He must condemn Yeshua (Bulgakov uses the Aramaic variant of Jesus's name), who announces in dangerously anti-Roman fashion that "every kind of power is a form of violence against the people, and that there will come a time when neither the power of the Caesars, nor any other kind of power will exist" (41; 22). And he must proclaim Yeshua's sentence "in the name of the Emperor Caesar" to his cohorts of soldiers, who respond with the traditional "Hail, Caesar" (51; 30), and to crowds of pilgrims preparing to celebrate the Jewish festival of Passover. Centurions, clad in burnished armor, then escort the hapless prisoners to their painful deaths, drawn out until the executioner, whispering, "Praise the merciful Hegemon" (i.e., Pilate), stabs the crucified men to death (189; 151). Bulgakov presents a classic narrative of the brutality of the powerful Roman state vis-à-vis a representative of faith-filled otherworldliness.

In apparent contrast to somber Yershalaim (Bulgakov's variant of Jerusalem), driven by carefully managed Roman authority, the novel's Moscow scenes have a carnivalesque quality and are characterized at first glance by an expanding power vacuum. During the visit of Woland and his band of followers, who include the jester-like cat Behemoth, the entire management of the Variety Theater is either killed or driven mad through a series of inexplicable occurrences. Women at Woland's magic show turn out to be clad only in their underwear when the new clothes bestowed upon them during the show disappear once they leave the theater. The staff of the Entertainment Commission find their director temporarily invisible and themselves singing uncontrollably; they land in the same insane asylum as the Master. Griboedov House, site of the Writers' Union, and several other buildings go up in flames merrily lit by Woland's henchmen. The head of the Writers' Union, Berlioz, meets his death early in the novel; twelve colleagues await him impatiently that night at Griboedov before learning that their leader has been decapitated.[11] Confused police search ineffectually for ways to capture Woland and his men. When they arrive at the notorious apartment that Woland has taken over from Styopa Likhodeyev, director of the Variety Theater, they see Behemoth, who challenges them to a duel and is met with a shower of bullets—but "not only was no one killed, no one was even wounded" (347; 291).

Russia and Roman Judea thus appear quite different, a conclusion that seems to gain credence from the conversation between Woland and his associate Azazello near the end of the novel that I have quoted as the epigraph to this section. And yet Russia, too, has its Roman elements, as Azazello's late, overt comment actually encourages the reader to recognize. Bulgakov inserts a series of references to Rome into the Moscow sections of his novel. Early in the novel, for instance, in a precursor to Woland and Azazello's conversation about Rome, two men with Roman-sounding names, Amvrosy and Foka, meet at Griboedov. Amvrosy, of course, recalls in name Ambrosius, well known to a reader of Briusov's *Altar of Victory* as an antipagan representative of a Christianity sanctioned by state authorities. Foka (Phocas) was the name given to both a universally disliked seventh-century Byzantine emperor and a second-century Christian martyr who later became a saint.[12] In this context, Amvrosy's insistence to Foka that he is "categorically opposed" (67; 47) to visiting a restaurant called the Coliseum certainly makes sense. (For his part, Foka has acknowledged that Amvrosy "know[s] how to live" [67; 47].) Further, the fires set by Woland's group recall the ones Nero set in Rome and then blamed on the "new sect" of Christians.[13] In addition, the surname of the Variety Theater's financial manager is Rimskii ("Roman"), thus implying that a Roman of sorts is in a position of power in the world of art that the Master has tried to inhabit. The Master, after all, has been banished from Soviet society for daring to pen the anti-Roman tale of Jesus. The additional links that Bulgakov, like Kuzmin, asserts between his ancient and modern settings through a series of repeated words, images, and gestures reinforce the suggestion of important similarities between the two cities.[14]

Bulgakov's inclusion of Roman elements in his depiction of Moscow suggests that, contrary to chaotic appearances, the capital must possess elements of imperial authority. The connections that have been suggested between Woland and Stalin, during whose purges and terror Bulgakov wrote his novel, support such a conclusion.[15] According to Andrei Siniavskii, for instance, a writer with his own experiences of an oppressive Soviet state, in *The Master and Margarita* Bulgakov "showed that history had entered a realm beyond human comprehension, a realm of demonic powers."[16] Siniavskii characterizes Stalin as "a Magician who, for a protracted period, was able to infuse [Soviet history] with the force and aspect of the fabulous fantastic, of a mad, nightmarish farce." Asserting a parallel between Stalin and Bulgakov's magician, he argues, "It's no accident that the events in Bulgakov's novel revolve around an insane asylum that ends by enveloping all of Moscow."[17] Siniavskii notes that the power-driven Stalin sought to reinstate aspects of tsardom, and in so doing became "a synonym for the entire state, for life on earth."[18] If one accepts this reading, Bulgakov's Roman references, taken together, hint at a Russian power structure more elusive than Pilate's, perhaps, but equally "Roman" in its strength and values. Establishing links between the Yershalaim and Moscow of his novel and implying further connections to his contemporary, Stalinist surroundings, Bulgakov portrayed his own Russia as a complex successor to the Roman Empire of Pilate's day.

Bulgakov's merged portrayal of Pilate's Yershalaim and Soviet Moscow parodies the notion of Russia as a messianic Third Rome. Rather, both cities resemble the Jerusalem of the anti-Roman Revelation 11:8, "the great city which is allegorically called Sodom and Egypt, where their Lord was crucified." For Bulgakov, who sets the ancient part of his novel specifically in Judea, Jews play a significant—and negative—role in this violation of a potential, sacred New Jerusalem. In Yershalaim, Yeshua is persecuted by the priest Kaifa (Caiaphas) and his fellow Jews, who do not permit Pilate to pardon Yeshua despite Pilate's wish to do so.[19] Bulgakov separates Yeshua further from the historical Jesus's Jewish roots and surroundings: Yeshua professes to have no family, though he says his father may be Syrian, and to have only one unwanted disciple, a Levite whose writings Yeshua himself dismisses as unconnected to his own sayings. In Moscow, meanwhile, the Master finds his life destroyed by the Soviet literary bureaucrats, clearly portrayed as Jews in an early draft of the novel.[20] Specifically, the Master's critics—Kaifa's successors—attack him for trying to "sneak into print an apologia for Jesus Christ" (151; 120).

Linking the Jesus figure of his ancient narrative to the spiritually minded Russian writer in his modern one,[21] Bulgakov echoes in a sense those fin-de-siècle thinkers such as Merezhkovskii who had posited a Jesus more Hellenistic (and thus connected to Russian spirituality) than Jewish.[22] Faith and "true" creativity are related for Bulgakov, and they are represented ideally by Yeshua and the Master. Instead, however, Kaifa and the literary critics continue to speak for religion and art, though they are in fact motivated by the secular power of their Roman cities rather than by the otherworldly concerns that Yeshua and the Master value. Rimskii's financial directives at the theater thus take on the resonance of the money changers at the Temple whom Jesus condemns in John 2:13–16. And, continuing the chain of profanations, Bishop Ambrosius's Russian "descendant" Amvrosy speaks fervently of fish, a symbol of Christ—but at Griboedov, where the well-fed and privileged Amvrosy makes his claims to gourmet status, the fish is consumed by the "false priests" of Soviet culture. Meanwhile, Woland, posing as a foreigner, is informed that international visitors generally stay at the Metropole (Metropolis) Hotel, but he chooses nonetheless to stay in Likhodeyev's apartment: Rome, the archetypal metropolis, encompasses any Russian home. "Holy Moscow" is beset by Rome and Jerusalem in their most earthly forms.

Thus, when Ivan Bezdomnyi, the writer who observes Berlioz's death, shows up at Griboedov defensively clutching an icon and desperate to share his experiences, he is received with utter lack of comprehension and then sent to the psychiatric clinic, where he meets the Master. In the world Bulgakov inhabited and portrayed, a besieged Russia, no longer able to accommodate the wisdom of its holy fools, instead expels them to insane asylums (one recalls Renan's words about sacred speech that in modern times is labeled insanity).

And yet, Bulgakov asserts, the holy fools still matter—and surprisingly, they matter to Rome, even as they perish at its behest. In Yershalaim, Pilate, whose name is synonymous with cruelty, is in fact moved by Yeshua's gentle philosophy of a temple of new truth and his intuitive understanding of Pilate's misery. In a remorseful dream after he has pronounced the death sentence, Pilate queries, "Could you with your intelligence really imagine that the procurator of Judea would ruin his career over a man who had committed a crime against Caesar?" (322; 272). His answer in the dream is tardily affirmative: "He would do anything to save the totally innocent mad dreamer and physician from death!" (322; 272). Pilate is guilt-stricken over his own weakness of character and dissatisfied with his vengeful murder of Judas and his subsequent gift of parchment to Levi Matvei, who will write down his own version of Yeshua's words. He is doomed to spend the next two thousand years longing for another chance to speak with Yeshua, to undo the damage done. The forgiving Yeshua, for his part, refrains from blaming Pilate for his death: during his lifetime, Yeshua's last word is "Hegemon" (189; 152), the title Pilate had insisted Yeshua use to address him.[23] Although Judea forms a part of Bulgakov's Rome, then, Roman power is redeemable, while Judea, it seems, is not.

The curious relationship between Yeshua and Pilate, or Christ and Rome, is duplicated to a degree in the interactions between the Russian Master and Woland. Like Pilate, Woland has a surprising side to him, one that appreciates the Master's narrative of Yeshua. In fact, the dangerously powerful Woland who runs the insane asylum that is Moscow, and, at his ball, entertains vicious criminals, concentrates his disruptive efforts on the literary community that has rejected the Master and his work. At Margarita's request, he rescues the Master from the clinic where he has been living anonymously and restores to him in full the manuscript the Master had partially burnt after the critics' attacks. At the end of the novel, Woland has Azazello poison the two lovers, but he then sees that they are resurrected and taken to a place of "peace." Tying together the ancient and modern settings and thus their participants, Yeshua becomes actively involved in the fate of the Master and Margarita when he requests this solution for the couple—who do not, he says at the same time, deserve his own "light."

Broadening the circle of relationships once again, critics have repeatedly linked the connection between the Master and Woland to the one between Bulgakov and Stalin. In 1930, after his plays had been attacked by vitriolic Soviet critics and banned, Bulgakov wrote to Stalin, who subsequently phoned him and told him to expect work at the Moscow Art Theater. Elena Sergeevna Bulgakova, Bulgakov's third wife and the prototype for Margarita,[24] asserted later that the conversation with Stalin may well have saved Bulgakov's life: without Stalin's help, Bulgakov might have committed suicide and never have written *The Master and Margarita*.[25] In later years, Bulgakov found an odd sort of vindication as the critics who had denigrated his work vanished in the dictator's purges.[26] While he himself faced a series of bitter disappointments in his career and constant fear over his own future, he remained alive. The multifaceted interactions between Bulgakov and Stalin reached their culmination in Bulgakov's last play, *Batum*, begun in 1938 as he was at work on *The Master and Margarita*. Its theme was Stalin's early life. Among the titles Bulgakov considered for his play were "The Master" and "The Pastor,"[27] linking his version of Stalin to the Russian writer in his novel (and, correspondingly, himself) and to Christ. Bulgakov further complicated his portrayal through a scene in which Stalin predicts a time when a devil, perhaps representative of Stalin himself, will steal the sun—a sign for Bulgakov of approaching apocalypse.[28] Thus in *Batum* Bulgakov infused his portrayal of Stalin with all the ambivalence he had come to feel toward the leader—an ambivalence reflected as well in *The Master and Margarita*'s violent but potentially redeemable magician, Woland.

Bulgakov, then, repeats Kuzmin's conflation of artist and emperor. Paralleling the link between Kuzmin's alter ego Pavel and Nero, Bulgakov's semiautobiographical Master establishes connections to Woland/Stalin. Unlike Yeshua, who treats Pilate with love, the Master appears to be motivated by fear and disbelief in his mortal interactions with Woland. Thus, unlike Yeshua, he compromises himself even as in a sense he uplifts his imperial double,[29] thereby providing possible justification for his unfitness in Yeshua's eyes for "the light." At the same time, though, through this contact, questionable though it may be, the Master serves as an example, albeit imperfect, of the Russian artist's ability to follow Yeshua in establishing links between Rome and Christianity. It is he, then, in a wiser, resurrected mode, who finishes Yeshua's story, telling the suffering Pilate to go and meet his murdered acquaintance from long ago: "Free! Free! He is waiting for you!" (383; 324). For Bulgakov, this second conversation, one he himself craved but did not have with Stalin, can occur only in an apocalyptic, artistically created framework. As David Bethea writes, "With the New Jerusalem still distant, only art can free Pilate, write history from actuality back into possibility."[30] Once the Master has uttered his postapocalyptic lines, both Yershalaim and Moscow, so unreceptive to Yeshua's story in secular time, then fade out, even as Babylon, symbolic of the oppressive Roman state, and then the entire "first heaven" and "first earth" vanish at the end of Revelation as the New Jerusalem at last approaches.[31]

Characterizing Russia through Yershalaim as a province of the Roman Empire, Bulgakov, like earlier modernists, claimed a complex Rome as a key to Russia's national identity. The leading figure in this scenario was Jesus, reconfigured to coincide with a twentieth-century Russian writer. Yeshua the provincial Galilean comes before the power of the Roman state to claim, as his bishops would in subsequent centuries, that "a new temple of truth will be created" (35; 17) in place of the Jewish Temple or Rome's edifice of power. Yet in his first discussion with Pilate, Yeshua startles the Roman procurator when he speaks not only his own Aramaic, but Greek and Latin as well. As Yeshua explains, in Latin, his philosophy of "good people" (38–39; 20), the procurator warms to him and his message, longing to take Yeshua to his home in

Caesarea instead of sending him to his death. Yeshua, then, can speak the language of Caesar and of Rome. This polyglot, rootless wanderer thus recalls the Russian lauded by Dostoevskii in his Pushkin Speech and then by Merezhkovskii and Ivanov in their visions of the Russian intellectual: in his ability to sacrifice his own identity, as he sloughs off family and associates, he can cross barriers of nationality to bring a spiritual truth home to the West. Bulgakov, writing another Rome text featuring an authorial alter ego, connects Yeshua, the Master, and himself. Yeshua's "Russian" quality of "all-human-ness," to cite Merezhkovskii's "On the Reasons for the Decline," redounds once again to the twentieth-century Russian writer, despite his imperfections.

Thus, in a new realm and era the Master's conciliatory Russian word as conceptualized by Bulgakov creates a literary, unified "Third Rome," as Pilate and Yeshua come together. Back in Moscow, the Master's "disciple" Ivan, successor to Merezhkovskii's Alexis and Tikhon, is privy, when the moon is magically full, to this otherworldly vision of reconciliation between Yeshua and Pilate, Christianity and empire. Bulgakov's novel thus in a sense brings a reader full circle back to Merezhkovskii's trilogy, written decades earlier, as it recalls the earlier writer's combination of contemporary despair and hope in the potential of Russian writers to create, if only in words and images, a unifying Russian ideal.

The Master and Margarita forms an important part of the "Rome text" of Russian modernism, a text that remained remarkably consistent despite radical changes in Russian politics and culture between 1890 and 1940. The fundamental elements of this text were the worldly empire and the kingdom of God—and the clash or unification of the two. For each writer, of course, the elements held different connotations, and historical realities and associated attitudes affected the assigned roles. As Russia's revolution progressed and a strong new state came into being, for instance, the players shifted. Revolutionaries, connected for Merezhkovskii, Briusov, and Blok with the Christians' conflict with the Roman state, for Ivanov, Kuzmin, and Bulgakov increasingly became embodiments of that state itself, as the erstwhile rebels consolidated power. Nonetheless, Rome in its various aspects continued to serve a powerful and constant role in discussions of Russian national identity.

Writing Russia as part of a multivalent Rome, the Russian modernists in this study asserted a membership, unique in its partially Eastern, "provincial" cast, in "Western civilization" as traditionally construed. In keeping with the archaeological discoveries and philosophical and historical fascinations of their era, these writers, witnesses to a radical, twentieth-century experiment—the creation of a Communist state—affirmed the ongoing value of myth when they placed the events around them into the context of an ancient and equally overwhelming story. Further, inserting into their Rome-based texts the alter egos that could act for them in a creative realm, they proclaimed an important role for the Russian artist in the midst of change, even when they were disillusioned with their actual contemporary Russia. Their works stand both as revisionist recreations of Rome in its many aspects and, simultaneously, as prescriptions, viewed through a Roman prism, for the future of the Russian nation—or the Russian artist. When Russians rediscovered the Silver Age as the Soviet empire collapsed a half-century after Bulgakov's death, they reencountered fin-de-siècle formulations of Rome—and reworked them in ways that the monk Filofei never could have imagined.

The Third Rome in the Post-Soviet Era

Currently the Russian appetite for its Italian cultural patrimony is extraordinary.
Joseph Brodsky, "The Russian Academy: Preliminary Notes," 1995

In the contemporary Russian writer Viktor Pelevin's novel *Zhizn' nasekomykh* (The Life of Insects, 1994), two human beings in the form of insects discuss Russia in the post-Soviet period:

> The road they were walking along ran past a deep foundation pit with the ruins of an unfinished building. Grass, bushes, and even young trees grew in the cracks of the walls, and the place looked less like a foundation dug for a new building than like a grave for a building that had died, or the excavated remains of an ancient city. Sam took a long look at it and walked on without speaking. Natasha also was silent.
>
> "Yes," said Sam, when the pit was behind them. "That's really fascinating. One odd thing I've noticed here. They say Russia's the Third Rome, right?"
>
> "Yes, that's right, the third. And the second Israel. Ivan the Terrible said that. I read it in the newspaper."
>
> "Well, if we write Third Rome in Russian, *Trety Rim,* and then turn the word for 'Rome' backward, we get *Trety Mir,* Third World."[32]

In their attention to the idea of the Third Rome, Pelevin's insects capture a phenomenon that has been widespread in various realms since the "decline and fall" of the Soviet state. Scholars, political and religious activists, artists, and entrepreneurs have seen in the increasingly malleable medieval term a formula diversely applicable to their changing society. Such fluidity is certainly suspect from the point of view of historical veracity. Noting that toward the end of the 1980s "the Third Rome reentered Russian historical studies with a vengeance," historian Paul Bushkovitch points to the problems inherent in this focus: "The story of the Third Rome in Russian historiography is a case of the triumph of the present over the past, of the anachronistic overemphasis placed by modern scholars, working from modern notions, on an idea of dubious importance."[33] Bushkovitch's concerns are echoed by his fellow historian Marshall Poe, who writes, "'Third Rome,' then, is the result of the projection of a modern idea . . . onto a superficially analogous early modern concept."[34] And yet, Poe acknowledges, it is precisely this process of projection that creates a legitimate field of inquiry for scholars of the Third Rome concept: how has the term been used to support pre-existing notions of Russian national identity, or to reflect their disappearance?

In 1991, as the Soviet empire collapsed, Andrei Fadin published an article titled "Tretii Rim v tret'em mire: Razmyshleniia na ruinakh imperii" (The Third Rome in the Third World: Musings on the Ruins of an Empire). Acknowledging that the Soviet world, previously a counterbalance to the "first world," or the West, had "fallen," Fadin wondered how Russia would overcome its loss of identity and disintegration of living standards in the years to come.[35] Ten years later, in a detailed article in a newsletter of the Russian Special Forces, Egor Kholmogorov provided one possible response to questions such as Fadin's when he noted that the very concept of the Third Rome provided Russians with a forceful national identity, "placing Russia in a position that cannot be compared with any in history." Kholmogorov maintained that "there is not a single somewhat educated Russian who would not know the words 'two Romes fell, and a third stands, and a fourth there shall not be.'" Intent on fulfilling a violently imperialistic interpretation of the term, he called for Russians to "drive off any possible pretenders to the Roman scepter with kicks, cudgels, and nuclear weapons—there is no other way."[36] The nationalist group Pamiat', too, has found the term useful.

Other paths, of course, are being advocated, less violent ones, which also make use of the Third Rome formula. The religious and mystical applications of the term over the past decade provide numerous examples. Articles on the quarrels between the Russian Orthodox Church and the Catholic Church or between Russian Orthodoxy and the Patriarchate of Constantinople have found in "Third Rome" a polemically useful substitute for "Russia." "The Third Rome has quarreled with the second," Aleksei Makarkin announced in an article written in 2000.[37] The two churches, he explained, were arguing over ecclesiastical jurisdictions, as they had so often in the past. Meanwhile, works that feature a Christian-apocalyptic worldview along with an assertion of Russia's messianic significance, particularly as compared with the decadent West, unsurprisingly abound; visions of prophetic gravity labeled "Third Rome" have appealed to painters as well as writers.[38] The theme has not, however, precluded an openness to the West: in an April 2003 article that recalls earlier reports from Russians visiting Rome, Ol'ga Dmitrieva wrote of the delight a denizen of the "Third Rome" finds when visiting the "First"—although she acknowledges, in a refrain common to Russian Rome usage, that the Romans are generally unaware of the Russians' status.[39]

The term has also come to be used on the level of kitsch to provide Russian flavor to a diverse variety of enterprises. At times the connections between these enterprises and Filofei's doctrine are decidedly curious. As of this writing, the Third Rome publishing house is a leading Russian publisher of automobile-related texts, including road atlases: "our leitmotif is automobiles and everything connected with them," the company's website advertises as it promotes its on-line shop.[40] A Russian bank is called "The Third Rome," as is a video game created in 1996 and dedicated rather anachronistically to Russian history of the twelfth and thirteenth centuries; "precisely at this time of savage struggle for the throne of the Ruler of Rus' . . . there arose the great Orthodox state, which shortly thereafter contemporaries would call the Third Rome," an advertisement for the game proclaims.[41] If one is mysteriously transported to Yalta, as *The Master and Margarita*'s Styopa Likhodeyev is when Woland takes over his apartment, one can dine at the Third Rome Restaurant and gamble at the Third Rome Casino (fig. 15). Meanwhile, a travel agency in Sochi, capitalizing on the area's history, calls itself the "Third Rome" and advertises family trips in the Black Sea region.[42] And it is tantalizing to imagine what Bulgakov the master satirist could have done with Moscow's annual "Miss Tretii Rim" (Miss Third Rome) pageant. At the eighth such pageant in 2001, contestants participated in a show that, according to the pageant organizer, connected contemporary life with the "distant past," as the backdrop for the festivities featured renderings of Rome, Constantinople, and Moscow.[43]

Fig. 15. The Third Rome Casino, Yalta, 2003

More substantively, an exhibit called "Moscow the Third Rome" opened in October 2003 at the Museum of the Church of Christ the Savior, and was devoted to spiritual and artistic works and manuscripts from several Russian archives, museums, and the Russian State Library.[44] Its organizers sought to draw connections between the Russian past, including its links to Byzantium, and contemporary Russia.

In addition, the display of the "Trojan treasure" (Sokrovishcha Troi) that opened in 1996 at Moscow's Pushkin Museum, founded by Ivan Tsvetaev at the beginning of the twentieth century, links contemporary Russian life with Russia's longstanding fascination with Western civilization and its complex origins—and their relationship to Russia. Although the gold has been dated at least one thousand years earlier than Homer's Troy, it is nonetheless often called "Priam's Treasure" after the defeated Trojan king of Homer's tales. When Heinrich Schliemann found the treasure in the 1870s, he disregarded Turkish law, smuggled his find into Greece, and, eventually, bequeathed the treasure to the German people. The gold remained on display in Berlin until the final stages of World War II, when Soviet soldiers confiscated it and brought it back to the Soviet Union. After that, the gold disappeared from view;

many presumed it lost forever, a casualty of war. It came to light definitively in October of 1994, when German museum officials thrilled scholars and art enthusiasts worldwide with the announcement that they had seen the gold at the Pushkin Museum.[45] Several countries quickly voiced claims to the treasure, including Turkey, Germany, Greece (after all, they won the Trojan War), and, of course, Russia.[46]

Claiming the treasure, these nations have in effect claimed the Trojan narrative in concrete form. The treasure represents an extraordinary heritage, and the tale of its discovery is one that bolsters the value the modern age has assigned to myth: Schliemann so believed in the Homeric tales that he used them—successfully—as his guide to the site of Troy. The exhibition and treasure claimed by Russia at the turn of the twenty-first century may thus be viewed in the context of the reception of antiquity during Russia's Silver Age a century earlier, when scholars and artists came together to explore a curiously vibrant ancient past. Indeed, beyond the concept of spoils of war (an idea lent added fuel by the purported German theft of Russia's famous Amber Room from the Catherine Palace during World War II), Russians have justified their current stewardship of the treasure by citing Schliemann's personal and professional links to Russia and by invoking the fin-de-siècle passion for archaeological exploration that his discoveries both epitomized and furthered in Russia as well as Europe. "After all, Schliemann, a German citizen, spent 18 years of his life in Russia as a successful businessman, amassing a substantial fortune. He received the title of honorary citizen of the city of St. Petersburg and there he learned the Russian language and married a Russian woman . . . who bore him three children. . . . Scholars maintain that he received important motivation for this [Troy-related] work in Russia," the official catalogue of the exhibit states.[47] Moreover, after his work in Troy, "anxious to retain his ties with Russia, with which he still felt deeply connected," Schliemann planned a new expedition, this time to Colchis.[48] As this site in Georgia had been absorbed by the Russian Empire earlier in the century, Schliemann contacted Tsvetaev for a recommendation letter. (Tsvetaev wrote the letter, but permission was denied.)

The connections between Schliemann and Tsvetaev, father of the poet Marina Tsvetaeva, once again call to mind the Silver Age environment that spurred the Russian modernists to create their Rome texts. The gold at the Pushkin Museum, which became available once more to Russian and international viewers, may be compared in this light to the texts themselves, many of them newly republished along with other

Silver Age texts in the post-Soviet period. Emerging from the collapse of the Soviet Empire and reinserting imperialist doctrines and trappings into their national discourse, Russians yet again have turned to Rome in an effort to assign meaning to the present—hence the profusion of "Third Romes" throughout Russia today. Finding in the "Eternal City" an inspiring predecessor and a benchmark for future goals, Russia continues to recreate and claim Rome.

Notes

Introduction

1. This quotation from the *Translatio Sancti Clementis* or *Legenda italica* of Leo of Ostia, composed in approximately 1100, is cited in Leonard Boyle, *A Short Guide to St. Clement's, Rome* (Rome: Collegio San Clemente, 1989), 33.

2. Boyle, *Short Guide to St. Clement's*, 5, 8. See also Tat'iana Iashaeva and Mariia Motovilina, *Krestnyi put' sviatogo Klimenta: Rim—Khersones* (Sevastopol: Inkermanskii Sviato-Klimentovskii Monastyr', 2002).

3. "'The Tale of the Vladimir Princes,' composed in the first half of the sixteenth century, introduced into the historical record a brother of Augustus, Prus, who presumably ruled the Prussian lands and was a direct ancestor of Riurik. It then traced the lineage of the Moscow princes back to Riurik" (Richard S. Wortman, *Scenarios of Power: Myth and Ceremony in Russian Monarchy*, 2 vols. [Princeton, N.J.: Princeton University Press, 1995–2000], 1:26). See, too, G. S. Knabe, *Russkaia antichnost'. Soderzhanie, rol' i sud'ba antichnogo naslediia v kul'ture Rossii. Programma-konspekt lektsionnogo kursa* (Moscow: Rossiiskii Gosudarstvennyi Gumanitarnyi Universitet, 2000), 100–101: Knabe notes that drawings at the Moscow Kremlin dating to the seventeenth century feature Augustus and his descendants.

4. Aspects of the respective associations of Moscow, Rome, and Constantinople have been discussed by historians, cultural semioticians, and others. See, for instance, Joel Raba, "Moscow—the Third Rome or the New Jerusalem," *Historische Veröffentlichungen: Forschungen zur osteuropäischen Geschichte* 50 (1995): 303, on the complex "character components" of the "triad Rome-Constantinople-Moscow": "the rulers of pagan Rome, who nevertheless were the masters of the world, become the forefathers of the rulers of Muscovite Russia; the rulers of Christian Byzantium transmitted the symbols of their power to the forefathers of the Russian autocrat elected by God." See, too, William K. Medlin, *Moscow and East Rome* (Geneva: Librarie E. Droz, 1952), 79,

on the legacy of Byzantium for Russian rulers: "temporal head of Orthodox Christendom and defender of the universal faith." Semioticians Iurii Lotman and Boris Uspenskii argue that "the idea of 'Moscow as the Third Rome' brings together two tendencies—the religious and the political. When the second aspect was being considered the connection with the *first Rome* was emphasized, this entailed a suppression of the religious aspect and underlined the secular or 'imperial' one. The primary figure in this case is Caesar Augustus, not Constantine" (Ju. M. Lotman and B. A. Uspenskij, "Echoes of the Notion 'Moscow the Third Rome' in Peter the Great's Ideology," in their *The Semiotics of Russian Culture,* ed. Ann Shukman [Ann Arbor: Department of Slavic Languages and Literatures, University of Michigan, 1984], 54). See, too, Lotman's discussion of St. Petersburg as characterized by "two archetypes: the 'eternal Rome' and the 'non-eternal, doomed Rome' (Constantinople)" (Yuri M. Lotman, *Universe of the Mind: A Semiotic Theory of Culture,* trans. Ann Shukman, intro. Umberto Eco [Bloomington: Indiana University Press, 1990], 194).

5. Tsvetaeva's essay "Geroi truda," devoted to Valerii Briusov, characterizes Briusov as a "Scythian Roman" (Marina Tsvetaeva, "Geroi truda [Zapisi o Valerii Briusove]," in her *Proza,* intro. Valentina S. Coe [Letchworth, U.K.: Bradda Books, 1969], 88).

6. For a helpful example of such a study, see Aleksei Kara-Murza, ed., *Znamenitye russkie o Rime* (Moscow: Izdatel'stvo Nezavisimaia Gazeta, 2001), which contains reactions of Russian visitors in Rome from the early nineteenth through the early twentieth centuries. Kara-Murza has compiled similar volumes on Venice (*Znamenitye russkie o Venetsii* [Moscow: Izdatel'stvo Nezavisimaia Gazeta, 2001]) and on Florence (*Znamenitye russkie o Florentsii* [Moscow: Izdatel'stvo Nezavisimaia Gazeta, 2001]).

7. "Just as the dimension of depth has vanished from the sphere of visual creation, so the dimension of historical depth has vanished from the content of the major works of modern literature. Past and present are apprehended spatially, locked in a timeless unity that, while it may accentuate surface differences, eliminates any feeling of sequence by the very act of juxtaposition" (Joseph Frank, *The Idea of Spatial Form* [New Brunswick, N.J.: Rutgers University Press, 1991], 63). Frank notes (62–63) that modern works "maintain a continual juxtaposition between aspects of the past and the present so that both are fused in one comprehensive view."

8. Cited in Peter Brown, *The Rise of Western Christendom* (Malden, Mass.: Blackwell Publishers, 1997), 6.

9. Ovid called the area "a barbarous land" and "the remotest part of the world" (Ovid, *Tristia,* in *Ovid in Six Volumes,* vol. 6, *Tristia, Ex Ponto,* trans. Arthur Leslie Wheeler, Loeb Classical Library [Cambridge, Mass.: Harvard University Press, 1988], 143, 153).

10. Brown, *The Rise of Western Christendom,* 126. See also Patrick J. Geary, "Barbarians and Ethnicity," in *Late Antiquity: A Guide to the Postclassical World,*

ed. G. W. Bowersock, Peter Brown, and Oleg Grabar (Cambridge, Mass.: Belknap Press of Harvard University Press, 1999), 109: "whenever the Slavs appear in sources, they do so not as peasants but as fierce warriors, loosely organized into short-lived bands."

11. This tendency is evident in the title of V. S. Pritchett's *The Gentle Barbarian: The Life and Work of Turgenev* (London: Chatto & Windus, 1977). See as well Queen Victoria's 1878 characterization of the Russians during the Russo-Turkish War: "the great barbarians, the retarders of all liberty and civilisation that exists" (cited in Walter L. Arnstein, "The Warrior Queen: Reflections on Victoria and Her World," *Albion* 30, no. 1 [1998]: 23).

12. See Edward Shils, "Center and Periphery," in his *The Constitution of Society* (Chicago: University of Chicago Press, 1982), 93–109. Shils notes in another essay that "every society, seen macrosociologically, may be interpreted as a center and a periphery. The center consists of those institutions (and roles) which exercise authority—whether it be economic, governmental, political, military—and of those which create and diffuse cultural symbols—religious, literary, etc.—through churches, schools, publishing houses, etc. The periphery consists of those strata or sectors of the society which are the recipients of commands and of beliefs which they do not themselves create or cause to be diffused, and of those who are lower in the distribution or allocation of rewards, dignities, facilities, etc." (Edward Shils, "Society and Societies," in *The Constitution of Society*, 59).

13. On the Greek trading colonies in the Black Sea region, dating back at least to the middle of the first millennium BCE, see E. D. Frolov, *Russkaia nauka ob antichnosti* (St. Petersburg: Izd. S.-Peterburgskogo Universiteta, 1999), 9; see also Charles King, *The Black Sea: A History* (Oxford: Oxford University Press, 2004), 26–42. On Roman views of the non-Roman world, Brown writes, regarding primarily the Western frontiers of the empire, "The reality was more complex than Roman stereotypes of the 'barbarians' would suggest" (*The Rise of Western Christendom*, 12).

14. For a fascinating treatment of America's preoccupation with Rome, see William L. Vance, *America's Rome*, 2 vols. (New Haven, Conn.: Yale University Press, 1989). The first volume deals with classical Rome in particular.

15. In the essay from which I have selected the epigraph to this section, Joseph Brodsky addresses the issue of these differing attitudes and argues that "Rome, which doctored the history of our civilization anyway, deleted the Byzantine millennium from the record" (Joseph Brodsky, "Flight From Byzantium," in *Less than One: Selected Essays* [New York: Farrar Straus Giroux, 1986], 414). Brodsky writes in relation to the trip to Istanbul that inspired his essay, "After all, I spent thirty-two years in what is known as the Third Rome, about a year and a half in the First. Consequently, I needed the Second, if only for my collection" (395). Before his death in 1996, Brodsky called for a Russian academy in Rome, asserting that "Italian culture is indeed the mother of Russian

aesthetics" and concluding, "Italy was a revelation to the Russians; now it can become the source of their renaissance" (Joseph Brodsky, "The Russian Academy: Preliminary Notes," *New York Review of Books*, 21 March 1996, 45). Knabe identifies three examples during the Soviet era of classical influence on Russian culture: the elegiac depictions of St. Petersburg in the literature of the 1920s; the monumental "Stalinist" architecture of the 1930s and 1940s; and, finally, the "Roman theme" in Brodsky's work from the 1980s to the beginning of the 1990s (*Russkaia antichnost'*, 201).

16. Indeed, the citizens of Byzantium called themselves "Romans" (King, *The Black Sea*, 65). As Helen C. Evans notes, the appellation endures in the title of the city's ecumenical patriarch: "Archbishop of Constantinople, New Rome" (Helen C. Evans, "Byzantium: Faith and Power [1261–1557]," in *Byzantium: Faith and Power [1261–1557]*, ed. Helen C. Evans [New York: Metropolitan Museum of Art; New Haven, Conn.: Yale University Press, 2004], 5).

17. Note, for instance, the inescapable equation of *Rim* (Rome) and *mir* (world) in Russian poetry (see V. N. Toporov, "Vergilianskaia tema Rima," in *Issledovaniia po strukture teksta*, ed. T. V. Tsiv'ian [Moscow: Nauka, 1987], 196–215).

18. Liah Greenfeld, *Nationalism: Five Roads to Modernity* (Cambridge, Mass.: Harvard University Press, 1992), 224–28.

19. Cited in Stephen Lessing Baehr, *The Paradise Myth in Eighteenth-Century Russia: Utopian Patterns in Early Secular Russian Literature and Culture* (Stanford, Calif.: Stanford University Press, 1991), 52–53. Baehr writes (53) that the nineteenth-century Slavophiles "went so far as condemning the westernizing historian T. N. Granovskii for arguing that Vineta [one of the supposed ancient Slavic kingdoms] was mythical rather than real."

20. Greenfeld, *Nationalism*, 254–55. (Pointing to the complexities in Russia's self-identification with Rome, Greenfeld titles the chapter she devotes to Russia "The Scythian Rome: Russia.") For an example of the distinctions some Russians drew between their nation and the West, see Merezhkovskii's proclamation regarding Russia's character as opposed to that of Europe: "Russia is the reverse of Europe. . . . To speak the language of Nietzsche, Apollo is found in you, in us—Dionysus . . . You love the golden mean, while we love extremes; you are sober, while we are constantly drunk . . . you know how to 'save your soul,' while we seek always to lose ours. You have the *City of the Present*, while we are the seekers of the *City of the Future*. . . . For you politics is a science, while for us it is a religion" (D. S. Merejkowsky, "Préface," in D[mitrii] Merejkowsky, Z[inaida] Hippius, and D[mitrii] Philosophoff, *Le tsar et la révolution* [Paris: Société du Mercure de France, 1907], 6–7).

21. Note, for example, Tsar Boris's acceptance of a rebuke from a holy fool in Aleksandr Pushkin's *Boris Godunov*.

22. See also Tiutchev's "Umom Rossiiu ne poniat'." On his messianic views of Russia and their relation to the idea of Moscow as the Third Rome, see N. V.

Sinitsyna, *Tretii Rim: Istoki i evoliutsiia russkoi srednevekovoi kontseptsii* (Moscow: Indrik, 1998), 16–21. For a detailed discussion of the Rome theme in Tiutchev's work, see G. S. Knabe, "Rimskaia tema v russkoi kul'ture i v tvorchestve F. I. Tiutcheva," in *Antichnoe nasledie v kul'ture Rossii*, ed. G. S. Knabe (Moscow: Rossiiskii Nauchno-issledovatel'skii Institut Kul'turnogo i Prirodnogo Naslediia, 1996), 115–58.

23. Peter Chaadaev, "Apology of a Madman," in *Readings in Russian Civilization*, 3 vols., ed. Thomas Riha (Chicago: University of Chicago Press, 1969), 2: 314 (the original was written in French). Compare this with Chaadaev's earlier statement from his "Letters on the Philosophy of History" (1829–1831): "Fundamentally, we Russians have nothing in common with Homer, the Greeks, the Romans, and the Germans; all that is completely foreign to us" (ibid., 307–8).

24. Mark Conroy describes the process an author may follow as he seeks legitimacy in previous texts: "To secure some cachet for one's own discursive status, one may seek a respectable lineage for one's key concept; cite various authorities to shore up the claims made for that concept; perhaps even attempt a line of filiation for the major texts one uses the concept to analyze" (Mark Conroy, *Modernism and Authority: Strategies of Legitimation in Flaubert and Conrad* [Baltimore, Md.: Johns Hopkins University Press, 1985], 16). See also Frederick T. Griffiths and Stanley J. Rabinowitz, *Novel Epics: Gogol, Dostoevsky, and National Narrative* (Evanston, Ill.: Northwestern University Press, 1990), 5: "How Aeneas will inevitably launch Rome would have intrigued the ancient reader less than whether Virgil would master or be mastered by the incomparable Homer, whom he rivaled and recreated line by line."

25. The first-century BCE historian Dionysius provides an example of the differing narratives about Aeneas that existed at that time: "It was necessary for me to relate these things and to make this digression, since some historians affirm that Aeneas did not even come into Italy with the Trojans, and some that it was another Aeneas, not the son of Anchises and Aphrodite, while yet others say that it was Ascanius, Aeneas' son and others name still other persons. And there are those who claim that Aeneas, the son of Aphrodite, after he had settled his company in Italy, returned home, reigned over Troy, and dying, left his kingdom to Ascanius, his son, whose posterity possessed it for a long time" (Dionysius of Halicarnassus, *Roman Antiquities*, 1.53–54, trans. Earnest Cary, in *Readings in the Classical Historians*, ed. Michael Grant [New York: Charles Scribner's Sons, 1992], 343–44).

26. "For these I set no limits, world or time, / But make the gift of empire without end" (Virgil, *The Aeneid*, trans. Robert Fitzgerald [New York: Vintage Books, 1984], 13). Aeneas's Trojan origins present both an opportunity and a challenge to Virgil. Through his story, the Trojans, the ancient enemy of the Greeks, manage to be reborn as Roman imperialists, and indeed to master the Greeks who had once defeated them. On the other hand, the Eastern-born Aeneas, stalwart father of the Roman Empire, is characterized by his Latin enemy

Turnus as "a Phrygian eunuch," with "lovelocks curled with hot iron, drenched with liquid myrrh" (371), thereby fitting into Roman stereotypes about the regions they consigned to the "East," which included Egypt and Greece along with Asia. Virgil's description of Aeneas's shield, for instance, contains an indictment of Cleopatra (unnamed but identifiable), associated along with her lover Antony with emotion, barbarism, and shame (254). An example of Roman disdain for Greece, construed along with other regions as Eastern, may be found in Juvenal's satires: "I cannot, citizens, stomach / a Greek-struck Rome. Yet what fraction of these sweepings / derives, in fact, from Greece? For years now Syrian / Orontes has poured its sewerage into our native Tiber—/ its lingo and manners, its flutes, its outlandish harps / with their transverse strings, its native tambourines, / and the whores who hang out round the race-course" (Juvenal, "From Satire III," in *The Norton Book of Classical Literature,* ed. Bernard Knox [New York: W. W. Norton, 1993], 819). While for his part Virgil attempts to sidestep the conundrum of Aeneas's identity by suggesting that his father, Anchises, has Italian ancestry, this connection complicates yet again the myths of origins in Virgil's text.

27. Wortman, *Scenarios of Power,* 1:26.

28. Ibid., 1:13; see also Knabe, *Russkaia antichnost',* 102.

29. While Peter also ordered translations to be made of Greek classics, the Roman model was for him a more all-encompassing one, as borne out by the architecture of his new capital and its political structure, Senate, titles, etc. On St. Petersburg's Roman qualities, see, for instance, Knabe, *Russkaia antichnost',* 185–87.

30. Frolov, *Russkaia nauka ob antichnosti,* 58–60.

31. Baehr, *The Paradise Myth,* 50.

32. On the Rome theme in the eighteenth century, see ibid., particularly chaps. 2 and 3; Stephen L. Baehr, "From History to National Myth: *Translatio imperii* in Eighteenth-Century Russia," *Russian Review* 37, no. 1 (1978): 1–13; Andrew Kahn, "Readings of Imperial Rome from Lomonosov to Pushkin," *Slavic Review* 52, no. 4 (1993): 745–68; Knabe, *Russkaia antichnost',* chaps. 6–8.

33. Baehr, "From History to National Myth," 8; see also Baehr, *The Paradise Myth,* 49–50.

34. King, *The Black Sea,* 140–47. Catherine's acquisitions were also intended to promote a new image of Russia as European, as opposed to "an Asiatic country, poor, plunged in ignorance, darkness and barbarity": classical antiquity became an important element of this quest, as existing Tatar place names were replaced by names with classical Greek roots (ibid., 162).

35. Irina Reyfman, "Catherine II as a Patron of Russian Literature," in *Russia Engages the World, 1453–1825,* ed. Cynthia Hyla Whittaker (Cambridge, Mass.: Harvard University Press, 2003), 64.

36. The southern coast of the Crimea was the only outpost of the Byzantine Empire on the northern shore of the Black Sea. It was the site of the ancient

Greek trading colony of Chersonesus, where the Romans later established a garrison to protect the grain supply. Chersonesus itself was besieged and captured under Prince Vladimir of Kievan Rus' in one of various raids the Russians undertook in the region in the tenth century (A. A. Vasiliev, *History of the Byzantine Empire 324–1453* [Madison: University of Wisconsin Press, 1952], 323), though they did not keep their hold on it. This area was lost by the Byzantines after the fourth Crusade in 1204, when Western crusaders sacked Constantinople, an act that heralded the disintegration of the Byzantine Empire. The Crimea eventually ended up under Ottoman suzerainty. When the Russian Empire annexed Georgia and the rest of the Caucasus in the course of the nineteenth century, it absorbed some territories that had been subject to Rome, starting after the Roman general Pompey's defeat of Mithridates, king of Pontus, in the first century BCE, and continuing through the first and second centuries CE, as the Roman Empire expanded eastward to reach the Caspian Sea.

37. Baehr, "From History to National Myth," 13.

38. See Baehr, *The Paradise Myth*, 161–62.

39. Knabe, *Russkaia antichnost'*, 132–33.

40. On Pushkin's use of classical materials in specific writings, see Knabe, *Russkaia antichnost'*, 145–53.

41. See *The Travel Diary of Peter Tolstoi: A Muscovite in Early Modern Europe*, trans. Max J. Okenfuss (DeKalb: Northern Illinois University Press, 1987). Tolstoi figures in Merezhkovskii's third novel, devoted to Peter I.

42. For a fascinating treatment of Gogol's stay in Rome, as well as his textual mythologizations of that city, see Griffiths and Rabinowitz, *Novel Epics*, particularly chap. 2, "Gogol in Rome." On his short story "Rim," which testifies to his attraction to the beauties of Rome, see Andreas Schönle, "Gogol, the Picturesque, and the Desire for the People: A Reading of 'Rome,'" *Russian Review* 59 (2000): 597–613; and Michael R. Kelly, "Gogol's 'Rome': On the Threshold of Two Worlds," *Slavic and East European Journal* 47, no. 1 (2003): 24–44.

43. George Heard Hamilton, *The Art and Architecture of Russia* (Harmondsworth, U.K.: Penguin Books, 1983), 363–67; *Nostalgia d'Italia: Russian Water-Colours of the First Half of the XIX Century*, ed. Eugenija Petrova and Claudio Poppi (Florence: Ponte alle Grazie, 1991), 7. In an 1839 letter to his father, Ivanov wrote, "You try to comfort me, saying that this won't be my last work, and I answer that it is, because after this one I'll come back to Petersburg, where common portraits and icons will turn me into a merchant. Oh! If only I could work in Rome!" (cited in *Nostalgia d'Italia*, 16). To the Romantic generation, Rome crystallized what was attractive in Italy as a whole; see Princess Volkonskaia's 1829 letter to a Russian friend: "Come to Italy, . . . come to collect marbles, lava, memories, poetry and especially to think under this cloudless sky" (*Nostalgia d'Italia*, 10). I am grateful to Christopher Ely for making this book available to me.

44. M. L. Gasparov, *Antichnost' v russkoi poezii nachala XX veka* (Pisa: Istituto di Lingua e Letteratura Russa, 1995), 10–11. While Homer's epics were translated

into Russian in the mid-eighteenth century and then again in the early nineteenth century (Frolov, *Russkaia nauka ob antichnosti,* 102–3), the Greek tragedians Aeschylus, Euripides, and Sophocles were not translated until the Symbolist period, by such figures as Viacheslav Ivanov, Innokentii Annenskii, Dmitrii Merezhkovskii, and Faddei Zelinskii.

45. For a survey of classical education in Russia during the nineteenth century, see A. A. Nosov, "K istorii klassicheskogo obrazovaniia v Rossii (1860—nachalo 1900-kh godov)," in Knabe, *Antichnoe nasledie v kul'ture Rossii,* 203–29. On classicism in the educational policy of the early nineteenth century, see Knabe, *Russkaia antichnost',* 121–24. Knabe discusses the efforts made—not always successfully—during this period to promote classical studies, including assigning Latin teachers to the more prestigious ninth class in the Table of Ranks, rather than the tenth class to which other teachers belonged.

46. Nosov, "K istorii klassicheskogo obrazovaniia," 204–6.

47. Ibid., 217.

48. Ibid., 217–18. Nosov also notes (211–13) the influence of P. M. Leont'ev and M. N. Katkov in formulating the 1871 program.

49. D. S. Merezhkovskii, "Avtobiograficheskaia zametka," in *Russkaia literatura XX veka (1890–1910),* 3 vols., ed. S. A. Vengerov (Moscow: Mir, 1914–16), 1:289.

50. A. V. Amfiteatrov, "Zakliuchenie," in his *Zver' iz bezdny,* 2 vols. (Moscow: Algoritm, 1996), 2:571.

51. Nosov, "K istorii klassicheskogo obrazovaniia," 221–23.

52. Iu. Asoian and A. Malafeev acknowledge that the Tolstoyan classical program was not popular among students, but they cite Vladimir Solov'ev and the scholar-brothers Trubetskoi as examples of its success (Iu. Asoian and A. Malafeev, "Faddei Zelinskii i programma kul'turologii," in their *Otkrytie idei kul'tury: Opyt russkoi kul'turologii serediny XIX–nachala XX vekov* [Moscow: OGI, 2000], 264–65). Nosov also argues that the "cultural renaissance of the Silver Age" could not have occurred without the classical gymnasium, citing Briusov, Belyi, Ivanov, Blok, and Nikolai Gumilev as examples of those who attended these institutions ("K istorii klassicheskogo obrazovaniia," 228). M. L. Gasparov writes, however, that the Tolstoyan program's lack of pedagogical and thematic inspiration left most Russian writers with a poor grasp of Greek and only an adequate grounding in Latin. He notes further that program reforms early in the twentieth century enabled the Russian gymnasium to join the ranks of the best schools in Europe by 1914 (*Antichnost' v russkoi poezii nachala XX veka,* 10–11). Zelinskii believed that school reforms in 1890 had weakened classical education and "entailed a general depression of the level of education on the young men who leave our Gymnasia" (Professor [Tadeusz] Zielinski, *Our Debt to Antiquity* [Port Washington, N.Y.: Kennikat Press, 1971, reissue of 1909 ed.], 13).

53. Cited in Robert Lee Wolff, "The Three Romes: The Migration of an Ideology and the Making of an Autocrat," *Daedalus* 88, no. 2 (1959): 291. For a recent detailed analysis of the doctrine, its sources, and its fate over the centuries, see

Sinitsyna, *Tretii Rim.* Her book is reviewed in Paul Bushkovitch, "N. V. Sinitsyna, *Tretii Rim: Istoki i evoliutsiia russkoi srednevekovoi kontseptsii,*" *Kritika* 1, no. 2 (2000): 391–99. For an enlightening discussion of the doctrine in the context of later Russian apocalypticism, see David M. Bethea, *The Shape of Apocalypse in Modern Russian Fiction* (Princeton, N.J.: Princeton University Press, 1989), 15–19.

54. Marshall Poe notes that while other texts, such as a fifteenth-century lamentation on the fall of Constantinople and Metropolitan Zosima's Paschal Canon, have been seen as containing elements of the idea of *translatio imperii* (and, therefore, of the Third Rome), Filofei was the first to state such a connection specifically. Poe writes further that scholars disagree on the number of letters penned by the Pskovian monk, and on their addressees; nonetheless, he concludes, "Filofei most likely introduced the idea in an epistle to a grand princely official written in 1523/24" (Marshall Poe, "Moscow, the Third Rome: The Origins and Transformations of a 'Pivotal Moment,'" *Jahrbücher für Geschichte Osteuropas* 49, no. 3 [2001]: 416).

55. The doctrine has also been used as an explanation for a later Russian expansionism: see, for instance, Mikhail Agursky, *The Third Rome: National Bolshevism in the USSR* (Boulder, Colo.: Westview Press, 1997). Daniel B. Rowland notes this common use and argues to the contrary that in fact sixteenth-century Russians associated themselves more with ancient Israel than with Rome (Daniel B. Rowland, "Moscow—the Third Rome or the New Israel?" *Russian Review* 55, no. 4 [1996]: 591–93). On the same subject see Raba, "Moscow—the Third Rome or the New Jerusalem," 297–308.

56. Nikolay Andreyev, "Filofey and his Epistle to Ivan Vasil'yevich," *Slavonic and East European Review* 38, no. 90 (1959): 29–30.

57. Poe, "Moscow, the Third Rome," 418–19. The term "Old Believers" refers to the group of Russian Christians who dissented from various reforms in Church practice and liturgy introduced by the Patriarch Nikon during the reign of Peter I's father, Aleksei Mikhailovich; they perceived these reforms as deviations from true Christianity that spelled the end of the world. They were persecuted by the state but survive to this day. Bethea writes that for Old Believers appalled by the Nikonian reforms, "If Moscow was turning its back on its heritage as the Third Rome, then there was only one conclusion to draw—it was not the holy city but the *unholy* city, the seat of the Antichrist. . . . Messianism was turned inside out into apocalypticism; Russia's manifest destiny as the *New* Rome and world savior was transformed into its manifest destiny as traducer of sacred (here 'old') tradition" (*The Shape of Apocalypse in Modern Russian Fiction,* 20). On the Old Believers' adherence to the formula, see, too, Dmitri Strémooukhoff, "Moscow the Third Rome: Sources of the Doctrine," *Speculum* 28 (1953): 100. Rome remained an operative trope, albeit one used to mark the nonrealization of an ideal, rather than to celebrate its potentiality.

58. See Sinitsyna, *Tretii Rim,* 13–15, for specific data about the publication of Filofei's works during this time.

59. On Ikonnikov's study, *Opyt issledovaniia o kul'turnom znachenii Vizantii v russkoi istorii,* see Poe, "Moscow, the Third Rome," 421–22.

60. Cited in Wortman, *Scenarios of Power,* 2:373.

61. On the political background of the doctrine, see, for example, Strémooukhoff, "Moscow the Third Rome: Sources," 99: he notes that the doctrine illustrates "new political concepts" and aided in "the creation of a strong centralized state." On the idea of a reunion of the churches, see Sinitsyna, *Tretii Rim,* chap. 3, sec. 4.

62. Cited in Sinitsyna, *Tretii Rim,* 22.

63. Wortman, *Scenarios of Power,* 2:345.

64. I. Kirillov, *Tretii Rim: Ocherk istoricheskogo razvitiia idei russkogo messianizma* (Moscow: Tip. Mashistova, 1914), 25–26.

65. V. S. Solov'ev, "Vizantizm i Rossiia," in *Sobranie sochinenii V. S. Solov'eva,* 10 vols., ed. S. M. Solov'ev and E. L. Radlov (St. Petersburg: Prosveshchenie, [1911–1914]), 7:285–86. For more information on Solov'ev's views of the Third Rome doctrine, see S. N. Nosov, "Ideiia 'Moskva—Tretii Rim' v interpretatsiiakh Konstantina Leont'eva i Vladimira Solov'eva," in *Russkaia literatura i kul'tura novogo vremeni* (St. Petersburg: Nauka, 1994), 156–65. On the theme of the ancient world in Solov'ev's work, see B. V. Mezhuev, "Antichnaia tema v russkoi filosofskoi mysli vtoroi poloviny XIX veka," in Knabe, *Antichnoe nasledie v kul'ture Rossii,* 191–200.

66. V. S. Solov'ev, "Panmongolizm," in *Chteniia o Bogochelovechestve; Stat'i; Stikhotvoreniia i poema; Iz "Trekh razgovorov," kratkaia povest' ob Antikhriste,* intro. A. B. Muratov (St. Petersburg: Khudozhestvennaia Literatura, 1994), 393.

67. As Viacheslav V. Ivanov notes, while Europe has tended to view Russia as Eastern, Russians have labeled "Eastern" those regions to their south. Ivanov argues that Russians combine within themselves both East and West (Viach. Vs. Ivanov, "Temy i stili Vostoka v poezii Zapada," in *Vostochnye motivy: Stikhotvoreniia i poemy,* comp. L. E. Cherkasskii and V. S. Murav'ev [Moscow: Nauka, 1985], 424). Edward A. Allworth writes that until the eighteenth century, "Russians felt rooted in the east. In that respect, they contrasted strikingly with other inhabitants of the continent, who showed little doubt about their European identity. Most Europeans saw the east, including Russia, as a mysterious, faraway area, little known and vaguely defined. That mystery would add to the confusion about the Russian orientation by contributing to its complex image a contagious romanticism—both in Europe about Russia and in Russia regarding the surrounding east" (Edward A. Allworth, "Russia's Eastern Orientation: Ambivalence toward West Asia," in Whittaker, *Russia Engages the World,* 142). V. E. Molodiakov argues that the plethora of associations with the term "East" gave rise at times to contradictions: Christ did not belong in the same region as "Eastern despotism." Thus the concept of the East was split, as in Solov'ev's poem "Ex oriente lux," in which the poet asked which East would triumph in Russia, that of Xerxes or that of Christ (V. E. Molodiakov, "Kontseptsiia dvukh

vostokov i russkaia literatura serebrianogo veka," *Izvestiia Akademii Nauk SSSR, Seriia Literatury i Iazyka* 49, no. 6 [1990]: 504). Molodiakov supplies a list of "Eastern" associations and locates "the birthplace of Christianity" specifically in the Near East. I would argue in addition, however, that for those writers who preferred not to associate Christ with his Jewish antecedents, another "Eastern" association was Greece as the wellspring of Russia's Orthodox faith.

68. In the context of longstanding discussions of Russia's national identity, the referent for "West" tended to be Europe, though the term had assumed the more general association of a geographical area and corresponding cultural tradition in response to which Russians had frequently defined themselves.

69. As the classicist Faddei Zelinskii wrote at the turn of the twentieth century, "never yet has classical study been so interesting as now." Pointing to excavations in Italy, Greece, and elsewhere, he explained this phenomenon in part by noting that "the material for study is constantly being enlarged by fresh discoveries" (*Our Debt to Antiquity*, 191–92). Certainly active excavation had been ongoing for centuries, but, as Claude Moatti notes, in the nineteenth century excavations became more scientific and scholarly, and their goal was no longer the acquisition of treasure (Claude Moatti, *The Search for Ancient Rome* [London: Thames and Hudson, 1993], 90).

70. "In the ignorant, childish—but already symbolic—unifying babble of wall paintings in the Christian catacombs, the ruptured link between art and religion arises once again and becomes more vital" (D. S. Merezhkovskii, *L. Tolstoi i Dostoevskii* [Moscow: Nauka, 2000], 183).

71. For information on the recovery of ancient Rome during the nineteenth century, see Moatti, *The Search for Ancient Rome*, chaps. 4 and 5. Moatti writes (92) that the Commission for Antique Monuments and Civic Buildings was replaced in 1811 with the Commission for the Embellishment of Rome.

72. Such expeditions began in the late eighteenth century once this territory was under Russian control; see Frolov, *Russkaia nauka ob antichnosti*, 125–37.

73. I. S. Sventsitskaia, "Izuchenie antichnogo nalsediia v universitetakh Rossii vo vtoroi polovine XIX veka," in Knabe, *Antichnoe nasledie v kul'ture Rossii*, 241.

74. Cited in N. G. Goncharova, "Neskol'ko slov o 'giperboreiskoi antichnosti' Serebrianogo veka i ee korniakh," in *Mifologi Serebrianogo veka*, 2 vols., ed. N. G. Goncharova (Moscow and St. Petersburg: Letnii Sad, 2003), 1:13.

75. Sventsitskaia, "Izuchenie antichnogo naslediia," 235, 239.

76. A. Zakharov, "Muzei iziashchnykh iskusstv imeni Imperatora Aleksandra III pri Moskovskom Universitete," *Germes* no. 9 (1 May 1912): 249–52; the reporter noted specific items in the museum, including copies of ancient monuments from the classical world and the ancient Near East. On Tsvetaev's career path and accomplishments, see Knabe, *Russkaia antichnost'*, 209–10.

77. Knabe, *Russkaia antichnost'*, 210.

78. Vasiliev, *History of the Byzantine Empire*, 11.

79. For university student Blok's positive assessment of Zelinskii's teaching, see Blok's 16 October 1901 letter to his father (Aleksandr Blok, *Sobranie sochinenii,* 8 vols. [Moscow and Leningrad: Khudozhestvennaia Literatura, 1960–63], 8:25–27).

80. In his links to writers of the day, Zelinskii was typical of the scholars who popularized the ancient world (Sventsitskaia, "Izuchenie antichnogo naslediia," 243). In another example of the connections between scholars and belletristic writers, Ivan Tsvetaev was the father of Marina Tsvetaeva.

81. Zielinski, *Our Debt to Antiquity,* 117–18. Zelinskii valued Nietzsche's philosophy as "the last major contribution of antiquity to contemporary thought" (F[addei] Zelinskii, "Nittsshe i antichnost'," in his *Iz zhizni idei* [St. Petersburg: Stasiulevich, 1905], 299). Zelinskii's fellow scholar M. Rostovtsev testified to his colleague's commitment to antiquity in a 1914 article marking the thirtieth anniversary of Zelinskii's scholarly endeavors: "for Zelinskii, antiquity has not lived past its time, is not dead, but is, rather, contemporary" (Mikhail Rostovtsev, "Faddei Frantsevich Zelinskii," *Germes* no. 3 [1 Feb. 1914]: 82). For a brief overview of Zelinskii's life and works, see S. S. Averintsev, "Zelinskii Faddei Frantsevich," in *Russkie pisateli 1800–1917: Biograficheskii slovar',* 5 vols., ed. P. A. Nikolaev (Moscow: Bol'shaia Rossiiskaia Entsiklopediia, 1992–), 2:336–37. For a more detailed analysis of Zelinskii's thought, see Asoian and Malafeev, "Zelinskii i programma kul'turologii," 243–72; Frolov, *Russkaia nauka ob antichnosti,* 282–88.

82. Asoian and Malafeev, "Zelinskii i programma kul'turologii," 263.

83. Cited in ibid., 250.

84. Zelinskii's ideas of a Slavic Renaissance influenced and echoed those of Viacheslav Ivanov. See Averintsev, "Zelinskii Faddei Frantsevich," 337; Asoian and Malafeev, "Zelinskii i programma kul'turologii," 261–62. While the idea of a Slavic Renaissance was a relatively popular one in this period, it is important to note that for Zelinskii the concept of a renaissance specifically entailed the resurrection of the culture of the classical world. See the review of the third edition of his *Drevnii mir i my* in the journal *Germes,* in which the reviewer wrote of Zelinskii's "favorite idea—the third Slavic Renaissance of antiquity" (*Germes* no. 9 [1 May 1911]: 210).

85. Zielinski, *Our Debt to Antiquity,* 120.

86. Viacheslav Ivanov would later recall that at the turn of the twentieth century Mommsen told his students that a new age of barbarism was pending; unlike Zelinskii, however, Mommsen was convinced that it was unavoidable (Asoian and Malafeev, "Zelinskii i programma kul'turologii," 251).

87. Zielinski, *Our Debt to Antiquity,* 37.

88. H. Stuart Hughes, *Oswald Spengler* (New Brunswick, N.J.: Transaction Publishers, 1992), 31–32.

89. On this transition in historical thought, see ibid., 34–49. Hughes includes in his discussion of cyclical theories summaries of the thought of Giambattista

Vico, author of *The New Science* (1725–1730), and of Nikolai Danilevskii, whose *Russia and Europe* came out in 1869. On the "shift in attention from the historical past to the personal past," see Stephen Kern, *The Culture of Time and Space 1880–1918* (Cambridge, Mass.: Harvard University Press, 1983), 63: Kern reads this shift as "part of a broad effort to shake off the burden of history."

90. James McFarlane writes that myth could be seen as "imposing order of a symbolic, even poetic, kind on the chaos of quotidian event" (James McFarlane, "The Mind of Modernism," in *Modernism 1890–1930,* ed. Malcolm Bradbury and James McFarlane [Sussex: Harvester Press Limited; Atlantic Heights, N.J.: Humanities Press, 1978], 82).

91. As Lauri Honko writes, "In terms of its *form,* a myth is a *narrative* which provides a verbal account of what is known of sacred origins" (Lauri Honko, "The Problem of Defining Myth," in *Sacred Narrative: Readings in the Theory of Myth,* ed. Alan Dundes [Berkeley and Los Angeles: University of California Press, 1984], 49).

92. Theodor H. Gaster, "Myth and Story," in Dundes, *Sacred Narrative,* 112.

93. Mircea Eliade, "Mythologies of Memory and Forgetting," *History of Religions* 2, no. 2 (1963): 343. Bronislaw Malinowski writes that "the really important thing about the myth is its character of a retrospective, ever-present, live actuality" (Bronislaw Malinowski, *Magic, Science, and Religion and Other Essays* [Garden City, N.Y.: Doubleday, 1948], 126).

94. Cited in L. A. Kolobaeva, "Total'noe edinstvo khudozhestvennogo mira (Merezhkovskii-Romanist)," in *D. S. Merezhkovskii: Mysl' i slovo,* ed. V. A. Keldysh, I. V. Koretskaia, and M. A. Nikitina (Moscow: Nasledie, 1999), 9.

95. Friedrich Nietzsche, *On the Advantage and Disadvantage of History for Life,* trans. Peter Preuss (Indianapolis: Hackett Publishing Company, 1980), 11.

96. See Gilbert Highet, *The Classical Tradition* (New York: Oxford University Press, 1949), 371.

97. Kern, *The Culture of Time and Space,* 29.

98. In her study of the French thinker Henri Bergson, Hilary L. Fink observes, "Late nineteenth-century thinkers no longer considered reality to be a closed system of phenomena, wholly discoverable by the laws of reason and mathematics; instead, reality was seen as dynamic, in many ways mysterious, accessible not through intellect or analysis but rather through religion, metaphysics, and intuition" (Hilary L. Fink, *Bergson and Russian Modernism, 1900–1930* [Evanston, Ill.: Northwestern University Press, 1999], 4). Professing to move beyond clocks and calendars, Bergson called upon the individual to experience time as "duration." "What I call 'my present,'" he explained, "has one foot in my past and another in my future" (Henri Bergson, *Matter and Memory* [New York: Zone Books, 1988], 138).

99. Valerii Briusov, *Dnevniki 1891–1900* (Moscow: Izd. M. i S. Sabashnikovykh, 1927; rpt., Letchworth, U.K.: Bradda Books, 1972), 13 (page citations refer to the reprint edition). As Avril Pyman writes, in the context of Russian

Symbolism, "The sign system which seemed so stable to the educated majority" was "no longer adequate to that which needed to be expressed" (Avril Pyman, "Symbolism and Philosophical Discourse," *Russian Literature* 36 [1994]: 372).

100. Viacheslav Ivanov, "The Testaments of Symbolism," in his *Selected Essays*, trans. and ann. Robert Bird, ed. and intro. Michael Wachtel (Evanston, Ill.: Northwestern University Press, 2001), 41.

101. Viacheslav Ivanov, "On the Joyful Craft and the Joy of the Spirit," in *Selected Essays*, 125.

102. As an example of the perhaps counterintuitive association between Decadence and progress, see Charles Baudelaire's characterization of progress in an 1855 essay as a "very fashionable error," and a "symptom of an already too visible decadence" (cited in Marshall Berman, *All That Is Solid Melts into Air: The Experience of Modernity* [Harmondsworth, U.K.: Penguin Books, 1988], 138). Regarding the connection between Decadence and barbarism, Renato Poggioli explains that Western Decadence is a "projection of the peculiar crisis of the modern mind," according to which the decadent, through his dissociation from the "essentials of civilization . . . discovers all too late that history has reverted to nature; and that the barbarian, being nature's child, is now becoming history's agent. At this point, the decadent recognizes that he is left no alternative but to play a passive, and yet theatrical, role on history's stage. That role is that of scapegoat or sacrificial victim; and it is by accepting that part, and acting it well, that he seals in blood the strange brotherhood of decadence and barbarism. . . . He thus often chooses to open the gates of the city to its barbaric besiegers, who will be its destroyers, as well as his executioners" (Renato Poggioli, "Qualis Artifex Pereo! Or Barbarism and Decadence," *Harvard Library Bulletin* 13, no. 1 [1959]: 136–38). David Weir points to Paul Verlaine's poem "Langueur" ("Je suis l'Empire à la fin de la decadence, / Qui regarde passer les grands Barbares blancs") as an instance of the "double image of barbarism and civilization" (David Weir, *Decadence and the Making of Modernism* [Amherst: University of Massachusetts Press, 1995], 25).

103. The Symbolist movement in Russia was originally known by critics of Dmitrii Merezhkovskii's and Valerii Briusov's work as "Decadence," in keeping with earlier French appellations (and with the critical attitude toward examples of the "new art"). For a study of the links between French and Russian Symbolism, see Georgette Donchin, *The Influence of French Symbolism on Russian Poetry* (The Hague: Mouton and Co., 1958).

104. Lotman writes, "The city, being the place where different national, social and stylistic codes and texts confront each other, is the place of hybridization, recodings, semiotic translations, all of which makes it into a powerful generator of new information. These confrontations work diachronically as well as synchronically: architectural ensembles, city rituals and ceremonies, the very plan of the city, the street names and thousands of other left-overs from past ages act as code programmes constantly renewing the texts of the past. The city

is a mechanism, forever recreating its past, which then can be synchronically juxtaposed with the present. In this sense the city, like culture, is a mechanism which withstands time" (*Universe of the Mind*, 194–95).

105. As Brown explains, the word "pagan" stems from the Christians' use of *paganus* in the late fourth century. While the word originally meant "second-class participant," Brown writes, in the early fifth century it took on the additional connotation of country-dwellers, those who lived in the *pagus;* thus, "cultivated polytheists, urban notables and even members of the Roman Senate, were told that theirs was the religion of countryfolk . . . worthy only of a stolid core of peasants" (*The Rise of Western Christendom*, 35–36). In this book I use "pagan" to convey its generally accepted meaning at the turn of the twentieth century: one who worships gods—with particular stress on the gods of the Greek and Roman pantheons—other than those of the Judeo-Christian tradition.

106. Dominic Lieven writes, "in one important respect the Soviet Union could be considered to stand in the Roman Christian tradition of empire, combining great power and territory with a would-be universalist and monotheistic world religion" (Dominic Lieven, *Empire: The Russian Empire and Its Rivals* [New Haven, Conn.: Yale University Press, 2000], 11). Describing the doctrine of Moscow as the Third Rome, Lieven argues, "Neither this doctrine nor the tsar's adoption of the double-headed eagle and other Byzantine symbols constituted any claim to former Byzantine territory, let alone to Byzantium's traditional ideology of universal empire" (237). However, for later Russians concerned at the turn of the twentieth century with issues of spiritual and worldly empire (interest in "reclaiming" Istanbul, or "Tsar'grad," was particularly high, in addition, during World War I), they clearly did.

107. Andrei Belyi, "Krizis soznaniia i Genrik Ibsen," in his *Arabeski* (Munich: Wilhelm Fink Verlag, 1969), 161.

108. V. F. Khodasevich, *Nekropol'* (Brussels: Les Editions Petropolis, 1939), 103.

109. Cited in Nicolas Zernov, *The Russian Religious Renaissance of the Twentieth Century* (London: Darton, Longman, and Todd, 1963), 87.

110. Andrei Belyi, "Vospominaniia o Bloke," in *Aleksandr Blok v vospominaniiakh sovremennikov*, 2 vols., ed. Vladimir Nikolaevich Orlov (Moscow: Khudozhestvennaia Literatura, 1980), 1:207.

111. Irina Paperno, "Introduction," in *Creating Life: The Aesthetic Utopia of Russian Modernism*, ed. Irina Paperno and Joan Delaney Grossman (Stanford, Calif.: Stanford University Press, 1994), 1.

112. Elizaveta Kuz'mina-Karavaeva, "Vstrechi s Blokom," in Orlov, *Aleksandr Blok v vospominaniiakh sovremennikov*, 2:62.

113. For both reasons I have reluctantly relinquished the Rome-related poetry of the Acmeist Osip Mandel'shtam; it is obviously familiar to readers as an integral element of Mandel'shtam's oeuvre and has been analyzed thoughtfully and incisively in various studies. See, for instance, Victor Terras, "Classical

Motives in the Poetry of Osip Mandel'štam," *Slavic and East European Journal* 10, no. 3 (1966): 251–67; Ryszard Przybylski, "Rome, or A Dream about the Unity of All Things," in his *An Essay on the Poetry of Osip Mandelstam: God's Grateful Guest*, trans. Madeline G. Levine (Ann Arbor, Mich.: Ardis, 1987), 11–44; Gregory Freidin, *A Coat of Many Colors: Osip Mandelstam and His Mythologies of Self-Presentation* (Berkeley and Los Angeles: University of California Press, 1987); and the collection *Mandel'shtam i antichnost': Sbornik statei*, ed. O. A. Lekmanov, Zapiski Mandel'shtamovskogo obshchestva, 7 (Moscow: Mandel'shtamovskoe Obshchestvo, 1995).

114. D. S. Mirsky, *A History of Russian Literature, comprising A History of Russian Literature and Contemporary Russian Literature*, ed. and abridged Francis J. Whitfield (New York: Knopf, 1949 [rpt. 1969]), 417.

Chapter 1. The Blueprint

1. The first novel of the trilogy was originally published under the title *Otverzhennyi* (The Outcast) in the periodical *Severnyi vestnik*, nos. 1–6 (1895), as Merezhkovskii did not wish to label his Julian an "apostate"; the novel was then published in book form, first in 1896, with the original title, and then in 1902, under the newer title by which it has continued to be known. The trilogy's second novel appeared in part in *Nachalo*, nos. 1–2, 4, 1899, under the title "Vozrozhdenie" (The Renaissance), and then in full under its present-day title in *Mir bozhii*, nos. 1–12, 1900, before being published in book form in 1901. The third novel was published in *Novyi put'*, nos. 1–5, 9–12, 1904, and *Voprosy zhizni*, nos. 1–3, 1905, and then in book form in 1905.

2. Nicolas Berdyaev, *Dream and Reality: An Essay in Autobiography* (London: Geoffrey Bles, 1950), 148–49.

3. D. S. Mirsky, *A History of Russian Literature, comprising A History of Russian Literature and Contemporary Russian Literature*, ed. and abridged Francis J. Whitfield (New York: Knopf, 1949 [rpt. 1969]), 414.

4. For comparisons to Sienkewicz and Zola, see for instance L. Obolenskii, "Vlechenie k drevnosti," *Knizhki nedeli* 10 (1896): 261. On Flaubert and France, see the memoirs of Merezhkovskii's wife, Zinaida Hippius (Z. N. Gippius-Merezhkovskaia, *Dmitrii Merezhkovskii*, in *D. S. Merezhkovskii, 14 dekabria. Z. N. Gippius-Merezhkovskaia, Dmitrii Merezhkovskii* [Moscow: Moskovskii Rabochii, 1990], 339). All three novels were translated into numerous languages. *Julian the Apostate* was translated into English, French, German, Italian, Polish, and Spanish; the following two novels were translated widely as well, though *Peter and Alexis* was not as popular in Europe as its predecessors. See Avril Pyman, *A History of Russian Symbolism* (Cambridge: Cambridge University Press, 1994), 395.

5. V[iktor] Burenin, "Kriticheskie ocherki," *Novoe vremia*, no. 9254 (7 [20] Dec. 1901): 2. Another reader wrote (inaccurately, as an unimpressed Burenin pointed out), "Until now we haven't had any Russian novels about foreign life,

and at present it seems that no one else is producing them." On the tense relations between Burenin and modernist writers including Merezhkovskii, see Pyman, *A History of Russian Symbolism,* 114; "Pis'ma D. S. Merezhkovskogo k P. P. Pertsovu," ed. M. I. Koreneva, *Russkaia literatura* 2 (1991): 163, and ibid. 3 (1991): 135n21.

6. Olga Matich, "Androgyny and the Russian Religious Renaissance," in *Western Philosophical Systems in Russian Literature,* ed. Anthony M. Mlikotin (Los Angeles: University of Southern California Press, 1979), 170.

7. In her memoirs, Liubov' Blok wrote that her husband, Aleksandr Blok, urged her to read Merezhkovskii's novels (Liubov Mendeleeva-Blok, "Facts and Myths about Blok and Myself," in *Blok: An Anthology of Essays and Memoirs,* ed. Lucy Vogel [Ann Arbor, Mich.: Ardis, 1982], 26). Vogel points to the influence of Merezhkovskii's *Leonardo da Vinci* on Blok's concept of the Renaissance artist and suggests that Blok "identified with" Merezhkovskii's Leonardo (Lucy E. Vogel, *Aleksandr Blok: The Journey to Italy* [Ithaca, N.Y.: Cornell University Press, 1973], 108–9). On Blok's relationship with Merezhkovskii, see Z. G. Mints, "Blok v polemike s Merezhkovskimi," in *Aleksandr Blok i russkie pisateli* (St. Petersburg: Iskusstvo-SPB, 2000), 541; as well as Avril Pyman, "Aleksandr Blok and the Merežkovskijs," in *Aleksandr Blok Centennial Conference,* ed. Walter N. Vickery (Columbus, Ohio: Slavica Publishers, 1984), 237–70. For an insightful discussion of the influence of Merezhkovskii's third novel on Mandel'shtam's "Na rozval'niakh," see Gregory Freidin, *A Coat of Many Colors: Osip Mandelstam and His Mythologies of Self-Presentation* (Berkeley and Los Angeles: University of California Press, 1987), 115–17. Merezhkovskii's modernist trilogy paved the way for the novels of Fedor Sologub and Andrei Belyi. L. A. Kolobaeva notes in addition Merezhkovskii's influence on Mikhail Bulgakov's *Master and Margarita,* as well as his impact on the works of Iurii Tynianov, Mark Aldanov, and A. N. Tolstoi (L. A. Kolobaeva, "Merezhkovskii—Romanist," *Izvestiia Akademii Nauk SSSR,* Seriia Literatury i Iazyka 50, no. 5 [1991]: 452).

8. The award went to Merezhkovskii's fellow émigré Ivan Bunin. After the Bolshevik takeover in 1917, which ran counter to their vision of a spiritually based revolution, Merezhkovskii and Hippius left the Soviet state in 1919.

9. Hippius wrote in her memoirs of the difficulties Merezhkovskii encountered when trying to publish his first "historical novel in the new style" (Gippius-Merezhkovskaia, *Dmitrii Merezhkovskii,* 327).

10. The reviewer did, however, express his conviction that Merezhkovskii's *Julian the Apostate* was "one of the most significant phenomena in our literary life over the past year" ("Novye knigi. D. S. Merezhkovskii. Otverzhennyi. Roman v dvukh chastiakh. Spb. 1896," *Russkoe bogatstvo,* no. 11 [Nov. 1895]: 60).

11. Obolenskii, "Vlechenie k drevnosti," 272–73.

12. V. Mirskii, "Nasha literatura. 'Smert' bogov' i 'Voskresshie bogi,' rom. D. S. Merezhkovskogo," *Zhurnal dlia vsekh,* no. 2 (1902): 234. Burenin, too,

argued, in his review of *Leonardo da Vinci,* that a Russian writer should stick to Russian themes (Burenin, "Kriticheskie ocherki," 2).

13. Skabichevskii's scathing review came after only the first three chapters of *Leonardo da Vinci* had appeared. Underlining Merezhkovskii's supposed insignificance and lack of talent, Skabichevskii proceeded to compare him to the less-than-renowned Nestor Kukol'nik (A[leksandr] Skabichevskii, "Tekushchaia literatura," *Syn otechestva,* no. 68 [12 (24) March 1899]: 2). For his part, Merezhkovskii had written critically of Skabichevskii, seeing the older writer as a relic of an outmoded Populist trend (D. S. Merezhkovskii, "O prichinakh upadka i o novykh techeniiakh sovremennoi russkoi literatury," in his *Polnoe sobranie sochinenii D. S. Merezhkovskogo,* 24 vols. [Moscow: Sytin, 1914], 17:201–9).

14. Avril Pyman writes, "The links between the novels are not the rational links of cause and effect, but are pictorial, musical and poetic. Merezhkovsky works and thinks through the medium of art alone" (Pyman, *A History of Russian Symbolism,* 126).

15. For analyses of the Nietzschean influences in *Julian the Apostate* and in the trilogy as a whole, see Bernice Glatzer Rosenthal, "Stages of Nietzscheanism: Merezhkovsky's Intellectual Evolution," in *Nietzsche in Russia,* ed. Bernice Glatzer Rosenthal (Princeton, N.J.: Princeton University Press, 1986), 74–86; Edith W. Clowes, *The Revolution of Moral Consciousness* (DeKalb: Northern Illinois University Press, 1988), 115–34; and Edith W. Clowes, "The Integration of Nietzsche's Ideas of History, Time, and 'Higher Nature' in the Early Historical Novels of Dmitry Merezhkovsky," *Germano-Slavica* 3, no. 6 (1981): 401–16.

16. Dmitrii Panchenko, "Leonardo i ego epokha v izobrazhenii D. S. Merezhkovskogo," in D. S. Merezhkovskii, *Voskresshie bogi: Leonardo da-Vinchi* (Moscow: Khudozhestvennaia Literatura, 1990), 635.

17. Andrei Belyi, "Trilogiia Merezhkovskogo," *Vesy,* no. 1 (1908): 80. Modern critics note Merezhkovskii's divergence in the trilogy from nineteenth-century Realist treatments of character development: see, for instance, Kolobaeva, "Merezhkovskii—Romanist," 448; Z. G. Mints, "O trilogii D. S. Merezhkovskogo 'Khristos i Antikhrist,'" in D. S. Merezhkovskii, *Khristos i Antikhrist,* 4 vols. (Moscow: Kniga, 1989–90), 1:10.

18. See, for instance, Obolenskii, "Vlechenie k drevnosti," 273–78; and P. Grinevich, "Zametki chitatelia," *Russkoe bogatstvo,* no. 4 (April 1900): 140. Rosenthal suggests that "'Art for art's sake' became the battle cry of the new movement"; as she notes later, however, "Though Merezhkovsky bitterly criticized populist didacticism in his art, his art was also purposive in nature. Art leads to higher truths, refines the soul, gives meaning to life, and creates an elevated national consciousness. . . . Nothing must distort the artist's creative vision, no authority be allowed to hamper his search. But the search did have an end. Art was not a goalless activity; pleasure was not its major function" (Bernice Glatzer Rosenthal, *Dmitri Sergeevich Merezhkovsky and the Silver Age: The Development of a Revolutionary Mentality* [The Hague: Martinus Nijhoff, 1975], 46, 54).

19. M. M. Bakhtin, "Epic and Novel," in *The Dialogic Imagination: Four Essays by M. M. Bakhtin,* ed. Michael Holquist, trans. Caryl Emerson and Michael Holquist (Austin: University of Texas Press, 1981), 7; see also 11.

20. Merezhkovskii's use of geographic designators, while rather heavy-handed, is not entirely consistent, not only from one novel to the next but also within individual novels. Nonetheless, there were associations in his mind that remained relatively constant, such as a "West" of freedom, beauty, and individualism as opposed to a more spiritual "East." His insistent repetition of these terms throughout the trilogy, despite their shifting connotations, deserves consideration, particularly since this repetition points to his ongoing belief in the importance of the artist as one who can inspire the synthesis of divided worldviews and cultural heritages. Indeed, Merezhkovskii's idées fixes on the subject of geographic unity and its relationship to art come through clearly in his 1910 review of Andrei Belyi's novel *Serebrianyi golub'* (The Silver Dove, 1910), planned at that time as the first part of a trilogy called *Vostok ili zapad* (East or West). He writes, "The Western, descending light—the truth about the earth and about man—is not a lesser light than the ascending, Eastern light—the truth about heaven, about God. Only the unification of these two lights, these two truths, will produce the noonday light, the perfected truth about Godmanhood. To the question, 'East or West?' there is only one answer: the rejection of the question itself, not East *or* West, but East and West." Merezhkovskii asserted that rather than echoing his characters' vacillations between East and West, an artist needed to assert his will in order to bring them together (D. S. Merezhkovskii, "Vostok ili zapad," in *Andrei Belyi: Pro et contra,* ed. D. K. Burlaka [St. Petersburg: Izd. Russkogo Khristianskogo Gumanitarnogo Instituta, 2004], 265–66).

21. See Friedrich Nietzsche, *On the Genealogy of Morals,* trans. Walter Kaufmann and R. J. Hollingdale (New York: Vintage Books, 1989), 34.

22. Frederick T. Griffiths and Stanley J. Rabinowitz, *Novel Epics: Gogol, Dostoevsky, and National Narrative* (Evanston, Ill.: Northwestern University Press, 1990). Griffiths and Rabinowitz discuss various Gogolian texts and Dostoevskii's *Brothers Karamazov.* It is interesting to note in this regard Skabichevskii's characterization of Merezhkovskii's novels as a "divine trilogy"; though sarcastic, Skabichevskii's comment clearly evokes Dante. Merezhkovskii published a study of Dante in 1939.

23. Griffiths and Rabinowitz, *Novel Epics,* 6.

24. Ibid.

25. Ibid., 2. Griffiths and Rabinowitz take issue with Bakhtin's "epic" category, as have other scholars. Bakhtin claims that "an absolute epic distance separates the epic world from contemporary reality, that is, from the time in which the singer (the author and his audience) lives" ("Epic and Novel," 13). Griffiths and Rabinowitz suggest rather that "it is not the lack of connection with the current time that characterizes the epic so much as the appropriation

of contemporary realities to create an importance like that of the past, a raid conducted on the present by a grander past" (*Novel Epics*, 36).

26. See Griffiths and Rabinowitz, *Novel Epics*, 5.

27. In an 1895 conversation that the writer Anatolii Viktorovich Polovtsov recorded in his diary, Merezhkovskii asserted that he wanted to convey Julian's era accurately, even as he brought out the links between Julian's day and his own (A. L. Sobolev, "D. S. Merezhkovskii v rabote nad romanom 'Smert' bogov. Iulian Otstupnik,'" in *D. S. Merezhkovskii: Mysl' i slovo*, ed. V. A. Keldysh, I. V. Koretskaia, and M. A. Nikitina [Moscow: Nasledie, 1999], 44–45).

28. Julian was frequently portrayed in nineteenth-century literature. For a wide-ranging survey of images from the eighteenth to the twentieth centuries, see Heinrich A. Stammler, "Julianus Apostata Redivivus. Dmitrij Merežkovskij: Predecessors and Successors," *Die Welt der Slaven* 11, nos. 1–2 (1966): 180–204. See also Jean Richer et al., *L'Empereur Julien: De la légende au mythe (de Voltaire à nos jours)* (Paris: Les Belles Lettres, 1981). One of the best-known nineteenth-century works about Julian is Henrik Ibsen's 1873 play *Emperor and Galilean*. For George Brandes's discussion of Merezhkovskii's first novel in the light of Ibsen's work, see G. Brandes, "Merezhkovskii," in *D. S. Merezhkovskii: Pro et contra*, ed. D. K. Burlaka (St. Petersburg: Izd. Russkogo Khristianskogo Gumanitarnogo Instituta, 2001), 313–21. Elaine Rusinko suggests as well that Merezhkovskii was influenced by Ibsen (Elaine Rusinko, "Rewriting Ibsen in Russia: Gumilyov's Dramatic Poem, 'Gondla,'" in *The European Foundations of Russian Modernism*, ed. Peter I. Barta in collaboration with Ulrich Goebel [Lewiston, N.Y.: Edwin Mellen Press, 1991], 193n3). G. N. Khrapovitskaia questions whether there was such influence, and posits a coincidence of sources and motivations for the two authors; she notes, for instance, that contemporary critics did not link Merezhkovskii's novel with Ibsen's play, which was translated into Russian first in 1903 (G. N. Khrapovitskaia, "Tri Iuliana," *Filologicheskie nauki* 5 [1996]: 15–24; see in particular 23n2). I would argue that the similarities between the two texts are too striking to be coincidental. Apollon Maikov's plays *Tri smerti* and *Dva mira* would also have contributed to Merezhkovskii's picture of Rome and early Christianity. On Merezhkovskii's evaluation of the latter, see K. A. Kumpan, "D. S. Merezhkovskii—Poet (U istokov 'novogo religioznogo soznaniia')," in D. S. Merezhkovskii, *Stikhotvoreniia i poemy*, Novaia Biblioteka Poeta (St. Petersburg: Akademicheskii Proekt, 2000), 61. Stammler ("Julianus Apostata Redivivus," 191) writes that Maikov apparently encouraged Merezhkovskii in the pursuit of the pagan-Christian theme in ancient Rome.

29. Critics such as Valerii Briusov and Aleksandr Amfiteatrov took Merezhkovskii to task for some factual errors in his exposition of Julian's life, but Merezhkovskii's portrayal is in general historically accurate. On Briusov, see M. L. Gasparov, "Briusov i antichnost'," in Valerii Briusov, *Sobranie sochinenii v semi tomakh*, 7 vols. (Moscow: Khudozhestvennaia Literatura, 1973–75), 5:548; for Amfiteatrov, see A. V. Amfiteatrov, "Russkii literator i rimskii imperator," in his

Sobranie sochinenii, 37 vols. (St. Petersburg: Prosveshchenie, n.d.), 25:17ff. Hippius recalled in her memoirs that Merezhkovskii was an assiduous researcher: he traveled to Italy, Greece, and Constantinople before writing this first novel, and subsequent trips to Italy and around Russia served to provide facts and setting for the later novels as well (*Dmitrii Merezhkovskii,* 328–29, 369). And yet, amid this profusion of details, Merezhkovskii's biases emerge clearly, most particularly in his views on the two conflicting faiths of Julian's era and their relevance in this Roman context to contemporary Russia. G. Ponomareva argues that Merezhkovskii's historical inaccuracies were largely intentional and reflect his concern with myth-making (G. Ponomareva, "Zametki o semantike 'pereputannykh tsitat' v istoricheskikh romanakh D. S. Merezhkovskogo," in *Klassitsizm i modernizm: sbornik statei,* ed. I. V. Abramets et al. [Tartu: Tartu Ulikooli Kirjastus, 1994], 102–11).

30. Rosenthal writes, "Julian represented Merezhkovsky, or more exactly, the new man Merezhkovsky hoped to become" (Rosenthal, "Stages of Nietzscheanism," 74). I would suggest, rather, that Julian in his contradictions echoed Merezhkovskii as he was at the time of his writing the novel, and that Merezhkovskii sought to overcome these contradictions.

31. Merezhkovskii, "O prichinakh," 212.

32. D. S. Merezhkovskii, *Smert' bogov (Iulian Otstupnik),* in his *Sobranie sochinenii v chetyrekh tomakh,* 4 vols. (Moscow: Pravda, 1990), 1:105. Further references to this work are cited parenthetically in the text.

33. The Alexandrian priest Arius and his followers perpetuated this brand of Christianity, started by Lucian in Antioch, Syria, in the second half of the third century. Arianism taught that Jesus was a created being, rather than of one essence with God. At the Council of Nicaea in 325, during the reign of Constantine, Arianism was condemned as heresy. Constantine later softened his position regarding Arianism, perhaps because he came to realize its popularity in the Eastern half of the Empire (A. A. Vasiliev, *History of the Byzantine Empire, 324–1453* [Madison: University of Wisconsin Press, 1952], 54–57). Despite the Nicaean edict, adherents of the rival doctrines continued to battle for supremacy. Constantius II, Constantine's son and Julian's predecessor, was an active promoter of Arianism.

34. Merezhkovskii's portrayal of these debates may have been influenced by Flaubert's *The Temptation of Saint Anthony,* in which Anthony is exposed to a similar myriad of fervently voiced Christian beliefs. I am grateful to Mikhail Leonovich Gasparov for this observation.

35. Juventinus's story recalls that of the Russian monk Theodosius, who persisted in the monastic life despite his mother's opposition and became abbot of the Kievan Crypt Monastery.

36. Merezhkovskii appears to exaggerate the extent to which the Roman Empire had been Christianized at the time of Julian's rule. Robert Browning refers to the "religious ambivalence of the age" (Robert Browning, *The Emperor*

Julian [London: Weidenfeld and Nicolson, 1975], 27). Ramsay MacMullen points out that with the limited evidence at our disposal, it is impossible to form a conclusive picture of the pagan-Christian dynamics at the beginning of this era. MacMullen notes, though, that Constantine's creation of a state cult of Christianity would have made pagans less likely to proclaim their allegiances. He also points out the army's predominantly pagan make-up and the persistence of paganism in various provinces, both as late as Julian's reign (Ramsay MacMullen, *Paganism in the Roman Empire* [New Haven, Conn.: Yale University Press, 1981], 131–33). And yet E. R. Dodds writes, "In the fourth century paganism appears as a kind of living corpse, which begins to collapse from the moment when the supporting hand of the State is withdrawn from it. And it is hard to believe that Julian's attempt to resuscitate it by a mixture of occultism and sermonising could have had any lasting success even if he had lived to enforce his programme" (E. R. Dodds, *Pagan and Christian in an Age of Anxiety* [Cambridge: Cambridge University Press, 1965], 132).

37. Gore Vidal, "A Note," in his *Julian* (Boston: Little, Brown, 1962), viii. Theodoret wrote an ecclesiastical history covering the period from 325 to 428 CE (Vasiliev, *History of the Byzantine Empire,* 120). Centuries later in Russia, faced with Tsar Alexander II's decision to emancipate the Russian serfs after his coronation in 1855, the Russian liberal Alexander Herzen would respond to the tsar with Theodoret/Julian's words (Nicholas V. Riasanovsky, *A History of Russia* [New York: Oxford University Press, 1984], 371; see also Irina Paperno, "The Liberation of the Serfs as a Cultural Symbol," *Russian Review* 50, no. 4 [1991]: 424–25). In a letter of 14 September 1894, Merezhkovskii wrote that he was thinking of using the famous phrase as the title for his novel (Sobolev, "D. S. Merezhkovskii v rabote," 40). In Ibsen's *Emperor and Galilean,* Julian uses this phrase shortly before his death (Henrik Ibsen, *Emperor and Galilean,* in *The Oxford Ibsen,* 8 vols., ed. and trans. James Walter McFarlane and Graham Orton [London: Oxford University Press, 1960–77], 4:452). Much of Julian's dying speech in Merezhkovskii's novel comes from the writings of Ammianus Marcellinus (who, while acquainted with Julian, was almost definitely not present at his deathbed [see Browning, *The Emperor Julian,* 213]), but Julian's final profession of faith in Christ does not. For an analysis of Ammianus's role in Merezhkovskii's novel, see Peter G. Christensen, "*Christ and Antichrist* as Historical Novel," *Modern Language Studies* 20, no. 3 (1990): 72, who argues that "history writing itself is invoked to reconcile the strife between Christianity and paganism."

38. The lilies will reappear in the next novel in the context of a Christian chant overheard by the "searcher" Giovanni Beltraffio, Leonardo's disciple. On the image of the lily as typical of fin-de-siècle aesthetics and taste, see David Weir, *Decadence and the Making of Modernism* (Amherst: University of Massachusetts Press, 1995), 65: "Blue china, kneebreeches, peacock feathers, lilies and sunflowers were among the paraphernalia required by the fashionable aesthete."

39. Given Merezhkovskii's initial refusal to use the word "apostate" in the novel's title, Arsinoe's assessment appears to reflect the author's own view.

40. Stammler, "Julianus Apostata Redivivus," 194–95. Merezhkovskii's Julian calls to mind Dostoevskii's Stavrogin in *Besy* (The Devils): Stavrogin admits the necessity of religious faith and yet cannot achieve it. Konstantin Mochulsky writes, "Nikolai Stavrogin . . . *knows* that he lacks the soil, *knows* that the only salvation is in Christ, *knows* that without faith he will perish—and *does not believe.* He acknowledges the existence of God and the necessity of religion intellectually, but his heart is not with God but with the devil" (Konstantin Mochulsky, *Dostoevsky: His Life and Work,* trans. Michael A. Minihan [Princeton, N.J.: Princeton University Press, 1967], 429).

41. D. S. Merezhkovskii, *Simvoly* (St. Petersburg: A. Suvorin, 1892).

42. D. S. Merezhkovskii, "Konets veka: Ocherki sovremennogo Parizha," in his *Stikhotvoreniia i poemy,* 421.

43. Ibid., 419, 423.

44. Ibid., 419.

45. D. S. Merezhkovskii, "Panteon," in his *Stikhotvoreniia i poemy,* 337.

46. D. S. Merezhkovskii, "Rim," ibid., 337.

47. Merezhkovskii, "Konets veka," 419.

48. Merezhkovskii, "Panteon," 337.

49. Hippius writes (*Dmitrii Merezhkovskii,* 328) that Merezhkovskii's own turn to Christ, while clearer in *Leonardo da Vinci,* began with *Julian the Apostate.*

50. D. S. Merezhkovskii, "Vozvrashchenie," in his *Stikhotvoreniia i poemy,* 348.

51. D. S. Merezhkovskii, "Volny," ibid., 335.

52. Merezhkovskii, "Konets veka," 428.

53. D. S. Merezhkovskii, "Smert': Peterburgskaia poema," in his *Stikhotvoreniia i poemy,* 249.

54. D. S. Merezhkovskii, "Mark Avrelii," in his *Polnoe sobranie sochinenii,* 17:27–28. In this article, a review of Ernest Renan's *Marc Aurèle et la fin du monde antique,* Merezhkovskii, perhaps identifying with Renan, wrote that Renan felt as alone in contemporary society as Marcus Aurelius had in ancient Rome (29). See also Merezhkovskii's 1891 poem "Mark Avrelii" (in his *Stikhotvoreniia i poemy,* 339–40).

55. "Hail, Caesar, we salute you, we who are about to die!" (see Suetonius, *Life of Claudius,* trans. Graves, 199); Merezhkovskii, "Smert': Peterburgskaia poema," 250. Similarly, in his essay "Akropol'," Merezhkovskii recalled that the sight of the Coliseum had evoked in him thoughts of the dead feeling of overthrown power (D. S. Merezhkovskii, "Akropol'," in his *Polnoe sobranie sochinenii,* 17:14). In his 1891 notebook, Merezhkovskii wrote that everything he did was permeated with the idea of his own impending death (D. S. Merezhkovskii, "Zapisnaia knizhka 1891 g.," ed. and ann. M. Iu. Korenevaia, in *Puti i mirazhi russkoi kul'tury,* ed. V. E. Bagno et al. [St. Petersburg: Severo-zapad, 1994], 348).

56. D. S. Merezhkovskii, "Semeinaia idilliia," in his *Stikhotvoreniia i poemy,* 358. On Merezhkovskii's concerns in regard to Russia's rapid industrialization, see Rosenthal, *Merezhkovsky and the Silver Age,* 8–9, 18–19, 37.

57. See Merezhkovskii, "Konets veka," 424. Even as she affirms Julian's hidden love of Christ, Arsinoe proclaims her exasperation with Julian and his few fellow pagans: "You are sick, you are too weak for your own wisdom! That is your curse, belated Hellenes! You have strength neither for good nor for evil. . . . You have sailed away from one bank, but you have not landed at the other. You believe, and you do not believe, you eternally change, you eternally waver, you will something, and cannot carry it out, because you do not know how to desire" (Merezhkovskii, *Smert' bogov,* 219).

58. See D. S. Merezhkovskii, "Gimn krasote," in his *Stikhotvoreniia i poemy,* 357; Merezhkovskii, "Konets veka," 425.

59. Richard Pipes, *Russia under the Old Regime* (New York: Charles Scribner's Sons, 1974), 222. Pipes notes, "Foreigners found dissenters to be the only Orthodox people in Russia familiar with the Holy Scriptures and able to discuss religious questions" (236).

60. On Old Believers, see note 57 in the introduction.

61. Cited in Glennys Young, *Power and the Sacred in Revolutionary Russia: Religious Activists in the Village* (University Park: Pennsylvania State University Press, 1997), 29–30.

62. Merezhkovskii, "O prichinakh," 229.

63. Pipes notes the *mir*'s collective emphasis: "The community restrained the unsocial impulses of the muzhik: the collective was superior to its individual members" (*Russia under the Old Regime,* 158). At the same time, given the provinciality of the Russian peasantry, Merezhkovskii's vision of the *mir* and of the world-welcoming nature of the Russian people was as exaggerated as Dostoevskii's had been; Pipes writes, "If foreign residents can be trusted many Russian peasants as recently as the nineteenth century did not know and would not believe that there were in the world other nations and other monarchs than their own" (159).

64. Merezhkovskii, "Konets veka," 422. Merezhkovskii's statement of the "Galilean's" triumph recalls Julian's dying words in *Julian the Apostate.*

65. A. Richard Turner, *Inventing Leonardo* (New York: Alfred A. Knopf, 1993), 100. Dmitrii Panchenko also notes the resources available to Merezhkovskii as he embarked upon the novel (D[mitrii] Panchenko, "Leonardo i ego epokha," 629). Merezhkovskii's associate Akim Volynskii published a work on Leonardo in 1900, shortly before Merezhkovskii's own novel appeared (Panchenko, "Leonardo i ego epokha," 632).

66. D. S. Merezhkovskii, *L. Tolstoi i Dostoevskii* (Moscow: Nauka, 2000), 189–90.

67. Merezhkovskii also added to the historical sources: there is no record, for example, of Leonardo's ever having met Machiavelli, or of his falling in love

with Mona Lisa as he painted her portrait, as Merezhkovskii suggests he did (Panchenko, "Leonardo i ego epokha," 630–31).

68. D. S. Merezhkovskii, *Voskresshie bogi (Leonardo da Vinchi),* in his *Sobranie sochinenii v chetyrekh tomakh,* 4 vols. (Moscow: Pravda, 1990), 2:128. Further volume and page references to this work are cited parenthetically in the text.

69. Mints has suggested that the figure of Savonarola in the novel can also be understood as a caricature of Lev Tolstoi, whose rejection of earthly pleasures appalled Merezhkovskii (Mints, "O trilogii D. S. Merezhkovskogo 'Khristos i Antikhrist,'" 18).

70. Evtikhii is a figure who has attracted surprisingly little critical attention, particularly given his importance in conveying Merezhkovskii's invocation of the Third Rome doctrine (as I discuss below) and, more broadly, in representing an alternative to the "Historic Christianity" of Savonarola and his like. I differ, therefore, with those scholars who feel that Merezhkovskii's portrayal of Christianity in this second novel is one-sided (see, for instance, Kumpan, "Merezhkovskii—Poet," 63).

71. For Merezhkovskii at this stage, the Third Rome was an inclusive concept that encompassed both Orthodox religion with its Hellenic roots and Roman imperialism. Thus even as Merezhkovskii lauded Russia's national traits and destiny, he did so, as Ben Hellman notes, in a universal context: "Russian spiritual greatness did not exclude other nations, and it did not represent a danger, but rather a blessing for the rest of the world, as it stood in the service of universalism" (Ben Hellman, *Poets of Hope and Despair: The Russian Symbolists in War and Revolution (1914–1918)* [Helsinki: Institute for Russian and East European Studies, 1995], 225). Hellman argues that Merezhkovskii rejected nationalism, relying instead on Dostoevskii's understanding of the Russian people as extraordinary precisely in their ability to embody within themselves, as had Pushkin, the traits of all peoples. Russians were to lead the world to a state of unity. Thus, for Merezhkovskii, Mamyrov's "Historic" Christian biases, manifest in his intolerance toward the Western tendencies that must take part in a true, Merezhkovskiian Third Rome, undermine his assertion of the Third Rome doctrine.

72. C. Harold Bedford, *The Seeker: D. S. Merezhkovskiy* (Lawrence: University Press of Kansas, 1975), 32. Merezhkovskii's portrayal of Leonardo follows the French nineteenth-century tradition (Turner, *Inventing Leonardo,* 143). Jules Michelet's Leonardo was attracted to paganism and to nature, while Edgar Quinet described Leonardo as a forerunner of modern humankind (ibid., 105–9). Meanwhile, Arsène Houssaye added Christianity to the French version of Leonardo: as Turner notes, Houssaye portrayed Leonardo as a "Christian-Artist-Hero," writing, "For Leonardo da Vinci, science illuminates the image of God with an ever brilliant light" (ibid., 113).

73. Christensen argues that Merezhkovskii's morally ambivalent Leonardo "has taken the path to salvation through creativity rather than through

obedience to traditional morality" and discusses the relationship between the ideas in Merezhkovskii's second novel and those of Berdiaev (Peter G. Christensen, "Merezhkovsky and Berdyaev: Leonardo and the Meaning of the Creative Act," *Symposium* 45, no. 3 [1991]: 177).

74. Irene Masing-Delic discusses the inability of Merezhkovskii's Leonardo to move from artistic creativity to life-creation in his painting of Mona Lisa: "da Vinci creates portraits full of accurately observed truth, even inner truth. He fails, however, to transcend experimental psychology. Therefore he also fails to transcend art, since detached analysis and aesthetic amelioration of the human model, however penetrating and beautifully executed, are not enough for the ultimate artistic act of life-creation. This act of genuine creation needs the powerful energy of passion and faith." She compares da Vinci to the European Decadents who were Merezhkovskii's contemporaries (Irene Masing-Delic, "Creating the Living Work of Art: The Symbolist Pygmalion and His Antecedents," in *Creating Life: The Aesthetic Utopia of Russian Modernism,* ed. Irina Paperno and Joan Delaney Grossman [Stanford, Calif.: Stanford University Press, 1994], 70).

75. N. K. Gudzii, "Povest' o novgorodskom belom klobuke," in *Khrestomatiia po drevnei russkoi literature XI-XVII vekov,* comp. N. K. Gudzii (Moscow: Gosudarstvennoe uchebno-pedagogicheskoe izdatel'stvo, 1962), 241. Dmitri Strémooukhoff writes, to the contrary, that it "is not, however, generally accepted that Dmitri Gerasimov is the author of this legend," though he associates the two in his own discussion (Dmitri Strémooukhoff, "Moscow the Third Rome: Sources of the Doctrine," *Speculum* 28 [1953]: 92).

76. Fedor Buslaev discussed the 1485 psalter, created by Fedor Kliment'ev Sharapov, which was located in St. Petersburg's Imperial Public Library (F. I. Buslaev, *Istoricheskie ocherki russkoi narodnoi slovesnosti i iskusstva,* 2 vols. [St. Petersburg: Obshchestvennaia pol'za, 1861], 2:201); Merezhkovskii did some of his research for the novel at that library (Sobolev, "D. S. Merezhkovskii v rabote," 35). Buslaev found Hellenic influence in the simple Christian images of the text and asserted that a fifteenth-century icon-painter combining classical art and Christian faith understood these images better than educated people of his own day (*Istoricheskie ocherki,* 203). Buslaev includes in his text reproductions of the drawings he discusses. Merezhkovskii appears to have been influenced by Buslaev's interpretation, echoing the latter's assessment of the significance of the psalter and the illustrations he singles out. For example, both Merezhkovskii (*Leonardo da Vinci,* 2:277) and Buslaev (204) refer to Psalms 42:1 ("As a deer longs for flowing streams, so my soul longs for you, O God") and link it to images in the psalter. Since Merezhkovskii's descriptions in *Leonardo da Vinci* suggest an acquaintance with drawings other than those reproduced in Buslaev's text, it is likely that he had been exposed to the original psalter as well.

77. See Malachi 3:1. See also variants in Matthew 11:10, Mark 1:2, and Luke 7:27.

78. Stammler notes the influence of Vladimir Solov'ev's poem "Ex oriente lux" on Merezhkovskii's depiction of Evtikhii's messianic visions of Russia and argues briefly that Evtikhii's revelation is a rejection of "earthly power and glory" in favor of Christ (Heinrich Stammler, "Russian Metapolitics: Merezhkovsky's Religious Understanding of the Historical Process," *California Slavic Studies* 9 [1976]: 128). While I agree that Merezhkovskii would come to this opinion by the time he was writing his third novel, the fact that he posited Leonardo, with his attraction to both Godman and Mangod, as a forerunner of future revelations suggests that the novelist was not at this point relinquishing hope for their coming synthesis in Russia.

79. Turner, *Inventing Leonardo,* 125. While Pater was criticized for incorporating his own artistic views into his reading of Leonardo's work, Wilde, for one, had no objections to such artistic evaluations, writing, "Nay, it is rather the beholder who lends to the beautiful thing its myriad meanings, and makes it marvellous for us, and sets it in some new relation to the age, so that it becomes a vital portion of our lives, and a symbol of what we pray for, or perhaps of what, having prayed for, we fear that we may receive" (cited in ibid., 129). Merezhkovskii's readings and reworkings of the "texts" of Rome and of the Western tradition—and his rendering them relevant to modern-day Russia—might be said to function in Pater's tradition.

80. Cited in Panchenko, "Leonardo i ego epokha," 633; Kumpan, "Merezhkovskii—Poet," 67. For further discussion of Merezhkovskii's *Dafnis i Khloia* (D. Merezhkovskii, *Vechnye Sputniki* [St. Petersburg: P. Pertsov, 1897]) and its links to his concept of the "new beauty" and its significance for cultural transformation, see Kumpan, "Merezhkovskii—Poet," 66–67.

81. "'What does it mean—symbols?' they asked me uncomprehendingly" (D. Merezhkovskii, "Avtobiograficheskaia zametka," in *Russkaia literatura XX veka (1890–1910),* 3 vols., ed. S. A. Vengerov [Moscow: Mir, 1914–16], 1:292). On Merezhkovskii's despair when an announcement for the new book spelled the title wrong ("Simvol'e"), see Kumpan's commentary in Merezhkovskii, *Stikhotvoreniia i poemy,* 804.

82. Cited in Pyman, *A History of Russian Symbolism,* 93.

83. Cited in ibid., 106.

84. Bedford, *The Seeker,* 113–14.

85. For a description of the Meetings' goals and history, see Gippius-Merezhkovskaia, *Dmitrii Merezhkovskii,* 353ff. See also Jutta Scherrer, *Die Petersburger Religiös-Philosophischen Vereinigungen* (Wiesbaden: Harrassowitz, 1973); and Avril Pyman, "The Church and the Intelligentsia with Special Reference to the Religious-Philosophical Meetings in St. Petersburg 1901–1903," in *Russian Thought and Society 1800–1917: Essays in Honor of Eugene Lampert,* ed. Roger Bartlett (Keele, U.K.: University of Keele, 1984), 181–219.

86. See, for instance, his 2 September 1899 letter to P. P. Pertsov in which he claimed that the salvation of the world lay in devotees of Russian culture and

correspondingly of the "Third Russian Rome—'and there will be no fourth'" ("Pis'ma D. S. Merezhkovskogo k P. P. Pertsovu," *Russkaia literatura* 2 [1991]: 136).

87. Pyman, "The Church and the Intelligentsia," 197.

88. In his "Avtobiograficheskaia zametka" (294), Merezhkovskii recalled, "Soon the meetings were forbidden by Pobedonostsev. I went to the late metropolitan Antonii to plead for them. He refused me, making reference to his subordination to secular powers."

89. "Peter, planning to make the Church his own weapon, instead turned out himself to be an instrument of the Divine Will" (Merezhkovskii, *L. Tolstoi i Dostoevskii,* 206). Bedford (*The Seeker,* 93) writes of Merezhkovskii, "He saw in the patriarchate the seeds of papacy; and he was convinced that, had the patriarchate continued to exist, the Orthodox Church would have followed the course of Catholicism. . . . He even went so far as to proclaim that Peter's control of the administration of the Church (though not of its canonical duties) in addition to his being the head of state would lead to a theocracy." See also Rosenthal, *Merezhkovsky and the Silver Age,* 103–4.

90. Merezhkovskii's Nietzscheanism had abated, and he had altered his ideas and terminology accordingly. While he continued to laud such "pagan" concepts as beauty, nature, and freedom, he now rejected blood lust, self-deification, and the will to power and consigned them to the realm of the Antichrist, which he rejected in favor of Russian Christian meekness (Bedford, *The Seeker,* 97).

91. D. S. Merezhkovskii, *Polnoe sobranie sochinenii,* 17 vols. (St. Petersburg and Moscow: M. O. Vol'f, 1911–13), 1:iii. These changes form part of Merezhkovskii's new three-stage model of history, reflected in *Peter and Alexis.* He now argued that the pagan (i.e., pre-Christian), "fleshly" reign of "the Father" was followed by the Christian, "spiritual" reign of "the Son." The third stage, ushered in by an Eternally Feminine Holy Ghost, was to bring the reconciliation of Father and Son, the Second Coming of Christ, and an apocalyptic theocracy. Thus a synthesis of spirit and flesh was deferred to a time beyond history (James P. Scanlan, "The New Religious Consciousness: Merezhkovskii and Berdiaev," *Canadian Slavic Studies* 4, no. 1 [1970]: 30–31; Temira Pachmuss, *D. S. Merezhkovsky in Exile* [New York: Peter Lang, 1990], 58). Some scholars have suggested that the Father-Son conflict in Merezhkovskii's philosophy, and the soothing feminine element, can be traced back to childhood problems with his father and his mother's efforts to reconcile the two. See, for example, Bedford, *The Seeker,* 4; Bernice Glatzer Rosenthal, "Eschatology and the Appeal of Revolution: Merezhkovsky, Bely, Blok," *California Slavic Studies* 11 (1990): 128. For analysis of the effects of the 1905 Revolution on Merezhkovskii's thought, see Rosenthal, "Eschatology," and C. H. Bedford, "Dmitry Merezhkovsky, the Intelligentsia, and the Revolution of 1905," *Canadian Slavonic Papers* 3 (1958): 27–42.

92. D. S. Merezhkovskii, *Antikhrist (Petr i Aleksei),* in his *Sobranie sochinenii v chetyrekh tomakh,* 4 vols. (Moscow: Pravda, 1990), 2:346. Further references to this work are cited parenthetically in the text.

93. Gippius-Merezhkovskaia, *Dmitrii Merezhkovskii,* 372–73. Apparently after several arguments with his wife, Merezhkovskii rewrote the scenes devoted to Peter; this may account for Peter's intermittent positive qualities in the novel. Kolobaeva writes ("Merezhkovskii—Romanist," 449) that Merezhkovskii presents a dualistic Peter, an Antichrist with nonetheless many good impulses, including his desire to save people during a flood in St. Petersburg.

94. Nicolas Berdyaev, *The Origin of Russian Communism* (New York: Charles Scribner's Sons, 1937), 9.

95. D. S. Merejkowsky, "Religion et révolution," in D. Merejkowsky, Z. Hippius, and Dm. Philosophoff, *Le tsar et la révolution* (Paris: Société du Mercure de France, 1907), 140–41. The article was published originally in French.

96. Ibid., 178.

97. Ibid., 144.

98. Merezhkovskii is not consistent in his portrayal of the sectarians of *Peter and Alexis,* however: he rejects those Old Believers, like the ones Tikhon encounters, whose path to God involves self-destruction or the destruction of others.

99. Peter's execution of Alexis at the end of the novel echoes Aeneas's brutal slaying of Turnus at the end of Virgil's *Aeneid.* In Virgil's case, the "old" is destroyed in the person of Turnus, and thus one can argue that the killing is justified so that Roman imperialism may come to be. In Merezhkovskii's case, Alexis is not the proponent of the "old" that he is often taken to be. Rather, he represents a potential, synthesizing future path, one that Peter rejects and one that must, therefore, give way to apocalypse.

100. Critics, too, have tended to read Alexis as strictly conservative: see, for instance, Clowes ("The Integration of Nietzsche's Ideas," 412), who argues that "Aleksei tries to preserve the old backward way of life."

101. Mints, "Blok v polemike," 541.

102. The appearance of John and the eventual apocalyptic ending to the work set Merezhkovskii's novel in the company of those modern Russian novels that can be characterized, according to David M. Bethea, as "apocalyptic fiction." Bethea provides a typology of such fiction (though he does not deal with Merezhkovskii's novel) in his "On the Shape of the Apocalypse in Modern Russian Fiction: Towards a Typology," *Issues in Russian Literature before 1917: Selected Papers of the Third World Congress for Soviet and East European Studies,* ed. J. Douglas Clayton (Columbus, Ohio: Slavica, 1989), 176–95.

103. Christensen argues that Alexis is purely "weak, masochistic, and despairing," and is "not really analogous to Christ, for the sword that Christ bore was not aimed against His Father" (Christensen, "*Christ and Antichrist* as Historical Novel," 74). If one reads Alexis as a more complex figure linked to the Russian intelligentsia of Merezhkovskii's own day, however, particularly in the

light of the author's other writings of the period and his hopeful vision regarding the intelligentsia, one may posit a clear linkage between Alexis and the holy and sacrificial.

104. D. S. Merezhkovskii, "Strashnyi sud nad russkoi intelligentsiei," in his *Polnoe sobranie sochinenii,* 17 vols., 11:130. This article, a tirade against the Church's rejection of the Westernized intelligentsia based on an incident in 1905, is significantly more favorable in its treatment of Peter than the novel is.

105. D. S. Merejkowsky, "Préface," in *Le tsar,* 10.

106. On these meetings, see Gippius-Merezhkovskaia, *Dmitrii Merezhkovskii,* 332–33; and Merejkowsky, "Religion," 226.

107. Merejkowsky, "Religion," 225. This evaluation of Dobroliubov appears to be more sympathetic than Merezhkovskii and Hippius's apparent earlier view; for their previous misgivings about Dobroliubov's spiritual quests, see "Pis'ma D. S. Merezhkovskogo k P. P. Pertsovu," *Russkaia literatura* 3 (1991): 155–56n7.

108. Merejkowsky, "Religion," 224.

109. Ibid., 233.

110. In his 1910 review of Belyi's *Silver Dove,* Merezhkovskii wrote that Peter had understood that moving Russia in the direction of the West was "a question of life and death for Russia" but compared the tsar to a Caesar because of the harshness of his methods in achieving this goal (Merezhkovskii, "Vostok ili zapad," 261).

111. Merejkowsky, "Préface," 12.

112. Valerii Briusov, "D. S. Merezhkovskii kak poet," in his *Dalekie i blizkie* (Letchworth, U.K.: Bradda Books, 1973), 56, 63.

113. Andrei Belyi, "Trilogiia," in his *Arabeski* (Munich: Wilhelm Fink Verlag, 1969), 417–18.

Chapter 2. Relinquishing Empire?

1. *Pis'ma V. Ia. Briusova k P. P. Pertsovu, 1894–1896 gg. (K istorii rannego simvolizma),* Teksty i materialy, 3 (Moscow: Gosudarstvennaia Akademiia Khudozhestvennykh Nauk, 1927), 22. Briusov referred to the novel as *Otverzhennyi,* the title under which it was serialized.

2. Valerii Briusov, "Pis'ma k M. V. Samyginu," in *Valerii Briusov i ego korrespondenty,* 2 vols., ed. N[ikolai] A[lekseevich] Trifonov, Literaturnoe nasledstvo, 98 (Moscow: Nauka, 1991–94), 1:389n6.

3. Martin P. Rice, *Valery Briusov and the Rise of Russian Symbolism* (Ann Arbor, Mich.: Ardis, 1975), 27–28.

4. On Merezhkovskii's influence, see ibid., 7; Joan Delaney Grossman, *Valery Bryusov and the Riddle of Russian Decadence* (Berkeley and Los Angeles: University of California Press, 1985), 73; see, too, *Pis'ma V. Ia. Briusova k P. P. Pertsovu,* 19: Briusov told Pertsov he was ready to "fall on his knees" before the

Leda of Merezhkovskii's 1895 poem of that name, devoted to the mother of Helen of Troy.

5. Valerii Briusov, *Dnevniki 1891–1900* (Moscow: Izd. M. i S. Sabashnikovykh, 1927; rpt., Letchworth, U.K.: Bradda Books, 1972), 13. Briusov seems initially to have used "Symbolism" and "Decadence" interchangeably. Later in the 1890s, however, he came to believe that "Decadence" described the mood of the fin de siècle, while "Symbolism" applied to the specific artistic method used to express this mood. These definitions changed over the course of his career: ten years later, for instance, he felt that Decadence had been a literary school, but was now dead, and that Symbolism was an eternal type of art. For further discussion, see Grossman, *Valery Bryusov and the Riddle of Russian Decadence,* chap. 3; Rice, *Valery Bryusov and the Rise of Russian Symbolism,* 65–70.

6. Grossman, *Valery Bryusov and the Riddle of Russian Decadence,* 99.

7. S. I. Gindin, "Valerii Briusov," in *Russkaia literatura rubezha vekov (1890-e—nachalo 1920-kh godov),* 2 vols., ed. V[sevolod] A[leksandrovich] Keldysh et al. (Moscow: Nasledie, 2000–2001), 2:19.

8. Further, Briusov increased Europeans' knowledge of Russian literature through yearly reports on the Russian literary scene to the English journal *The Athenaeum* (Valerii Briusov, "Avtobiografiia," in *Russkaia literatura XX veka (1890–1910),* 3 vols., ed. S. A. Vengerov [Moscow: Mir, 1914], 1:113). Impressed by his efforts, Western critics would label him a "Peter the Great" in the cultural sphere; see Georgette Donchin, *The Influence of French Symbolism on Russian Poetry* (The Hague: Mouton, 1958), 11; and Renato Poggioli, *The Poets of Russia, 1890–1930* (Cambridge, Mass.: Harvard University Press, 1960), 101. Critics have noted, too, that various Briusovian texts may be viewed as forays into genres common to Western European literature. Konstantin Mochul'skii sees Briusov's first novel, *Ognennyi angel* (The Fiery Angel, 1907–1908), as an attempt to create in Russia a Western European adventure story (Konstantin Mochul'skii, *Valerii Briusov* [Paris: YMCA Press, 1962], 135); on Western tendencies in Briusov's stories as well, see S. S. Grechishkin and A. V. Lavrov, "Briusov-novellist," in Valerii Briusov, *Povesti i rasskazy* (Moscow: Sovetskaia Rossiia, 1983), 7–8.

9. In his diary, Briusov noted that Merezhkovskii had shown him his collections of books on Leonardo and on Peter (*Dnevniki,* 98; see also 96).

10. Valerii Briusov's *Altar' pobedy, povest' IV veka* was published in *Russkaia mysl',* nos. 9, 11, 12 (1911), 1–6, 8–10 (1912); it then came out, with Briusov's commentary, in vols. 12 and 13 of his collected works in 1913. The unfinished *Iupiter poverzhennyi* was first published in Briusov's posthumous *Neizdannaia proza* (Moscow and Leningrad: Gosudarstvennoe Izdatel'stvo Khudozhestvennoi Literatury, 1934). Both works were republished in vol. 5 of Briusov's *Sobranie sochinenii v semi tomakh,* 7 vols. (Moscow: Khudozhestvennaia Literatura, 1973–75); citations in the text refer to the latter edition.

11. Briusov returned to the novel during the winter of 1917/18. On the dates Briusov worked on the second novel, see M. L. Gasparov, "Primechaniia k

romanu 'Iupiter poverzhennyi,'" in Briusov, *Sobranie sochinenii,* 5:656. Gasparov questions the dating of the work to the end of 1913 by Briusov's wife, I. M. Briusova, in her notes to Briusov's *Neizdannaia proza,* 171.

12. See, for instance, Igor' Postupal'skii, "Proza Valeriia Briusova," in Briusov, *Neizdannaia proza,* 161–66; E. S. Litvin, "Evoliutsiia istoricheskoi prozy Briusova (Roman 'Altar' pobedy')," *Russkaia literatura* 2 (1968): 159; L. M. Chmykhov, "Nekotorye voprosy Briusóvskoi teorii istoricheskogo romana," in *Briusovskii sbornik,* ed. V. S. Dronov et al. (Stavropol': Stavropol'skii gosudarstvennyi pedagogicheskii institut, 1974), 26.

13. Interestingly, Aleksandr Amfiteatrov, who wrote *Zver' iz bezdny,* a history of imperial Rome containing clear references to modern Russia (for instance, a chapter on Rome in the first century BCE was titled "Roman Decembrists"), gave credit to Merezhkovskii and Briusov, along with Henryk Sienkiewicz, for having increased public interest in the ancient world through their Rome-related novels (A. V. Amfiteatrov, "Zakliuchenie," in his *Zver' iz bezdny,* 2 vols. [Moscow: Algoritm, 1996], 2:576). For a comparison of their approaches to the historical novel, see Pierre Hart, "Time Transmuted: Merežkovskij and Brjusov's Historical Novels," *Slavic and East European Journal* 31, no. 2 (1987): 187–201. Hart focuses predominantly on Briusov's *Fiery Angel* and does not touch upon the Roman novels, however.

14. Cited in A. N. Malein, "V. Ia. Briusov i antichnyi mir," *Izvestiia Leningradskogo universiteta* 2 (1930): 186. Malein's article is quoted in M. L. Gasparov, "Briusov i antichnost'," in Briusov, *Sobranie sochinenii,* 5:548.

15. Cited in P. N. Berkov, "Problemy istorii mirovoi kul'tury v literaturnokhudozhestvennom i nauchnom tvorchestve Valeriia Briusova," in *Briusovskie chteniia 1962 goda,* ed. K[azar] V[artanovich] Aivazian (Erevan: Armianskoe Gos. Izd., 1963), 22.

16. Gasparov warns, however, against exaggerating Briusov's scholarly credentials: he notes that the novelist seems to have relied upon approximately ten of the many sources he lists in the novel's bibliography, and that many of his Latin quotations were taken from secondary sources (Gasparov, "Briusov i antichnost'," 548; see also his "Neizdannye raboty V. Ia. Briusova po antichnoi istorii i kul'ture," in *Briusovskie chteniia 1971 goda,* ed. K[azar] V[artanovich] Aivazian [Erevan: Aiastan, 1973], 194–95). Berkov, on the other hand, insists upon Briusov's erudition ("Problemy," 21). In a posthumously published description of a planned fictional project on world cultures, Briusov wrote that his goal was to paint a portrait of the past that would be more alive to readers than what they might find in authentic documents or in the work of historians, "told dryly, coldly, and calmly," but he nonetheless insisted that the reader would find "only verifiable historical facts" in his texts (Briusov, *Neizdannaia proza,* 6). Although, as I note below, his novelistic and historical tendencies sometimes come into conflict, I differ with Joachim T. Baer's assertion that "faithfulness to historical detail does not possess an overriding significance for Briusov" (Joachim T.

Baer, "The Dark Power of Fate in Briusov's Prose on Ancient Rome," *Transactions of the Association of Russian-American Scholars in the U.S.A.* 26 [1994]: 344).

17. Aleksandr Blok, *Sobranie sochinenii,* 8 vols. (Moscow and Leningrad: Khudozhestvennaia Literatura, 1960–63), 7:128.

18. Letter to Briusov, cited in Grechishkin and Lavrov, "Briusov-novellist," 5. The critic Vsevolod Setschkareff expresses a preference for *The Altar of Victory* over Merezhkovskii's historical novels (V[sevolod] Setschkareff, "The Narrative Prose of Brjusov," *International Journal of Slavic Linguistics and Poetics* 1/2 [1959]: 237). As his article is a broad survey of Briusov's prose, he does not analyze the Roman novels in depth.

19. S. Adrianov, "Kriticheskie nabroski," *Vestnik Evropy,* no. 7 (1912): 349. For an interesting discussion of Briusov's "use of a Latin lexicon in Russian garb," see Joachim T. Baer, "Valerij Brjusov's *Altar' pobedy* and Symbolist Poetics," in *Studies in Slavic Literatures and Culture in Honor of Zoya Yurieff,* ed. Munir Sendich (East Lansing, Mich.: Russian Language Journal, 1988), 23–26.

20. Vl. Kr. [V. P. Kranikhfel'd], "Valerii Briusov: Polnoe sobranie sochinenii i perevodov," *Sovremennyi mir,* no. 11 (1913): 280.

21. L. Gurevich, "Khudozhestvennaia literatura," *Ezhegodnik gazety "Rech'" na 1913 god* (1912): 387.

22. Dmitrii Maksimov suggests that the areligious Briusov did not want to record the Christian victory and therefore did not complete *Jupiter Overthrown* (Dmitrii Maksimov, *Briusov: Poeziia i pozitsiia* [Leningrad: Sovetskii Pisatel', 1969], 187).

23. See Briusov's article on Pushkin's *Mednyi vsadnik* in his *Sobranie sochinenii,* 7:31–32: Briusov wrote critically that Merezhkovskii divided Pushkin's characters in this work into representatives of either Christianity or paganism.

24. In his commentary to *The Altar of Victory* (594), Briusov notes that the historian Edward Gibbon wrote that Gratian donned Scythian garb in order to offend public taste. Briusov himself insists, via numerous references, upon the Scythian nature of the forces his pagan characters see threatening Rome. In his 1899 poem "Skify" (The Scythians), he wrote of them as his forebears (*Sobranie sochinenii,* 1:152).

25. Christopher Hibbert, *Rome: The Biography of a City* (Harmondsworth, U.K.: Penguin, 1985), 70.

26. Cited in Christopher Woodward, *In Ruins* (New York: Pantheon, 2001), 6.

27. See M. L. Gasparov's notes to *Iupiter poverzhennyi,* in Briusov, *Sobranie sochinenii,* 5:666.

28. I am grateful to Mikhail Leonovich Gasparov for this observation.

29. Gasparov, "Neizdannye raboty," 195–96. Gasparov cites Briusov's comments in his unpublished "Zolotoi Rim" (Golden Rome), found in Briusov's archives in the Russian State Library.

30. Gasparov ("Briusov i antichnost'," 546) notes that Briusov saw Russian and European culture of his own day as similar to that of fourth-century Rome:

strong but nonetheless threatened by impending clashes with "barbarian" forces.

31. Briusov, *Dnevniki,* 61.

32. Valerii Briusov, "Rimskaia imperiia," in "Svetoch mysli: Venok sonetov," in his *Sobranie sochinenii,* 3:385. This cycle was written in 1917–1918 and published posthumously.

33. N. P. Kolosova points out that Junius's Christian wife in the second novel is kind and gentle, but that Junius is nonetheless bored by her meekness and timidity and leaves her for the more interesting and compelling Hesperia (N. P. Kolosova, "Poet, istorik, uchenyi," in Valerii Briusov, *Izbrannaia proza* [Moscow: Pravda, 1986], 18).

34. Maksimov, *Briusov: Poeziia i pozitsiia,* 185n1. Though written in 1919, after the Bolshevik Revolution had rendered Christianity a political liability, these words seem consonant with Briusov's prior beliefs. Despite a brief interlude when Merezhkovskii and Hippius attempted to interest him in their new religion (see below), Briusov remained true to an upbringing in which "faith in God seemed as much of an absurdity as faith in household spirits or water nymphs" (Briusov, "Avtobiografiia," 102); he was never an adherent of any form of Christianity.

35. While Ambrosius's extant letters reveal the bishop's view of the Christian era as a new one and his firm rejection of Symmachus's request, they do not suggest the corresponding disdain for the Roman Empire as a whole that Briusov portrays. Indeed, the very political Ambrosius's letters were written to an emperor (see R. H. Barrow, ed., *Prefect and Emperor: The "Relationes" of Symmachus A.D. 384* [Oxford: Clarendon Press, 1973]). Writing at the end of the nineteenth century, Gaston Boissier notes that those seeking in his own day to separate the church from the state ironically might find justification for their viewpoint in the writings of St. Ambrose (Gaston Boissier, *La fin du paganisme,* 2 vols. [Paris: Librairie Hachette, 1891], bk. 6, 2:291). The usually scholarly Briusov crafted an Ambrosius consistent with the separation the novelist posited between the Roman Empire and the Christian age; here Ambrosius and Augustine seem in a sense to merge. Novelist and scholar also clash in the treatment of Symmachus, who actually headed two embassies regarding the Altar of Victory; his exchange with Ambrosius took place during the second one, when Valentinian ruled the Western Empire. Briusov the novelist posits a dramatic personal meeting between Symmachus and Ambrosius during Gratian's reign; in his notes to the novel (591), Briusov the historian acknowledges this change and identifies the ancient sources (the writings of both men).

Briusov's Ambrosius carries the rejection of the past into his personal life also: a member of the ancient Aurelius family, Ambrosius now considers himself "born again" and no longer answers to the family name. Although Symmachus at first insists on calling the bishop "Aurelius," he renounces this form of address after hearing Ambrosius's essentially treasonous words and announces that he now considers the bishop an enemy of the state (127). Briusov, who sought in a sense throughout his career to be born again, frequently used the name "Avrelii" (Aurelius) as a pseudonym, as in his "Svoboda slova," written in response to Lenin in 1905 (see below). Grossman suggests that "the reference was to Aurelius d'Aquapendente, a follower of Agrippa von Nettesheim" (Grossman, *Valery Bryusov and the Riddle of Russian Decadence,* 285n60). It is tempting to posit in addition a connection with the Aurelius of Briusov's novel, though the most immediate explanation for the pseudonym is that "Avrelii" is an anagram of Briusov's first name, Valerii.

36. See, too, Grossman, *Valery Bryusov and the Riddle of Russian Decadence,* 285: "The free poet draws his inspiration solely from those things that touch his inner life, whether they be public events or no."

37. Virgil, *The Aeneid,* trans. Robert Fitzgerald (New York: Vintage Books, 1984), 104.

38. V. Ia. Briusov, "Otvetnaia rech'," in *Valeriiu Briusovu: Sbornik, posviashchennyi 50-letiiu so dnia rozhdeniia poeta,* ed. P. S. Kogan (Moscow: Izd. KUBS'A V.L.Kh.I., imeni Valeriia Briusova, 1924), 57.

39. Maksimilian Voloshin, *Liki tvorchestva* (Leningrad: Nauka, 1988), 415. Voloshin's article was first published in 1907.

40. Ibid.

41. V. F. Khodasevich, "From 'Bryusov,'" in *The Diary of Valery Bryusov (1893–1905), with Reminiscences by V. F. Khodasevich and Marina Tsvetaeva,* trans. and intro. Joan Delaney Grossman (Berkeley and Los Angeles: University of California Press, 1980), 158.

42. Marina Tsvetaeva, "Geroi truda (Zapisi o Valerii Briusove)," in her *Proza,* intro. Valentina S. Coe (Letchworth, U.K.: Bradda Books, 1969), 88. Tsvetaeva is referring here to the hard-working Briusov's famous poem "V otvet" (In Response), with its line "Vpered, mechta, moi vernyi vol" (Forward my dream, my faithful ox) (Briusov, *Sobranie sochinenii,* 1:278). On Tsvetaeva's characterization of Briusov, see Roman Voitekhovich, "Briusov kak rimlianin v 'Geroe truda' Mariny Tsvetaevoi," in *Russkii simvolizm v literaturnom kontekste rubezha XIX–XX vv.,* Blokovskii sbornik, 15 (Tartu: Tartu Ulikooli kirjastus, 2000), 182–95.

43. B. I. Purishev, "Vospominaniia ob uchitele," in *Briusovskie chteniia 1963 goda,* ed. K[azar] V[artanovich] Aivazian (Erevan: Aiastan, 1964), 518.

44. Briusov, *Dnevniki,* 139–40.

45. Briusov, *Sobranie sochinenii,* 1:36.

46. Briusov, *Dnevniki,* 69–70.

47. Ibid., 16.

48. See Gasparov, "Neizdannaia rabota," 191–92.

49. See, for example, the poem "K Tikhomu Okeanu" in *Stephanos* (Briusov, *Sobranie sochinenii,* 1:423).

50. See Briusov's poem "K sograzhdanam," in *Stephanos* (ibid., 1:425). Briusov was referring to the early Roman custom (beginning in 494 BCE) of a

plebeian general strike; the plebeians would meet on the Aventine (M. Cary and H. H. Scullard, *A History of Rome Down to the Reign of Constantine,* 3rd ed. [New York: St. Martin's Press, 1975], 66). Anna Frajlich-Zajac compares Briusov's use of the image of the Aventine in this poem to Osip Mandel'shtam's in his "Obizhenno ukhodiat na kholmy" (Anna Frajlich-Zajac, "The Image of Ancient Rome in the Poetry of Russian Symbolists" [Ph.D. diss., New York University, 1990], 104). Anna Frajlich's *The Legacy of Ancient Rome in the Russian Silver Age* (Amsterdam: Rodopi, 2007) appeared as this book was going to press.

51. Valerii Briusov, "Tsusima," in his *Sobranie sochinenii,* 1:426–27. "Briusov could call Russia the 'Third Rome' . . . but this was clearly just a historical reflex, as the notion of Russia as the preserver of true Christianity was irrelevant to the irreligious Briusov" (Ben Hellman, *Poets of Hope and Despair: The Russian Symbolists in War and Revolution (1914–1918)* [Helsinki: Institute for Russian and East European Studies, 1995], 15).

52. Valerii Briusov, "Iulii Tsezar'," in his *Sobranie sochinenii,* 1:427. For an analysis of this poem, see Anna Frajlich-Zajac, "Three Great Romans in Briusov's Poetry," in Sendich, *Studies,* 158–60.

53. Valerii Briusov, "Iulii Tsezar'," 427.

54. Valerii Briusov, "Dovol'nym," in his *Sobranie sochinenii,* 1:432.

55. Grossman, *Valery Bryusov and the Riddle of Russian Decadence,* 283.

56. Valerii Briusov, "Griadushchie gunny," in his *Sobranie sochinenii,* 1:433. I. V. Koretskaia notes that in this poem, Briusov altered Ivanov's paradigm in which the role of the artist was to be like Attila and his horsemen; Briusov's artist in "Griadushchie gunny" is meant instead to preserve culture (I. V. Koretskaia, *Nad stranitsami russkoi poezii i prozy nachala veka* [Moscow: Radiks, 1995], 169). As will be noted, however, the stance of Briusov's poetic hero in this poem is complex.

57. The article was republished by S. I. Gindin in *Literaturnaia gazeta,* no. 34/5308 (20 August 1990): 6, and then reprinted in Valerii Briusov, *Mirovoe sostiazanie,* intro. V. E. Molodiakov (Moscow: AIRO-XX, 2003), 95–100.

58. V. I. Lenin, "Partiinaia organizatsiia i partiinaia literatura," in his *Polnoe sobranie sochinenii,* 55 vols. (Moscow: Gosudarstvennoe Izdatel'stvo Politicheskoi Literatury, 1958–82), 12:99–105, esp. 100–103. For an English translation, see *Marxism and Art: Essays Classic and Contemporary,* ed. Maynard Solomon (New York: Alfred A. Knopf, 1973), 179–83.

59. Valerii Briusov, "Svoboda slova," in his *Mirovoe sostiazanie,* 98. On Briusov's article see also Gérard Abensour, "Léninisme et vie intellectuelle: La polémique de 1905 entre Brjusov et Lenin," *Cahiers du monde russe et soviétique* 21, no. 2 (1980): 159–71.

60. V. Ia. Briusov, "Pis'ma k A. A. Shesterkinoi," in *Valerii Briusov,* Literaturnoe nasledstvo, 85 (Moscow: Nauka, 1976), 654.

61. V. Ia. Briusov, "Strashnykh zrelishch zriteliami my," in V. E. Molodiakov,

"V. Ia. Briusov, Stikhotvoreniia 1918–1921 gg.," *De Visu,* no. 4 / 5 (1993): 6; rpt. in *Mirovoe sostiazanie,* 159–60.

62. Molodiakov, "V. Ia. Briusov, Stikhotvoreniia 1918–1921 gg.," 5.

63. "But this was perfectly consistent," Khodasevich declares ("From 'Bryusov,'" 159), "for he saw before him a 'strong power,' one of the variants of absolutism—and he bowed down before it, it offered him sufficient protection against *demos,* the lower classes, the mob. It cost him nothing to declare himself a Marxist—for it was all the same to him in what name it ruled, as long as there was a power. In Communism he worshipped a new autocracy." Indeed, in the 1918 poem cited above, Briusov greeted representatives of the future despite his misgivings. In his 1914 short story "Reia Silviia," Briusov had also insisted on the need to go forward, again in a Roman context. Briusov portrayed a sixth-century Roman woman named Maria who assumes the name Rhea Sylvia and goes mad because of her inability to accept the death of the Roman Empire; spending much of her time in Nero's ruined Golden House, the woman eventually gives birth to a stillborn monstrosity rather than the twins, reminiscent of Romulus and Remus, she had expected to bear. Litvin ("Evoliutsiia istoricheskoi prozy Briusova," 160) refers to the story as an epilogue to Briusov's Roman novels, as does Setschkareff ("The Narrative Prose of Brjusov," 262). For an intriguing analysis of the story as an indictment of Symbolist dreams, see Pierre R. Hart, "Myth and History: Brjusov's 'Rhea Sylvia,'" *Slavic and East European Journal* 20 (1976): 231–38.

64. Berkov, "Problemy," 51. In this light, it is worth noting that a January 1924 poem praised Lenin as one who had brought about a new era (Valerii Briusov, "Lenin," in his *Mirovoe sostiazanie,* 180).

65. Cited in Gasparov, "Briusov i antichnost'," 546–47.

66. Mochul'skii, *Valerii Briusov,* 175; Frajlich-Zajac, "The Image," 56.

67. Russian State Library, coll. 386, box 49, item 9.

68. Briusov's 1921 tragedy *Diktator* (The Dictator), published for the first time by S. I. Gindin only in 1986, betrays his ongoing misgivings about the Soviet government for which he was working. The play is filled with terms that would have been familiar to a Russian audience of the revolutionary period (references to soviets and comrades, for instance, abound), but the government has become a dictatorship. Once again, Briusov cast his political commentary in Roman terms: a plot against the dictator is explicitly compared to that against Julius Caesar (Valerii Briusov, *Diktator,* in *Sovremennaia dramaturgiia,* no. 4 [1986], 182). On the history of this tragedy, see E. I. Kolesnikova, "Tragediia V. Briusova 'Diktator,'" *Russkaia literatura,* no. 2 (1991): 197–204.

69. Briusov, *Dnevniki,* 109, 115.

70. Ibid., 118.

71. Ibid., 133. See, too, Dmitrii Maksimov, "Valerii Briusov i 'Novyi put,'" in *Russkii simvolizm,* Literaturnoe nasledstvo, 27–28 (Moscow: Zhurnal'no-gazetnoe Ob"edinenie, 1937), 276–98.

72. Briusov, *Dnevniki*, 136. The estrangement was short-lived: by 1907 Briusov had already allied himself with them again in literary polemics.

73. Valerii Briusov, "V zashchitu ot odnoi pokhvaly," in his *Sobranie sochinenii*, 6:101.

74. See, for instance, Avrelii [V. Briusov], "Vekhi. V. Misticheskie anarkhisty," *Vesy*, no. 8 (1906): 44; Avrelii [V. Briusov], "Vekhi. IV. Fakely," *Vesy*, no. 5 (1906): 56. As Martin Rice explains, as early as 1906, the "biggest problem facing Brjusov during the remaining years of his association with the [Symbolist] movement was how to survive as a nonpartisan litterateur in a literary society dominated by various schools and philosophies vying for recognition as the true faith" (Martin P. Rice, "The Aesthetic Views of Valerij Brjusov," *Slavic and East European Journal* 17 [1973]: 57–58).

75. Valerii Briusov, "O 'rechi rabskoi,' v zashchitu poezii," in his *Sobranie sochinenii*, 6:178–79.

76. N. S. Ashukin, ed., *Valerii Briusov v avtobiograficheskikh zapisiakh, pis'makh, vospominaniiakh sovremennikov i otzyvakh kritiki* (Moscow: Federatsiia, 1929), 264.

77. Joan Delaney Grossman, "Briusov's Defense of Poetry and the Crisis of Symbolism," in *Issues in Russian Literature before 1917*, ed. J. Douglas Clayton (Columbus, Ohio: Slavica, 1989), 201.

78. Valerii Briusov, "Kliuchi tain," in his *Sobranie sochinenii*, 6:87–91.

79. Valerii Briusov, "Sviashchennaia zhertva," ibid., 6:97.

80. Valerii Briusov, "Iz pisem Briusova k Petrovskoi," in *Valerii Briusov*, 791.

81. Ibid., 790.

82. Cited in A. E. Margarian, "Valerii Briusov i Rene Gil'," in *Briusovskie chteniia 1966 goda*, ed. K[azar] V[artanovich] Aivazian (Erevan: Aiastan, 1968), 529. It is worth noting that despite Briusov's admiration for Ghil, when the latter served as French correspondent for *Vesy* beginning in 1904, Briusov was at times overwhelmed by Ghil's productivity (Avril Pyman, *A History of Russian Symbolism* [Cambridge: Cambridge University Press, 1994], 171).

83. V. Ia. Briusov, "Literaturnaia zhizn' Frantsii: Nauchnaia poeziia," in his *Sobranie sochinenii*, 6:165–67.

84. Ibid., 6:167.

85. Ibid., 6:174.

86. Grossman, focusing on Briusov's poetry, writes of his "near-conversion" to scientific poetry in 1907, but states that he did not "formally declare himself for scientific poetry" until his last two verse collections (Grossman, *Valery Bryusov and the Riddle of Russian Decadence*, 314–15). Regarding his later poetry, see M. L. Gasparov, "Ideia i obraz v poetike 'Dalei,'" in *Briusovskie chteniia 1983 goda*, ed. Ia[kov] I[vanovich] Khachikian et al. (Erevan: Sovetakan Grokh, 1985), 106–13; rpt. in M. L. Gasparov, *Akademicheskii avangardizm: Priroda i kul'tura v*

poezii pozdnego Briusova (Moscow: Rossiiskii Gumanitarnyi Universitet, 1995), 6–15. In addition, Briusov's incomplete project "Sny chelovechestva" (Dreams of Humankind), on which he worked from 1909 until at least 1913, recalled Ghil's "Oeuvre" (an ongoing work) in its vast historical scope and was to be dedicated to Ghil ("Primechaniia," in Briusov, *Sobranie sochinenii,* 2:459). "Scientific poetry" is a general term, using "poetry" in the broad, Aristotelian sense, which can include prose. A. V. Lavrov notes that features of scientific poetry appear in Briusov's prose works before they become evident in his poetry (A. V. Lavrov, "Proza poeta," in V. Ia. Briusov, *Izbrannaia proza* [Moscow: Sovremennik, 1989], 17).

87. See Lavrov, "Proza poeta," 16–17.

88. Indeed, Ghil noted the "synthetic" quality of Briusov's novel. Responding to Briusov's initial plans for *Altar' pobedy,* Ghil wrote that the novel appeared to present a "synthétique épopée de cette Byzance et de Rome au IV siècle,—de ces magnificences, de ces pourpres cruautés et de ces arguties philosophiques et religieuses,—décadences d'étrange éclat, en même temps que genèse d'un monde nouveau" (Letter from Ghil to Briusov, 21 May 1911, Russian State Library, coll. 386, box 82, item 28). (The letter is partially published in Russian translation in Margarian, "Valerii Briusov i Rene Gil'," 534–35, but this relevant passage is missing.)

89. Briusov, "Avtobiografiia," 101, 104–7.

90. See for instance Briusov, *Dnevniki,* 6–9, 12.

91. See Valerii Briusov, *Velikii Ritor. Zhizn' i sochineniia Detsima Magna Avsoniia. S prilozheniem perevodov stikhov Avsoniia* (Moscow: Russkaia mysl', 1911). As Briusov explained in a 1910 interview, "I am captivated not by the authors of the Golden Age, not by the verbose Ovid and not by Virgil, though he is, of course, magnificent, but by the latest writers of the fourth century. I would say that not only are they not inferior to [the earlier writers], but in fact they achieve an even greater level of perfection" (Ashukin, *Valerii Briusov v avtobiograficheskikh zapisiakh,* 263).

92. It is interesting to note too that Junius regrets attempts made to convert his wife and sister to Christianity, even as Briusov was discomfited by the magic wrought on his own wife and sister by the newly spiritual Aleksandr Dobroliubov during a visit to the Briusov home (*Dnevniki,* 44); Khodasevich records that Briusov refused to go home while Dobroliubov remained there (Khodasevich, "From 'Bryusov,'" 155).

93. Briusov, *Dnevniki,* 12.

94. Khodasevich, "From 'Bryusov,'" 156.

95. Valerii Briusov, "Iunomu poetu," in his *Sobranie sochinenii,* 1:100.

96. Valerii Briusov, "Rodnoi iazyk," in his *Sobranie sochinenii,* 2:66.

97. Briusov, "Sviashchennaia zhertva," 99.

98. Diana Lewis Burgin, "Mythical Ballads and Metaballadic Myth in

Bryusov's Verse," in *Studies in Russian Literature in Honor of Vsevolod Setchkarev,* ed. Julian W. Connolly and Sonia I. Ketchian (Columbus, Ohio: Slavica, 1986), 64–65.

99. Irene Masing-Delic, "Limitation and Pain in Brjusov's and Blok's Poetry," *Slavic and East European Journal* 19, no. 4 (1975): 390–92.

100. Valerii Briusov, "Kleopatra," in his *Sobranie sochinenii,* 1:153.

101. Valerii Briusov, "Antonii," ibid., 1:392. For detailed analysis of this poem, see M. L. Gasparov, *Antichnost' v russkoi poezii nachala XX veka* (Pisa: Istituto di Lingua e Letteratura Russa, 1995), 44–52; M. M. Girshman, "V. Briusov. 'Antonii,'" in *Poeticheskii stroi russkoi liriki,* ed. G[eorgii] M. Fridlender (Leningrad: Nauka, 1973), 199–210. Girshman (201) notes that passion becomes the main character of the poem.

102. Briusov, "Kliuchi tain," 93.

103. Valerii Briusov, "Strast'," in *Biblioteka russkoi kritiki: Kritika russkogo simvolizma,* 2 vols., ed. N. A. Bogomolov (Moscow: Olimp, 2002), 1:135. On this article, see Joan Delaney Grossman, "Valery Briusov and Nina Petrovskaia: Clashing Models of Life in Art," in *Creating Life: The Aesthetic Utopia of Russian Modernism,* ed. Irina Paperno and Joan Delaney Grossman (Stanford, Calif.: Stanford University Press, 1994), esp. pages 134–37.

104. Voloshin, *Liki tvorchestva,* 415.

105. Mochul'skii, *Valerii Briusov,* 118.

106. Poggioli, *The Poets of Russia, 1890–1930,* 101.

107. Cited in Mochul'skii, *Valerii Briusov,* 110.

108. Valerii Briusov, "Predislovie," in Nikolai Kliuev, *Sosen perezvon* (Moscow: V. I. Znamenskii, 1912), 9.

109. Indeed, as N. A. Bogomolov has recently demonstrated, published versions of Briusov's diaries have deleted "spiritualism" from the writer's firmly stated intention to become the leader of the Decadent movement; the original diary entry paired Decadence and spiritualism as leading fields of the future that Briusov sought to head (compare Briusov, *Dnevniki,* 93, with N. A. Bogomolov, "Spiritizm Valeriia Briusova: Materialy i nabliudeniia," in his *Russkaia literatura nachala XX veka i okkul'tizm: Issledovaniia i materialy* [Moscow: Novoe Literaturnoe Obozrenie, 2000], 281). At the turn of the twentieth century, Briusov participated in numerous spiritualist séances. The documented experience of his colleague Aleksandr Lang while in a state of trance distinctly calls to mind Briusov's descriptions in *The Altar of Victory* of Junius's state of mind when overcome by Rhea's attractions (see Bogomolov, "Spiritizm," 284).

110. Cited in Briusov, *Dnevniki,* 61.

111. In this light, it is interesting to consider Briusov's brief outline for the completion of *Jupiter Overthrown:* Junius was to progress "to Hesperia and through her to Theodosius and, subsequently, to God" (*Neizdannaia proza,* 174).

112. S. V. Shervinskii, "Briusov i Rim," in Kogan, *Valeriiu Briusovu,* 52.

113. Valerii Briusov, "V Damask," in his *Sobranie sochinenii,* 1:311. On this poem see Leonid Livak, "The Making of a Symbolist Metaphor: Valerij Brjusov's Poem 'V Damask,' the Holy Bible and *The Book of The Thousand Nights and a Night,*" *Russian Literature* 45 (1999): 149–65.

114. Tsvetaeva, "Geroi truda," 88.

Chapter 3. A "Roman Bolshevik"

1. Blok began "Catiline" on 22 April 1918 and completed it on 17 May 1918. The article was first published by Alkonost, St. Petersburg, 1919.

2. Aleksandr Blok, "Katilina," in his *Sobranie sochinenii,* 8 vols., ed. V. N. Orlov, A. A. Surkov, and K. I. Chukovskii (Moscow and Leningrad: Khudozhestvennaia Literatura, 1960–63), 6:86. Further references to the article appear in the text in my own translation, with page numbers cited parenthetically. As this book goes to press, the volume of Blok's *Polnoe sobranie sochinenii i pisem v dvadtsati tomakh* (ed. Rossiiskaia Akademiia Nauk [Moscow: Nauka, 1997–]) containing his later prose has not yet appeared; consequently, although I cite his *Polnoe sobranie sochinenii* (identified thus) when possible, citations from "Catiline" and other late prose works are drawn from his earlier *Sobranie sochinenii* (identified thus).

3. The relationship between Blok and Merezhkovskii was longstanding and complex. On the connections between "Catiline" and Merezhkovskii, see Z. G. Mints, "Blok i russkii simvolizm," in *Aleksandr Blok: Novye materialy i issledovaniia,* 5 vols., ed. V[ladimir] R[odionovich] Shcherbina, Literaturnoe nasledstvo, 92 (Moscow: Nauka, 1980–83), 1:153; see, too, "Blok v polemike s Merezhkovskimi," in Z. G. Mints, *Aleksandr Blok i russkie pisateli* (St. Petersburg: Iskusstvo-SPb., 2000), 619. Mints ("Blok v polemike," 619) suggests that the phrase "scribes and corpses" refers to Merezhkovskii (see also 551 for her discussion of Blok's dismissal, in a letter to Andrei Belyi, of Merezhkovskii's "dead philology"). Merezhkovskii had linked Catiline to the fall of Rome in his 1906 article "Griadushchii Kham" (see commentary in Blok, *Polnoe sobranie sochinenii,* 5:342). On the influence of Merezhkovskii's trilogy as a whole on Blok's thought, see Mints, "Blok v polemike," 541; despite his concerns over Merezhkovskii's schema, Mints states that *Julian the Apostate* was Blok's favorite novel. Lucy Vogel notes the influence of Merezhkovskii's novel about Leonardo in the formation of Blok's views of the Renaissance artist (Lucy E. Vogel, *Aleksandr Blok: The Journey to Italy* [Ithaca, N.Y.: Cornell University Press, 1973], 107–9). In a 1909 review article, Blok presented a sympathetic view of Merezhkovskii as one who "was born an artist and will die an artist," and who was equally entranced by Rome and Byzantium ("Merezhkovskii," in his *Sobranie sochinenii,* 5: 365). In his 1902 "Zametka o Merezhkovskom," however, he had assessed Merezhkovskii more critically (*Sobranie sochinenii,* 7:67–68). For more information

on the relationship between Blok and Merezhkovskii, see Avril Pyman, "Aleksandr Blok and the Merežkovskijs (New Materials and General Survey)," in *Aleksandr Blok Centennial Conference,* ed. Walter N. Vickery (Columbus, Ohio: Slavica, 1984), 237–70; in this article (238), Pyman cites D. E. Maksimov's contention that Blok ended up rejecting the older writer's tendency toward schematization and "'accepting Merežkovskij first and foremost as an artist whose value is not in his ideas but in his quests, doubts and those extensive cultural foundations which, according to Blok, form the basis of genuine art.'"

4. Mircea Eliade writes, "By virtue of . . . paradigmatic models revealed to men in mythical times, the Cosmos and society are periodically regenerated" (Mircea Eliade, *The Myth of the Eternal Return,* Bollingen series, 46 [Princeton, N.J.: Princeton University Press, 1965], xiv). See, too, Eliade's *Myth and Reality:* "He who recites or performs the origin myth . . . becomes 'contemporary' with the events described. . . . One emerges from a profane, chronological time and enters a time that is of a different quality, a 'sacred' Time at once primordial and infinitely recoverable" (Mircea Eliade, *Myth and Reality* [New York: Harper and Row, 1963], 18).

5. While Blok had shifted earlier in his career from the mythologization of the personal to a focus on the connection between the poet and his age, in "Catiline" he asserts that the poet's own experiences, albeit derived from his surroundings rather than his personal life, still form the basis of his art (see Avril Pyman, *The Life of Aleksandr Blok,* vol. 2, *The Release of Harmony, 1908–1921* [Oxford: Oxford University Press, 1980], 304).

6. Vladimir Orlov, *Gamaiun* (Leningrad: Sovetskii Pisatel', 1978), 621; see also "Primechaniia" to Blok's *Sobranie sochinenii,* 6:503.

7. Orlov, *Gamaiun,* 595–96; Anatolii Iakobson, *Konets tragedii* (Vilnius and Moscow: Vest', 1992), 73. See also the commentary to Blok's "Dvenadtsat'" in *Polnoe sobranie sochinenii,* 5:340–42.

8. In a contemporary review of "Catiline," N. Kashin asserted that readers' knowledge of Catiline's plot stemmed from their schooldays (N. Kashin, "Aleksandr Blok: Katilina," *Vestnik teatra,* no. 45 [1919]: 15). Interestingly, Mikhail Kuzmin refers to Catiline, whom he compares, among other figures, to Pechorin, the leading character of Mikhail Lermontov's 1840 novel *Geroi nashego vremeni* (A Hero of Our Time), in a notebook entry published in 1922. He also mentions Suetonius and "Caesar's speech in the Senate" (Mikhail Kuzmin, "Cheshuia v nevode," in his *Proza,* ed. V[ladimir] Markov et al., vol. 11, *Kriticheskaia proza,* bk. 2 [Oakland, Calif.: Berkeley Slavic Specialties, 2000], 147). Kuzmin was certainly familiar with Blok's oeuvre and may well have had Blok's essay in mind when he made these notes.

9. For information on Blok's early classical training, see K. A. Kumpan, "O prepodavanii 'drevnikh iazykov' vo Vvedenskoi gimnazii (eshche raz k voprosu 'Blok i antichnost' ')," in *Aleksandr Blok: Issledovaniia i materialy,* ed. Iu[rii] K. Gerasimov et al. (Leningrad: Nauka, 1991), 151–57. Blok began his university

studies in Petersburg University's Faculty of Law, but then transferred to the Philological Faculty, where he excelled. Kumpan notes (152) that for his Latin examination during his first year of university, Blok chose to translate sections of Virgil's *Aeneid* and Cicero's *Orations against Catiline*. For further information about Blok's classical studies and interests, see D. M. Magomedova, "Blok i antichnost'," *Vestnik Moskovskogo universiteta,* ser. 9, Filologiia, no. 6 (1980): 42–49. See also in the same publication Blok's translation from Ovid's *Amores* (A. Blok, "Perevod 'Amores' 3, 5 Ovidiia," ed. D. M. Magomedova, 50–51). It is unlikely, however, that Blok would have turned to Latin sources when writing his essay: on the inaccuracies in his translation from Latin in his "Epitafiia Filippo Lippi" (1914), see M. L. Gasparov and N. V. Kotrelev, "Blok i latyn'," *Novoe literaturnoe obozrenie,* no. 36 (1999): 169–71. I am grateful to Mikhail Leonovich Gasparov for this observation.

10. Virgil's *Aeneid* and Dante's *Inferno* paint lurid pictures of Catiline: see Virgil, *The Aeneid,* trans. Robert Fitzgerald (New York: Vintage Books, 1984), 253, for an overt reference; and Dante, *The Inferno,* trans. Robert Pinsky (New York: Noonday Press, 1996), 207, for an implied one. For a history of Catiline's reception, see Peter Barta, "Re-Figuring the Revolutionary: Blok, Ibsen, and Catiline," *New Comparison* 19 (Spring 1995): 49–51. See also Renée Poznanski, "Catilina, le Bolchevik romain," *Revue des études slaves* 54, no. 4 (1982): 632–35.

11. Given the Acmeists' rejection of Ibsen, one might posit a polemical intent in Blok's assertion in "Catiline" of Ibsen's ongoing relevance to Russian culture (for a discussion of the Symbolists' and Acmeists' divergent opinions of Ibsen, see Elaine Rusinko, "Rewriting Ibsen in Russia: Gumilyov's Dramatic Poem, 'Gondla,'" in *The European Foundations of Russian Modernism,* ed. Peter I. Barta in collaboration with Ulrich Goebel [Lewiston, N.Y.: Edwin Mellen Press, 1991], 189–218). See also Nils Ake Nilsson, *Ibsen in Russland* (Stockholm: Almqvist & Wiksell, 1958). For more information on the relationship between Blok's essay and Ibsen's play, see Barta, "Re-Figuring the Revolutionary."

12. Henrik Ibsen, "Catiline: Preface to the Second Edition," in *The Oxford Ibsen,* 8 vols., ed. and trans. James Walter McFarlane and Graham Orton (London: Oxford University Press, 1960–77), 1:110.

13. "Critical history is a history which breaks with itself, debases itself in order to make room for the present and the future. What is left of history is a phantasm of history which tells a story about fictional genealogies, invented predecessors, a history which is a 'poetic elaboration and . . . spirited retelling'" (Dragan Kujundzic, *The Return of History: Russian Nietzscheans after Modernity* [Albany, N.Y.: SUNY Press, 1997], 18). Nietzsche discusses "critical history" in his "On the Uses and Disadvantages of History for Life," part of his *Untimely Meditations,* which was in Blok's Petersburg library (V. M. Papernyi, "Blok i Nitsshe," *Tipologiia russkoi literatury i problemy russko-estonskikh literaturnykh sviazei,* Uchenye zapiski Tartuskogo gosudarstvennogo universiteta, issue 491 [1979]: 93n51). Both Nietzsche and Blok decry a pious treatment of the past;

both celebrate the dangerous revolutionaries who are willing to go against the accepted order, terrifying their contemporaries and endangering themselves in the process; and both condemn the scholars who are so concerned with details that they cannot see the forest for the trees (see in particular Nietzsche, *On the Uses and Disadvantages of History for Life,* trans. Peter Preuss [Indianapolis, Ind.: Hackett Publishing Company, 1980], 22, 20; Blok, "Katilina," 70, 83). While Blok's familiarity with this text cannot be confirmed (Papernyi, "Blok i Nitsshe," 104n103), the Symbolist milieu was saturated with Nietzsche's thought, and Blok may well have absorbed these Nietzschean ideas along with many others.

14. See Barta, "Re-Figuring the Revolutionary," 62n61; Poznanski, "Catilina, le Bolchevik romain," 639.

15. Aleksandr Blok, *Zapisnye knizhki 1901–1920* (Moscow: Khudozhestvennaia Literatura, 1965), 402. When Blok read "Catiline" as a lecture at Petrograd's School of Journalism shortly after completing it, he told his audience that he had chosen his subject for its contemporary relevance (Aleksandr Blok, "Predislovie k lektsii o Katiline, chitannoi v shkole zhurnalizma," in his *Sobranie sochinenii,* 6:451–52).

16. Orlov, *Gamaiun,* 596.

17. *Pravda*'s headline on 19 January 1918, for example, proclaimed the "fire of the world revolution" that was "spreading" (Sergei Hackel, *The Poet and the Revolution* [Oxford: Clarendon Press, 1975], 54).

18. Aleksandr Blok, "Chto seichas delat'? Otvet na anketu," in his *Sobranie sochinenii,* 6:59.

19. Aleksandr Blok, "Silent Witnesses," trans. Vogel, in her *Aleksandr Blok: The Journey to Italy,* 189.

20. Ibid., 182. Blok reworked the preface in 1918.

21. On Blok's distinction between bourgeoisie and intelligentsia, see his "Intelligentsiia i revoliutsiia," written several months before "Catiline" (*Sobranie sochinenii,* 6:17).

22. Cited in Pyman, *Life,* 2:247.

23. Orlov, *Gamaiun,* 585.

24. For a similar characterization by Blok of his own contemporary Russia, see "Intelligentsiia i revoliutsiia," 17–18, where he also writes that World War I showed that "Europe has gone mad" (10). His attention to the war suggests yet another parallel between his visions of Rome and Russia: in "Catiline," he comments on the wars of first-century BCE Rome. In "Intelligentsiia i revoliutsiia" (11), he writes of World War I that "under this sign, no one will be liberated," once more evoking Emperor Constantine's Christian "sign" and the ancient world.

25. As Barta notes, Blok dismisses the "philologists" as the successors to Sallust and Cicero, upon whom they rely indiscriminately. Barta suggests, however, that Blok appears to have made use of the works of the Russian scholar I. K. Babst, who in 1856 published an article on Sallust that presages Blok's own

comments on the Roman historian (Barta, "Re-Figuring the Revolutionary," 53–55). See, too, Mints ("Blok v polemike," 619) on Blok's earlier linkage of philologists and Merezhkovskii.

26. Aleksandr Blok, *Dnevniki*, in his *Sobranie sochinenii*, 7:318. In this context it is interesting to note Blok's reactions to the Italian city Ravenna, which he visited with his wife as part of their journey to Italy in 1909 and commemorated in a poem ("Ravenna") that year. Blok was impressed by the city's preservation of "early art, the transition from Rome to Byzantium," as he wrote in a 13 May 1909 letter to his mother (*Sobranie sochinenii*, 8:284); as Vogel observes, "Here was a place which had chosen to die a natural death rather than surrender to that all-conquering monster—modernity" (*Blok: The Journey to Italy*, 86). The Bloks had planned to visit Rome on this trip, but were disenchanted with "big cities" after Florence and changed their itinerary (*Sobranie sochinenii*, 8:287).

27. Blok, *Dnevniki*, 336. Instead of the letter, Blok sent Hippius a poem that she did not understand, and the misunderstanding between the two continued.

28. Blok, "Chto seichas delat'? Otvet na anketu," 59.

29. Blok, "Intelligentsiia i revoliutsiia," 20. As D. M. Magomedova notes, "The Intelligentsia and the Revolution" may be read as a response in part to Merezhkovskii and Hippius's negative reaction to the Bolshevik takeover; Magomedova posits the two as significant "addressees" of Blok's message (D. M. Magomedova, "A. A. Blok v polemike s D. S. Merezhkovskim v 1917–1918 gg.," in *D. S. Merezhkovskii: Mysl' i slovo*, ed. V. A. Keldysh, I. V. Koretskaia, and M. A. Nikitina [Moscow: Nasledie, 1999], 274).

30. Mints notes that the Nietzschean, "one great man" pathos of Merezhkovskii's novels may be contrasted with Blok's vision of a wind independent of human will ("Blok v polemike," 619). See also Evelyn Bristol, "Blok between Nietzsche and Soloviev," in *Nietzsche in Russia*, ed. Bernice Glatzer Rosenthal (Princeton, N.J.: Princeton University Press, 1986), 157. For further analyses of the relationship between Blok's thought and that of Nietzsche, see V. M. Papernyi, "Blok i 'Proiskhozhdenie tragedii' Nitsshe (K probleme 'Blok i Nitsshe')," in *Tezisy I Vsesoiuznoi (3) Konferentsii "Tvorchestvo A. A. Bloka i russkaia kul'tura XX veka"* (Tartu: Tartuskii Gosudarstvennyi Universitet, 1975), 107–12; Papernyi, "Blok i Nitsshe," 84–106; Raoul Labry, "Alexandre Blok et Nietzsche," *Revue des études slaves* 27 (1951): 201–8; Rolf-Dieter Kluge, *Westeuropa und Rusland im Weltbild Aleksandr Bloks* (Munich: Otto Sagner, 1967), chap. 4; A. V. Lavrov, "Motivy 'Zaratustry' v tsikle 'Zakliatie ognem i mrakom,'" in Gerasimov et al., *Aleksandr Blok: Issledovaniia i materialy*, 172–77.

31. Gaius Sallustius Crispus, *The Jugurthine War/The Conspiracy of Catiline*, trans. and intro. S. A. Handford (London: Penguin Books, 1963), 185. See Blok, "Katilina," 67, for his paraphrase of Sallust.

32. See Blok's 12 May 1918 notebook comment: "One thing only makes a human being human: the knowledge of social inequality" (*Zapisnye knizhki*, 406).

33. Although the Russian song "Marsel'eza" shares the title of the French revolutionary anthem "La Marseillaise," the words are not in fact the same.

34. Henrik Ibsen, letter to George Brandes, 17 February 1871, in *Letters of Henrik Ibsen,* trans. John Nilsen Laurvik and Mary Morison (New York: Fox, Duffield, 1905), 208. Significantly for Blok's purposes (though Blok does not quote these lines), Ibsen follows this outburst in his letter with the exclamation, "The state must be abolished! In that revolution I will take part." For Blok's full citation from the letter, see "Katilina," 89–90. It is worth noting that the Russian translation he used makes a distinction in the first line of this quotation between two words that the English translator has rendered as "liberty" and "liberties." The Russian translation distinguishes between *svoboda* and *vol'nosti:* thus, "What you call freedom, I call liberties" (*Sobranie sochinenii,* 6:90). Ibsen's statement is relevant to Blok's earlier interest in "mystical anarchism": along with Viacheslav Ivanov and Georgii Chulkov, Blok had called for complete freedom, particularly in the political sphere.

35. Aleksandr Blok, "Iskusstvo i revoliutsiia," in his *Sobranie sochinenii,* 6:25.

36. In Blok's idea of perpetual revolution one might note the influence of the writer Evgenii Zamiatin, with whom Blok was in contact at this time (James Forsyth, *Listening to the Wind: An Introduction to Alexander Blok* [Oxford: Willem A. Meeuws, 1977], 113).

37. Aleksandr Blok, "Dvenadtsat'," in his *Polnoe sobranie sochinenii,* 5:7.

38. For a list of the parallels between "Catiline" and "The Twelve," see Iakobson, *Konets tragedii,* 73; Mints, "Blok i russkii simvolizm," 160. For a comparison of nighttime scenes in "Catiline" and "The Twelve," see the commentary to the poem in Blok, *Polnoe sobranie sochinenii,* 5:371–372. Iakobson (74–76) evaluates the two works differently, labeling "Catiline" a "monstrous," "tendentious" twin to "The Twelve." Konstantin Mochulsky refers to "Catiline" as a "half-comic misunderstanding" (Konstantin Mochulsky, *Aleksandr Blok,* trans. Doris V. Johnson [Detroit, Mich.: Wayne State University Press, 1983], 407). Two of Blok's contemporaries were kinder in their appraisal: both Andrei Belyi and Maksim Gor'kii acclaimed the article (*Aleksandr Blok: Novye materialy i issledovaniia,* 3:485n10, 4:237; for Belyi's comments see also "Primechaniia" to Blok, *Sobranie sochinenii,* 6:503–4).

39. As I noted in chapter 1, one may see echoes of Merezhkovskii's *Peter and Alexis* in this portrayal of the Russian people.

40. Blok, "Intelligentsiia i revoliutsiia," 15.

41. Kornei Chukovsky, *Alexander Blok as Man and Poet,* trans. and ed. Diana Burgin and Katherine O'Connor (Ann Arbor, Mich.: Ardis, 1982), 19.

42. Iakobson, *Konets tragedii,* 55.

43. Blok, *Zapisnye knizhki,* 428.

44. Ibid., 439.

45. Blok, *Dnevniki,* 325.

46. Blok, *Zapisnye knizhki,* 417.

47. Friedrich Nietzsche, *The Birth of Tragedy and The Case of Wagner,* trans. Walter Kaufmann (New York: Vintage Books, 1967), 123.

48. Blok, *Zapisnye knizhki,* 84.

49. Ibid., 78–84. See Papernyi, "Blok i Nitsshe," 93n51, for a list of Nietzschean texts in Blok's library. See also *Biblioteka A. A. Bloka: Opisanie,* 3 vols., comp. O. V. Miller, N. A. Kolobova, and S. Ia. Vovina, ed. K. P. Lukirskaia (Leningrad: Biblioteka Akademii Nauk SSSR, 1984–86), 3:243, 278.

50. Blok, *Zapisnye knizhki,* 84.

51. Nietzsche, *The Birth of Tragedy,* 41. "A tempest seizes everything that has outlived itself, everything that is decayed, broken, and withered, and, whirling, shrouds it in a cloud of red dust to carry it into the air like a vulture," Nietzsche proclaimed (123). Regarding Blok's Dionysianism as expressed in his *Snezhnaia maska* (Snow Mask), see in particular Papernyi, "Blok i Nitsshe," 95; and Lavrov, "Motivy 'Zaratustry,'" 174. See also Avril Pyman, *The Life of Aleksandr Blok,* vol. 1, *The Distant Thunder, 1880–1908* (Oxford: Oxford University Press, 1979), 263.

52. Blok, *Zapisnye knizhki,* 78. As Papernyi notes, although this phrase is found in the midst of Blok's citations from Nietzsche and is not set apart from them in the published version of the notebooks, it is in fact Blok's own addition (Papernyi, "Blok i Nitsshe," 92n47).

53. Although Blok was most closely associated with Ivanov in the period after the 1905 Revolution, it seems clear from Blok's postrevolutionary prose that Ivanov's Dionysianism had a lasting impact on Blok's work.

54. James West, *Russian Symbolism* (London: Methuen, 1970), 79; Bernice Glatzer Rosenthal, "Introduction," in *Nietzsche in Russia,* ed. Bernice Glatzer Rosenthal (Princeton, N.J.: Princeton University Press, 1986), 19.

55. Rosenthal, "Introduction," 22.

56. Viacheslav Ivanov, "Religiia Dionisa," *Voprosy zhizni,* no. 7 (1905): 139.

57. For references to Renan's influence on the Christ of "The Twelve," see Forsyth, *Listening to the Wind,* 121; Irene Masing-Delic, *Abolishing Death: A Salvation Myth of Twentieth-Century Literature* (Stanford, Calif.: Stanford University Press, 1992), 213; I. S. Prikhod'ko, "Obraz Khrista v poeme A. Bloka 'Dvenadtsat','" *Izvestiia Akademii Nauk SSSR,* Seriia literatury i iazyka 50 (1991): 434; O. P. Smola, *"Chernyi vecher, belyi sneg . . ."* (Moscow: Nasledie, 1993), 74; Blok, *Polnoe sobranie sochinenii,* 5:330. These sources do not explore the connection in detail, however.

58. Ernest Renan, *The Life of Jesus,* intro. John Haynes Holmes (New York: Modern Library, 1927), 224.

59. Ibid., 225.

60. Ibid., 235.

61. Ibid., 269.

62. Ibid., 154.

63. Ibid., 304.

64. Ibid., 293–94.

65. Ibid., 156.
66. Ibid., 389.
67. Ibid., 98.
68. Ibid., 292 (see Matthew 10:34).
69. Ibid., 389.
70. Ibid., 298.
71. Aleksandr Blok, "Skify," in his *Polnoe sobranie sochinenii,* 5:79.
72. In this chapter I do not attempt to provide an in-depth analysis of this poem or, later, Blok's "Scythians"; rather, by looking at these poems in the context of "Catiline," I seek to provide additional insights into the essay and Blok's reception of the Bolshevik takeover.
73. Blok, "Dvenadtsat'," 20.
74. For a summary of public reaction to "The Twelve," see Pyman, *Life,* 2: 285, 302–3; for a more thorough treatment of this subject, see the commentary to the poem in Blok's *Polnoe sobranie sochinenii,* 5:301–81. Analyses of the Christ figure in "The Twelve" are legion (see Blok, *Polnoe sobranie sochinenii,* vol. 5, esp. 321–43 and 376–79). For Blok's own reaction, see Chukovsky's memoirs: "I remember the time in June, 1919 when Gumilev was delivering a lecture about Blok's poetry at the Institute of Art History and said in passing that the end of 'The Twelve' (the place where Christ appears) seemed artificially tacked on, and that the sudden appearance of Christ was a purely literary effect. Blok was in the audience and listening as always with an unchanging expression on his face, but at the end of the lecture he said thoughtfully and cautiously, with a kind of preoccupied air: 'I don't like the end of "The Twelve" either. I wanted it to turn out differently. When I got to the ending, I was surprised myself: why Christ? But the closer I looked the more clearly I saw Christ. And so I made a mental note: "Yes, unfortunately, Christ."'" Gumilev, Chukovsky reports, "looked at [Blok] with his usual arrogance: . . . he didn't like it when poets acted like passive victims of their own poetry" (Chukovsky, *Blok as Man and Poet,* 25). See also Blok's description to Nadezhda Pavlovich of his vision of Christ in a storm (Smola, *"Chernyi vecher, belyi sneg . . . ,"* 80; Blok, *Polnoe sobranie sochinenii,* 5:343).
75. For appraisals of Blok's Christ as feminine, see Smola, *"Chernyi vecher, belyi sneg . . . ,"* 84; Papernyi, "Blok i Nitsshe," 101n91; Hackel, *The Poet and the Revolution,* 119; Blok, *Polnoe sobranie sochinenii,* 5:336–38; see also Avril Pyman, ed., *Alexander Blok: Selected Poems* (Oxford: Pergamon Press, 1972), 216, regarding the Christ of Blok's earlier poem "Vot on—Khristos—v tsepiakh i rozakh." Blok himself referred to Christ at one point as feminine: "But I myself sometimes hate that feminine phantom" (*Dnevniki,* 330). On the crown of white roses worn by the Christ of "The Twelve," see in particular Blok, *Polnoe sobranie sochinenii,* 5:379–81. The idea of a Dionysus-Christ figure combining strength and gentleness recalls the ideal figure Merezhkovskii had sought at the end of *Julian the Apostate;* this image could have made its way into Blok's poem. Blok

discussed the "poison of contradictions" in his "Art and Revolution" (Blok, "Iskusstvo i revoliutsiia," 24–25), specifically in a discussion of Wagner's simultaneous love and hatred of Christ.

76. Papernyi, "Blok i Nittsshe," 92.

77. Nietzsche, *The Birth of Tragedy*, 26–27; for a Nietzschean reference not present in the commentary to Blok's *Polnoe sobranie sochinenii*, see Forsyth (*Listening to the Wind*, 121), who notes that Nietzsche's Zarathustra "also comes on dancing feet wearing a chaplet of roses," but does not develop this idea further.

78. Blok, "Dvenadtsat'," 19. For a discussion of this laughter, see L. Dolgopolov, "Mnogogolosie epokhi i pozitsiia avtora ('Dvenadtsat'' A. Bloka)," *Voprosy literatury* 9 (1978): 189. On its Nietzschean overtones, see Masing-Delic, *Abolishing Death*, 218–19.

79. Aleksandr Blok, "Krushenie gumanizma," in his *Sobranie sochinenii*, 6:114.

80. Nietzsche, *The Birth of Tragedy*, 141; see also 52.

81. Ibid., 141.

82. Nietzsche explained further (ibid., 122–24), "We can understand why so feeble a culture hates true art; it fears destruction from its hands"; nonetheless, he called upon his readers to "dare to be tragic men." Only then might an observer conclude, as one would have in ancient Greece, "how much did this people have to suffer to be able to become so beautiful!" (144).

83. Blok, "Krushenie gumanizma," 111–12.

84. It is important to note that while the Bolsheviks represented a transformation of enormous significance to Blok, he was never a Party member, and his concept of Bolshevism was not a political one. Instead, he saw the revolution in cosmic terms and told his acquaintance Evgenii Zamiatin in 1920 that Bolshevism and revolution did not exist in Moscow or Petersburg but were, rather, to be found "in the depths of Russia, perhaps in the countryside" (*Polnoe sobranie sochinenii*, 5:347).

85. Blok, *Zapisnye knizhki*, 407.

86. Ibid., 402.

87. Cited in Pyman, *Life*, 2:339.

88. Blok, *Zapisnye knizhki*, 403. Blok's first reference to "Attis" can be found in his 1912 diary; he noted that the poet Maksimilian Voloshin had introduced him to the poem (Blok, *Dnevniki*, 160).

89. On the gender ambiguities in the poem, see Kenneth Quinn, ed., *Catullus: The Poems* (London: Macmillan, 1970), 286–87.

90. Intent on merging life and art, Blok once again reveals a distinctly modernist sensibility, one alien to the ancient writers from Euripides to Catullus who had implored the gods to leave them free of the transformative madness besetting the characters they described. By asserting an identification between one who describes the perilous madness and one who willingly enters into it, René Girard suggests, the writer commits sacrilege: "He is exposed to a form of

hubris more dangerous than any contracted by his characters; it has to do with a truth that is felt to be infinitely destructive, even if not fully understood" (René Girard, *Violence and the Sacred* [Baltimore, Md.: Johns Hopkins University Press, 1979], 135).

91. Aleksandr Etkind, "Revoliutsiia kak kastratsiia: Mistika sekt i politika tela v pozdnei proze Bloka," in his *Sodom i Psikheia: Ocherki intellektual'noi istorii Serebrianogo veka* (Moscow: ITs-Garant, 1996), 62.

92. Ibid., 80, 105.

93. Masing-Delic points to the influence of Vladimir Solov'ev in this characterization (*Abolishing Death,* 216; see also 116), and Etkind specifies that of several of Blok's contemporaries, including Merezhkovskii, Berdiaev, and Kliuev ("Revoliutsiia kak kastratsiia," 74).

94. Masing-Delic, *Abolishing Death,* 217.

95. Blok rejects the nineteenth-century Russian poet Afanasii Fet's translation of the poem and cites the Latin instead. M. L. Gasparov explains that while Blok was in fact influenced by Fet's work, Fet's simplification of the galliambic meter removed the irregularity of the original, an irregularity that Blok, in keeping with Sallust's description, associated with Catiline's walk (Gasparov, "Frigiiskii stikh na vologodskoi pochve," *Russian Linguistics* 18, no. 2 [1994]: 199).

96. B. M. Eikhenbaum, "Sud'ba Bloka," in his *Skvoz' literaturu: Sbornik statei* (Leningrad: Academia, 1924), 222–23. Eikhenbaum notes further that "speaking of Catullus, Blok allegorically speaks of himself" (223); he also equates Blok with Ibsen (228). Iakobson argues that the Catullus-Blok parallel in "Catiline" is forced (*Konets tragedii,* 74).

97. Blok, *Dnevniki,* 317.

98. Nicholas V. Riasanovsky writes that Blok "presented his Russian-Scythians not simply as Asiatics, but rather as an independent third element between Europe and Asia, which had for centuries protected the West" (Nicholas V. Riasanovsky, "The Emergence of Eurasianism," *California Slavic Studies* 4 [1967]: 68). Blok was affiliated at the time he wrote "Catiline" with a group called the Scythians, headed by the literary critic Ivanov-Razumnik. Shortly before Blok began to work on "Catiline," he heard excerpts of Ivanov-Razumnik's article "Ispytanie v groze i bure," an analysis of Blok's "The Twelve" and "The Scythians." E. A. D'iakova asserts this article's influence on "Catiline" (E. A. D'iakova, "Khristianstvo i revoliutsiia v mirosozertsanii 'Skifov,'" *Izvestiia Akademii Nauk SSSR,* Seriia literatury i iazyka 50, no. 5 [1991]: 422). Ivanov-Razumnik proclaimed the importance of exploding the European old world from within, as Christianity had once exploded the "old world" of Rome. He also wrote that Europeanness existed in Russia as well as in Europe and called upon Russian Scythians to summon Europe to a new era of freedom. See Ivanov-Razumnik, "Ispytanie v groze i bure," in his *Alexander Blok. Andrei Bely,* intro. M. H. Shotton (Letchworth, U.K.: Bradda Books, 1971), 164–67. For further information on Russian Scythianism, see Stefani Hoffman, "Scythian Theory

and Literature, 1917–1924," in *Art, Society, Revolution: Russia 1917–1921*, ed. Nils Ake Nilsson (Stockholm: Almqvist & Wiksell, 1979), 138–64. It is worth noting that, as Pyman writes (*Life*, 2:292), Blok "made a mistake in confusing Mongols and Scythians," seeing both groups as different from and indifferent to European culture; he learned from S. F. Ol'denburg that the Scythians had not, in all likelihood, been Asians (Blok, *Polnoe sobranie sochinenii*, 5:477).

99. Blok, "Skify," 77.

100. Ibid., 80.

101. Blok, *Dnevniki*, 317.

102. Ibid., 316.

103. Blok, *Zapisnye knizhki*, 434.

104. Ibid., 409.

105. Ibid., 430. See, too, Blok's relative's reminiscence of the poet's association of "socialist construction" with his lack of inspiration to write following the spring of 1918 (*Polnoe sobranie sochinenii*, 5:346), as well as Blok's recently published 1919 notebook entry referring to the Bolshevik government as an autocracy (Magomedova, "A. A. Blok v polemike," 278). One may interpret Blok's 1921 speech "O naznachenii poeta" (On the Calling of the Poet), dedicated to Pushkin, in which he called for freedom for art, in this light. Significantly, despite Blok's rejection in "Catiline" of the excessive schemas of *Christ and Antichrist*, he maintained in a 1920 speech on the staging of Merezhkovskii's play *Tsarevich Aleksei* (a reworking of *Peter and Alexis*) that Merezhkovskii was "an artist." The play evoked the vanished "World of Art" milieu of the early twentieth century and thus served as a manifestation of the ability of culture to endure, he added (Blok, "O Merezhkovskom," *Sobranie sochinenii*, 6:394–95). On this speech, see Pyman, "Aleksandr Blok and the Merežkovskijs," 260.

106. Blok, *Dnevniki*, 388.

107. Pyman, *Life*, 2:366.

108. Quoted in Vogel, *Blok: The Journey to Italy*, 50–51.

109. Cited in Pyman, *Life*, 2:339.

110. Blok, "Otvet na anketu," 59.

Chapter 4. The Third Rome in Exile

1. Fotiev includes the poems from Ivanov's later "Rimskii dnevnik 1944 goda" in this assessment, but privileges the sonnets, referring to them as "the most perfect hymn to the Eternal City in Russian literature" (K[irill] Fotiev, "Ierarkhiia blagoveniia [Zametki o tvorchestve Viacheslava Ivanova]," *Grani*, no. 55 [1964]: 227–28). In a 1935 article, the philosopher Nikolai Berdiaev described Ivanov as "the most refined and universal-in-spirit representative not only of Russian culture at the beginning of the twentieth-century, but perhaps of Russian culture as a whole" (Nikolai Berdiaev, "Russkii dukhovnyi renessans nachala XX v. i zhurnal 'Put','" *Put'*, no. 49 [Oct.–Dec. 1935]: 9).

2. Viacheslav Ivanov began the sonnets upon his arrival in Rome in September 1924; he sent the nine sonnets, titled "Rimskie sonety," to his friend Mikhail Gershenzon in Moscow the following January. While several sonnets were published in translation (German and Italian) in subsequent years, the sonnets were not published as a cycle until 1936, in *Sovremennye zapiski*, vol. 62. At this point Ivanov moved the sonnet he had written second, "Monte Pincio," to the end of the cycle (Olga Deschartes, "Primechaniia," in Viacheslav Ivanov, *Sobranie sochinenii*, 4 vols., ed. Dmitrii V. Ivanov and Olga Deschartes [Brussels: Foyer Oriental Chrétien, 1971–86], 3:849–50). I will be citing the text of the sonnets from that edition: *Sobranie sochinenii*, 3:578–82.

3. Lidiia Ivanova, *Vospominaniia: Kniga ob ottse*, ed. John Malmstad (Moscow: Kul'tura, 1992), 50.

4. "During the nine semesters which he spent at the University of Berlin from the autumn of 1886 until the spring of 1891, he worked on the history of Ancient Rome and of the Byzantine Empire, specializing in questions such as the system of state taxation in Egypt under the Roman Empire, Latin and Greek paleography, Roman law, the exarchate of Ravenna, and Byzantine institutions in Southern Italy" (Pamela Davidson, *The Poetic Imagination of Vyacheslav Ivanov: A Russian Symbolist's Perception of Dante* [Cambridge: Cambridge University Press, 1989], 26). For more information on Ivanov's studies in Berlin, as well as a list of his courses and instructors, see Michael Wachtel, "Viacheslav Ivanov, student Berlinskogo universiteta," *Cahiers du monde russe* 35, nos. 1–2 (1994): 353–76. Ivanov's dissertation, *De societatibus vectigalium publicorum populi romani*, was published in 1910 and reprinted in 1972. The Russian historian Mikhail Rostovtsev encouraged Ivanov to pursue its publication; see G. M. Bongard-Levin, M. Wachtel, and V. Iu. Zuev, "Mikhail Ivanovich Rostovtsev i Viacheslav Ivanovich Ivanov (Novye materialy)," *Vestnik drevnei istorii*, no. 4 (1993): 213–14.

5. Viacheslav Ivanov, "Avtobiograficheskoe pis'mo," in his *Sobranie sochinenii*, 2:21.

6. Deschartes notes the parallels between Zinov'eva-Annibal's and Shvarsalon's unions with Ivanov in Rome (Olga Deschartes, "Vvedenie," in Ivanov, *Sobranie sochinenii*, 1:134).

7. On Ivanov's courses at Baku University, as well as his popularity among the students there, see N. V. Kotrelev, "Viacheslav Ivanov—Professor Bakinskogo Universiteta," in *Uchenye zapiski Tartuskogo gosudarstvennogo universiteta*, vol. 209, *Trudy po russkoi i slavianskoi filologii. XI. Literaturovedenie* (Tartu: Tartuskii Gosudarstvennyi Universitet, 1968), 326–27. On Ivanov in Baku, see M. Al'tman, *Razgovory s Viacheslavom Ivanovym* (St. Petersburg: Inapress, 1995).

8. While Ivanov clearly seems to have had no intention of returning to Russia, in fact he quit the country as a representative of the new Soviet state, with the (meagerly) paid assignment—ultimately on his part unsuccessful—of forming a Russian Academy in Rome (see Andrei Shishkin, "Viacheslav Ivanov i Italiia,"

in *Russko-ital'ianskii arkhiv,* comp. Daniela Rizzi and Andrei Shishkin [Trento: Dipartimento di Scienze Filologiche e Storiche, 1997], 517). A Soviet citizen who appears never to have renounced this citizenship explicitly (though it lapsed in 1936), Ivanov took on the official status of "one who had not returned" only in 1929, when his annual request for a renewal of his stipend and extension of his stay was rejected; the Narkompros (People's Commissariat of Public Education) considered his "business trip" to have gone on for quite long enough and ordered him, fruitlessly, back to the Soviet Union (Shishkin, "Viacheslav Ivanov i Italiia," 520; John Glad, *Russia Abroad: Writers, History, Politics* [Tenafly, N.J.: Birchbark Press, 1999], 258, 341, 554).

9. Viacheslav Ivanov, "Laeta," in his *Sobranie sochinenii,* 1:638.

10. Viacheslav Ivanov, "Dnevnik 1924 goda," in his *Sobranie sochinenii,* 3:851.

11. Ivanova, *Vospominaniia,* 139–48.

12. Dimitri Ivanov, "Un'amicizia: Ettore Lo Gatto–Venceslao Ivanov," in *Studi in onore di Ettore Lo Gatto,* ed. Antonella D'Amelia (Rome: Bulzoni Editore, 1980), 101.

13. Muratov and Ivanov were well acquainted and spent time together in Italy, as Ivanova recalls in her memoirs; see Ivanova, *Vospominaniia,* 152. Like Ivanov, Muratov writes of Rome's fountains, of Gogol's presence in the city, and of the links between Rome and various European cultural figures (see, for instance, Pavel Muratov, *Obrazy Italii,* 3 vols. [Berlin: Grzhebin, 1924], 2:15, 26–27, 34–35).

14. Vasily Rudich, "The Tower Builder: The Works and Days of Vyacheslav Ivanov," *Arion: A Journal of Humanities and the Classics* 5, no. 3 (1998): 57.

15. Viacheslav Ivanov, "The Testaments of Symbolism," in his *Selected Essays,* trans. and ann. Robert Bird, ed. and intro. Michael Wachtel (Evanston, Ill.: Northwestern University Press, 2001), 44.

16. Dmitri Ivanov, "Recurrent Motifs in Ivanov's Work," in *Vyacheslav Ivanov: Poet, Critic and Philosopher,* ed. Robert Louis Jackson and Lowry Nelson, Jr. (New Haven, Conn.: Yale Center for International and Area Studies, 1986), 374.

17. On the Dionysian and Apollonian interplay in this process, see Carol Anschuetz, "Ivanov, Critic of Modern Culture," in *Vjačeslav Ivanov. Russischer Dichter—europäischer Kulturphilosoph. Beiträge des IV. Internationalen Vjačeslav-Ivanov-Symposiums,* ed. Wilfried Potthoff (Heidelberg: Universitätsverlag C. Winter, 1993), 22-23.

18. "I poet chemu-to uchit, / . . . / Uchit on—vospominat'" (Viacheslav Ivanov, "Rimskii dnevnik 1944 goda," in his *Sobranie sochinenii,* 3:592).

19. Viacheslav Ivanovich Ivanov and Mikhail Osipovich Gershenzon, "A Corner-to-Corner Correspondence," in *Russian Intellectual History: An Anthology,* ed. Marc Raeff (Atlantic Highlands, N.J.: Humanities Press, 1978), 383. (The original is found in Ivanov, *Sobranie sochinenii,* 3:383–415.)

20. "Thus the god is preceded by the cult, the cult by the victim, the victim by ecstasy. God, priest, and victim are one and the same, a notion corroborated

by modern anthropology" (Rudich, "The Tower Builder," 53). See also Fausto Malcovati, "The Myth of the Suffering God and the Birth of Greek Tragedy in Ivanov's Dramatic Theory," in Jackson and Nelson, *Vyacheslav Ivanov: Poet, Critic, and Philosopher,* 291; as well as Anschuetz, "Ivanov, Critic of Modern Culture," 21: "as the orgiast came to perceive the god as one who suffered death like him, he also came to experience himself as one who is born again like the god. That is the individual aspect of orgiasm. It enables the orgiast to perceive Dionysus as a metaphysical reality that Ivanov equates with truth." In his equation of worshipper and worshipped in an orgiastic context, one observes Ivanov's links to Blok and his Catiline.

21. Davidson, *Poetic Imagination,* 123.

22. Viacheslav Ivanov, "Ad Rosam," in his *Sobranie sochinenii,* 2:449–50. See Davidson, *Poetic Imagination,* 208–18, for an analysis of this poem.

23. Michael Wachtel, "Viacheslav Ivanov: From Aesthetic Theory to Biographical Practice," in *Creating Life: The Aesthetic Utopia of Russian Modernism,* ed. Irina Paperno and Joan Delaney Grossman (Stanford, Calif.: Stanford University Press, 1994), 159–62.

24. Ivanov and Gershenzon, "A Corner-to-Corner Correspondence," 380–81, 379, 376. One of Ivanov's books was titled *Cor Ardens* (A Flaming Heart). On the importance of the motif of the burning heart in Ivanov's texts, see Wachtel, "From Aesthetic Theory to Biographical Practice," 165. On the connections between the sonnets and the "Correspondence" regarding water imagery, see Elena Takho-Godi, "'Ostaetsia issledovat' istochniki voli i prirodu zhazhdy' (O 'Rimskikh sonetakh' Viacheslava Ivanova)," in *Viacheslav Ivanov: Tvorchestvo i sud'ba,* ed. and comp. E. A. Takho-Godi (Moscow: Nauka, 2002), 65–66.

25. Ivanov, "Dnevnik 1924 goda," 852.

26. Vasilii Rudich, "Viacheslav Ivanov i antichnyi Rim," in *Cultura e memoria,* vol. 2, *Kul'tura i pamiat',* ed. Fausto Malcovati (Florence: La Nuova Italia Editrice, 1988), 134. In the pre-Roman period, Cumae was "the oldest permanent settlement of Greeks on the Italian mainland" (M. Cary and H. H. Scullard, *A History of Rome Down to the Reign of Constantine,* 3rd ed. [New York: St. Martin's Press, 1975], 16). It was the site of the oracle of Apollo. Ivanov's stress on Cumae as the site of Aeneas's vision of Rome's future accords with his conviction that Italy had absorbed and perpetuated aspects of the Greek heritage he loved. See Shishkin, "Viacheslav Ivanov i Italiia," 503, on Ivanov's praise of Italy's acceptance of the Hellenic heritage. As Rudich notes, the nonimperialist Ivanov's interest in ancient Rome focuses on the eschatological: "hence his interest in Virgil" (Vasily Rudich, "Vyacheslav Ivanov and Classical Antiquity," in Jackson and Nelson, *Vyacheslav Ivanov: Poet, Critic, and Philosopher,* 278). On the Trojan theme and the links between Rome and Russia in Ivanov's poem "Laeta," see Robert Bird, "Viacheslav Ivanov za rubezhom," in *Kul'tura russkoi diaspory: Samorefleksiia i samoidentifikatsiia,* ed. A. Danilevskii and S. Dotsenko (Tartu: Tartu Ulikooli Kirjastus, 1997), 70–71.

27. Ivanov, "Dnevnik 1924 goda," 850. See also Rudich, "Viacheslav Ivanov i antichnyi Rim," 141. Dmitrii Ivanov notes that for his father, "Rome was the land of the refound spirit" ("Un'amicizia: Ettore Lo Gatto–Venceslao Ivanov," 100).

28. When Ivanov sent the sonnets to Gershenzon in 1925, he had assigned a title to each. The titles, along with the notes Ivanov appended to the sonnets upon their publication as a cycle in 1936, are found in Deschartes's commentaries in Ivanov, *Sobranie sochinenii,* 3:850.

29. In a review of the sonnets, the poet Vladislav Khodasevich suggested that Ivanov had perhaps overestimated the erudition of his readers, since he had attached so few notes to his complex poems (Vladislav Khodasevich, "Knigi i liudi," *Vozrozhdenie,* 25 Dec. 1936, 9).

30. On the Russian subtext to the poem, and its resonances, see Alexis Klimoff, "The First Roman Sonnet in Vyacheslav Ivanov's Roman Cycle," in Jackson and Nelson, *Vyacheslav Ivanov: Poet, Critic, and Philosopher,* 127, 131–32; Alexis Rannit, "O Viacheslave Ivanove i ego 'Svete vechernem,'" *Novyi zhurnal,* no. 77 (1964): 82; Bird, "Viacheslav Ivanov za rubezhom," 69; Shishkin, "Viacheslav Ivanov i Italiia," 514–15; Takho-Godi, "'Ostaetsia issledovat' istochniki voli i prirodu zhazhdy,'" 60.

31. Viacheslav Ivanov, "Lettre à Charles Du Bos," in his *Sobranie sochinenii,* 3:420. Aeneas's city is engulfed in flames when he departs.

32. In the ancient world, the cypress was associated with the cult of the dead (V[asilii] I[vanovich] Kuzishchin et al., eds. *Slovar' antichnosti* [Moscow: Progress, 1989], 262).

33. "All the sufferings, losses, feats of Aeneas, starting with his flight from burning Troy, are for the sake of Rome" (V. N. Toporov, "Vergilianskaia tema Rima," in *Issledovaniia po strukture teksta,* ed. T[at'iana] V[ladimirovna] Tsiv'ian [Moscow: Nauka, 1987], 198).

34. "On quitting Rome travellers used to take a draught from this fountain and throw a coin into the basin, in the pious belief that their return was thus ensured" (Karl Baedeker, *Central Italy* [New York: Charles Scribner's Sons, 1909], 185); the custom is ongoing to this day. In his sense of connection to Rome, Ivanov echoes Briusov, whose 1908 poem "Na Forume" also stresses the arches of the city, its palaces, and the theme of memory.

35. This archaic pronunciation of *reve* was often used in rhymes during the Pushkin era of Russian poetry, though during the earlier period the word would not have been coupled with "Trevi," an inexact rhyme.

36. In a 1931 article on Virgil, Ivanov argued that Aeneas had wanted to spare Turnus, but the gods would not let him do so; again, Aeneas's future—and that of Rome—were divinely planned and sanctioned (Viacheslav Ivanov, "Vergils Historiosophie," *Corona* 1, no. 6 [1931]: 764).

37. Virgil, *The Aeneid,* trans. Robert Fitzgerald (New York: Vintage Books, 1984), 190.

38. Ivanov, "Vergils Historiosophie," 766–67; see, too, Rudich, "Viacheslav Ivanov i antichnyi Rim," 139–40; Vasilii Rudich, "Vergilii v vospriiatii Viach. Ivanova i T. S. Eliota," *Europa orientalis* 21, no. 1 (2002): 339–51.

39. Viacheslav Ivanov, "On the Russian Idea," in his *Selected Essays*, 132.

40. Ibid., 133.

41. Ivanov notes that in this sense, "instead of a traditional heroic saga filled with fame and suffering," Aeneas's life story might be compared to a saint's life, or that of a figure from the Bible ("Vergils Historiosophie," 771).

42. Ibid., 769–70; Rudich, "Vergilii v vospriiatii," 349–50.

43. Ivanov, "Vergils Historiosophie," 761, 773–74; see also his "On the Russian Idea," 235. Pollio was instrumental in bringing about an agreement between Marc Antony and Octavian (later Augustus Caesar), one facet of which was the marriage of Antony and Octavia, the future emperor's sister. It was hoped at the time that such a union might bring to an end the years of civil war that had brought suffering to Rome and to Virgil's own family (Guy Lee, "Introduction," in Virgil, *The Eclogues* [Harmondsworth, U.K.: Penguin Books, 1984], 19–20). As Ivanov notes ("Vergils Historiosophie," 773–74), Rome's first Christian emperor, Constantine, was the first to publicize a view of the eclogue as "messianic," a prediction of the birth of Christ.

44. See Viacheslav Ivanov, "Legion i sobornost'," in his *Sobranie sochinenii*, 3: 254–61.

45. Rudich, "Viacheslav Ivanov i antichnyi Rim," 138–39; Rudich, "Vergilii v vospriiatii," 349.

46. Ivanov, "Lettre," 424–26; see also Deschartes, "Vvedenie," 174.

47. Ivanov, "Lettre," 424.

48. F[edor] Stepun, "Viacheslav Ivanov," in Ivanova, *Vospominaniia*, 388. Ivanov described a meeting with Zinov'eva-Annibal in the Coliseum in his poem "V Kolizee" (In the Coliseum) in his *Sobranie sochinenii*, 1:521; he wrote further of their early meetings in his "Avtobiograficheskoe pis'mo," 10.

49. Wachtel explains that Ivanov "uses his verses to *respond*," writing further, "We find in Ivanov's poetics far less patricide than we do ancestor worship" (Michael Wachtel, "The 'Responsive Poetics' of Vjačeslav Ivanov," *Russian Literature* 44 [1998]: 303–4). On Ivanov's relationship to Dante, see in particular Davidson's *Poetic Imagination;* see also her "Vyacheslav Ivanov and Dante," in Jackson and Nelson, *Vyacheslav Ivanov: Poet, Critic, and Philosopher*, 147–61. On Ivanov's relationship to Augustine, see A[ndrzej] Dudek, "Idei blazhennogo Avgustina v poeticheskom vospriiatii Viach. Ivanova," *Europa orientalis* 21, no. 1 (2002): 353–65. Dudek (355) divides the Augustinian references in Ivanov's work into two categories: direct citations and constructions, and similarities for which it is difficult to trace a direct connection. He notes that three Augustinian texts were particularly important to Ivanov: *Confessions, City of God*, and *On True Religion*. For a brief synopsis of Ivanov's links to Augustine,

in terms of both ideas and life experiences, see A. A. Kondiurina et al., eds., "Perepiska V. I. Ivanova i O. A. Shor," in *Archivio Russo-Italiano III,* ed. Daniela Rizzi and Andrei Shishkin (Salerno: Convivium, 2001), 194–95n20.

50. Ivanova, *Vospominaniia,* 124.

51. Ivanov, "Legion i sobornost'," 257–58. For a fuller list of Ivanov's direct references to Augustine, see Dudek, "Idei blazhennogo Avgustina," 363.

52. Kondiurina et al., "Perepiska V. I. Ivanova i O. A. Shor," 193; see, too, Deschartes, "Vvedenie," 175. Deschartes also notes—in connection with Ivanov's move to the University of Pavia in 1926—the fact that Augustine's remains were buried there.

53. Alexis Klimoff, "Dionysus Tamed: Two Examples of Philosophical Revisionism in Vjačeslav Ivanov's 'Roman Diary of 1944,'" in Malcovati, *Cultura e memoria,* 1:164.

54. In a 6 December 1928 letter to Ol'ga Shor (Olga Deschartes), Ivanov, who was in Pavia, listed the books that he wanted Shor to send him from Rome. The first two items—on a list that included Ivanov's dissertation and early books of verse, Zelinskii's study of Hellenistic religions, and Afanas'ev's *Russkie narodnye skazki*—were "1) Virgili. Opere (1 tom)" and "2) S. Augustini. Confessionum" (Kondiurina et al., "Perepiska V. I. Ivanova i O. A. Shor," 339n3).

55. Saint Augustine, *Confessions,* trans. R. S. Pine-Coffin (Harmondsworth, U.K.: Penguin Books, 1961; rpt., 1988), 62, 68.

56. Augustine's mother, Monica, herself a convert to Christianity, prays constantly that her son will follow in her footsteps.

57. On Augustine's text as a "transformation and rewriting of the *Aeneid,*" see Sarah Spence, *Rhetorics of Reason and Desire* (Ithaca, N.Y.: Cornell University Press, 1988), 56–59, as well as 139n2, where Spence provides further sources on Virgil's influence on Augustine. See, too, Sabine MacCormack, *The Shadows of Poetry: Vergil in the Mind of Augustine* (Berkeley: University of California Press, 1998).

58. Davidson, "Vyacheslav Ivanov and Dante," 149–50.

59. Ibid., 151.

60. On the influence of Dante on three of Ivanov's poetry collections, see Davidson, *Poetic Imagination,* chap. 5.

61. My literal translation. All other quotations from this work are from *The Inferno of Dante,* trans. Robert Pinsky (bilingual edition) (New York: Noonday Press, 1996), 2.

62. Ibid., 7.

63. Ibid., 11. I am grateful to Ruth Rischin for suggesting in the early stages of this project that I explore this passage from Dante.

64. "Uzheli ia tebia, Ellada, razliubil?" (Viacheslav Ivanov, "Palinodiia," in his *Sobranie sochinenii,* 3:553). For a helpful explication of this poem, see Pamela Davidson, "Hellenism, Culture and Christianity: The Case of Vyacheslav

Ivanov and His 'Palinode' of 1927," in *Russian Literature and the Classics,* ed. Peter I. Barta, David H. J. Larmour, and Paul Allen Miller (Amsterdam: Harwood Academic Publishers, 1996), 83–116.

65. See Deschartes, "Vvedenie," 174–76.

66. "This new brand of Christianity based on Dionysiac mysticism was the spiritual ideal which Ivanov proposed for his age" (Davidson, *Poetic Imagination,* 33). James West writes, "To an extent matched by none of his contemporaries, he turned to the Eastern Christian tradition, and the threads that link it to the mysteries of ancient Greek religion, perceived as the matrix from which Christianity sprang" (James West, "Criticism, Mysticism and Transcendent Nationalism in Vjačeslav Ivanov's Thought," *Russian Literature* 44 [1998]: 349). In his "Avtobiograficheskoe pis'mo" (12), Ivanov wrote that at age seven, he had fallen in love with Christ for life. See also Bernice G. Rosenthal, "From Decadence to Christian Renewal: The Parallel Paths of Merezhkovsky and Ivanov," *Slavic and East European Arts* 6, no. 2 (1990): 33–50. For more on the relationship between Ivanov and Merezhkovskii, especially regarding Merezhkovskii's *Leonardo da Vinci,* see Gennadii Obatnin, *Ivanov-mistik: Okkul'tnye motivy v poezii i proze Viacheslava Ivanova (1907–1919)* (Moscow: Kafedra Slavistiki Universiteta Khel'sinki, Novoe Literaturnoe Obozrenie, 2000), 110; on Ivanov's seventieth birthday greetings to Merezhkovskii as marking a new collaboration between Ivanov and the Russian émigré community, see Aleksei Klimov, "Viacheslav Ivanov v Italii (1924–1949)," in *Russkaia literatura v emigratsii: Sbornik statei,* ed. N. P. Poltoratskii (Pittsburgh, Pa.: Department of Slavic Languages and Literatures, University of Pittsburgh, 1972), 159; for a comparison of the two thinkers, see Avril Pyman, "Vjačeslav Ivanov and *Novyi put':* Lico ili maska? A disagreement between Merežkovskij and Ivanov as to how to put across the attitudes of the 'returning intelligencija' without shocking the people of the Church," in Potthoff, *Vjačeslav Ivanov. Russischer Dichter—europäischer Kulturphilosoph,* 289–306. Pyman notes that Merezhkovskii, "however ineptly, had jogged the memory of the Russian Orthodox and suggested new insights into old sources" (300), adding, however, that Ivanov questioned Merezhkovskii's allegorical approach as nonartistic (305).

67. Davidson, *Poetic Imagination,* 8.

68. On the water imagery of Ivanov's "Roman Sonnets" as linked to his earlier views of Dionysus, as well as the connections between Ivanov's fountain imagery and that of the poet Rainer Maria Rilke, see Takho-Godi, "'Ostaetsia issledovat' istochniki voli i prirodu zhazhdy,'" 61–64.

69. Ivanov, "Dnevnik 1924 goda," 852.

70. Fotiev, "Ierarkhiia blagoveniia," 22.

71. Ivanov, "Dnevnik 1924 goda," 852.

72. Despite Hannibal's links to Spain (see Cary and Scullard, *A History of Rome,* 124ff.), his roots were in Carthage, and the war was seen by the Romans

largely as a struggle between a Carthaginian East and a Roman West. Looking back on the Punic Wars, Virgil provided a pretext for them in his *Aeneid* through the story of the ill-fated love affair between Aeneas and the Carthaginian Dido. Moreover, as Ivanov noted in his "Vergils Historiosophie" (765), Virgil managed in his rendering of the Trojan War to take the conflict out of its traditional Greek context (in which the Trojans were the Eastern foes of a Western Greece) and to cast the Trojans instead as carriers of a Western ideal. This reading is convenient for Ivanov, who would go on to claim that the Russians, too, had ended up as carriers of Roman universalism. For both Virgil and Ivanov, geographic associations were, once again, malleable and dependent upon context.

73. Ivanov, "On the Russian Idea," 129.

74. Ibid., 130.

75. Ibid., 133.

76. Ibid., 138–39.

77. Ibid., 142.

78. Viacheslav Ivanov, "On the Joyful Craft and the Joy of the Spirit," in his *Selected Essays,* 120.

79. Ivanov, "On the Russian Idea," 138.

80. Olga Deschartes, "Vyacheslav Ivanov," *Oxford Slavonic Papers* 5 (1954): 48.

81. Tomas Venclova, "Viacheslav Ivanov and the Crisis of Russian Symbolism," in *Issues in Russian Literature before 1917,* ed. J. Douglas Clayton (Columbus, Ohio: Slavica, 1989), 210.

82. As West notes, Ivanov distinguishes between "Russia as an ethnogeographical entity" and Holy Russia as "a spiritual entity, a universal" ("Criticism, Mysticism, and Transcendent Nationalism," 353).

83. Ivanov, "On the Russian Idea," 132.

84. Ibid.

85. Ibid., 133.

86. Ben Hellman, *Poets of Hope and Despair: The Russian Symbolists in War and Revolution (1914–1918)* (Helsinki: Institute for Russian and East European Studies, 1995), 117.

87. Viacheslav Ivanov, "Budi, budi," in his *Sobranie sochinenii,* 4:51. The title of his poem and its epigraph refer to the title of a chapter in Fedor Dostoevskii's *Brat'ia Karamazovy* (Brothers Karamazov, 1880), in which the intellectual seeker Ivan Karamazov tells the saintly Father Zosima that "the Church ought to include the whole State, and not simply occupy a corner in it, and, if this is, for some reason, impossible at present, then it ought, in reality, to be set up as the direct and chief aim of the future development of Christian society!" Ivan argues further that this course of action had not taken place in the Roman Empire, which "included the Church but remained a pagan State in very many of its departments" (Fyodor Dostoyevsky, *The Brothers Karamazov,* trans. Constance Garnett [New York: Modern Library, 1950], 69–70).

88. See, for example, Viacheslav Ivanov, "Chasha Sviatoi Sofii," in his *Sobranie sochinenii,* 4:36; "Pol'skii messianizm kak zhivaia sila," ibid., 4:660, 664; "Dukhovnyi lik slavianstva," ibid., 4:667–72.

89. Hellman, *Poets of Hope and Despair,* 84.

90. Viacheslav Ivanov, "Gimn," in his *Sobranie sochinenii,* 4:60.

91. On Ivanov's view of the revolution as areligious, see in particular his 1917 essay "Revoliutsiia i narodnoe samoopredelenie" (Revolution and Popular Self-Determination), in *Sobranie sochinenii,* 3:354–64. Ivanov criticized Kerenskii, who became the head of the Provisional Government, for a lack of spirituality in his dealings with a disaffected Russian soldier (361). On the mystical roots of Ivanov's response to the revolution, as well as a discussion of this essay as an early sign of his disillusionment, see Obatnin, *Ivanov-mistik,* 164–65.

92. See his "Pesni smutnogo vremeni," in his *Sobranie sochinenii,* 4:72–75. In her "Viacheslav Ivanov's 'Malicious Counter-Revolutionary Verses': *Pesni smutnogo vremeni* Reconsidered" (*Canadian-American Slavic Studies* 26, nos. 1–3 [1992]: 77–96), Carol Ueland argues that in the poems Ivanov puts Russia's recent troubles into the context of earlier Russian history, thereby asserting the possibility of resurrection in his own dark times.

93. Viacheslav Ivanov, "Lazar'," in his *Sobranie sochinenii,* 4:77.

94. Ivanov, "Dnevnik 1924 goda," 852.

95. Ivanov, "Lettre," 424. Ivanov himself debated Soviet Commissar of Education Anatolii Lunacharskii on matters of reason and faith in the early days following the Bolshevik coup and then again in 1924 before his departure. Lunacharskii advocated Bolshevik atheism, while Ivanov spoke, with passion, for Christ (Deschartes, "Vvedenie," 160).

96. Ivanov, "Lettre," 424. In his description of Russia's revolutionary frenzy, Ivanov uses the word *neistovstvo* (427), as Blok had in "Catiline." His description of Russia's "angel" with "sick wings" (423) may be contrasted with Blok's more positive vision of the Red Guards as winged.

97. Scholars disagree on the extent of the continuity of Ivanov's thought. James West writes that "Ivanov's thought is striking for its relative lack of evolution over a period of some forty years. It did not need to evolve; what he wrote in 1904, or 1907, or 1910, or in some of the blackest times in 1921 was sufficiently mature and well-expressed that the almost, seventy-year-old poet-sage felt no pressing need to completely restate it" (James West, "Ty esi . . . ," in Malcovati, *Cultura e memoria,* 1:233). On the other hand, Klimoff asserts a "striking degree of discontinuity" in Ivanov's creative path, noting, for instance, the seventeen years following the "Roman Sonnets" during which he wrote almost no poetry, after a highly prolific period between 1903 and 1912; Klimoff analyzes the "philosophical revisionism" of two of Ivanov's later works (Klimoff, "Dionysus Tamed," 163). Each argument is somewhat tempered, however. Klimoff (167) notes that in one of the works he discusses Ivanov does not appear to sacrifice "the hope of ultimate redemption." West, meanwhile, writes

that the poet's early optimism "was perhaps one of the few components of Ivanov's thinking that was subject to later revision" ("Ty esi . . . ," 235). I argue that although Ivanov underwent certain important shifts, much of his fundamental vision remained intact.

98. Ivanov wrote the letter on 7 December 1935 to the Russian émigré A. G. Godiaev; it is cited in his *Vjačeslav Ivanov: Dichtung und Briefwechsel aus dem deutschsprachigen Nachlass*, ed. Michael Wachtel (Mainz: Liber Verlag, 1995), 18.

99. Ivanov, *Dichtung und Briefwechsel*, 18.

100. Ivanov, "Lettre," 428.

101. Robert Bird, "Notes," in Ivanov, *Selected Essays*, 280.

102. Ivanov, "On the Joyful Craft and the Joy of the Spirit," 120. The widely traveled Anacharsis was, as Charles King explains, "one of the only men of Scythia whom Herodotus thought worth describing in any detail." King writes further, "In Greek literature, Anacharsis was celebrated as the embodiment of practical wisdom despite his barbarian origins." He continued to be celebrated in European literature through the eighteenth century, though it is unclear whether in fact he truly existed. See Charles King, *The Black Sea: A History* (Oxford: Oxford University Press, 2004), 37–40.

103. Ivanov, "Lettre," 424.

104. The formal aspect of Ivanov's rendering of Rome is underscored by the fact that the sonnets are an example of ecphrasis. Thus Ivanov's poetry becomes part of a further chain, as he describes previous artistic creations and, in keeping with his theories of art, perpetuates an ongoing sequence of acts of memory and inspiration. For a discussion of ecphrasis in Russian modernism, see Maria Rubins, *Crossroad of Arts, Crossroad of Cultures: Ecphrasis in Russian and French Poetry* (New York: Palgrave, 2000).

105. Rudich notes that the "first" Rome and the "third" come together in the first sonnet to create a picture of "Eternal Rome" (Rudich, "Viacheslav Ivanov i antichnyi Rim," 141). See also Piero Cazzola, "L'idea di Roma nei *Rimskie sonety* di Viaceslav Ivanov (con richiami a Gogol' e a Herzen)," in Malcovati, *Cultura e memoria*, 1:86. Cazzola argues that the first sonnet recalls Filofei's vision, as well as Faddei Zelinskii's dreams of a "Slavic Renaissance." As I will show, the interlacing of Romes found in the first sonnet continues in various ways throughout the cycle.

106. As Robert Bird writes in a discussion of Ivanov's myth of Rome, "Rome would not have been Rome for Viacheslav Ivanov" if it had not inspired the poet to new thoughts of his homeland, Russia ("Viacheslav Ivanov za rubezhom," 77).

107. Klimoff, "The First Roman Sonnet in Vyacheslav Ivanov's Roman Cycle," in Jackson and Nelson, *Vyacheslav Ivanov: Poet, Critic and Philosopher*, 124, 129. Ivanov wrote a total of 219 sonnets, including two sonnet-garlands; see Deschartes, "Vyacheslav Ivanov," 56–58. The traditional Petrarchan sonnet has fourteen lines, divided into two quatrains and two tercets. The rhyme

scheme in the quatrains is generally *abba abba;* although the rhyme scheme of the tercets is often more varied, Georgii Shengeli asserts that the canonical form is *ccd ede* (G[eorgii] Shengeli, *Tekhnika stikha* [Moscow: Khudozhestvennaia Literatura, 1960], 303–4). Of Ivanov's nine "Roman Sonnets," only three (II, VI, and IX) follow this pattern. Lawrence J. Zillman notes, however, that the rhyme scheme of the sonnet "has, in practice, been widely varied despite the traditional assumption of limited freedom in this respect" (Lawrence J. Zillman, "Sonnet," in *Princeton Encyclopedia of Poetry and Poetics,* ed. Alex Preminger [Princeton, N.J.: Princeton University Press, 1974], 781). In the context of the "Roman Sonnets," Ivanov's choice of poetic form complements his rejection in the sonnets of a narrow nationalism and his acceptance instead of a universal ideal: the sonnet itself originated in Italy and then spread to other European national traditions.

108. Ivanov and Gershenzon, "A Corner-to-Corner Correspondence," 396.

109. Ivanov told Du Bos that culture, through memory, means that "the instruments of natural disunity—space, time, and inert matter—" are transformed into instruments of harmony, in keeping with divine unity ("Lettre," 428).

110. Klimoff, "The First Roman Sonnet," 127. See, too, Toporov's analysis of Ivanov's use of *rim* and *roma* in the sonnets. Toporov notes as well that Virgil's linkage of Rome with the world finds particularly fitting expression in Russian, where the two words are mirror images (*rim* and *mir*). Reworking the traditional linkage of *Roma* and *Amor,* Ivanov uses the *rim-mir* palindrome at various points in the cycle to underline his dominant theme of universality ("Vergilianskaia tema Rima," 207–8, 211–12).

111. Ivanov's use of blue recalls Belyi's "Pervoe svidanie" (which in turn refers back to Solov'ev's "Tri svidaniia" and, through Solov'ev's reference, to Lermontov; see Ivanov, *Sobranie sochinenii,* 4:739), as well as Belyi's *Zoloto v lazuri* and Blok's similar use of these colors to connote heavenly glory. Gold and azure are linked in Symbolist poetry with the concept of Sophia.

112. Baedeker notes that the Quirinal was populated by the Sabines, whose union with the settlement on the Palatine is said to have led to the formation of the city of Rome (*Central Italy,* 177). The hill was named for the Sabine god Quirinus (*Rome,* Michelin Green Guide [Paris, 1985], 153).

113. Silver Age poets did, however, use *saga.* I am grateful to Mikhail Leonovich Gasparov for these observations.

114. The pope's name was Felice Peretti—hence the aqueduct's name. See Baedeker, *Central Italy,* 189; Mrs. Charles MacVeagh, *Fountains of Papal Rome* (New York: Charles Scribner's Sons, 1915), 22.

115. Ivanov's use of the Old Church Slavic "prag" (threshold) in line 8 recalls its use in the poetry of the Pushkin period, including repeated instances in Nikolai Gnedich's translation of Homer's *Iliad* (1:591, 15:23, 22:70, 23:202, 24:527), as well as Ivanov's own "V Kolizee."

116. MacVeagh, *Fountains of Papal Rome,* 197–98. The piazza's name comes from the location, since the seventeenth century, of the Spanish Embassy to the Vatican. At the time Ivanov was writing, however, the area around the piazza had been known for some time for its British population (Baedeker, *Central Italy,* 183; Michelin, *Rome,* 96).

117. On the links between Ivanov's sonnets and Gogol's own responses to Rome, see Cazzola, "L'idea di Roma."

118. *Baedeker's Rome* (New York: Prentice-Hall, 1991), 101.

119. Baedeker, *Central Italy,* 185.

120. In the passage from the *Inferno* quoted as an epigraph in this chapter, Dante, already accompanied by Virgil, encounters Homer, Horace, Lucan, and Ovid. On Ivanov's attention in sonnet V to Bernini and Piranesi, see Rannit, "O Viacheslave Ivanove i ego 'Svete vechernem,'" 83–86.

121. Respighi also wrote "The Fountains of Rome." On Ivanov's acquaintance with Respighi, see Ivanova, who notes that the composer's "Pines of Rome" was performed the first year the Ivanovs were in Italy (*Vospominaniia,* 146).

122. Kuzishchin, *Slovar' antichnosti,* 55.

123. Ivanov's sequence in this line recalls Blok's 1912 poem "Noch', ulitsa, fonar', apteka," though Ivanov's focus on resurrection differs from Blok's more pessimistic picture (on this point, see, too, Cazzola, "L'idea di Roma," 94).

124. Ivanov's final note to the poems identifies the Aqua Virgo as the source of the Trevi Fountain.

125. Referring to Peter's martyrdom, Rudich writes that "pagan and imperial Rome through the agony of self-destruction and annihilation was transformed into Christian Rome" ("Viacheslav Ivanov i antichnyi Rim," 141).

126. M. M. Bakhtin, "Prilozhenie. Iz lektsii po istorii russkoi literatury. Viacheslav Ivanov," in *Estetika slovesnogo tvorchestva,* comp. S. G. Bocharov, ann. S. S. Averintsev and S. G. Bocharov (Moscow: Iskusstvo, 1979), 377.

127. Taddeo Zielinski, "Introduzione all'opera di Venceslao Ivanov," *Il Convegno* 14, nos. 8–12 (25 Dec. 1933, XII): 241.

128. "Vyacheslav, don't you realize that now at last your orchestras come alive," an ecstatic Andrei Belyi would cry, to Ivanov's distress, at the sight of the first Soviet mass rallies (Rudich, "The Tower Builder," 61).

Chapter 5. Emperors in Red

1. A[ndrei] Belyi, "The Diary of a Writer: Why I Cannot Work in a Civilized Fashion," *Zapiski mechtatelei* 2–3 (1921): 115, cited in B[oris] M. Eikhenbaum, "Blok's Fate," in *Blok: An Anthology of Essays and Memoirs,* ed. and trans. Lucy Vogel (Ann Arbor, Mich.: Ardis, 1982), 134.

2. Kuzmin pointed out that in his *Dnevnik pisatelia* Belyi had tried to prove that at present he could not write articles—"and with that writes an article"

(M[ikhail] Kuzmin, "Mechtateli," in his *Uslovnosti: Stat'i ob iskusstve* [Petrograd: Poliarnaia Zvezda, 1923], 154–55).

3. *Smert' Nerona,* in M. Kuzmin, *Teatr v chetyrekh tomakh (v dvukh knigakh),* 4 vols. in 2, ed. Vladimir Markov and George Cheron, comp. A. G. Timofeev (Oakland, Calif.: Berkeley Slavic Specialties, 1994), 1:322–80. The play was first published in M. A. Kuzmin, *Sobranie stikhov,* 3 vols., ed. John E. Malmstad and Vladimir Markov (Munich: Wilhelm Fink Verlag, 1977–78), 3:569–613, after having been preserved in the archive kept by Ol'ga Gildebrandt-Arbenina, wife of Kuzmin's longtime companion Iurii Iurkun (the three formed a ménage-à-trois of sorts from 1921 until Kuzmin's death in 1936). On the history of this archive, as well as Gildebrandt-Arbenina's despair when she thought Kuzmin's and Iurkun's papers, including *Smert' Nerona,* had been lost, see "O. N. Gildebrandt-Arbenina: Pis'mo Iu. I. Iurkunu, 13.02.46," intro. G. A. Morev, in *Mikhail Kuzmin i russkaia kul'tura XX veka,* ed. G. A. Morev (Leningrad: Sovet po Istorii Mirovoi Kul'ture AN SSSR, 1990), 244–52; on the archive see also Gleb Morev, "Oeuvre posthume Kuzmina: Zametki k tekstu," *Russian Literature* 46 (2000): 474; S. V. Shumikhin, "Dnevnik Mikhaila Kuzmina: Arkhivnaia predistoriia," in Morev, *Mikhail Kuzmin i russkaia kul'tura XX veka,* 139–45; and, briefly, "M. A. Kuzmin v dnevnikakh E. F. Gollerbakh," intro. E. A. Gollerbakh, ibid., 230. Malmstad and Markov note that the typewritten manuscript from which they published the play was marked by a large number of errors: in the case of certain words or phrases, they had to guess at Kuzmin's original intent (John E. Malmstad and Vladimir Markov, "Primechaniia," in Kuzmin, *Sobranie stikhov,* 3:737). In addition, at least one entire scene (Act Two, Scene 6, devoted apparently to the great fire of Rome) is missing.

4. John E. Malmstad and Nikolay Bogomolov, *Mikhail Kuzmin: A Life in Art* (Cambridge, Mass.: Harvard University Press, 1999), 314.

5. In presenting Acte as a Christian, Kuzmin most likely follows Henryk Sienkiewicz's example in *Quo Vadis* (1896); neither Suetonius nor the historian Tacitus describes her as such (Malmstad and Markov, "Primechaniia," 739).

6. Chicherin's letter of 15 August 1904 to Kuzmin is cited in Malmstad and Bogomolov, *A Life in Art,* 51.

7. "M. A. Kuzmin v dnevnikakh E. F. Gollerbakh," 227. Kuzmin died on 1 March 1936.

8. In the fall of 1905, Kuzmin first read to acquaintances his "Aleksandriiskie pesni" (Alexandrian Songs) and his short novel *Kryl'ia* (Wings); both works met with praise. The latter was published in *Vesy* in 1906 and created a scandal because of its open portrayal of homosexuality (see Malmstad and Bogomolov, *A Life in Art,* 93–97; John E. Malmstad, "Bathhouses, Hustlers, and a Sex Club: The Reception of Mikhail Kuzmin's *Wings,*" *Journal of the History of Sexuality* 9, nos. 1–2 [2000]: 85–104).

9. Kuzmin was certainly not atypical in his pre-1905 lack of interest in politics, which was shared by Merezhkovskii, Briusov, Blok, and Ivanov.

However, while some writers were inspired to revolutionary sympathy following 1905 (Blok carried a red flag at the time, much to his friends' bemusement), Kuzmin responded with a rejection of revolution—thus making his eventual, albeit brief, acceptance of the Bolsheviks all the more surprising to those who knew him.

10. "Iz perepiski s G.V. Chicherinym (1905–1914)," in Mikhail Kuzmin, *Stikhotvoreniia: Iz perepiski*, ed. N.A. Bogomolov (Moscow: Progress-Pleiada, 2006), 355.

11. M. Kuzmin, *Dnevnik 1905–1907* (St. Petersburg: Ivan Limbakh, 2000), 57.

12. Ibid., 59.

13. Ibid., 64, 77. Kuzmin's correspondence with Chicherin clearly brings out their differing opinions of the motivation and character of the Black Hundreds. Chicherin, seemingly in the role of instructor or guide to his less politically savvy and more aesthetically motivated friend, criticizes Kuzmin's sympathy for the Black Hundreds and repeatedly underlines the worthlessness of such groups. Kuzmin somewhat defensively maintains his position, but by January 1906 his interest in the group appears to cool as he acknowledges that "for me . . . politics is a closed book." See, for example, "Iz perepiski s G.V. Chicherinym (1905–1914)," 384, 387, 390–95, 404.

14. Malmstad and Bogomolov, *A Life in Art*, 91, 87.

15. Kuzmin, *Dnevnik 1905–1907*, 79. N. A. Bogomolov and S. V. Shumikhin wrote in 1991 that Kuzmin's anti-Semitism had been even more of a taboo topic for Soviet literary scholars than his homosexuality (N. A. Bogomolov and S. V. Shumikhin, "Mikhail Kuzmin, Dnevnik 1921 goda," *Minuvshee* 12 [1991]: 429).

16. Kuzmin, *Dnevnik 1905–1907*, 77.

17. Mikhail Kuzmin, "Histoire édifiante de mes commencements," ed. S. V. Shumikhin, in Morev, *Mikhail Kuzmin i russkaia kul'tura XX veka*, 152.

18. In a letter of 17 May 1895 to Chicherin, Kuzmin wrote that he was "transported, intoxicated" by his journey, which included Constantinople, Greece, and Alexandria (Satho Tchimichkian, "Extraits de la correspondance Mihail Kuzmin—Georgij Čičerin," *Cahiers du monde russe et soviétique* 15, nos. 1–2 [1974]: 153).

19. Anastasia Pasquinelli, "Les thèmes italiens dans la poésie de Mihail Kuzmin: l'Italie comme théâtre de la mémoire," *Cahiers du monde russe* 35, no. 4 (1994): 806–7.

20. Cited in Malmstad and Bogomolov, *A Life in Art*, 37.

21. In a diary entry of 6 April 1929, Kuzmin noted that religion and love were the most important aspects of his life (Malmstad and Bogomolov, *A Life in Art*, 262; N. A. Bogomolov and John E. Malmstad, *Mikhail Kuzmin: Iskusstvo, zhizn', epokha* [Moscow: Novoe Literaturnoe Obozrenie, 1996], 209).

22. Kuzmin would write later in life that he considered himself particularly knowledgeable in three areas, one of which was Gnosticism, an otherworld-focused movement linking Greek philosophy and Christianity that challenged

the developing Christian church in the second century (Malmstad and Bogomolov, *A Life in Art*, 341).

23. See, for instance, Kuzmin, *Dnevnik 1905–1907*, 95.

24. Vladimir Markov, "Italy in Mikhail Kuzmin's Poetry," *Italian Quarterly* 20 (1977–1978): 5–18.

25. Charles Rougle, "The Intelligentsia Debate in Russia 1917–1918," in *Art, Society, Revolution: Russia 1917–1921*, ed. Nils Ake Nilsson (Stockholm: Almqvist and Wiksell International, 1979), 101.

26. Malmstad and Bogomolov, *A Life in Art*, 254.

27. Rougle, "The Intelligentsia Debate," 60–61; Bogomolov and Malmstad, *Iskusstvo*, 200.

28. Cited in Malmstad and Bogomolov, *A Life in Art*, 259.

29. Cited in Bogomolov and Malmstad, *Iskusstvo*, 203–4.

30. N. A. Bogomolov, "Liubov'—vsegdashniaia moia vera . . . ," in his *Mikhail Kuzmin: Stat'i i materialy* (Moscow: Novoe Literaturnoe Obozrenie, 1995), 42; Bogomolov and Malmstad, *Iskusstvo*, 206. See also Bogomolov and Shumikhin, "Mikhail Kuzmin, Dnevnik 1921 goda," 429–30, for more information on Kuzmin's reaction to the revolution and its aftermath.

31. On these events see Malmstad and Bogomolov, *A Life in Art*, 266–69.

32. Two decades later, in 1938, Iurkun was shot, two years after Kuzmin's own death from natural causes.

33. Mikhail Kuzmin, "Plen," in M. Kuzmin, *Stikhotvoreniia* (St. Petersburg: Gumanitarnoe Agenstvo "Akademicheskii Proekt," 2000), 638. For further analysis of "Plen," see Bogomolov, "Liubov'—vsegdashniaia moia vera," 43.

34. Malmstad and Bogomolov, *A Life in Art*, 296.

35. George Cheron, "The Drama of Mixail Kuzmin" (Ph.D. diss., University of California at Los Angeles, 1982), 70; Bogomolov and Malmstad, *Iskusstvo*, 243.

36. Leon Trotsky, *Literature and Revolution* (Ann Arbor: University of Michigan Press, 1960), 28–29. For analysis of Trotsky's comments, see Bogomolov and Malmstad, *Iskusstvo*, 253.

37. John E. Malmstad, "Mixail Kuzmin: A Chronicle of His Life and Times," in Kuzmin, *Sobranie stikhov*, 3:286.

38. Ibid., 232–33; Bogomolov and Malmstad, *Iskusstvo*, 211–12.

39. During the 1920s Kuzmin's friendship with the writers Konstantin Vaginov, Aleksandr Vvedenskii, and Daniil Kharms, all members of Leningrad's avant-garde OBERIU (Association for Real Art), influenced his style. Reflecting in addition his interest during this period in German Expressionism, his post-revolutionary works feature characters, motifs, and events that take on differing meanings throughout the text, so that the reader is forced to search for clues in stanzas or scenes that appear at first glance to be completely disconnected. On Kuzmin's relations with the Oberiuty, see George Cheron, "Mixail Kuzmin and the Oberiuty: An Overview," *Wiener Slawistischer Almanach* 12 (1983): 87–101. Cheron notes ("Oberiuty," 93–95) that Vvedenskii wrote a play in 1926

entitled "Minin i Pozharskii," in which Nero was a character. Perhaps the play influenced Kuzmin's own choice of theme when he wrote *The Death of Nero.*

40. Mikhail Kuzmin, "Cheshuia v nevode," in his *Proza,* ed. V[ladimir] Markov et al., vol. 11, *Kriticheskaia proza,* bk. 2 (Oakland, Calif.: Berkeley Slavic Specialties, 2000), 146.

41. Mikhail Kuzmin, "Struzhki," ibid., 329.

42. Ibid., 331.

43. Ibid., 335.

44. See Kuzmin, "Pis'mo v Pekin" (A Letter to Peking), in *Uslovnosti,* 163; on Kuzmin's vision of "contemporaneity" in art, see also his "Skachushchaia sovremennost'" (Galloping Contemporaneity), ibid., 152.

45. Given Briusov's comparison of Lenin's views on culture to those of Caliph Omar, it is intriguing to note the reappearance of Omar in Kuzmin's postrevolutionary assessment of early Christianity and its links to socialism. The legend that Omar burned the library of Alexandria was exaggerated, Kuzmin asserted, since the Egyptian anchorites had already destroyed much of the library as an example of the "pagan and diabolical" culture that they abhorred ("Struzhki," 331).

46. Mikhail Kuzmin, *Smert' Nerona,* in his *Teatr,* 1:350; further references to this work are cited parenthetically in the text.

47. Kuzmin embellishes Suetonius's account, which reads, "Nero therefore grew up in very poor circumstances under the care of his aunt Domitia Lepida, who chose a dancer and a barber to be his tutors" (Gaius Suetonius Tranquillus, *The Twelve Caesars,* trans. Robert Graves [Harmondsworth, U.K.: Penguin Books, 1957; rpt., 1982], 216; page numbers refer to the reprint edition.)

48. Here Kuzmin condenses Suetonius: Nero's return to fortune came in stages, as he first regained his family inheritance and only later was adopted by Claudius (see ibid., 216–17). Suetonius writes that Claudius adopted Nero when he was ten.

49. A. G. Timofeev points here to the "parodic usage of canonical forms" in the application of religious terms to Nero (A. G. Timofeev, "Teatr 'nezdeshnikh vecherov,'" in Kuzmin, *Teatr,* 1:414).

50. On Nero's visions of the dead Agrippina, see Suetonius, *Twelve Caesars,* 232.

51. In Nero's confusion at this idea, one notes the influence on Kuzmin of Dostoevskii: the intellectual Ivan Karamazov protests to his brother Alesha in Dostoevskii's *The Brothers Karamazov* that he "never could understand how one can love one's neighbours. It's just one's neighbours, to my mind, that one can't love, though one might love those at a distance" (Fyodor Dostoyevsky, *The Brothers Karamazov* [New York: Modern Library, 1950], 281). Malmstad writes that Dostoevskii is the only Russian writer to appear frequently in the letters Kuzmin wrote during a personal crisis of 1898 (Malmstad, "Chronicle," 51). In addition, other Kuzminian texts rely heavily on Dostoevskii: Kuzmin's novel

Tikhii strazh (1914–1915), for example, has been characterized as a parody of *The Brothers Karamazov* (Andrew Field, "Mikhail Kuzmin: Notes on a Decadent's Prose," *Russian Review* 22, no. 3 [1963]: 299).

52. Suetonius, *Twelve Caesars*, 225.

53. "As [his companions] bustled about obediently he muttered through his tears: 'Dead! And so great an artist!'" (ibid., 243).

54. "Virtually every city and every town in Russia marked Lenin's funeral day with a demonstration of some kind. Typically the residents gathered in the center of the town and listened to speeches and marching bands playing funeral music. And at precisely 4:00 Moscow time [when Lenin's body was placed in its vault] they all bared their heads and stood at attention while sirens blew and rifles and cannon shot salutes to the dead leader" (Nina Tumarkin Fosburg, "The Lenin Cult: Its Origins and Early Development" [Ph.D. diss., Harvard University, 1975], 298–99). Petrograd's demonstration was the largest; presumably Kuzmin attended or heard about the event. See also Nina Tumarkin, *Lenin Lives* (Cambridge, Mass.: Harvard University Press, 1983), 162–63.

55. Cited in N. A. Bogomolov, "Vokrug 'Foreli,'" in Morev, *Mikhail Kuzmin i russkaia kul'tura XX veka*, 206. This article was reprinted with some changes in Bogomolov, *Mikhail Kuzmin: Stat'i i materialy*, 174–78. For further Kuzminian references to Lenin's death, see also Bogomolov and Malmstad, *Iskusstvo*, 308n11. For a discussion of Lenin as both utopian and antiutopian, see Richard Stites, "Revolution: Utopias in the Air and on the Ground," in his *Revolutionary Dreams: Utopian Vision and Experimental Life in the Russian Revolution* (New York: Oxford University Press, 1989), 41–46.

56. See Morev, "Oeuvre posthume," 468–70.

57. O. N. Gildebrandt, "O Iurochke," in M[ikhail] Kuzmin, *Dnevnik 1934 goda* (St. Petersburg: Ivan Limbakh, 1998), 160–61. Also on Iurkun, see Eric de Haard, "Proza Iur. Iurkuna mezhdu neosentimentalizmom i emotsionalizmom (Literaturnye otnosheniia s M. Kuzminym)," *Russian Literature* 46 (2000): 411–35.

58. For comparisons of Nero and Stalin, see Marie-Luise Bott, "O postroenii p'esy Mixaila Kuzmina 'Smert' Nerona' (1928–29 g.)," in *Studies in the Life and Works of Mixail Kuzmin*, ed. John E. Malmstad (Vienna: Wiener Slawistischer Almanach, 1989), 143; Cheron, "The Drama of Mixail Kuzmin," 259–60. In addition to the parallels with Lenin and Stalin, Kuzmin links the Bolshevik leaders to an Italian dictator who ruled long after Nero, namely, Mussolini. Mussolini formed his Fascist Party in 1919, the year Kuzmin chose for his play's opening scene, and the criminals who entice Pavel into becoming involved in setting his hotel on fire mention the "Fascist delegation" that has been staying at that hotel. When one considers the fact that Mussolini spoke of reestablishing the Roman Empire, thereby linking himself with the Roman Caesars, and the fact that the Fascists felt that the ultimate end of history was the state, rather than the individual, further links to Kuzmin's play and to his concept of Soviet reality become evident.

59. Suetonius, *Twelve Caesars*, 246.

60. Robert C. Tucker, *Stalin as Revolutionary, 1879–1929* (New York: W.W. Norton, 1973), 462. Bott points out that the final scene of the play can be read as a reference to the rumors of saintliness that follow a tyrant's death, and she notes the existence of such rumors after Lenin's death (Bott, "O postroenii p'esy Mixaila Kuzmina 'Smert' Nerona,'" 149). Her article was written before Kuzmin's diary entry of 28 January 1924 became available, however, and does not explore the idea of the political personality cult as it is addressed in his play.

61. Fosburg, "The Lenin Cult," 308, 313.

62. Ibid., 322.

63. Ibid., 326.

64. Given Petrograd's transformation into Leningrad, it is worth noting Suetonius, *Twelve Caesars*, 245: "The month of April . . . became Neroneus; and Rome was on the point of being renamed 'Neropolis.'"

65. Ibid., 221.

66. Mikhail Kuzmin, "Tri Marii," in his *Stikhotvoreniia: Iz perepiski*, 125–26. I am grateful to N. A. Bogomolov for this observation.

67. Plato, "Phaedrus," in *Phaedrus and Letters VII and VIII*, trans. and intro. Walter Hamilton (London: Penguin Books, 1973), 54. Timofeev suggests that Pavel and Nero are linked through the similar mediocrity of their art ("Teatr 'nezdeshnikh vecherov,'" 415). I would suggest, on the contrary, that the similarities between Pavel's play and Kuzmin's own undercut the credibility of Pavel's critics.

68. Again one notes the influence of Dostoevskii: in a scene reminiscent of *The Brothers Karamazov*, Marie goes down on her knees before Pavel, lauding his generosity as she promises to marry him.

69. Kuzmin, "Plen," 643. See also Bogomolov and Malmstad, *Iskusstvo*, 207.

70. Mikhail Kuzmin, "Piat' razgovorov i odin sluchai," *Russian Literature* 46 (2000): 485.

71. Ibid., 490.

72. Ibid.

73. Karl Mannheim, *Ideology and Utopia*, trans. Louis Wirth and Edward Shils (San Diego: Harcourt Brace Jovanovich, 1985), 259.

74. Ibid., 259–60.

75. Cheron further defines the expressionistic qualities of another Kuzminian text of this period, *Progulki Gulia* (Hull's Strolls, 1924), noting its similarities to "the drama of transfiguration or metamorphosis of the German expressionists with their constant wanderings where the dynamic, episodic structure mirrors the inner turmoil and awareness of chaos in the soul of the central figure" ("Mixail Kuzmin and the Oberiuty," 90).

76. Kuzmin, "Struzhki," 333. See also Bogomolov and Malmstad, *Iskusstvo*, 245.

77. Mannheim, *Ideology and Utopia*, 259. On Kuzmin's ability to find strength

in the past in order to survive the present, see A[leksandr] Lavrov and R[oman] Timenchik, "'Milye starye miry i griadushchii vek': Shtrikhi k portretu M. Kuzmina," in Mikhail Kuzmin, *Izbrannye proizvedeniia* (Leningrad: Khudozhestvennaia Literatura, 1990), 15. I quote the word "idealism" here advisedly, taking it to refer to an artistic belief in the value of imagination over realism, rather than to the generalized and unrealizable utopian mindset that Kuzmin condemned in his play and other writings.

78. As a writer with a broad variety of interests, Kuzmin certainly had phases in which some areas of fascination were more prominent than others. In his letter to Chicherin of 29 April 1905, he compared his shifts of interest to the motion of a pendulum ("Iz perepiski s G.V. Chicherinym [1905–1914]," 325; see also N. A. Bogomolov's commentary to this letter [ibid., n.1], where he discusses the two men's use of the term "pendulum" to describe how Kuzmin tended during this period to alternate between Russian and Western European influences). I am focusing, however, on the acknowledged continuities in Kuzmin's creative worldview, as discussed further in the text.

79. Neil Granoien, "Mixail Kuzmin: An Aesthete's Prose" (Ph.D. diss., University of California at Los Angeles, 1981), 44–48.

80. Mikhail Kuzmin, *Chudesnaia zhizn' Iosifa Bal'zamo, grafa Kaliostro,* in his *Proza,* 8:8–9.

81. John E. Malmstad and Gennady Shmakov, "Kuzmin's 'The Trout Breaking through the Ice,'" in *Russian Modernism: Culture and the Avant-Garde, 1900–1930,* ed. George Gibian and H. W. Tjalsma (Ithaca, N.Y.: Cornell University Press, 1976), 145–46.

82. Irina Paperno, "Dvoinichestvo i liubovnyi treugol'nik: Poeticheskii mif Kuzmina i ego pushkinskaia proektsiia," in Malmstad, *Studies,* 61–62.

83. See John Malmstad, "Mikhail Kuzmin and the Autobiographical Imperative," *Slavonica* 4, no. 2 (1997–98): 23. Malmstad writes, "The deepest roots of the art are in no way necessarily equivalent with life, as Kuzmin used his 'autofictions' (to borrow Edmund White's coinage) not only to offer an *apologia pro vita sua* and register immediate experience, but to structure it and himself."

84. Satho Tchimichkian-Jennergren, "L'art en tant que résurrection dans la poésie de M. Kuzmin," in Malmstad, *Studies,* 50.

85. Ibid., 48.

86. Mikhail Kuzmin, "Emotsional'nost' i faktura," in his *Uslovnosti,* 177. Timofeev ("Teatr 'nezdeshnikh vecherov,'" 414) writes that one can view Kuzmin's text as "the last play of Kuzminian emotionalism," and, therefore, that one can see it not simply as political satire but, through the stories of Pavel and Nero, as an expression of Kuzmin's own personal experiences.

87. Malmstad ("Chronicle," 293) has described the play as "one of the most curious Russian plays of the century," a characterization with which I concur. Marie-Louise Bott maintains that compared with Kuzmin's other works, *The Death of Nero* represents "something completely new" ("O postroenii p'esy

Mixaila Kuzmina 'Smert' Nerona,'" 141); I argue, rather, that the play has many similarities to Kuzmin's earlier texts.

88. Paperno, "Dvoinichestvo i liubovnyi treugol'nik," 60.

89. Suetonius mentions (245) that Nero did indeed carry a doll as a good luck charm, but he does not name this figure; nor does he write that she was lost. Nero "lost some very valuable objects in a shipwreck" (238), but Suetonius does not include the doll among them. Kuzmin, student of the classics, may have gotten the idea for the doll's name from a late fourth-century BCE cult in honor of Tiukhe, which is mentioned by Epicurus. The cult is discussed briefly in E. R. Dodds, *The Greeks and the Irrational* (Berkeley and Los Angeles: University of California Press, 1951), 259. Dodds attributes this ancient reverence for chance to "the deep impression left on men's minds in the late fourth century by the occurrence of unpredictable revolutionary events" (259). Kuzmin, writing at a time of great turbulence, may have found an oblique reference to this cult appealing.

90. See, too, Tchimichkian-Jennergren, "L'art en tant que résurrection," 53, on life emerging from water as symbolized by Tiukhe.

91. Simon Karlinsky, "Kuzmin, Gumilev and Cvetaeva as Neo-Romantic Playwrights," in Malmstad, *Studies*, 19.

92. See Kuzmin, *Dnevnik 1905–1907*, 61, and 453n34; as well as his remark in his diary on 19 June 1906 that one did not discuss Merezhkovskii and Nietzsche during "rendezvous" and escapades with lovers (177). Kuzmin's review of Merezhkovskii's play is found in his *Uslovnosti*, 90–94. On Kuzmin and Blok, see Gennadii Shmakov, "Blok i Kuzmin (novye materialy)," in *Blokovskii sbornik II* (Tartu: Tartuskii Gosudarstvennyi Universitet, 1972), 341–64; Kuzmin praised Blok's "Dvenadtsat' " as "one of [his] highest achievements" (Mikhail Kuzmin, "Golos poeta," in *Uslovnosti*, 170; see, too, Shmakov, "Blok i Kuzmin," 357).

93. See, for instance, Kuzmin, "Cheshuia v nevode," 144.

94. Kuzmin would continue his "internal and constant polemic with Christianity" in his 1934 diary, in which he maintained in a 9 October entry that religion was a personal or national, rather than international, phenomenon. Christianity initially had been an acceptably "idealistic, Jewish heresy," he wrote, but it had turned into "an odious Jewish thing." He also, however, wrote with distaste of the earliest Christians, whom he compared to revolutionaries such as Leonid Kannegiser (also a Jew). Again, Kuzmin's views here are not entirely consistent, and, as volume editor Gleb Morev notes, they do not coincide with his 1897 vision of a pagan-influenced Christianity. See Kuzmin, *Dnevnik 1934 goda*, 118, 327.

95. On potential Kuzminian influence on Bulgakov's novel, see Bott, "O postroenii p'esy Mixaila Kuzmina 'Smert' Nerona,'" 149–50.

Conclusion

1. Merezhkovskii's 1932 *Iisus neizvestnyi* may provide an exception, though its date and the fact that it was written over a decade after Merezhkovskii's

1919 emigration from Russia separate it from Russia's modernist Rome texts. Andrew Barratt notes similarities between *Iisus neizvestnyi* and Bulgakov's novel (Andrew Barratt, *Between Two Worlds: A Critical Introduction to "The Master and Margarita"* [Oxford: Clarendon Press, 1987], 182n9).

2. Miron Petrovskii, "Mifologicheskoe gorodovedenie Mikhaila Bulgakova," *Teatr,* no. 5 (May 1991): 21. Barratt writes of the influence of Symbolism, particularly Symbolist views of Christ, on Bulgakov (*Between Two Worlds,* 315–17). I. F. Belza discusses the influence of Briusov's *Fiery Angel* on Bulgakov's portrayal of black magic (I. F. Belza, "Genealogiia *Mastera i Margarity,*" in *Kontekst* [Moscow: Nauka, 1978], 193), and L. A. Kolobaeva suggests the influence of Merezhkovskii's *Leonardo da Vinci* in that regard (L. A. Kolobaeva, "Total'noe edinstvo khudozhestvennogo mira [Merezhkovskii-Romanist]," in *D. S. Merezhkovskii: Mysl' i slovo,* ed. V. A. Keldysh, I. V. Koretskaia, and M. A. Nikitina [Moscow: Nasledie, 1999], 16). It should be noted, though, that Bulgakov expressed distaste for what he called "symbolist rubbish" in a 16 January 1925 diary entry (*Manuscripts Don't Burn: A Life in Diaries and Letters,* comp. J. A. E. Curtis [London: Harvill, 1992], 61).

3. On the influence of Renan's *Life of Jesus* on Bulgakov's novel, see, for instance, J. A. E. Curtis, *Bulgakov's Last Decade: The Writer as Hero* (Cambridge: Cambridge University Press, 1987), 152; Lesley Milne, *Mikhail Bulgakov: A Critical Biography* (Cambridge: Cambridge University Press, 1990), 232.

4. For a survey of approaches in the voluminous literature on Bulgakov's novel, see Andrew Barratt, "The Master and Margarita in Recent Criticism," in *The Master and Margarita: A Critical Companion,* ed. Laura D. Weeks (Evanston, Ill.: Northwestern University Press, 1996), 84–97.

5. Bulgakov referred thus to his novel, which he continued to edit as he lay dying (Ellendea Proffer, "Afterword," in Mikhail Bulgakov, *The Master and Margarita,* trans. Diana Burgin and Katherine Tiernan O'Connor [New York: Vintage Books, 1996], 368). Parenthetical references to this work in the text cite first the Russian edition (Mikhail Bulgakov, *Master i Margarita* [Moscow: Khudozhestvennaia Literatura, 1988]) and then the English translation by Burgin and O'Connor, whose transliterations for names and places I have used as well.

6. Colin Wells, *The Roman Empire* (Stanford, Calif.: Stanford University Press, 1984), 30–31.

7. Norman Perrin and Dennis C. Duling, *The New Testament: An Introduction,* 2nd ed. (New York: Harcourt Brace Jovanovich, 1982), 17–19.

8. Ibid., 19–20.

9. L. H. Feldman, "Financing the Colosseum," *Biblical Archaeology Review,* July–Aug. 2001, 20–31.

10. In his portrayal of the remorseful Pilate, Bulgakov appears to have been influenced by the "Acts of Pilate," part of the apocryphal Gospel of Nicodemus, which asserts Pilate's innocence and blames the execution of Jesus on the Jewish people. The Gospel of Nicodemus may be found in *The Other Bible,* ed. and

intro. Willis Barnstone (San Francisco: Harper and Row, 1984), 359–80. In this text the emperor Tiberius seeks Jesus's help, finds out that Pilate has permitted his execution, and has Pilate executed as well. Pilate is welcomed by one of God's angels, however, so that the narrative ends up asserting the innocence of the Romans and the guilt of the Jews in Jesus's death. I. F. Belza and Ellendea Proffer note that the Gospel of Nicodemus presented Bulgakov with the names of the two criminals executed with Jesus (Belza, "Genealogiia *Mastera i Margarity*," 177; Ellendea Proffer, "Commentary," in Bulgakov, *The Master and Margarita*, 341). Boris Gasparov notes that Bulgakov, who clearly knew of the apocryphal gospels and made use of their content in his novel, stated that he was not a historian (Boris Gasparov, "Novyi Zavet v proizvedeniiakh M. A. Bulgakova," *Neue Russische Literatur* 4–5 [1981–1982]: 159). Rather, he was creating a noncanonical account to which he ascribed greater truth than that found in traditionally accepted narratives.

11. As Proffer writes, events one associates with the traditional Gospel narratives are displaced into the Moscow sections of the novel, while characteristics of the Stalinist era find their way into the Yershalaim sections of the text; thus Berlioz has the disciples Yeshua is missing (see, for example, Ellendea Proffer, *Bulgakov: Life and Work* [Ann Arbor, Mich.: Ardis, 1984], 555, 559).

12. Interestingly, St. Phocas tends to be portrayed in a white garment, holding various objects—an image that calls to mind the poet Ivan Bezdomnyi, who responds to his meeting with the devil by appearing at Griboedov in his underwear, clutching an icon. Gasparov points out that Amvrosii and Foka recall two Roman bishops, one of whom was killed under Trajan, and notes the Coliseum reference that follows and the name Rimskii (Boris M. Gasparov, "Iz nabliudenii nad motivnoi strukturoi romana M. A. Bulgakova 'Master i Margarita,'" *Slavica Hierosolymitana* 3 [1978]: 216).

13. "Nero fabricated scapegoats—and punished with every refinement the notoriously depraved Christians (as they were popularly called). Their originator, Christ, had been executed in Tiberius' reign by the governor of Judea, Pontius Pilatus" (Tacitus, *The Annals of Imperial Rome*, trans. Michael Grant [Harmondsworth, U.K.: Penguin, 1982], 365). On the fires, see, too, Gasparov, "Iz nabliudenii," 223. Gasparov also (ibid., 224) connects Nero's epoch with Moscow at the end of the 1920s–1930s and Tiberius's with the beginning of the 1920s, asserting that Bulgakov's writing of the late 1930s is thus "a parable about . . . a world that has perished" but, unaware of this, continues to exist. Gasparov's interpretation recalls Blok's words about the Rome that continued to exist after the birth of Jesus, though it was already dead. Somewhat similarly, Petrovskii ("Mifologicheskoe gorodovedenie Mikhaila Bulgakova," 25–26) writes that Bulgakov's texts deal with the death of the City.

14. On a semantic level, words and phrases are repeated in both settings of the novel. Pilate's cry to the gods to give him poison as he interrogates Yeshua is repeated in the narrator's similar call as he observes the inhabitants of the

Writers' Union at Griboedov House. The rose oil Pilate detests in Yershalaim is used to bathe Margarita when she serves as the hostess of Woland's ball. Yeshua's hoarse voice during the scene of his execution is mirrored in Woland's hoarseness as he prepares for his evening's entertainment. Gestures also recur from one setting to another. Most strikingly, although Yeshua's execution is not labeled a crucifixion, the image of crucifixion is repeated throughout the novel. Varenukha, the house manager of the Variety Theater where Woland performs his black magic, lifts his arms "like someone crucified" when confronted with Woland's tricks (116/89). Frieda, the lone sinner at Woland's ball to whom Margarita is permitted to grant absolution, spreads herself out in the shape of a cross as she hears Margarita's judgment. And in Yershalaim, Judas's body lies with arms outflung after he is murdered at Pilate's instigation by the chief of the secret police, Afranius, and his men. For a detailed discussion of such connections, see Gasparov, "Iz nabliudenii," 215–18.

15. Bulgakov himself insisted that his Woland had no prototypes (Marietta Chudakova, *Zhizneopisanie Mikhaila Bulgakova* [Moscow: Kniga, 1988], 462); he made this statement in the late 1930s, however, an exceptionally dangerous time. Lesley Milne takes specific issue with "the Woland-Stalin identification" (*Bulgakov: A Critical Biography,* 244). It is beyond the scope of this chapter to explore the many other intriguing readings of Bulgakov's Woland.

16. Andrei Sinyavsky, *Soviet Civilization,* trans. Joanne Turnbull with Nikolai Formozov (New York: Arcade Publishing, 1990), 108.

17. Ibid., 107. See, too, M. Keith Booker, *Stalin and Modern Russian Fiction: Carnival, Dialogism, and History* (Westport, Conn.: Greenwood Press, 1995).

18. Sinyavsky, *Soviet Civilization,* 108–9, 104.

19. Kaifa is convinced that Yeshua is a Roman agent, a provocateur intent on inciting the Jewish populace to revolt; such a revolt would then justify a full-scale Roman takeover of Judea (see Proffer, *Bulgakov,* 548). For Bulgakov, therefore, his motives are political rather than religious.

20. The first draft of *The Master and Margarita* featured a scene at the Writers' Union where Ivan, fresh from his meeting with Woland, accuses his listeners of being Jewish executioners of Christ, using derogatory terms such as "zhid zlodei" and "sekretar' zhidovskii" (Chudakova, *Zhizneopisanie Mikhaila Bulgakova,* 304–5 and 490n). Bulgakov changed some of the words in this draft, but the meaning remained the same. The fact that several of the critics who had attacked his own work were Jewish did not escape Bulgakov, whose Master is to a strong degree autobiographical.

21. Chudakova notes that the first version of *The Master and Margarita* featured a scene in which the devil forced Ivan to step on a picture of Jesus by accusing him of being a member of the intelligentsia, an episode that further supports the links between Yeshua and the Master (ibid., 302).

22. Yeshua is in this regard quite different from the atheistic Briusov's "Jewish Christ"—though both writers, like Kuzmin, associate Jews with the Communist forces they find distasteful.

23. Yeshua's last words and thoughts in the novel are in fact somewhat unclear. A dream Ivan has in the psychiatric clinic is assumed to be the same as the Master's novel, and the dream shows Yeshua pronouncing the procurator's title as his last word. Afranius, the secret police chief, leaves this out of the account of Yeshua's execution that he presents to Pilate, but he adds that Yeshua blamed no one for his death. Afranius's motives are opaque, and the Master's text has unmistakable authority in the novel; Yeshua's last word, then, is most likely "Hegemon." For more on Afranius as unreliable, see Barratt, *Between Two Worlds*, 214.

24. In her memoirs Elena Sergeevna stated that as soon as she met Bulgakov, although she was already married, she understood that there was no meaning in life without him; this instant dedication characterizes Margarita as well (E. S. Bulgakova, "O p'ese 'Beg' i ee avtore," in *Vospominaniia o Mikhaile Bulgakove*, comp. E. S. Bulgakova and S. A. Liandres [Moscow: Sovetskii Pisatel', 1988], 387).

25. Curtis, *Manuscripts Don't Burn*, 113–14.

26. Elena Sergeevna's usually restrained diaries of the period are marked with satisfaction as she records certain arrests and imprisonments. See, for example, Elena Sergeevna Bulgakova, *Dnevnik Eleny Bulgakovoi* (Moscow: Knizhnaia Palata, 1990), 137, 140.

27. A[natolii] M. Smelianskii, *Mikhail Bulgakov v Khudozhestvennom teatre* (Moscow: Iskusstvo, 1989), 352.

28. Gasparov, "Novyi Zavet," 171. On the complex relationship between Bulgakov and the Soviet state, see, too, Vsevolod Sakharov, *Mikhail Bulgakov: Pisatel' i vlast'* (Moscow: Olma-Press, 2000). Gregory Freidin has explored the relationship between Mandel'shtam and Stalin, and writes of the writer-state relationship during the Soviet period, "The authority of one both undermined and supported the authority of the other, in a relation of mutually reinforced rivalry" (Gregory Freidin, *A Coat of Many Colors: Osip Mandelstam and His Mythologies of Self-Presentation* [Berkeley and Los Angeles: University of California Press, 1987], 268). Presumably referring to Bulgakov's agreement to write *Batum*, Stalin is said to have pronounced, "Our strength lies in the fact that we got even Bulgakov to work for us" (Smelianskii, *Bulgakov v Khudozhestvennom teatre*, 378). See, too, Stalin's 1929 reaction to Bulgakov's play *Dni Turbinykh* (The Days of the Turbins): "*The Days of the Turbins* is a demonstration of the all-powerful might of Bolshevism. Of course the author is 'not guilty' of this demonstration, but what is that to us?" (cited in Milne, *Bulgakov: A Critical Biography*, 110).

29. See, again, Freidin on Mandel'shtam: "he could not disentangle himself from a poetics in which the charisma of the author was predicated on the authority of a supreme ruler assigned the role of the poet's other" (*A Coat of Many Colors*, 250). Freidin notes (254) that Stalin asked Boris Pasternak whether Mandel'shtam was a "Master."

30. David M. Bethea, *The Shape of Apocalypse in Modern Russian Fiction* (Princeton, N.J.: Princeton University Press, 1989), 228.

31. See Revelation 18:10, 21:1–2.

32. Victor Pelevin, *The Life of Insects,* trans. Andrew Bromfield (New York: Farrar, Straus and Giroux, 1998), 59. Pelevin's usage here recalls the *Rim/mir* wordplay of earlier Russian texts. His reference to Ivan the Terrible also brings to mind Sergei Eisenstein's scenario for his *Ivan the Terrible,* in which the tsar cites the Third Rome doctrine and concludes, "And in that Third Rome—as ruler of Muscovy—as sole Master from this day forth shall I reign ALONE!" (Sergei M. Eisenstein, *Ivan the Terrible,* trans. Ivor Montagu and Herbert Marshall, ed. Ivor Montagu [New York: Simon and Schuster, 1962], 56).

33. Paul Bushkovitch, "N. V. Sinitsyna, *Tretii Rim: Istoki i evoliutsiia russkoi srednevekovoi kontseptsii,*" *Kritika* 1, no. 2 (2000): 392, 399.

34. Marshall Poe, "Moscow, the Third Rome: The Origins and Transformations of a 'Pivotal Moment,'" *Jahrbücher für Geschichte Osteuropas* 49, no. 3 (2001): 429.

35. Andrei Fadin, "Tretii Rim v tret'em mire: Razmyshleniia na ruinakh imperii," *Nezavisimaia gazeta,* 12 Sept. 1991, 5; excerpted from a longer version published in *Vek XX i mir* 9 (1991).

36. Egor Kholmogorov, "Tretii Rim," *Spetsnaz Rossii* 63, no. 12 (25 Dec. 2001).

37. Aleksei Makarkin, "Tretii Rim possorilsia so vtorym," *Segodnia,* 9 Nov. 2000, http://www.segodnya.ru/w3s.nsf/Archive/2000_250_news_text_makarkin4.html.

38. For works with an apocalyptic tone, see, for example, Oleg Slavin's ongoing "novel-hypothesis" *V pritsele Tretii Rim* (Moscow: Vagrius, 2001), which predicts the near future based on Biblical prophecy, or Mikhail Nazarov's *Taina Rossii* (Moscow: Russkaia Ideia, 1999). The latter book, full of anti-Semitic conspiracy theories, juxtaposes the New World Order (the Kingdom of the Antichrist) to the Russian Idea and includes a section entitled "Tretii Rim—Sviataia Rus'." The complete book appears in electronic form on several sites. For examples of various artistic treatments of the Third Rome theme, see Boris Lavrent'ev's painting *Tretii Rim* (1997) (http://www.artni.ru/lavrentev/gallery1/pict01.html [accessed 15 May 2003; site now discontinued]), Nikolai Komarov's mixed-media *Tretii Rim* (1991) (http://www.artsalon.ru/artists/komarov/3rim/big/), and a work by computer graphics student Oksana Pyshniak (http://www.charity.orthodoxy.ru/moscow9.htm).

39. Ol'ga Dmitrieva, "Moska po-ital'ianski znachit 'mukha': Rimliane vriad li dogadyvaiutsia o tom, chto Moskva—'tretii Rim,'" *Nezavisimaia gazeta,* 16 April 2002.

40. *Izdatel'stvo Tretii Rim,* http://www.tretiy.ru/izdatelstvo/index.php (accessed 15 May 2003; site now discontinued).

41. "Tretii Rim: Bor'ba za prestol," http://ogl.ru/pc/1964/main/ (accessed 28 Dec. 2004).

42. See http://www.kurortinfo.ru/tour/22/215.shtm (accessed 28 Dec. 2004).

43. Roman Ukolov, "Miss 'Tretii Rim,'" *Nezavisimaia gazeta*, 25 July 2001.

44. See http://www.museum.ru/N14763 (accessed 28 Dec. 2004).

45. For a detailed account, see Konstantin Akinsha and Grigorii Kozlov, *Beautiful Loot: The Soviet Plunder of Europe's Art Treasures* (New York: Random House, 1995), 3–11.

46. John Noble Wilford, "Archaeologists Rally to Defense of Flawed Giant," *New York Times*, 16 Jan. 1996.

47. Irina Antonova, "Introduction," in Vladimir Tolstikov and Mikhail Treister, *The Gold of Troy: Searching for Homer's Fabled City*, trans. Christina Sever and Mila Bonnichsen (New York: Harry N. Abrams, 1996), 7.

48. Anon., "Heinrich Schliemann: A Brief Biography," ibid., 13.

Index

Page numbers in italics refer to illustrations.

Acmeism, 217n113, 245n11

Acte, 266n5; Kuzmin's characterization of, 163, 174, 266n5

Aeneas: Briusov's translation of *Aeneid*, 90; Ivanov and, 31, 130, 135–36, 139–40, 141, 142–43, 145, 147, 152, 257n36, 258n41, 261n72; St. Augustine and, 142; Trojan narrative in Russian culture, 10, 25, 136–38, 147, 151, 200, 257n33; variations in ancient narratives about, 207n25; Virgil's characterization of, 10, 89, 207–8n26, 231n99, 260–61n72

Agrippina, 269n50; Kuzmin's characterization of, 170, 171, 177

Akhmatova, Anna, 22

Alexander I, Tsar, 11–12

Alexander II, Tsar, 18, 224n37

Alexander III, Tsar, 18

Alexander the Great, 41, 42

Alexander VI, Pope, 53

"Alexandrian Songs" (Kuzmin), 266n8

Alexis (Merezhkovskii's characterization of), 64, 66, 69–71, 231n99, 231n103

alphabet, Cyrillic, 3–4, 8

The Altar of Victory (Briusov), 29–30, 77–88, 93, 98, 100, 101, 104, 105, 190, 235n24

Ambrosius (St. Ambrose), 79, 87, 236n35; Briusov's characterization of, 79, 87, 88, 236–37n35; Bulgakov's Amvrosy linked to, 190, 192, 275n12

Amfiteatrov, Aleksandr, 14, 222–23n29, 234n13

Ammianus Marcellinus, 78, 84, 224n37; Merezhkovskii's characterization of, 40, 44, 224n37

Amvrosy (fictional character), 190, 192, 275n12

Anacharsis, 150, 224n37, 263n102

Anchises, 135, 138, 207n25, 208n26

androgyny, 59, 103, 122–23, 126

Annenkov, Iurii, 127

Annenskii, Innokentii, 23, 210n44

"Anthony" (Briusov), 101

Antichrist: in Dostoevskii's works, 72; in Kuzmin's works, 174, 177; in Merezhkovskii's works, 42, 54, 56, 65, 69, 71, 81, 231n93; Old Believers and, 211n57; Solov'ev's characterization of the, 18

The Antichrist: Peter and Alexis (Merezhkovskii), 35, 63–74, 64, 218n1

apocalypticism: artist's unifying role and, 194; Bolshevik revolution as context for, 26; Briusov and, 85, 93, 95; Bulgakov and, 32, 186–87, 193–94, 274–75n10; in Catiline's Rome, 186–87, 189; fall of Rome and, 25; in

apocalypticism (*continued*)
Merezhkovskii's works, 28, 41, 64, 69, 71–75, 84–85, 93, 95, 104, 230n91, 231n99, 231n102; messianism and, 198, 211n57; modernism and, 26; Old Believers and, 69; during Peter I's reign, 211n57; in recent works, 278n38; in Russian novel tradition, 231n102; Solov'ev and Symbolists' use of, 18, 32; Third Rome doctrine and, 15–16, 18, 25, 198
Apollo, 57, 117, 150, 206n20, 256n26; Apollonian/Dionysian dichotomy, 117–18, 120–21, 124, 125, 126, 127, 249n53
"Apology of a Madman" (Chaadaev), 10, 207n23
Appearance of Christ before the People (Ivanov, painting), 12
Appian Way, 18–20, *19*
"Aqua Virgo" (Ivanov), 137–38, 143, 152–53, 158–59
archaeology: as context for renewed interest in Rome, 19–22, 53; identification of Rome with Russia linked to, 195–96, 200–201; Merezhkovskii and, 37, 53; Russia's excavations of Greek trading colonies, 22
Arianism, 41, 43, 48, 223n33
Arnheim, Fraulein (fictional character), 66, 70
Arsinoe (fictional character), 40, 41, 42, 43–44, 63, 225n39, 226n57
Art and Revolution (Wagner), 115, 117
"art for art's sake," 37, 220n18
the artist: as alter ego of the author, 99, 164, 175, 194, 195, 196, 271n67, 272n86; Blok's conceptions of, 106, 107, 117, 120–28, 123, 244n5; Bolshevik "creativity" and, 171–73; Briusov's conceptions of, 88, 92–93, 96–99, 101, 104; Bulgakov's conceptions of, 32, 188, 189, 194; as connected to his age, 106, 123, 244n5; as failure, 168–72, 176–77; freedom as essential to, 92–93, 101, 104, 167–68, 253n105; Ivanov's conceptions of, 133, 144, 154–56, 158; Kuzmin's conceptions of, 164, 169–72, 176–77, 271n67; life creation as role of, 27, 181, 228n74; Merezhkovskii's conceptions of, 35, 40–41, 44, 52–53, 56–57, 66; as messianic or redemptive figure, 32, 164 (*see also* self-sacrifice of *under this heading*); as mythmaker, 7, 27, 29, 117, 133–35; nature and, 144, 154–56, 158; as revolutionary, 31–32, 74, 117, 120–28, 126, 162; Russian Orthodox Church and excommunication of, 48–49; self-sacrifice of, 99, 107, 117, 120–28, 133; unification or synthesis as role of, 32, 54, 124, 130, 180–82, 194; *zhiznetvorchestvo* and role of, 27
Asclepius, 156–58, 160
Asoian, Iu., 23, 210n52
"Attempt at Self-Criticism" (Nietzsche), 119–20
"At the Forum" (Briusov), 78, 257n34
Attila the Hun, 92, 238n56
"Attis" (Catullus), 31, 106, 122–25, 126, 127, 251n88
Augustine. *See* St. Augustine
Augustus Caesar, 10, 79, 83, 109, 187, 203–4n5
Ausonius, 98–99

Baehr, Stephen L., 11, 206n19
Baer, Joachim, 234–35n16
Bakhtin, Mikhail, 23, 37, 160–61, 221–22n25
Bakhtin, Nikolai, 23
Bal'mont, Konstantin, 89
barbarians: Blok's conceptions of, 18, 31, 121, 124–25, 125–26, 252–53n98; Briusov's conceptions of, 82, 92, 102; chaos and, 102; Christians as, 41, 48–49, 82; as constructed in classical antiquity, 7–8, 205n13; culture or "spirit of music" and, 121; Decadence linked to, 25, 216n102; the Dionysian linked to, 125, 147, 150; East linked with, 18, 125; European constructions of Russians as, 54–55, 66, 205n11; Ivanov and, 129, 150; Kuzmin's conceptions of, 165, 168; Merezhkovskii and, 41, 48–49, 54–55, 57, 66, 82; as revolutionaries,

125, 165; Russian self-identification as, 121, 125–26; Slavs as, 8, 204–5n10; Symbolism and interest in, 18; twentieth century as new age of barbarism, 214n86
Barta, Peter, 246–47n25
Batum (Bulgakov), 193–94
Baudelaire, Charles, 37, 39, 216n102
Bedford, C. Harold, 230n89, 230n90
Belinskii, Vissarion, 39
Beltraffio, Giovanni (fictional character), 52, 224n38
Belyi, Andrei, 14, 26, 62, 75; Bolshevism and, 162, 265–66n2, 265n128; Briusov's aesthetic disagreements with, 95; Merezhkovskii as influence on, 35; Merezhkovskii on, 221n20
Berdiaev, Nikolai, 34, 50, 67, 253n1
Bergson, Henri, 215n98
Berlioz (fictional character), 192, 275n11
Bernini, Lorenzo, 132, 154
Bethea, David, 194, 211n57, 231n102
Bezdomnyi, Ivan (fictional character), 192, 275n12
Bird, Robert, 263n106
Birth of Tragedy (Nietzsche), 24, 117, 119–21, 249n51
Black Hundreds, 165, 267n13
Blok, Aleksandr: anti-revolutionary forces in works of, 110–11; Apollonian/Dionysian dichotomy and, 117–18, 120–21, 124, 125, 126, 127, 249n53; and the artist as self-sacrificing, revolutionary figure, 107, 117, 120–28; Bolshevism and, 30, 105, 109, 111–12, 116–17, 119–20, 121, 126–27, 251n84, 253n105, 267n9; Briusov and, 79, 105; critical reception of works, 107–8, 250n74; on decline of civilization, 112, 116, 120–21, 128; as historian and Latin scholar, 108–9, 244–45n9; Ibsen and, 108, 114–15, 245n11, 248n34; Ivanov and, 128; and linguistic markers to in dicate Rome, 109; Merezhkovskii and, 35, 105, 107, 128, 219n7, 243–44n3, 253n105; mythmaking and, 107, 117, 120–28; Nietzsche as influence on, 117, 119–21, 249n51, 251n77; Renan as influence on, 118–19; and revolution as transformative destruction, 116, 117–19, 126–27; Scythians as constructed by, 18, 31, 124–25, 252–53n98; self-identification with historical and mythic figures, 107, 124–25, 252n96; Wagner as influence on, 120; Zelinskii as influence on, 22–23
Blok, Liubov', 219n7
Blok, works of: "Catiline," 30–31, 106–8, 113–16, 119, 123–24; "The Collapse of Humanism," 120–21; "The Intelligentsia and the Revolution," 112, 115–16, 247n29; "The Scythians," 18, 31, 124–25; "Silent Witnesses," 110; "The Twelve," 31, 106, 107, 110, 250–51n75; "Venice," 174
the body and embodiment: androgyny, 59, 122–23, 126; castration, 122–23, 126; Christianity and rejection of the, 53–54, 63, 72–73, 227n69; Kuzmin's assessment of Bolshevik "creativity" as scatological, 172; mortification of the body, 41
Bogomolov, Nikolai, 163, 165, 242n109
Boissier, Gaston, 22, 87, 236n35
Bolshevism: as anti-religion, 186, 236n34, 262n95; apocalypticism as response to, 26; Belyi and, 162; Blok and, 30, 105, 109, 111–12, 116–17, 119–20, 121, 126–27, 251n84, 253n105, 267n9; Briusov and, 30, 76–77, 92–94, 104, 239n63, 239n68; Bulgakov and, 26, 186, 277n28; intelligentsia linked to, 31–32; Ivanov and, 31, 149, 186, 262n95; Kuzmin and, 31–32, 58, 162, 167–68, 171–74, 176–77, 266–67n9, 270n26; Merezhkovskii and, 219n8, 247n29; perceived as linked to Christianity, 30–31, 106, 111, 112, 116, 119–20, 121; rejection of Christianity by, 148–49; Rome linked to, 26, 30
Borgia, Cesare, 52, 53
Boris Godunov (Pushkin), 12
Bott, Marie-Luise, 271n60, 272n87
bourgeoisie, 25, 110–11, 115, 121
Brandes, George, 114

Briullov, Aleksandr, 12
Briullov, Karl, 12; painting by, *13*
Briusov, Valerii: as areligious, 77–78, 86–87, 95–96, 235n22, 236n34, 238n51; artistic theories of, 88, 92–93, 96–99, 103, 104–5; authorial insertion in works of, 88, 94–95, 97–98; Blok and, 105; Bolshevism and, 30, 76–77, 92–94, 104, 239n63, 239n68; chaos and the barbaric admired by, 102; critical reception of works, 76, 78–79, 101–2, 233n8, 235n18; Decadence and, 216n103, 233n5; East/West dichotomy in works of, 81–82; editorial career of, 77, 89–90, 99; Ghil as influence on, 96–97, 240n82, 241n86, 241n88; as historian and Latin scholar, 78–79, 80, 87, 90, 94, 98–99, 234n16, 235n24, 236n35, 241n91; identification of Rome with Russia in works of, 88, 90, 238n51; individualism and, 90, 97, 104; Ivanov and, 89, 92, 105; Kuzmin and, 105; Merezhkovskii and, 29–30, 75, 78–79, 81–84, 90, 94–95, 97–98, 104, 222–23n29, 232–33n4; messianism and, 99; paganism in works of, 77, 79–83, 85–88, 104, 235n24; "scientific" aesthetics of, 30, 96–97, 103–4, 240–41n86; spiritualism as interest of, 242n109; Symbolism and, 6, 25, 30, 62, 76–77, 78, 95–96, 216n103, 233n5, 240n74; Western literature and, 233n8; works as negative response to Merezhkovskii, 29–30, 84–85, 95
Briusov, works of: *The Altar of Victory,* 29–30, 77–98, 100, 101, 104, 105, 190, 235n24; "Anthony," 101; "At the Forum," 78, 257n34; *Chefs d'oeuvre,* 76–77; "Cleopatra," 100–101; "The Coming Huns," 92; *Dictator,* 239n68; "Dreams of Humankind," 240n86; *The Fiery Angel,* 29, 233n8; "A Holy Sacrifice," 96; "I," 76; "Julius Caesar," 91; *Jupiter Overthrown,* 29–30, 77, 79–81, 83, 88, 93, 98–101, 235n22, 242n111; "The Keys to the Mysteries," 96, 101; "On 'Servile Speech,' in Defense of Poetry," 95; "Passion," 101; "The Present," 90; "Rhea Sylvia," 239n63; *Tertia vigilia,* 76–77; "To Damascus," 103; "To the Satisfied," 91–92; "To the Young Poet," 99; "We Are Experiencing an Epoch of Creativity," 89
Brodsky, Joseph, 7, 196, 205–6n15
The Brothers Karamazov (Dostoevskii), 72, 261n87, 269n51, 271n68
Brown, Peter, 205n13, 217n105
Browning, Robert, 223–24n36
Bulgakov, Mikhail: and Bolshevism, 26, 186, 277n28; the carnivalesque in works of, 189; critical reception of works, 193, 276n20; "holy fool" archetype and, 192; Kuzmin compared to, 184, 194; Merezhkovskii and, 191–92; Stalin and, 193–94, 277n28; Symbolism and, 6, 26, 32, 274n2; Third Rome doctrine and, 186, 191–92, 195
Bulgakov, works of: *Batum,* 193–94; *Master and Margarita,* 32, 184, 186–96, 198, 275–76n14
Bulgakova, Elena Sergeevna, 193, 277n24
Bulwer-Lytton, Edward, 164
Bunin, Ivan, 219n8
Burenin, Viktor, 34–35
Burgin, Diana, 100
Bushkovitch, Paul, 197
Buslaev, Fedor, 22, 57, *58,* 228n76
Byzantium, 16–18, 29, 203–4n4, 205n15. *See also* Constantinople
"Byzantium and Russia" (Solov'ev), 17–18

Caligula, 66, 170
Caliph Omar (Hazrat Omar bin Khattab), 92–93, 269n45
"Captivity" (Kuzmin), 168, 176–77
carnivalesque, Bulgakov and the, 189
castration, 122–23, 126
catacombs, 19, *20,* 21, 43
Catherine II, 11–12
Catholicism. *See* Roman Catholic Church
Catiline, 108, 186–87, 189; Blok's characterization of, 30, 105, 106, 113–16, 119, 123–24; depictions in literary tradition, 108, 113, 245n10

"Catiline" (Blok), 30–31, 113–16, 119, 123–24; critical reception of, 107–8
Catullus, 106–7, 109, 122–25, 251–52n90; Blok and, 122, 252n96
Chaadaev, Petr, 5–6, 10, 207n23
"The Chalice of Holy Sophia" (Ivanov), 148
Chefs d'oeuvre (Briusov), 76–77
Cheron, George, 271n75
Chersonesus, 4, 22, 208–9n36
Chicherin, Georgii, 164, 165, 183, 267n13, 267n18
Christ. *See* Jesus Christ
Christ and Antichrist (Merezhkovskii), 218n1; atemporality in, 36–37; critical reception of, 28, 34–35; Third Rome as theme in, 28–29
Christianity: apocryphal gospels, 274–75n11; Arianism, 41, 43, 48, 223n33; Bolshevism perceived as linked to, 30–31, 106, 111, 112, 116, 119–20, 121; early church and Slavic culture, 3–4, 8; "Historic" Christianity in Merezhkovskii's works, 38, 41–42, 43, 53, 227n70; in Kuzmin's works, 163, 166–67, 169; Merezhkovskii and, 35, 38, 41–42, 43, 53, 227n70; *narod* linked to "true faith," 49; as orgiastic, 30, 80–81, 117; paganism linked to, 166–67; Roman persecution of early Christians, 188; Socialism linked to, 26, 30, 166–67, 169; true Christian religion seen as inheritance of Russia, 15–16, 57–59, 203–4n4, 238n51. *See also* Jesus Christ; Russian Orthodox Church
Chudakova, Marietta, 276n21
Chukovsky, Kornei, 250n74
Chulkov, Georgii, 167–68
Chulkov, Mikhail, 9
Cicero, 12, 30, 108, 113, 246–47n25
Cicero Denouncing Catiline before the Senate (Maccari), *114*
City of God (St. Augustine), 63, 140–41
civilization: Blok on death of, 112, 116, 120–21, 128; classical heritage and, 23; revolution as threat to art and culture, 92–93; Russian assertion of membership in Western, 4, 129–31, 195–96, 205n15; Western Decadence and, 128
Claudius, 170, 171, 269n48
Clement XIII, Pope, 158
"Cleopatra" (Briusov), 100–101
Colchis, 200
"The Collapse of Humanism" (Blok), 120–21
"The Coming Huns" (Briusov), 92
Communism: Briusov and, 239n63; Ivanov on revolution and, 145–46, 149
Confessions (St. Augustine), 141
Conroy, Mark, 207n24
Constantine, 6, 40, 45, 83, 188, 223n36, 258n43
Constantinople: fall of, 15, 51; as irrelevant, 86; Ivanov and, 148, 149; Orthodox Christianity and, 6, 11; Russian links to, 6, 203–4n4; as "Second Rome," 9, 33. *See also* Byzantium
Constantius, 41, 42
"A Corner to Corner Correspondence" (Ivanov and Gershenzon), 133, 151, 256n24
"Cumae" (Ivanov), 135, 256n26
Cybele (Blok's characterization of), 122–23, 125, 127
cyclical concept of time and history, 24–25; atemporality in Merezhkovskii's works, 36–37; Blok and, 107, 110, 112, 127–28; death and resurrection in Ivanov's works, 130; decline or fall and, 110; in Ivanov's sonnets, 137, 157, 159; memory and, 159; modernism and, 33; Rome/Russia identification linked to, 146
Cyril, St., 3–4, 6, 8

Dante Alighieri, 142, 144; epic tradition and, 39–40; Ivanov and, 130, 141–45, 156, 258–59n49; Merezhkovskii and, 39–40, 221n22; passage from *The Inferno*, 135, 265n120
Daphnis and Chloe (Merezhkovskii trans.), 62

Davidson, Pamela, 134, 141, 144, 254n4, 260n66
Dead Souls (Gogol'), 12
The Death of Nero (Kuzmin), 31–32, 169–78, 182, 269n47, 269n48, 271n67; as commentary on Lenin and Stalin, 162; contexts of writing, 162–63, 268–69n39
Decadence, 73, 215n102; barbarism linked to, 25, 216n102; Briusov and, 98–99; Briusov and abandonment of, 96; Lenin's rejection of, 92; Merezhkovskii and, 36, 37, 59, 73, 216n103; progress linked to, 216n102; resurrection or rebirth linked to, 74; Russian Symbolists and, 36, 216n102, 216n103, 233n5
the Decembrists, 12
Decline and Fall of the Roman Empire (Gibbon), 22
decline or fall, 15; in Blok's works, 109–10, 121–24; in Briusov's works, 83; of Constantinople, 51; of Europe or the West, 50–51; in Ivanov's sonnets, 31; Merezhkovskii and theme of, 35, 40, 42, 47, 50–51, 59; of revolutionary spirit, 121–22; of Rome, 122; of the Soviet state, 196–97; spiritual failings linked to, 17–18, 47
Deschartes, Olga (Ol'ga Shor), 147, 259n54
The Devils (Dostoevskii), 225n40
Diagilev, Sergei, 62–63
Dictator (Briusov), 239n68
Dido, 89, 141, 145, 261n72
the Dionysian: Apollonian/Dionysian dichotomy, 24–25, 206n20; the artist and awakening, 120–21; barbarians linked to, 125, 147, 150; in Blok's works, 117–18, 120–21, 124, 125, 126, 127, 249n53; in Ivanov's works, 117, 131, 133, 144, 147, 150, 249n53, 250n75, 255–56n20, 260n66, 260n68; in Merezhkovskii's works, 25, 44, 52, 54, 59, 63, 72, 206n20; in Nietzsche, 117–18, 120, 206n20; as orgiastic, 24, 72, 117; Russia linked to, 125–26, 147, 150; Symbolists and fascination with, 25
the Dioscuri (Castor and Pollux), 137, 145, 152, 153
Divine Comedy (Ivanov trans.), 130, 141–42
Dobroliubov, Aleksandr, 73–74, 232n107, 241n92
Dodds, E. R., 224n36, 273n89
Dostoevskii, Fedor, 17, 72, 145, 149, 225n40, 261n87, 269n51, 271n68; Kuzmin as influenced by, 271n68
doubling: Bulgakov's framing device and double plot in *Master and Margarita,* 188, 193, 275–76n14; "double plot" in novel epics, 38–39; in Merezhkovskii's works, 56; twins and doubles in Kuzmin's works, 180–81, 182
"Dreams of Humankind" (Briusov), 240n86
Du Bos, Charles, 136, 140, 144, 149, 150

eagle, as symbol of both Rome and Russia, 16, 54, 199, 217
education: classical gymnasia as model for Russian, 13–15; popularization of classical antiquity through, 22–23, 210n52
Eikhenbaum, B. M., 252n96
Eisenstein, Sergei, 278n32
Eliade, Mircea, 24
"Emotionalism and Style" (Kuzmin), 181
"The End of the Century: Sketches of Contemporary Paris" (Merezhkovskii), 45–48
epics, 38–39, 221–22n25
Erenburg, Il'ia, 94
Etkind, Aleksandr, 122–23
Europe: as in decline, 50–51, 111–12; freedom linked to, 46, 70, 104, 221n20, 230n90; as modern Rome, 59
Evtikhii Paiseevich Gagara (fictional character), 52, 53–54, 56–57, 59, 62–63, 72, 84, 227n70, 229n78
"Ex oriente lux" (Solov'ev), 212–13n67, 212n67, 229n78
Expressionism, 163, 179, 268–69n39, 271n75

Fadin, Andrei, 197
faith: Bulgakov and link between creativity and, 191–92; "double faith"

in Merezhkovskii's works, 44, 48, 49–50; the East as associated with, 68–69, 72; fall or decline as rooted in spiritual failure, 17–18; *narod* and "true," 35, 40, 49, 61–62, 69, 70, 74; as Russian quality, 10; Third Rome doctrine and, 16–17; "true" Christian religion seen as inheritance of Russia, 15–16, 57–59, 203–4n4, 238n51. *See also* Russian Orthodox Church
fascism, 270n58
February Revolution of 1917: Blok and, 110; Briusov and, 29; Ivanov and, 148–49, 262n91; Kuzmin and, 167
Fet, Afanasii, 12
The Fiery Angel (Briusov), 29, 233n8
Filofei, 198, 263n105; formulation of "Third Rome Doctrine," 15–18, 211n54
Filosofov, Dmitrii, 63
Fink, Hilary L., 215n98
fire or flame, imagery in Ivanov's works, 134, 147
"Five Conversations and One Event" (Kuzmin), 172, 176–77, 178
Flaubert, Gustave, 84, 223n34
flight, in Merezhkovskii's works, 55, 57
"Flight to Byzantium" (Brodsky), 7
Foka (fictional character), 190, 275n12
Forum in Rome (ca. 1821), 21, *21*
Fotiev, Kirill, 129, 253n1
Frajlich-Zajac, Anna, 238n50
France: French Symbolists as influence on Russian authors, 37, 76; Paris as modern Rome, 45–46
Francis of Assisi, St., 55
Frank, Joseph, 204n7
Frazer, James, 25
freedom: Blok on, 114–15, 119, 121, 126, 128, 248n34, 253n105; Briusov's theory of artistic seeking and, 92–93; Europe/the West linked to, 46, 70, 104, 221n20, 230n90; Kuzmin and artistic, 167–68; in Merezhkovskii's works, 41, 44, 46, 70, 221n20; Paris linked to, 46; Rome linked to, 9, 46
Freedom to Art (organization), 167
Freidin, Gregory, 277n28, 277n29
French Symbolism, 37, 76
Freud, Sigmund, 35
"The Future Rome" (Merezhkovskii), 48

galliambic meter, 123–24, 252
Gasparov, M. L., 210n52, 234n16, 235–36n30
genre, 6; "apocalyptic fiction" in Russian novel tradition, 231n102; Ivanov's use of sonnet form, 151–52, 263–64n107; "novel epics," 38–39; trilogy novels, 38–39
geographical designators: barbarians linked to the East, 18, 125, 212n67; Briusov and, 81–82; faith or spirituality linked with the East, 26, 28, 40, 68–69, 72; Godman/Mangod and, 38; Ivanov and, 212–13n67, 261n72; Merezhkovskii and, 28, 35, 38, 44–45, 46, 49, 51, 68–69, 70, 72, 81–82, 206n20, 221n20; paganism linked with the West, 38, 46; rationality linked with the West, 18, 26, 28, 72; Rome as origin of, 51; Russia and synthesis of the East and the West, 6, 10, 17–18, 28, 32, 49, 51–52, 148; Russian constructions of "the East," 212–13n67; Russian constructions of "the West," 213n68; Russian national identity and, 195–96, 212–13n67, 213n68; secularism linked with the West, 28; Solov'ev's "Third Rome" and, 17–18; Symbolists' use of geographic designators, 18
Gerasimov, Dmitrii, 56–57, 228n75
Gershenzon, Mikhail, 133, 151, 254n2
Ghil, René, 96–97, 240n82, 241n86, 241n88
Gibbon, Edward, 22, 235n24
Gildebrandt-Arbenina, Ol'ga, 172, 180
Girard, René, 251–52n90
Gnosticism, 32, 169, 179, 267–68n22
Godman/Mangod dichotomy: in Ivanov's works, 144–45; Merezhkovskii and, 38, 45, 55–56, 73, 221n20, 229n78; Nietzschean Superman as Mangod, 53; Solov'ev and, 17, 38

Goethe, Johann Wolfgang von, 98, 134, 147
Gogol', Nikolai, 3, 12, 38, 129–30, 151, 153–54
Gollerbakh, Erikh, 164–65
Gor'kii, Maksim, 35, 101
Gratian, 79–80, 235n24, 236n35
Greenfeld, Liah, 9
Griffiths, Frederick T., 38–39, 221–22n25
Grossman, Joan Delaney, 91–92
Gumilev, Nikolai, 168, 210n52, 250n74

Hannibal, 146, 260n72
Helen of Troy, 137, 150
Hellman, Ben, 148, 227n71
Herod, 186–87
Herzen, Alexander, 224n37
Hesiod, 151
Hesperia (fictional character), 80–82, 83, 87–88, 94, 99–101, 102, 104
Hibbert, Christopher, 82–83
Hippius, Zinaida, 26, 52, 63, 64, 66, 94, 95, 111–12, 219n8, 219n9, 236n34, 237n27, 237n29
Historical Sketches of Russian Folk Literature (Buslaev), plate from, *58*
history: Blok's study of, 108–9, 244–45n9; Briusov's study of, 78–79, 80, 87, 90, 94, 98–99, 234n16, 235n24, 236n35, 241n91; "critical history," 245–46n13; historicity of Homer, 22; Ivanov's study of, 21, 131, 214n86, 254n4; Kuzmin's study of, 163, 171, 175, 269n47, 269n48, 273n89; Merezhkovskii's study of, 22, 36–37, 47, 52, 78–79, 222n27, 222n29; modernism and preoccupation with, 24–25, 33, 195–96; myth and, 24–25; Nietzsche and modern approach to, 24–25; relevance of, 94. *See also* archaeology; cyclical concept of time and history
"holy fools," 10, 192, 206n21
"A Holy Sacrifice" (Briusov), 96
Homer, 22, 38, 162, 207n24, 265n120
homosexuality, 180, 182, 266n8, 267n15
Honko, Lauri, 215n91
Hull's Strolls (Kuzmin), 271n75
"Hymn" (Ivanov), 148

"I" (Briusov), 76
Ibsen, Henrik, 108, 114–15, 222n28, 224n37, 245n11, 248n34
Ideology and Utopia (Mannheim), 178–79
Ikonnikov, Vladimir, 16
Il Tritone Fountain, *155*
"Il Tritone" (Sonnet V, Ivanov), 143, 144, 154–56, 158
Images of Italy (Muratov), 132
imperialism, 32; Briusov and, 90–91; Briusov as literary empire builder, 89–90; and the dynamic between literature and power, 161; Ivanov's ambivalence toward, 139; Merezhkovskii and, 35, 53, 64, 65, 67; Rome and Russian, 6, 11–12, 65–66, 195–96; Third Rome and, 16–17, 203–4n4
individualism: Apollonian tendency and, 24; Briusov and, 90, 97, 104; "egotism" of modern poets, 97; Kuzmin and, 163, 164, 167, 169, 179; Merezhkovskii and, 37, 45, 76; as un-Russian, 147
industrialization, 37, 47
The Inferno (Dante), 135
the intelligentsia: Blok and, 35, 110, 112, 115–16, 128, 247n29; Ivanov and, 146–47; Kuzmin and, 31, 146–47, 176–77; Merezhkovskii and, 35, 41, 62, 63, 69–72, 74, 128; *narod* in relationship to, 35, 71–72; Russian Orthodox Church and, 63
"The Intelligentsia and the Revolution" (Blok), 112, 115–16, 247n29
Iurkun, Iurii, 168, 172, 180, 266n3, 268n32
Ivan III, Tsar, 16
Ivanov, Aleksandr, 12, 151
Ivanov, Dmitrii, 131, 132, 133, 154, 257n27
Ivanov, G. I., 22
Ivanov, Viacheslav: Aeneas, Ivanov's self-identification with, 31, 130, 142–43, 152; authorial insertion in works, 129–30, 142–43, 145, 153–54, 159–60; Blok and, 117, 128; Bolshevism and, 31, 149, 186, 262n95; Briusov and, 89, 92, 105; Catholicism and, 130, 139–40, 144, 149–50, 160; critical reception of works, 129, 140, 160–61, 257n29; Dante and, 130,

140–45, 156, 258–59n49; death and resurrection as themes of, 130, 133–34; the Dionysian in works of, 117, 131, 133, 144, 147, 150, 249n53, 250n75, 255–56n20, 260n66, 260n68; Du Bos correspondence, 136, 140, 144, 149, 150; as expatriate, 129, 254–55n8, 263n106; geographical designators and, 212–13n67; as historian and scholar, 21, 131, 214n86, 254n4; languages blended in works of, 150–51, 152, 158; and memory as creative act, 130, 136–37, 151, 159; Merezhkovskii and, 260n66; Mommsen as influence on, 21, 131, 214n86; mythmaking and, 117, 133–35, 161; nature and culture in works of, 144, 154–56, 158; on orgiastic spirituality, 117, 255–56n20; religion and, 31, 117, 139, 140, 142–45, 262n96; resurrection as theme in works, 31, 135, 136, 147, 149, 151, 160; on revolution and Communism, 145–46, 148–49, 161, 262n91; St. Augustine and, 130, 258–59n49, 259n52; Symbolism and, 6, 95, 132–33, 146, 156, 160; Third Rome doctrine and, 31, 146, 147–48; Virgil's significance to, 31, 130, 138–42, 144, 145, 260–61n72; Zelinskii and, 23

Ivanov, works of: "The Chalice of Holy Sophia," 148; "A Corner-to-Corner Correspondence," 133, 151, 256n24; "Cumae," 135; *Divine Comedy* (trans.), 130, 141–42; "Hymn," 148; "Joys," 131–32; "Lazarus," 149; "Legion and *Sobornost'*," 139, 140; "Letter to Charles Du Bos," 136; "On the Joyful Craft and the Joy of the Spirit," 150, 263n102; "On the Russian Idea," 138–39, 146, 150; "Palinode," 144; "Polish Messianism as a Living Force," 148; "The Religion of Dionysus," 117; "Revolution and Popular Self-Determination," 262n91; "Roman Diary," 133; "Roman Sonnets," 31, 130–33, 149–50, 254n2, 263–64n107, 263n104; "So Be It, So Be It," 148, 261n87; Sonnet I, 20–21, 129, 135–36, 152; Sonnet II, 138, 152; Sonnet III, 143, 153; Sonnet IV, 143–45, 153–54; Sonnet V, 143, 144, 154–56, 158; Sonnet VI, 143, 145–46, 156, 264n107; Sonnet VII, 143, 156–57, 159; Sonnet VIII, 137–38, 143, 152–53, 158–59; Sonnet IX, 143, 159–60; "The Spiritual Face of Slavdom," 148; "The Testaments of Symbolism," 133; "Two Cities," 140

Ivanova, Lidiia, 131, 132, 140

Jerusalem: Bulgakov's Yershalaim, 188, 191; New Jerusalem, 82, 188, 191, 194; as part of Roman empire, 82, 187

Jesus Christ: as androgynous figure, 123; Arianism and concept of, 223n33; Blok's characterizations of, 123, 126, 250–51n75, 250n74; Briusov's characterization of, 276n22; Bulgakov's characterization of Yeshua, 32, 188–89, 276n14, 276n19, 276n21, 276n22, 277n23; as Dionysian figure, 117–18, 134, 144, 250–51n75; as historical figure, 187–88; Judaism and, 118; Kuzmin's Nero as false Christ figure, 163, 170, 173–74, 177; as revolutionary figure, 106, 112, 117, 119–20, 250–51n75; Socialism conflated with, 26; Symbolism and use of Christian imagery, 96

Jews and Judaism: in Briusov's works, 82, 103; Bulgakov's works and, 276n20; Christ as Jew, 118; Kuzmin and anti-Semitism, 165–66; linked to Communism, 276n22; in Merezhkovskii's works, 53; in Roman Jerusalem, 186–87

John of the Apocalypse, 69, 71, 73, 231n102

John the Baptist, St.: da Vinci's painting of, 52, 54, 59, *60*; icon of, *61*; in Merezhkovskii's works, 43, 52, 57, 59

John the Baptist (painting by da Vinci), in Merezhkovskii's works, 54

"Joys" (Ivanov), 131–32

Julian: as anachronistic, 37; as constructed in Christian thought, 42–43; in eighteenth-century literature, 222n28; Merezhkovskii's characterization of, 28–29, 40–45, 74–75

Julian the Apostate (Merezhkovskii), 28–29, 39–50, 218n1; critical reception of, 36; decline and fall as theme in, 59; East/West dichotomy and, 44–45, 51; pagan/Christian clash, 39–40
Julius Caesar, 85–86, 91, 109, 142, 239n68
"Julius Caesar" (Briusov), 91
Junius Norbanus (fictional character), 30, 77, 80–82, 83–88, 101–4, 236n33; similarities to Briusov, 91–92, 97–100, 241n92; similarities to Merezhkovskii's Julian, 80–81
Jupiter Overthrown (Briusov), 29–30, 79–81, 83, 88, 93, 98–101; as unfinished work, 77, 235n22, 242n111
Juvenal, translation of works into Russian, 12

Kannegiser, Leonid, 168
Kerchensk Gymnasium, performers pictured, *14*
Kerenskii, Aleksandr, 148–49
Kern, Stephen, 25, 215n89
"The Keys to the Mysteries" (Briusov), 96, 101
Kheraskov, Mikhail, 11
Khodasevich, Vladislav, 26, 90, 239n63, 257n29
Kholmogorov, Egor, 197
King, Charles, 263n102
Kirillov, I., 17
Klimoff, Alexis, 152, 262–63n97
Kliuchevskii, Vasilii, 17, 22
Kliuev, Nikolai, 102
Knabe, G. S., 12
Kondrat'ev, A. A., 79
Kreiman, Franz, 14
Kuzmin, Mikhail: anti-Semitism and, 165–66, 267n15, 273n94; as apolitical, 164–65, 167–68, 266–67n9; artistic freedom and, 167–68; artistic theories of, 179, 181; Bolshevism and, 26, 31–32, 162, 167–68, 171–74, 176–77, 266–67n9, 270n26; Briusov and, 105; Bulgakov compared to, 184, 194; Chicherin correspondence with, 164, 165, 183, 267n13, 267n18; Christianity linked to socialism by, 166–67, 169, 183; critical reception of works, 163, 168–69, 266n8, 271n67, 271n75; Dostoevskii as influence on, 271n68; Expressionism and, 163, 179, 268–69n39, 271n75; Gnosticism and neo-Platonism of, 32, 169, 179, 267–68n22; historical research and works of, 163, 171, 175, 269n47, 269n48, 273n89; homosexuality and, 177, 180, 182, 266n3, 266n8, 267n15; individualism and, 163, 164, 167, 169, 179; intelligentsia and, 31, 146–47; memory linked to artistic creation by, 181; paganism and, 163, 166–67; on revolution as barbarism, 165; Stalin linked to Nero by, 31, 162, 172–73; Symbolism and, 6, 183; syncretism as interest of, 169, 174; utopianism rejected by, 31–32, 163–64, 166–67, 172, 174, 176–78, 183, 272n77; water imagery in works of, 182
Kuzmin, works of: "Alexandrian Songs," 266n8; "Captivity," 168, 176–77; *The Death of Nero,* 31–32, 162–63, 169–78, 182, 268–69n39, 269n47, 271n67; "Emotionalism and Style," 181; "Five Conversations and One Event," 172, 176–77, 178; *Hull's Strolls,* 271n75; "The Ladder," 178; "Roman Marvels," 169; "Scales in the Net," 169; "Shavings," 169, 174, 179; "Sophia," 169; "Three Marys," 174; "The Trout Breaks the Ice," 182; "Wings," 180, 266n8
Kuz'mina-Karavaeva, Elizaveta, 27

L. Tolstoi and Dostoevskii (Merezhkovskii), 51, 59, 63
"La Barcaccia" (Sonnet IV, Ivanov), 143–45, 153–54
"The Ladder" (Kuzmin), 178
The Last Day of Pompeii (Briullov, painting), 12, *13*
The Last Days of Pompeii (Bulwer-Lytton), 164
La Tartarughe Fountain, *157*
"Lazarus" (Ivanov), 149

"Legion and *Sobornost'*" (Ivanov), 139, 140
Lenin, Vladimir: Briusov and, 92–94, 103–4; cult of, 172, 173, 270n54, 271n60; Kuzmin's Nero and, 31, 162
Leonardo da Vinci: Merezhkovskii's characterization of, 34–35, 50–53, 55–57, 59, 62, 66, 70, 226–27n67, 227n72, 228n74, 229n78; painting of St. John the Baptist by, 52, 54, 59, *60*
"Leonardo da Vinci" (poem, Merezhkovskii), 50
Leo X, Pope, 53, 56
Lermontov, Mikhail, 244n8
"Letter to Charles Du Bos" (Ivanov), 136
Lieven, Dominic, 217n106
The Life of Art (magazine), 168
The Life of Insects (Pelevin), 196–97
Life of Jesus (Renan), 118
lilies, as symbol, 224n38
Literature and Revolution (Trotsky), 168
Livy, 12
Lomonosov, Mikhail, 9
"longing for Italy," 12
Lotman, Iurii, 25, 203–4n4, 216–17n104
Lukin, Pavel (fictional character). *See* Pavel Lukin (fictional character)

Machiavelli, 52, 226–27n67
MacMullen, Ramsay, 224n36
madness: ancient attitudes toward, 251–52n90; in Blok's works, 110, 114, 118–19, 122, 127, 251–52n90; in Bulgakov's works, 189, 192; "holy fools," 10, 192, 206n21; in Kuzmin's works, 176
Maiakovskii, Vladimir, 116, 167
Maikov, Apollon, 15
Maikov, Vasilii, 11
Makarkin, Aleksei, 198
Malafeev, A., 23, 210n52
Malinowski, Bronislaw, 215n93
Malmstad, John, 163, 165, 180, 272–73n87
Mamyrov, Danilo (fictional character), 54–55, 56, 69, 227
Mandel'shtam, Osip, 35, 106, 217n113, 277n28, 277n29
Mannheim, Karl, 178–79
Marcus Aurelius, 47
Margarita (fictional character), 188, 193, 276n15, 277n24
marginalization: Russia as "periphery" turned "central," 10; of Russia in Western narrative of culture, 9
Marius the Epicurean (Pater), 19
Marxism, 26; Briusov and, 239n63; Christianity as literary surrogate for, 26; Merezhkovskii and concerns regarding, 37
Masing-Delic, Irene, 100, 123, 228n74
Master and Margarita (Bulgakov), 32, 184, 186–96, 198, 275–76n14; Jerusalem as setting of, 188; parallel structure of plots and images in, 275–76n14
materialism, 37
McFarlane, James, 215n90
Meierkhol'd, Vsevolod, 167, 235n18
memory: in Briusov's work, 257n34; as creative act, 130, 136–37, 181; Ivanov and, 31, 130, 133, 136–37, 151, 152, 156, 159, 263n104, 264n109; Kuzmin and, 181; as unifying or synthesizing force, 159
Merezhkovskii, Dmitrii: ambivalence in protagonists of, 40, 74; apocalypticism and, 28, 41, 64, 69, 71–75, 84–85, 93, 95, 104, 230n91, 231n99, 231n102; artists as characters in works, 35, 40–41, 44, 56–57; authorial insertion in works of, 74; autocracy as mistrusted by, 64, 65; Belyi and, 35; Blok and, 35, 105, 128, 219n7, 243–44n3; Bolshevism and, 219n8, 247n29; Briusov and, 29–30, 75, 78–79, 81–84, 94–95, 97–98, 104, 232–33n4; Buslaev as influence on, 228n76; Christianity in works of, 38; critical reception of works, 28, 34–35, 36–37, 75, 220n13, 222–23n29, 235n18; cyclical nature of time and history in works of, 36–37; death as preoccupation of, 225n55; Decadence and, 36, 37, 59, 73, 216n103; decline or fall as theme in works of, 40; "double faith" in works of, 44, 48; on education, 13–14; geographic designators in works of, 38, 44–45, 46, 49, 51,

Merezhkovskii, Dmitrii (*continued*) 68–69, 70, 72, 81–82, 221n20; Godman/Mangod dichotomy in works of, 45, 104; as historian, 22, 36–37, 47, 52, 78–79, 222–23n29, 222n27; and "Historic" Christianity, 38, 41–42, 43, 48, 53, 227n70; Ibsen and, 222n28; imperialism and, 35, 53, 64, 65, 67; industrialization and Marxism in works of, 47; Ivanov and, 260n66; literary reputation of, 35; messianism and, 38, 52, 56–57, 63, 95; on mythical narrative and national identity, 24; Nietzsche as influence on, 36, 37, 41, 53, 230n90; paganism in works of, 28–29, 36, 38, 41, 42, 46–47, 52, 53, 226n57, 230n90, 230n91; Religious-Philosophical Meetings of St. Petersburg and, 63–65; revolutionary interests of, 65, 74; Rome as symbol of unity in works of, 49; schematization and works of, 75, 81–82, 104, 106–7, 221n20, 253n105; secularism as theme in works of, 68; "seekers" in works of, 74–75; Symbolism and, 6, 95–96, 229n81; Third Rome doctrine and, 28–29, 36, 38, 40, 49–52, 54, 63, 75, 227n70, 227n71; "Third Testament" and apocalyptic Christianity in works of, 64, 73, 84–85, 230n91; "true" Christianity in works of, 43–44, 49, 55, 59, 62; "two truths" of, 37–38, 40–41, 65

Merezhkovskii, works of: *The Antichrist: Peter and Alexis*, 28–29, 34–37, 63–74; *Christ and Antichrist* (trilogy), 28–29, 34–37, 218n1; *Daphnis and Chloe* (trans.), 62; *Death of the Gods: Julian the Apostate*, 28–29, 36, 39–50, 51, 59, 218n1; "The End of the Century: Sketches of Contemporary Paris," 45–48; "The Future Rome," 34, 48; *L. Tolstoi and Dostoevskii*, 51, 59, 63; "On the Reasons for the Decline and on New Tendencies in Contemporary Russian Literature," 40, 49, 195; "The Pantheon," 46; "Petersburg Poem," 47; "Religion and Revolution," 68, 73–74; *The Resurrected Gods: Leonardo da Vinci*, 28–29, 34–35, 50–63, 218n1; "The Return," 47; "Rome," 46; *Symbols*, 45–46, 59, 76, 229n81; "Waves," 47

messianism: apocalypticism and, 198, 211n57; Briusov and rejection of, 99; Bulgakov and parody of Russian, 191–92; identification of Russia with Rome, 25–26; Ivanov and, 130, 148; Ivanov and Russian or Slavic, 148; Lenin-cult and leader worship, 173–74; Merezhkovskii and, 38, 52, 56–57, 63, 95, 229n78; Russia's as salvation of the West, 17–18, 52, 57, 148, 191, 198, 229n78; Slavic Renaissance and, 23; Third Rome doctrine as expression of, 16, 33, 38, 191; Zelinskii and Slavic, 23–24

Methodius, St., 3–4, 6, 8

Mints, Z. G., 227n69, 243n3, 247n30

Mirra (fictional character): in Briusov's works, 84; in Merezhkovskii's works, 42, 43–44, 49

Mirskii, V., 36

Mirsky, D. S., 28, 34

Mochul'skii, Konstantin, 102, 233n8

modernism: apocalypticism and, 26; Blok and, 251–52n90; da Vinci as symbol of modern man, 227n72; history as preoccupation of, 33; Nietzsche and, 24–25

Molodiakov, V. E., 212–13n67

Mommsen, Theodor, 21, 131, 214n86

"Monte Pincio" (Sonnet IX, Ivanov), 143, 159–60

Morev, Gleb, 172

Moscow: as setting in Bulgakov's *Master and Margarita*, 186, 188, 190–91, 194, 195; Third Rome doctrine and, 4, 15, 67, 198–99, 203–4n4, 211n57, 217n106

Muratov, Pavel, 132, 255n13

Mussolini, Benito, 270n58

Mystical Anarchists (literary group), 95, 96, 248n34

mythmaking: artist's role as mythmaker, 7, 27, 29, 117, 133–35; Blok and, 107, 117, 120–28; as both personal identity and artistic project, 27, 29, 133–35; Briusov and, 97; history and, 24, 215n91; Ivanov and, 31, 133–35; Kuzmin and, 163; Merezhkovskii and, 24, 36; as ordering of chaos, 215n90; as Roman project, 10–11; Rome as tool for Russian literary, 6–7, 10–11, 25–27, 36, 163, 194–95; Symbolism and, 10, 18, 25, 27, 36, 133, 183; Third Rome doctrine and literature as, 6–7, 16–18; *zhiznetvorchestvo* and, 27

names: place names as evidence of Westernization, 208n34; significance of characters', 49, 54, 80, 81, 84, 101, 184, 190, 273n89

narod: Blok on cultural vitality of the, 121; the intelligentsia in relationship to, 35, 71–72; Merezhkovskii's depiction of the, 35, 40, 49, 57, 61–62, 69–70, 71–72; "true faith" of, 35, 40, 49, 61–62, 69, 70, 74

nationalism, 130, 227n71

Nero, 187; Briusov's interest in, 90; as characterized in history, 177, 269n47, 269n48; Kuzmin's characterization of, 31–32, 162, 169–74, 177, 181–82, 271n67, 273n89; Suetonius's characterization of, 170, 171–72, 173, 177, 273n89

The New Path (journal), 63, 95

Nicholas, Father (fictional character), 80, 82, 87–88

Nicholas II, Tsar, 16, 17

Nietzsche, Friedrich, 7, 9–10, 25; Blok and, 117, 119–20, 249n51, 251n77; Briusov and attempted abandonment of Nietzschean thought, 96; Merezhkovskii and, 36, 37, 38, 41, 53, 55, 73, 230n90; modernism and, 24–25

Nosov, A. A., 14, 210n52

OBERIU (Association for Real Art), 268–69n39

Obolenskii, L., 36

October Revolution of 1917 (Bolshevik Revolution): Blok and, 106, 110–12, 115–16, 119–22, 125–28, 246n15, 251n84, 253n105; Briusov and, 30–31, 93–94, 233–34n11, 239n63, 239n68; Bulgakov and, 195; Ivanov and, 145–46, 149, 158, 159, 161, 262n95, 262n96, 265n128; Kuzmin and, 163–64, 167–69, 172–74, 176–78, 179, 183; Merezhkovskii and, 219n8, 247n29

The Odyssey (Homer), 162

Old Believers, 15–16, 48, 57, 68–69, 166–67, 211n57, 231n98

Omar, Caliph (Hazrat Omar bin Khattab), 92–93, 269n45

"On 'Servile Speech,' in Defense of Poetry" (Briusov), 95

On the Advantage and Disadvantage of History for Life (Nietzsche), 24

"On the Joyful Craft and the Joy of the Spirit" (Ivanov), 150, 263n102

"On the Reasons for the Decline and on New Tendencies in Contemporary Russian Literature" (Merezhkovskii), 40, 49, 195

"On the Russian Idea" (Ivanov), 138–39, 146, 150

openendedness, 37

Orpheus, 134

Our Debt to Antiquity (Zelinskii), 23

Ovid, 7–8, *8*, 12

paganism: Blok and, 163; Bolshevism and, 26, 235–36n30; Briusov and, 77, 79–83, 85–88, 104; Christianity linked to, 54, 57, 166; Christian/pagan clash in Rome, 26, 39–40, 77, 81–83, 139, 163, 188; classical, as linked to Russian Orthodox Church, 52; Ivanov and, 142–43, 144; Kuzmin and, 163, 166–67; Merezhkovskii and, 28–29, 36, 38, 41, 42, 46–47, 52, 53, 230n90; origins and use of word, 217n105; in Symbolist works, 30; the West linked to, 38, 46

"The Pagan School" (Baudelaire), 39

painting. *See* visual arts

Paleologue, Zoe, 16

"Palinode" (Ivanov), 144

"Panmongolism" (Solov'ev), 18

"The Pantheon" (Merezhkovskii), 46

Paperno, Irina, 27, 180
Paris, France, 45–46
"Party Organization and Party Literature" (Lenin), 92
"Passion" (Briusov), 101
Pater, Walter, 19, 59, 229n79
Paul, St., 103, 142–43
Pavel Lukin (fictional character), 162–64, 174–78, 181–82, 184, 270n58, 271n67
Pavlovich, Nadezhda, 250n74
Pelevin, Viktor, 196, 278n32
Pertsov, Petr, 76, 102
Pertsov, Viktor, 168
Peter I, Tsar: imperial Rome as model for, 11, 65–66, 208n29; Merezhkovskii's characterization of, 29, 63–74, 230n89, 231n93, 231n99; Westernization and, 62, 65–66, 70, 74
"Petersburg Poem" (Merezhkovskii), 47
Petrovskaia, Nina, 96
Phocas (Foka), St., 190, 275n12
Pindar, 153, 154
"Pines of Rome" (Respighi), 156
Plato, 8, 162, 175, 179
Plotinus, 179–80
plotting and plot structure: Bulgakov's framing device and double plot in *Master and Margarita,* 188, 193, 275–76n14; "double plot" in novel epics, 38–39; openendedness, 37
Plutarch, 108, 124
Poe, Edgar Allan, 37
Poe, Marshall, 16, 197, 211n54
Poggioli, Renato, 102, 216
"Polish Messianism as a Living Force" (Ivanov), 148
Polivanov, Lev, 14
Pollio, 258n43
Polovtsov, Anatolii Viktorovich, 222n27
Pontius Pilate, 187; Bulgakov's characterization of, 32, 188–89, 191–95, 274–75n10
popularization of classical antiquity, 28
"The Present" (Briusov), 90
progress, 9, 25, 36, 71, 216n102
Prus (mythical brother of Caesar), 4, 203n3
Punic Wars, 146, 261n72
Punin, Nikolai, 167
Purishev, B. I., 90
Pushkin, Aleksandr, 4, 5, 12
Pushkin Museum, 199–200
Pyman, Avril, 64, 215n99, 220n14, 244n3, 253n98, 260n66

Rabinowitz, Stanley J., 38–39, 221–22n25
Radishchev, Aleksandr, 12
Ravenna, Italy, 247n26
Realism, 37, 96, 132–33
"Regina Viarum" (Queen of the Roads, Sonnet I, Ivanov), 20–21, 129, 135–36, 152
religion. *See* Christianity; Gnosticism; Jews and Judaism; paganism; Roman Catholic Church; Russian Orthodox Church
"Religion and Revolution" (Merezhkovskii), 68, 73–74
"The Religion of Dionysus" (Ivanov), 117
Religious-Philosophical Meetings of St. Petersburg, 63–65, 230n88
Renaissance: as "missed" by Russia, 8; as setting for Merezhkovskii's works, 29, 34, 35–36, 37, 44, 50–54; "Slavic Renaissance," 23, 29
Renan, Ernest, 117, 118–19
Respighi, Ottorino, 156
The Resurrected Gods: Leonardo da Vinci (Merezhkovskii), 28–29, 50–63, 218n1; critical reception of, 34–35; "Slavic Renaissance" as context for writing of, 50–51
resurrection: in Blok's works, 127–28; in Bulgakov's works, 193, 194; Decadence and rebirth, 74; Ivanov and theme of, 133–34, 136, 147, 149, 151, 156–60, 256n20, 262n92, 265n123; in Kuzmin's works, 178, 180, 182; in Merezhkovskii's works, 71; Rome and, 135, 146–47; of St. Clement, 4, 6; "Slavic Renaissance" and cultural, 51–52; of Third Rome doctrine in post-Soviet Russia, 196–201

"The Return" (Merezhkovskii), 47
revolution: as artist's work, 117; Blok and, 112–17, 121–22, 126–27; as "bureaucratic" disappointment, 126–27; Christianity as, 26, 70–72, 93, 195–96; as context for identification with Rome, 25–26, 92–93; cyclical nature of, 116–17, 121–22; as depersonalizing, 105; Ivanov on, 145–46, 148–49, 262n91; Jesus Christ as revolutionary figure, 106, 112, 117, 119–20, 250–51n75; Mannheim on disillusionment with, 178–79; in Merezhkovskii's works, 29; millennialism and optimism about, 167; Second Punic War compared to Russian, 146; as threat to art and culture, 92–93; as transformative destruction, 116, 117–19, 121–22, 126–27; as "wind" beyond human control, 112–15, 117, 122, 247n30, 249n51, 250n74. *See also* Bolshevism
"Revolution and Popular Self-Determination" (Ivanov), 262n91
Rhea (fictional character), 80–81, 84, 86–87, 93, 96, 100–102
"Rhea Sylvia" (Briusov), 239n63
Rice, Martin, 240n74
Rimbaud, Arthur, 35
Riurik, 4, 203n3
Roman Catholic Church, 4–5, 51, 65, 197–98, 230n89; Ivanov's conversion to Catholicism, 130, 139–40, 144, 149–50, 160; Kuzmin and, 166–67; Rome as symbol of, 9
"Roman Diary" (Ivanov), 133
"Roman Elegies" (Goethe), 98
Roman Marvels (Kuzmin, unfinished work), 169
"Roman Sonnets" (Ivanov), 31, 130–31; contexts of writing, 131–33, 149–50; forms and rhyme schemes used in, 263–64n107; publication of, 254n2; visual art as subject of, 263n104. *See also specific sonnets under* Ivanov, works of
Romanticism, "longing for Italy" and, 12, 209n43
Rome: in Blok's works, 106, 109–10; Bolsheviks linked to, 26; in Briusov's works, 88, 90; Christian/pagan clash in, 26, 39–40, 77, 81–83, 139, 163, 188, 223–24n36; as constructed in Western cultural narrative, 9; cyclical view of history and, 146; eagle as symbol of, 16, 54, 199, 217; East/West dichotomy and, 51; as eternal, 130, 263n105; Europe as modern, 45–46, 59; fall of, 15, 25, 122; freedom linked to, 9, 46; identification of Russia with, 6–7, 25–26, 33, 75, 88, 106, 109–10, 130–31, 146, 195–96 (*see also* Third Rome doctrine); imperialism and, 11–12, 65–66, 161, 195–96; Ivanov's visits to, 129; in Kuzmin's works, 169; linguistic markers related to, 109–10; "longing for Italy" and, 12; in Merezhkovskii's works, 1, 34, 35, 40, 49, 75, 82–83; as multivalent and inclusive, 2, 25, 86, 102, 127, 195–96; mythmaking and, 6–7, 10–11, 25–27; as new Troy, 136; *rim* (Rome)/*mir* (world) wordplay, 152, 206n17, 264n110, 278n32; Roman Republic as inspirational to Russians, 12; Russian literary mythmaking and, 6–7, 10–11, 25–27, 36, 163, 194–95; Russian travel to, 12; as Russia's cultural heritage, 4–6, 51, 203–4n4; Symbolism and, 25; as symbol of dynamic between literature and power, 161; as symbol of Roman Catholic Church, 9; as symbol of unity, 49, 147, 151–61; Trinità dei Monti Church and Spanish Steps, *143*; as trope on both personal and national level, 27; as unifying or synthesizing, 49, 51–52, 130–31, 147, 151–61; universalism and, 138–39. *See also* Third Rome doctrine
"Rome" (Merezhkovskii), 46
Rougle, Charles, 167
Rudich, Vasily, 132, 256n26, 263n105, 265n125
Russia: Christian character of, 147–48; as constructed in Western narrative, 7–10, 212–13n67; the Dionysian linked

Russia (*continued*)
to, 125–26, 147, 150; as inheritor of "true" Christian religion, 15–17, 57–59, 203–4n4, 238n51; messianic role of, 17–18, 25–26, 52, 57, 148, 191, 198, 229n78; Moscow as representative of, 4, 15, 67, 198–99, 203–4n4, 211n57, 217n106; as Rome's cultural heir, 51, 129; universality of, 146–47, 149–50, 195; as vital and life-giving, 111–12
"The Russian Academy: Preliminary Notes" (Brodsky), 196, 205n15
Russian national identity: as constructed by Europeans, 212–13n67; geographical designators and, 195–96, 212–13n67, 213n68; Rome and constructions of, 7, 27, 29, 32, 33, 75, 163, 185, 194–98; Troy narrative and, 200
Russian Orthodox Church: as alien to Rome, 9; as anti-intellectual, 48; excommunication of artists by, 48–49; Greek heritage of, 38; Merezhkovskii's critique of "Historic Christianity" in, 38, 63; Peter I and, 67; true religion as Russian inheritance, 17
Russian Revolution of 1905: Blok and, 267n9; Briusov and, 29, 90–93; Ivanov and, 146; Kuzmin and, 165–66; Merezhkovskii and, 29, 68
Russo-Japanese War, 90–91, 146; Briusov and, 90–91

"Sailing to Byzantium" (Yeats), 27
St. Amrose (Ambrosius), 79, 87, 236n35; Briusov's characterization of, 79, 87, 88, 236–37n35; Bulgakov's Amvrosy linked to, 190, 192, 275n12
St. Augustine, 63, 130, 139, 140, 144, 259n52, 259n56; Aeneas and, 142; Ivanov and, 130, 258–59n49, 259n52
St. Clement, 3–4, 6
St. Cyril, 3–4, 6, 8
St. Francis of Assisi, 55
St. John the Baptist: da Vinci's painting of, 52, 54, 59, *60*; icon of, *61*; in Merezhkovskii's works, 43, 52, 57, 59
St. Methodius, 3–4, 6, 8
St. Paul, 103
St. Petersburg, Rome as model for, 11
St. Petersburg Academy of Sciences, 11
St. Phocas (Foka), 190, 275n12
saints. *See specific names*
Sallust (Gaius Salustius Crispus), 108, 113, 246–47n25
Savonarola, 52, 53; as caricature of Tolstoi, 227n69
"Scales in the Net" (Kuzmin), 169
The Scales (journal), 89, 92, 99
Schliemann, Heinrich, 21–22, 199–201
"scientific poetry," 96–97, 240–41n86, 240n86
Scythians, 18, 105, 150, 235n24, 263n102; literary group, 252–53n98
"The Scythians" (Blok), 18, 31, 124–25
self-sacrifice: Blok and the artist as self-sacrificing, revolutionary figure, 107, 117, 120–28; Briusov and the need for artistic, 99; castration and self-sacrifice, 122–23, 126; Ivanov's concepts of artistic, 133; Merezhkovskii's Alexis and, 231–32n103; revolutionary martyrdom, 71–72; Russia and Dionysian self-destruction, 147; Russia's redemptive role and, 38; St. Peter's martyrdom, 265n125; *sobornost'* and, 147–48
Sharapov, Fedor Kliment'ev, psalter of, 57, 228n76
"Shavings" (Kuzmin), 169, 174, 179
Shchedrin, Sil'vestr, 12
Shervinskii, S. V., 103
Shils, Edward, 205n12
Shmakov, Gennadii, 180
Shor, Ol'ga (Olga Deschartes), 147, 259n54
"A Short Story of the Antichrist" (Solov'ev), 18
Shvarsalon, Vera, 131, 134
Sienkiewicz, Henryk, 234n13, 266n5
"Silent Witnesses" (Blok), 110
The Silver Dove (Belyi), 221n20
Siniavskii, Andrei, 190–91
Skabichevskii, Aleksandr, 36, 220n13
Slavic Renaissance, 214n84, 263n105

"So Be It, So Be It" (Ivanov), 148, 261n87
sobornost', 147–48, 151–61
Socialism: Briusov and, 30; Christianity linked to, 26, 30, 166–67, 169; Roman pagan/Christian clash and, 26
Sokolov, Fedor, 22
Solov'ev, Sergei, 22
Solov'ev, Vladimir, 7, 17–18, 25, 46, 70, 125, 140, 210n52, 212n67, 229n78; belief in Russia as synthesizing Third Rome, 17–18; Merezhkovskii as influenced by, 38, 229n78
"Sophia" (Kuzmin), 169
"The Spiritual Face of Slavdom" (Ivanov), 148
Stalin, Joseph, 186, 270n58, 277n28; Bulgakov's Woland linked to, 191, 276n15; Kuzmin's Nero and, 31, 162
Stammler, Heinrich A., 229n78
Stepun, Fedor, 140
Suetonius, 163, 170–73, 177, 266n5, 273n89
Sventsitskaia, I. S., 22
Symbolists, Russian: Blok and, 6, 30–31, 95, 248n34; Briusov and, 6, 25, 30, 62, 76–77, 78, 95–96, 216n103, 233n5, 240n74; Bulgakov and, 6, 26, 32, 274n2; Christian imagery used by, 96; crisis of 1910 and schism in, 30, 95–96; Decadence and, 36, 216n102, 216n103, 233n5; French Symbolists as influence on, 37; geographic designators, 18; Ivanov and, 6, 95, 132–33, 146, 156, 160; Kuzmin and, 6, 183; Merezhkovskii's role in, 35, 36, 62, 229n81; mythmaking and, 10, 18, 25, 27, 36, 133; Solov'ev as influence on, 17, 18; visual arts and, 62–63; Zelinskii as influence on, 22–24
Symbols (Merezhkovskii), 45–46, 59, 76, 229n81
Symmachus, 188, 236n35; Briusov's characterization of, 79, 80, 82, 83, 87, 93, 236–37n35
synaesthesia, in Ivanov's sonnets, 152
syncretism: in Ivanov's works, 144–45; Kuzmin's interest in, 169, 174
Tacitus, 12
"Tale of the White Cowl" (legend), 15–16, 56–59, 275n12
The Temptation of Saint Anthony (Flaubert), 84, 223n34
Tertia vigilia (Briusov), 76–77
"The Testaments of Symbolism" (Ivanov), 133
Theodoret, Bishop of Cyprus, 42–43
The Theogony (Hesiod), 151
"These Poor Settlements" (Tiutchev), 10
Third Rome doctrine, 4, 6, 7, 203–4n4; apocalypticism and, 15–16, 18, 25, 198; Briusov and, 238n51; Bulgakov and, 186, 191–92, 195; faith or spirituality and, 16–17; Filofei and formulation of, 15–18, 211n54; imperialism and, 16–17; Ivanov and, 31, 146, 147–48; kitsch and popular culture references to, 198–99; Merezhkovskii and, 28–39, 36, 38, 40, 49–52, 54, 63, 75, 227n70, 227n71; messianism and, 16, 33, 38, 191; Moscow as representative of Russia in, 4, 15, 67, 198–99, 203–4n4, 211n57, 217n106; nationalism and, 146–47; post-Soviet resurrection of, 196–201; religious debate and, 197–98; resurrection and, 51–52; Russian national identity and, 197; *sobornost'* and, 147–48; Solov'ev's geographic designators and, 17–18
"Three Marys" (Kuzmin), 174
Thus Spake Zarathustra (Nietzsche), 24–25, 119–20
Tiberius, 187, 189, 275n10, 275n13
Tikhon Zapol'skii (fictional character), 64, 69, 72–74
time, 36–37; anachronistic ideas in works, 36–37; Blok and the artist connected to his age, 106, 123, 244n5; Rome as eternal and unchanging, 136; temporality in Ivanov's sonnets, 152. *See also* cyclical concept of time and history
Tiukhe (fictional character), 173, 181–82, 273n89
Tiutchev, Fedor, 10
"To Damascus" (Briusov), 103

Tolstoi, Aleksei N., Merezhkovskii as influence on, 35
Tolstoi, Dmitrii, 13
Tolstoi, Lev, 35, 227n69
Tolstoi, Petr Andreevich, 12
"To the Satisfied" (Briusov), 91–92
"To the Young Poet" (Briusov), 99
translations of classical works into Russian, 12, 62, 90, 130, 141–42, 208–9n36, 244–45n9
Trinità dei Monti Church and Spanish Steps, *143*
Trotsky, Leon, 168
"The Trout Breaks the Ice" (Kuzmin), 182
Troy: Russian national identity and narrative of, 200; Schliemann's discoveries, 21–22, 199–200; Trojan themes in Ivanov's works, 136–38, 147, 151
Tsvetaev, Ivan, 22, 199–200, 214n80
Tsvetaeva, Marina, 6, 90, 105, 204n5, 214n80
Tucker, Robert C., 173, 271n60
Turner, A. Richard, 50
"The Twelve" (Blok), 31, 106, 107, 110, 250–51n75
"Two Cities" (Ivanov), 140

Ueland, Carol, 262n92
unification: art as unifying force, 18, 32, 49–50, 54–56; artist's role in creation of unity, 32, 54, 124, 130, 180–82, 194; in Briusov's works, 241n88; da Vinci as representative of, 55–56; "double faith" in Merezhkovskii's works, 44, 48, 49–50; in Ivanov's works, 151–61, 264n109; Kuzmin's concept of the neo-Platonic soul and, 179–81; memory as synthesizing force, 159; in Merezhkovskii's works, 40, 49, 51–52, 55–56, 73; Rome as symbol of unity, 49, 147, 151–61; Russia as representative of "third principle," 17; Russian as unifying or synthesizing, 17–18, 32, 49, 51–52, 148; *sobornost'* and, 147, 151–61; sonnet form and, 151; Symbolists' interest in, 26–27, 160; visual art as representation of, 57
Union of Art Workers, 167
universality: Dostoevskii and, 145, 149–50; Ivanov's Rome and, 130, 146–47, 149–51, 260–61n72, 264n110; Merezhkovskii's Rome and, 49, 227n71; Russia and, 146–47, 149–50, 195; of Russian Revolution, 74
Uritskii, Moisei, 168
Uspenskii, Boris, 203–4n4
Uvarov, Sergei, 27

Valeria (fictional character), 102–3
"Valle Giulia" (Sonnet VII, Ivanov), 143, 156–57, 159
Vasilii III, Tsar, 15
Venclova, Tomas, 147
"Venice" (Blok), 174
Venus, 49–50, 65, 66, 107
"verbal instrumentation," 96–97
Virgil, 10, 11, 22, 81, 131, 207–8n26, 207n24, 207n25, 261n72; Ivanov and, 31, 130, 138–42, 144, 145, 260–61n72; Merezhkovskii and, 39; translation of works into Russian, 12
visual arts: Buslaev's scholarship as influence on Merezhkovskii, 228n76; da Vinci's painting of St. John the Baptist, 52, 54, 59, *60*; ecphrasis in Ivanov's sonnets, 263n104; Romanizing tradition in sculpture, 11; Roman subjects in Russian painting, 12, *13*; synthesis represented in literary works, 57; World of Art group, 62–63
Vogel, Lucy, 243n3
Voloshin, Maksimilian, 89–90, 101–2, 251n88
Vvedenskii, Aleksandr, 268–69n39

Wachtel, Michael, 134, 258n49
Wagner, Richard, Blok as influenced by, 115, 120, 250–51n75
water imagery: in Ivanov's works, 134, 135, 143, 153–54, 156, 159, 260n68; in Kuzmin's works, 182
"Waves" (Merezhkovskii), 47
"We Are Experiencing an Epoch of Creativity" (Briusov), 89
West, James, 260n66, 262–63n97
Westernization, 9; Briusov and, 29–30;

Merezhkovskii and, 40, 47, 50, 70; Peter I and, 65–66, 70, 74; Symbolism and, 62–63
Wilde, Oscar, 59, 229n79
Winckelmann, Johann, 24
wind and storm imagery in Blok's works, 112–13, 114, 115, 117, 122, 247n30, 249n51, 250n74
"Wings" (Kuzmin), 180, 266n8
Woland (fictional character), 186, 188, 189–91, 192, 193–94, 198, 275–76n14, 276n15
"The Word and Culture" (Mandel'shtam), 106
World of Art group, 62–63
World War I, 125, 146, 148, 167, 246n24
Wortman, Richard S., 11, 17

Yeats, William Butler, 27
Yeshua. *See* Jesus Christ

Zabelin, Ivan, 22
Zelinskii, Faddei (Tadeusz Zielinski), 22–24, 50, 161, 210n52, 213n69, 214n81, 214n84, 263n105
zhiznetvorchestvo, 27
Zinov'eva-Annibal, Lidiia, 131, 133–34, 140, 258n48